THE MAN WHO THOUGHT HE OWNED WATER

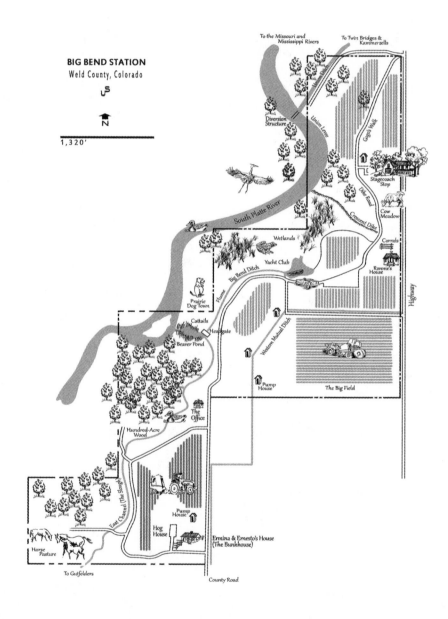

BIG BEND STATION

Weld County, Colorado

N

1,320'

To the Missouri and
Mississippi Rivers

To Twin Bridges &
Kammerzells

Diversion
Structure

Union Levee

Goose Walk

Stagecoach
Stop

Dike Road

Cow
Meadow

South Platte River

Crescent Dike

Wetlands

Corrals

Yacht Club

Ronnie's
House

Big Bend Ditch

Prairie
Dog Town

Flume

Highway

Cattails

Headgate

Western Mutual Ditch

Beaver Pond

Pump
House

The Big Field

The
Office

Hundred-Acre
Wood

East Channel (The Slough)

Pump
House

Hog
House

Ermina & Ernesto's House
(The Bunkhouse)

Horse
Pasture

To Gutfelders

County Road

THE MAN WHO THOUGHT HE OWNED WATER

On the Brink with American Farms, Cities, and Food

TERSHIA D'ELGIN

UNIVERSITY PRESS OF COLORADO

Boulder

© 2016 by Tershia d'Elgin

Published by the University Press of Colorado
5589 Arapahoe Avenue, Suite 206C
Boulder, Colorado 80303

The University Press of Colorado is a proud member of
The Association of American University Presses.

The University Press of Colorado is a cooperative publishing enterprise supported, in part,
by Adams State University, Colorado State University, Fort Lewis College, Metropolitan State
University of Denver, Regis University, University of Colorado, University of Northern Colorado,
Utah State University, and Western State Colorado University.

The paper used in this publication meets the minimum requirements of the
American National Standard for Information Sciences—Permanence of Paper for
Printed Library Materials. ANSI Z39.48-1992

ISBN: 978-1-60732-495-9 (paperback)
ISBN: 978-1-60732-496-6 (ebook)
DOI: 10.5876/9781607324966

Library of Congress Cataloging-in-Publication Data

Names: D'Elgin, Tershia, author.
Title: The man who thought he owned water : on the brink with
American farms, cities, and food / Tershia d'Elgin.
Description: Boulder : University Press of Colorado, [2016]
Identifiers: LCCN 2015042582 | ISBN 9781607324959 (pbk.) | ISBN 9781607324966 (ebook)
Subjects: LCSH: D'Elgin, Tershia. | Women environmentalists—Colorado—Biography. | Water
resources development—Colorado—History. | Water-supply, Rural—Colorado—History.
Classification: LCC GE195.9 .D45 2016 | DDC 333.91/309788—dc23

LC record available at http://lccn.loc.gov/2015042582

Cover photograph © kavram/Shutterstock.

for Diego Lynch,
a man who

CONTENTS

PROLOGUE

Truth has no special time of its own. Its hour is now—always.
—ALBERT SCHWEITZER, *ON THE EDGE OF THE PRIMEVAL FOREST*

Like most of us, the man made assumptions about water. Water was an entitlement, a long shower, fluid in the radiator, and the reason his wife wore rubber gloves after dinner. Then he moved his family to Big Bend Station, a farm that sits atop a hefty aquifer and next to the most important river on Colorado's Front Range. The farm's location, deeded water rights, and Rocky Mountain snowmelt made my father "The Man Who Thought He Owned Water." He was a version of all who trust that weather, rivers, and government will deliver the wet stuff. Yet, his is a story no other water book, no other farm book, no other climate book is telling.

Lots of people fantasize about a country life, but few grasp the desperate and complex water issues that challenge the American-grown food on which we all depend. Is it common for trespassers to divert water at gunpoint? For water conflicts to result in suicides? Why is America's most irrigated crop one we can't even eat? Is costly flooding inevitable? Who sanctions oil and gas infrastructure a stone's throw from water and food supplies?

Farmers always face hard knocks, but it never occurred to my father that water might fail in Colorado. After all, eighteen other states plus Mexico depend on Colorado snowmelt too. Even so, in the early twenty-first century, radical administrative changes separated over 100,000 acres of Colorado farmland—the nation's eleventh most-productive agricultural region—from the groundwater on which it depended. This land included my father's spread. Panicky, I began writing, as a way of explaining to myself how this might possibly have happened. Drought intensified the losses, and in ensuing years many Colorado farmers and ranchers lost their livelihoods. Some took their lives. I learned that shocks like these are seizing other ag regions across the country too, making my parents' unsought custodianship of the Earth broadly and critically relevant.

These throes along the Platte are the unintentional outcome of "growth" that began in the 1870s, when many people, including my great-great-grandfather Ben Eaton, first began diverting water from natural drainages. Ben Eaton, himself a farmer, was Colorado's fourth governor and a historic "father of irrigation." His labors led to water doctrine that still defines development and water management throughout the arid West.

One hundred and fifty years later, a guy in a cowboy hat and BMW now pulls up to a struggling farm and says, "Hi, pal, thought about unloading your water rights?" Such profiteering turns water into a commodity, skyrocketing its price. Energy-intensive infrastructure reroutes that water away from the land for city-dweller consumption. Doing so at the expense of farmland robs us of US-grown crops, just when fuel costs and tainted, nutrient-deficient food imports make them so critical. Storm water and wastewater leave population centers full of pharmaceuticals and other contaminants. As for the natural world? It is an expanding graveyard.

For me, this progression of "spectacles"—from small wonder to outrage—evokes what was and could be again our essential union with land, water, and natural resources. You'll see. Incidents at a single, deeply known, deeply felt place—Big Bend Station—suggest that our biological, political, economic, culinary, horticultural, and cultural worlds can immediately come together over this topic: *water*. We'll unravel little-understood intricacies of water law and its interpretation of "beneficial use." We'll contemplate why so many farmers raise corn, and plot the water savings, climate benefits, and potential income from changing crops. With a toxicologist, we'll explore contaminants introduced into the river from municipal wastewater. In rubber boots, we'll walk through fields down to the Platte, and then follow the slough upstream to the seep with a hydrologist. We'll become students of restoration ecology to revitalize the riparian woods. The goal is to direct conflicting interests to positive outcome on a single farm, possibly as an example for other farms. A dynamic waterway, the South Platte is now hobbled between interstates and functioning as a workhorse for Colorado's Front Range populations. What can be done to free and celebrate its untamed soul?

Please settle into this riff on food, water, and the natural world. My hope is that you'll find my family's capers narrow the chasm between farming and cities. Our experience demonstrates that you don't need a farm, nor even so much as a backyard, to connect better with resources. You need simply attention, bravery, and a timely idea. All of us can live more in concert with water, with wildlife, and with nearby food supplies. *The Man Who Thought He Owned Water*'s direction aspires to and *demonstrates* a way back to the source.

There are these two young fish swimming along, and they happen to meet an older fish swimming the other way, who nods at them and says, "Morning boys, how's the water?" And the two young fish swim on for a bit, and then eventually one of them looks over at the other and goes, "What the hell is water?"

—DAVID FOSTER WALLACE, FROM A COMMENCEMENT ADDRESS
GIVEN AT KENYON COLLEGE, 2005

THIRST FOR THE KNOWN

Where to act is to be free and to be free is to act.
—GUY-ERNEST DEBORD, *SOCIETY OF THE SPECTACLE*

Meet William Eaton Phelps. It's 1941. All limbs, the tall thirteen-year-old has prowled his way into a rough Denver neighborhood, west of the then-dreaded Wazee Street with its filth and its panhandlers. Look for a kid below the boulevard where the wide South Platte River swallows its tributary, Cherry Creek. Not the cultivated urban wetland that it is today, it's a dark, sunken no-man's land, a place for loneliness and pranks, a teenage boy's refuge. Take a deep breath, and then run with him up the creek.

Near water and even in water as he jumps from shore to rock and back again, you race with this nimble human against the flow. It feels good. Weightless. The long strides outdistance his childhood. Does he want solace without admitting it? Do you? Want revenge but uncertain why? He, and you too, settle for throwing every muscle at whatever happens next, near water.

In no time, you've run over two miles. Access to the creek abruptly becomes impossible. High fencing swallows the waterway into the manicured grounds of the Denver Country Club. Some might drool over this vista. Many acres of impeccable golf course and woods unfurl along Cherry Creek. On the south are mansions built by Denver's early mining and cattle barons. On the north is an exclusive neighborhood planned in the early twentieth century by nationally renowned landscape architects, the Olmsted brothers. This teenager doesn't live in a mansion or even a house, though. He resides right at the Denver Country Clubhouse, upstairs with the old gentlemen lodgers. His mother has only just deposited him there, this young man called Bill, on the privileged side of the fencing.

·········▬··▬·········

Bill's parents took off without him when the United States entered World War II. His mother, preparing to follow his father to Washington, DC, where he was stationed in the adjutant general's office, said goodbye at the clubhouse. She didn't give Bill the bike or pistol he wanted. Her long fingers opened in his palm, dropping a heavy reminder of his heritage—a gold ring engraved with her family crest. On it, a beady-eyed griffin held a fluttering standard in its talons. The standard bore the words *Veritas Alles Vincit.*

Learning that this meant "Truth Conquers All," Bill knew better than to register disappointment.

Truth and conquest—isn't that what teenagers do? Throughout the war, Bill communed primarily with other country-club lodgers: widowers and divorced gentlemen many times his age who drank a lot. The club chef made sack lunches for Bill, who rarely went to school. With no one to stop him, he improvised, playing snooker, caddying on the club golf course for pocket money, and hanging around the club ice rink, where he was reputed to have dazzled girls with dance maneuvers on used hockey skates. Growing up unsupervised at an exclusive country club, the only thing Bill lacked was anyone who cared.

Four years later, the war ended. His parents returned to Colorado to find that Bill was already a man. He had learned what some people never learn—to be wary, opportunistic, and to shoulder his own future.

In autumn 1947, this long, lean renegade invited a girl he had met on the club ice rink, a girl who cared, to overnight at a farm settled by his grandparents on his mother's side, the Eatons. They drove north into Colorado prairie farmland on the rural highway that had once been the South Platte Trail. Bill's mother chaperoned, lodged between the young pair in the front seat. Even so, the day glistened with possibilities. Cottonwood foliage cast fluttering gold over the South Platte River banks, where it sparkled for miles in the mirror of the winding river. And beyond the gleam, the Front Range rose as purple and majestic as any mountain view in America. The nineteen-year-old watched the road and sometimes looked past his mother at his pretty sweetheart, Dorothy Ann.

Gogo, as she was known, was only seventeen years old. With a single occupation, Bill, she could hardly contain her excitement. Though stealing glances at Bill's hands, Bill's fingers, Bill's fingernails on the wheel, she appeared to meditate on the white veil of snow on Long's Peak to the west. City scenery rolled away behind them into a backdrop of pastures, silos, and haystacks. She noticed an enormous forked cottonwood next to the road at the little farm town of Brighton.

"I'd like to be like that with Bill," Gogo fantasized, "a tree with two trunks."

They passed Fort Lupton and Fort Vasquez, towns that had grown around old trapper trading posts on the South Platte, and progressed from there through Greeley, then only a few thousand in population. They drove slowly through the town of Eaton, named after Bill's great-grandfather, author of *truth conquers all*. A few miles west at Woods Lake was the Eatons' farm. As their car rolled under the lofty porte-cochère east of the house, Bill's girl was giddy, agape. Under a green copper roof, the brick house was massive—three stories high. His mother got out and ran ahead. Bill had Gogo by the elbow as he flung open the beveled-glass door.

The grounds were a gentleman farmer's compendium—glass-paned hot-houses, seasonal garden, barn, coops, paddocks, the impressive lake that tied the holdings to water, and a nine-hole pitch-and-putt golf course, all rimmed with recently mown fields. Before that autumn day was finished, she saw all this, and more. After a formal dinner with candelabra and finger bowls, with serving staff in black uniforms and starched white aprons, Bill pulled Gogo into the living room. Halfway across the fifty-foot expanse was a mantle. Flames chased up the flue. The overstuffed furniture seemed built for Titans. It held down a Persian rug with colors as saturated as scarab gems. The lanky man, then the age my son is now, bent over to wind up the Victrola.

Is not spontaneous motion, intuitively taken, similar to lovemaking? From watching animals, and people who move with grace—whose appendages press as inquisitively against air, water, and ground as against flesh—I believe it is true. Bill there, in remote Weld County, Colorado, would have scoffed at theories about navigating through space as one would move over a woman's body. Scoff or not, he did it that night; he followed his instincts. Grabbing his trim sweetheart by the waist, he twirled Gogo across the parquet that edged the carpet. The song was "Cheek to Cheek."

After they'd circled the enormous room twice, it was time to rewind the Victrola handle. Their twirls eddying around the enormous room, they rewound Irving Berlin over and over again, until their sides ached, until laughter buckled them. Breathless, spent, they drifted to separate bedrooms, sinking into monogrammed linens so smooth and cool that they seemed refrigerated. Night passed, chasing dreams of lust and ambition over the horizon.

In the predawn darkness, Bill knocked on her bedroom door.

This was the signal.

Gogo dressed quickly and hurried to meet him on the east porch, where he had positioned a ladder. The sun's first semaphores shown to the east. He following her, they climbed onto the roof, moving quietly so as not to awaken his mother and uncle. Then they lay down on their bellies at the crest, facing west so they could peer over Woods Lake, still in profound blackness.

"I don't see anything," she whispered, leaning into his shoulder to keep warm.

"Wait."

Content to be together, she was quiet.

Dawn is soundless, until it's not. A rooster crowed out there, or a rabbit screamed in a coyote's fast jaws, or a door creaked. And at once the obsidian surface of the lake stirred. A flying carpet stitched of a thousand silent mallards lifted into the autumn morning, up and up, each wing paired with another wing, gaining purchase on the approaching daybreak. The birds flapped in unison. The flapping was so close to the two young people that their hair moved, splatters of water dampened their clothing, their cheeks pinkened, their clothing pressed closer to their skin and they, naturally, pressed closer to each other. The whirling air was an invitation, that they might join the drakes and their hens as they whooshed from the water up over the house and into the newly mown cornfield, the young people who would soon be my parents.

·········■■··■■·········

Bill and Gogo took the mallards' invitation. Two years later, Bill's own stint in the army was over. The twenty-one-year old then set his uncommon trajectory. His grandfather's affluence was spread too thinly among too many children to yield much, but still wearing the signet ring, Bill committed to his "truth." His object was not to lodge in close quarters at the country club or even the grander prospects of staying in a manor along its edges. He didn't aspire to white collars, ties, jackets, and wingtips; nor to a mahogany desk in a high rise. What he wanted was to buy and build his own version of his maternal forbearer's gentlemanly farmer life on the water. And this—minus many acres, live-in help, golf course, limousine, and any peace of mind—Bill would eventually do.

His goal was autonomy. It was an American dream, not of a picket fence, but of a "spread." This freedom demanded *owning* land, not leasing it or buying it over time. And the land needed to be healthy, with good soil, diverse opportunities, and wildlife as rich as those flocks of mallards that lent dawn such awe at his grandfather's farm. There wasn't any question that habitation, farming, and nature could be compatible. Without all three, there'd be no surviving. Owning land with mineral rights was desirable. Owning land with water rights was critical. These ambitions had ties to an old West of count-your-fence-posts and brook-no-transgressions. In 1950 Bill married Gogo and bought his own Victrola.

They didn't know it, but their life together began at the same time as in faraway France, a provocateur named Guy Debord shouted for do-it-yourself trajectories such as theirs. Sure, there were clear differences between Guy and Bill—Debord was a Marxist rabble-rouser and my father was an aspiring property owner—but both disdained the "normal" lifestyles imposed on them by civilization. Neither wished to lose their innermost ability to connect wholeheartedly with whatever they did. Debord's message was "Don't forfeit your sensuality, your free will, your rights!" Bill and Gogo didn't. *Move as your nature dictates instead.* And they did.

By the time I was out of the bassinet and ambulatory, Debord (whose work would provide a basis for contemporary urban planning) had coined the term *psychogeography*, a concept important to our story. *Psychogeography*, in Debord's terms, is the innate ability to navigate over the ground on which we live.[1] Each of us has, buried in our consciousness, a sort of compass—passed along with our genes from generation to generation—that "knows" Earth's forms and can intuitively navigate them, just as water does.

Debord claimed that the most important psychogeographic strategy is the *dérive,* pronounced "day-reeve." A dérive is a way of acting. In a dérive, persons—persons who are more like wild animals, and perhaps like you for that matter—stop moving through life as automatons. In a dérive, people let themselves be drawn by the attractions of the terrain and the encounters they find there. A dérive demands following one's instincts.[2] My parents were naturals. And I, like most two-year-olds, had already

Dérive

In the word *dérive,* the *rive* comes from the French word for "riverbank," as in the banks on either side of Paris's River Seine: the Rive Droite and Rive Gauche.

mastered acts of psychogeography if not its lexicon. I demonstrated by clambering willy-nilly between newborn siblings, food, and water.

A dérive is worth thinking about, but it's even more worth doing. Bill's dérive began from scratch, with little education, no inheritance, and hard work. He, my mother, my sister, brother, and I lived in Denver for the twenty years it took Bill to hit his mark. My father began humbly, working as a milkman from midnight until dawn. To economize, he set the milk-truck brakes lightly on the descending streets, such that the milk truck could roll downhill while he wasn't in it. The beanpole named Bill ran zigzags back and forth between the houses and the slow-rolling vehicle, carrying fresh milk, cottage cheese, and butter from local dairies to houses throughout the Cherry Creek neighborhood. In the afternoons, he progressed to real estate sales and from there to professional ranch and resort management. With three young children and few options, he was what you'd call a "go-getter."

In the 1960s, when I was thirteen myself, Bill made his first farmland purchase north of Denver on the South Platte River, about half hour from his grandfather's house on Woods Lake at Eaton. Through the window of my own adolescent disenfranchisement, his initial 300 acres looked dicey. The slope included a windowless cinderblock structure called the "Hog House" with an interior too awful to contemplate. Almost as cheerless was a long trailer we nonplussed city children referred to as "Early Raunch." Undaunted, Bill kept making land deals and at last accumulated 800 adjacent acres, a forty-five-minute drive from the Rockies' Front Range. The spread encompassed not just Hog House and trailer, but two little farmhouses and barns, and a larger clapboard house. The latter is a former stagecoach stop built in 1864. The property's name, "Big Bend Station," is in tribute to its location where the northbound river takes a wide right turn to the east. Looking at the house today, one needs no great imagination to picture trappers, coaches, horses, mules, wagons, and worn-out vagabonds pulling in under the enormous cottonwoods. The stairs are concave from wear and the bathroom floor is a bit off-plumb, enough so that we must correct for it to keep our seat on the toilet.

Of the hoards that tromped and rolled along the South Platte Trail during the second half of the nineteenth century and the early twentieth, many must have availed themselves of Big Bend Station's amenities. Lacking roads, travelers *had* to follow waterways. The South Platte River is one of two main tributaries of the Platte River, the North Platte being the other. The two merge near North Platte, Nebraska, and flowing east, ultimately meet the Missouri River, which flows to the Mississippi. The Platte River valley is broad, as noted by the

The Platte Basin.

French trappers who christened it *la Platte*, which means "flat" in French. In the Old West, the Platte represented a significant middle chunk of the Oregon Trail and the Mormon Trail, first for trappers, then for settlers and freighters. As many as a quarter million hopefuls traveled along the river during the Gold Rush.[3] Whereas northbound travelers took the North Platte fork, the South Platte that runs through what is now Bill's farm marked travelers' shortest and best route to and from Denver and Colorado's mountainous gold and silver cache directly west.

Throughout our teen years, Gogo and Bill dragged us from Denver to the farm for weekends. There I imagined myself a hostage: not just a hostage, but also a changeling. To buoy my teen spirits, I'd gaze on the extravagant view to the west—the girder of Rocky Mountain peaks, many over 14,000 feet in height. Their vigorous mass stretches above the aspen, ponderosa, and lodgepole pine forests. At the time I regarded them as a lovely setting. Now I know that like everything on our watery planet, the peaks are the product of climate change and dynamic geology. It is hard to fathom that these nearly vertical surfaces are residual ocean floor, uplifted by recondite geologic forces such as *subduction* and *volcanic arcing*. Over the multimillennia, water and soil froze in crevices of rock that then fissured, split, and eroded away, sculpting the peaks, leaving them in skirts of glaciated granite and alpine tundra.

While we gawk at the remarkable mountains, downhill tumbles an incessant, nearly invisible cascade of tiny mountain fragments. At high altitude near the South Platte's headwaters, the accumulations of crumbling granite are thin. Yet 130 miles downstream on the Plains, the river bottom and banks are thick with

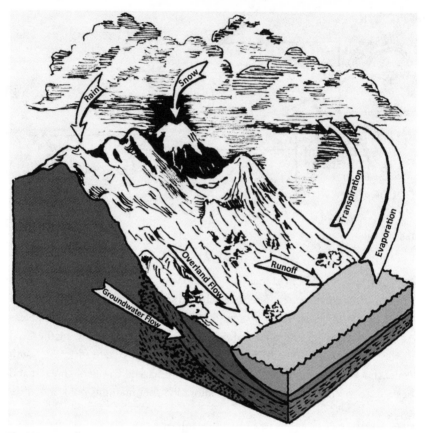

The Water Cycle.

permeable deposits of the stuff. A handful of soil from the farm feels gravelly between the fingers. Its sandy components were once mountain, and if it weren't for water and time, still would be.

And where does this water come from? Colorado's precipitous ranges are so close to the heavens that they make lovers of weather systems. Mountains massage the clouds, creating seasonal orgies of snow, hail, and rain. Utah, Nevada, California, Arizona, New Mexico, Kansas, Wyoming, Nebraska, Oklahoma, Texas, Iowa, Missouri, Arkansas, Louisiana, Illinois, Kentucky, Mississippi, Tennessee, and even Mexico all depend in part on this precipitation, as does Colorado itself. Colorado's snowfall is so abundant that mountain snow can remain many feet deep for the entire winter. In the spring, the sun begins chomping away at the snowfields, thawing them into rivulets, gullies, creeks, and rivers, unleashing an approximate average of 16 million acre-feet of water

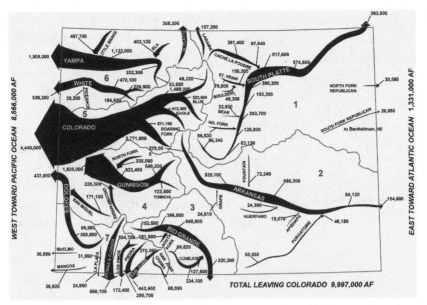

Colorado historic average annual stream flows (acre-feet). Prepared by the Hydrographic Branch (2011 Revision). Historic averages obtained from the USGS Water-Data Report. Office of the State Engineer Colorado Division of Water Resources.

in all directions, millions of acre-feet that reach as many as 50 million people, by the time that runoff meets oceans. However, within the continental United States, Colorado is the one state that uses only its own water; all the water in Colorado—above or below surface—comes either from mountain runoff or the sky.

The South Platte, though hardly a gusher, still constitutes a "major river" in arid-West terms. Long before any of us were born the waterway used to braid and unbraid, changing course, but it is now hobbled between roaring interstates, with tightly controlled banks. The Platte functions not just as a river, but as a workhorse for Front Range urban populations. It is also the principal source of water for eastern Colorado, which has been among the top-yielding agricultural areas in the country for decades. Though but an average of 1.4 million acre feet flow into the South Platte

Acre-Foot

An acre-foot is one acre, a foot deep in water or 325,851 gallons. This is equal to 43,560 cubic feet of water.

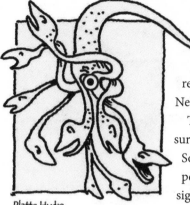

Platte Hydra

Bold, black dot marks Big Bend Station. The tail curls toward Nebraska, just as does the South Platte River.

annually, Coloradans use several times that amount, because water, once used, recharges the river, then is rediverted. That Platte water is reused countless times before it flows into Nebraska at Julesburg.[4]

Then there is groundwater in the Platte's surficial aquifer. To understand where the South Platte Aquifer is and where it isn't, I peered at a hydrology map. Following out of sight and under the river, the aquifer's shape and boundaries are a wider, more rotund version of the river's trajectory. It is a mistake to draw parallels between so vital an underground repository and a monster. Nevertheless, more than 300 miles long on the Colorado map, it has the look of a hydra, with heads sprouting from a long serpentine tail. The "heads" face south and west toward the Front Range. The aquifer's broader portions downstream of Big Bend Station (marked by dot on the graphic) constitute its "belly." They're as wide as fifteen miles. In its eastern reaches, still shadowing the river's course, the aquifer's "tail" is as narrow as one mile. Directly underfoot along the Front Range and yet invisibly so, the aquifer ranges from 20 to 200 feet deep and holds an average of over 10 million acre-feet of water derived of precipitation and irrigation recharge.[5]

Surficial Aquifers

These *aquifers* are near the soil surface and consist of unconsolidated sand and limestone that may date to the Pliocene-to-Holocene periods. Water there is otherwise unconfined and moves along the hydraulic gradient from areas of recharge to rivers and streams.

The mythical Lernaean hydra, Hercules's hydra, resided, not in Colorado of course, but in an ancient Greek farm region, then as wracked by drought as Colorado and all the West presently is. There, Poseidon came to the rescue of a lovely woman, Amymone, whom he instructed to pull his trident from a rock. When she did, a spring gushed forth from the aquifer below. The Greek farms were saved from drought, but unfortunately Poseidon's trident unleashed the poison-breathed hydra. That's how it is with gods. Better to let sleeping hydras lie? Hence, the second of Hercules's labors—right after doffing the lion pelt—was drawing the Lernaean hydra from its lair, then slaying the monster one head at a time. This was no easy trick, because the hydra's heads grew back, just as the South Platte Aquifer's nine "heads" recharge with water seasonally and during years with average precipitation. Historically, over 900,000 acre-feet recharge the aquifer annually.[6] As coming chapters, or "spectacles," unfold, the real monstrosity may become cavalier treatment of the aquifer and its contents.

My father's purchases, recorded on titles and deeds, came with the right to pump from this dynamic and recharging subterranean repository: the South Platte Aquifer. For additional water, he bought ample shares in two private irrigation ditches that deliver water diverted from the South Platte, the kind of ditches, if not the very ditches that his great-grandfather Ben Eaton, a historic waterman, had dug a century prior. All the water rights were guaranteed by the state of Colorado, the property rights by the Constitution. Bill's succession of farm purchases took two decades.

Leaving Denver to move to Big Bend Station was my father's grand design, not my mother's, a distinction perceptible only to her. Not until a "For Sale" sign hung in front of our vine-covered house in that tony Denver Country Club neighborhood did Gogo's misgivings overwhelm her good-sport nature. At the former stagecoach stop, Bill and she were doing reconnaissance upstairs. There was no ignoring that low ceiling, built for small statures the century before. It was practically *on* Bill's head. To Mom, it seemed miniaturized, for Lilliputians or Borrowers or elves. Tears began to flow. Bill took her into his arms, saying that it wasn't too late to change their minds, that they didn't need to move to the country, that they could take down the "For Sale" sign in Denver.

"Whatever you want, Gogo. It's up to you."

Up to me? Gogo peered out at the fields to the west. The windowpanes, made of uneven old glass, warped the cottonwoods beyond so they seemed slightly to wiggle. They batted like eyelashes, she said. Seeing that and with Bill next to her as he'd been on the roof out at Woods Lake all those years before, Gogo's pioneer spirit kicked in. She said, "No, let's do it." And she never complained about the move again, even though the reasons for so doing were already budding like hydra heads.

So we moved. Welcoming us was a plague of cutworm moths, millions of them, and they weren't much smaller than hummingbirds. We timid city folks took refuge inside. During the day, moths snoozed in powdery brown masses on the window screens, as thick as café curtains. Once the sun went down, they were unstoppable in their pursuit of light. We moved stealthily between boxes and disarray, keeping the doors closed and lights off. Everything seemed normal enough as long as it remained dark, but with a flick of the switch, the rooms erupted into a frenzied horror, something midway between *The Birds* and *Mothra*. Particularly the rooms that gave off to the outdoors were alive with hundreds, make that hundreds and hundreds, of startled moths. This siege went on for days.

My father's hard work had carried us over two decades like a silk balloon, with few bumps or tears. In moving, we cut ties with many Denver resources and people, whose hot air had until then passed as oxygen. Decamping to the farm couldn't be justified in the same way as acquiring a weekend house in Vail or Aspen. My parents' logic was lost on the city set. Not a resort getaway with nearby shops and activities, the farm was in the middle of nowhere. Some Denverites made the hour drive to see my family, but you could see it in their eyes: they thought my parents had lost their minds. Gogo and Bill felt it and sometimes said it: "Well, now we know who are real friends are."

And their "real" children. Cutworm moths and abandoned Denverites didn't faze my fourteen-year-old brother, Will, not at all. For Will, life was a hunt. He took to the outback like a Mohican. Already a gifted tracker and amateur taxidermist, he cut his hair in a Mohawk and struck up friendships with farmers' children, several of whom emerged from his lair at the trailer sporting Mohawks of their own. My sister, Annzo, was not so easily acclimatized. Poor thing sequestered herself on an island of civility upstairs, barely moving from a chaise longue except to get to her car and to Denver.

I had graduated from high school. While most people my age got stoned and got laid, I gathered up my books, my antiques, my carpet, and even my curtains hoping to cloister myself at Big Bend Station . . . in the Lilliputian sector. But it was hopeless. Yes, meadowlarks singing from the fence lines were poetic, but I couldn't wait to get away from what seemed like bumpkinland. My family was going to have to adjust to the isolation, the lack of sophistication, and the smell of manure without me. Under pretext of going to cooking school, I fled to Paris, where I could macerate in culture, where my thigh-high boots weren't at risk of cow pies, where Guy Debord was railing at people my age to *dérive*. Childhood was over, irremediably over.

The City of Lights was its own reward and a far cry from our expanse of pastures. Not for over eighteen months did I return, not to live, but to pop in intermittently on the farm, an *Animal Planet*. Big Bend Station's kitchen window opened onto frolicking bunnies and little quail trailing after bigger quail to hide under the junipers. If I'd tied a Tershia-cam to my noggin, there would have been footage of dickcissel flocks bursting from alfalfa pastures and solitary kill-deers hovering erratically before descending again to feed on insects. Mourning dove "dules" migrated through in the fall, clinging to the paddock, gleaning in cornfields and trying not to become fricassee. Belted kingfishers monitored the river buffet from snags lodged in the sediment. As it turned colder, thousands of mallards, wood ducks, and snipe lit on the river on their way south. They too foraged in the fields, though foxes and coyotes hunted there too. These wild canines were so crafty that one spotted them only peripherally; a second look rarely confirmed that they were there at all. Around Christmas, enormous dark chevrons of migrating Canada geese, miles long, appeared in sky. With for-mations resembling colossal arrows that might have been launched across the Plains from unseen mountain-dwelling archers, hundreds of thousands, indeed *millions* of honking, migrating birds aimed at prairie farmland.

Wild Will soon managed to shoot two geese with one shot, making himself a hero among meat eaters. His room was already full of glass-eyed animals that he'd killed then subjected to taxidermy, the beaver holding an ashtray next to his bed most unpardonably. He sported clothes made from pelts he'd tanned and whipstitched with rawhide. His carnage, plus filet mignons still in the form of cattle just over the fence, had turned Annzo into a vegetarian. She'd left home too by then and was making a success of modeling for Head Skis at inter-national resorts.

Every time I visited, my father took me on an excursion down to the river and back. Known as "the tour," the trip's object was wildlife emersion. Because the slough never froze, ducks fed there on wild watercress year-round, but they almost always took flight as we approached, sounding soft applause as their webbed feet met resistance in the water at takeoff. In their absence, Pop and I closely examined the muddy banks. This palimpsest marked the itinerary of passing paws. One could gauge how many hours or days before the prints occurred by their dryness, by whether they were one on top of another, whether there were fallen leaves in them. Not that we toured down on all fours, moving along on our knuckles. Pop simply gestured here and there, waving his hand toward raccoon prints, which he claimed were evidence of coons poking for crayfish. Dragging tail prints indicated the short work beaver were making of cottonwood saplings. Deer, though the largest critters, were hard to spot in their stiff tan coats (hiding from my brother), except when their heads appeared above a line of sight. It was easiest to see them in the spring and summer when they grouped with their fawns. Pairs of bald eagles lifted dripping carp from the

Platte to treetops, where they tore at and swallowed them. Great blue herons soared along the horizon, their prehistoric shapes reflected in the timeless water. This was Pop's life. And experiencing all this with him was very different from gazing up at Chagall's ceiling at the Garnier Opera in Paris. It was primal. Here, I wasn't a spectator; I was *in* it. It was eyes, ears, and nose about water proximity.

SPECTACLE 2

THE NUISANCE OF HINDSIGHT

*The people who support these boondoggle projects are always talking about the
vision and principles that made this country great. "Our forefathers would have
built this project!" they say. "They had vision!" That's pure nonsense. It wasn't the
vision and principles of our forefathers that made this country great. It was the
huge unused bonanza they found here . . . We've been so busy spending money
and reaping the fruits that we're blind to the fact that there are no more fruits. By
trying to make things better, we're making them worse and worse.*
—GLENN SAUNDERS, THEN CHIEF COUNSEL FOR THE DENVER WATER
BOARD, QUOTED IN MARC REISNER, *CADILLAC DESERT*

Back in the 1950s, all Denver schoolchildren were subjected to Colorado state
capitol building fieldtrips. There, guides greeted us with smiles, and then
boasted about the capitol's construction materials—*all* mined, cut, panned, and
manufactured in Colorado. The subject of Colorado's "inexhaustible resources"
was of little interest to us grade schoolers. Our attention flitted.

The capitol's massive dome, covered in gold leaf, is impressive, but it was the
west portico that most captivated me. It is exactly one mile above sea level. As a
landlocked first-grader, I stared down at the phrase "5,280 feet above sea level"
chiseled in the granite step. Puzzled, I bit my nail, wondering. Was an underground sea right there beneath my feet? My imagination fixed on that deeply
buried, briny somewhere with breaking waves, barking seals, and dunes strewn
with sand dollars.

Soon, guides nudged me and my classmates, like a segmented worm, through
the portico and up, up the grand staircase with brass balustrades that we fogged
up with hot child breath, past the murals, legislative chambers, committee rooms

and offices, to a dangerously narrow spiral staircase. Single file, we ascended ninety-four additional stairs, to arrive winded 180 feet farther above sea level.

Inlaid in the rotunda are portraits of sixteen notable pioneers, rendered in stained glass. My great-great-grandfather's portrait would be among them, my father had told me, so I tried to keep my mind from wandering.

There he was! "Benjamin Harrison Eaton." Colorado's first water man and fourth governor was widely credited with bringing large-scale water availability to the Front Range. Its farm region, which includes our Big Bend Station, became one of the most productive agriculture areas in the nation thanks to Ben Eaton's dedication. Such a legacy might have carried clout among my peers—and even sparked my own interest in historic Colorado, as my father hoped it would— had it not been for the unfortunate caption under my great-great-grandfather's portrait.

Picture me, sticky from my ascent in wide petticoats, coat, hat, and gloves, staring across the gallery at my esteemed relative and sounding out, in my early reader way, the words below his name: " A-N H-O-N-E-S-T P-L-O-D-D-E-R." What an odd epithet! Why not "problem solver" like Governor John Evans? Or "determined and compassionate" like educator Emily Griffith? An Honest Plodder? And only leave it to my vicious classmates to increase my mortification. For this shame I had distanced myself from the subterranean sea?

This episode at the age of six or seven made "forward momentum" my biggest priority. I refused to read about my venerable ancestor. Whenever anyone mentioned the word *pioneer* my ears air-locked. What next: outhouses and quilting? I couldn't wait to get away from the subject of water in the West. Not until recently, when water resources became first the object of my activism, then my profession, did I consider that *the past might answer the future.*

It's that line of inquiry that I now ponder. I'm not exploring the whole arid West or the whole arid world. I'm picking up details of personal history, in the hope of crafting a fix for one place, Big Bend Station, and through that fix, a more optimistic future.

For my backward glance, I chose 1803 as a point of departure, thirty years before my illustrious plodder's birth. America's expansionism had just resulted in the Louisiana Purchase, which included Colorado's northeastern flank, where some hint of Big Bend Station (an Arapaho campsite, maybe) might already have existed. This date makes a decent springboard because the Louisiana Purchase, like most purchases, concerned water resources.

In 1819, the federal government dispatched an engineer named Major Stephen Harriman Long to weigh the worth of the acquisition.[1] Long and his party rode west with increasing pessimism before reaching the immense Rockies, indivisible from the sky. Long wrote that the Plains were *not* full of potential, but were a dry, dry expanse unfit for anything except buffalo, snakes, cactus and antelope. Even so, Coloradans named one fourteener mountain peak after him—this cynic, a man who didn't even *like* Colorado. Long's Peak looms in front of our farm like a taunt. It does! And it is the favorite landmark of my mother, Gogo.

Despite Long's skepticism, the West's panoramas seemed limitless to nineteenth-century Americans. An assumption of inexhaustibility took hold. At the capitol building 150 years later, guides still extolled the inexhaustible resources. With so much distance between boundaries, few thought of the West as anything other than infinitely big. Screw up one place? Fail to reap enough? One could always move on. This perception of limitless horizons with limitless opportunities made Americans lax about stewardship and disrespectful of resources. This has certainly been my generation's behavior. And groundwater abuse is The Water Story today.

Now dabbling in hindsight, I consider the historic disconnect. Like any quantity of land, the Plains were not limitless; they were actually *finite*. Scientists might say that their immutable proportions suggest a predictable "carrying capacity."

To get your mind around *carrying capacity*, envision an area as big as a city block. Why not take the city block where Colorado's capitol building is? Imagine that this block is *all the land there is*. An island. Nothing comes in, except precipitation. Nothing goes out, except evaporation. All the food eaten on that block must be cultivated on that block. All the waste that accumulates on that block—including feces, dead humans, and dead animals—stays on that block. Whatever is not usable will take up space, a signature of *entropy*. With few resources and hardly any room, the trick is to keep entropy to a minimum. The finite block is a responsibility and an opportunity for everyone and everything on it. Imagine the care that would go into survival there on that small footprint, if there were *no other options*.

Entropy

Entropy is a measure of the energy that is *not* available for work during a thermodynamic process.

Entropy = Unavailable Energy

$$S = -k_B \sum_i p_i \ln p_i$$

Interestingly, an additional meaning of *entropy* is the doctrine of inevitable social decline and degeneration.

For a start, you had better begin chiseling at all that Colorado granite, to find tillable land as well as a source and receptacle for fresh water.

What Stephen Harriman Long called the "Great American Desert,"[2] hemmed between the Missouri River and the Rockies, is billions of times larger than that Denver city block, but just as finite. By the time Long saw the High Plains, low precipitation had shrunk its ability to sustain forests. Nevertheless, it did support thriving numbers of Plains Indians, in addition to evident buffalo, snakes, cactus, and antelope, whose numbers were excellent indicators of the land's carrying capacity. And the Plains Indians practiced tenets of sustainability that white settlers might've then learned from . . . but didn't.

Carrying capacity isn't immutable. It varies, with ecological shifts and with climate. Centuries before Major Long arrived, eastern Colorado was wet enough for Native American tribes to farm, to cultivate maize, beans, squash, marshelder, and sunflowers on the high grass plains.[3] Subsequent drought pushed the indigenous farmers toward the Missouri, where they lived in relatively fixed settlements.[4] There was little strife between tribes.

Speed

The average velocity of an object moving through displacement during an interval

$$v = \frac{\Delta x}{\Delta t}$$

By the early nineteenth century, however, settler expansion, armed incursions by tribes pinched by that expansion, and the growing fur trade destabilized the Missouri River region. Escalating tension drove the Cheyenne to the western Plains.[5] Horses provided opportunity. *Speed* did to the Native Americans what the automobile has done to us all. Once hunters climbed astride horses and felt what it was to gallop, felt the scenery zoom by, they were hooked. Using horses, trading for horses, herding and training wild horses, and raiding horses to hunt, they became nomadic. The Cheyenne expanded their range, concentrating on the bison-rich region between the two forks of the Platte.[6] And while the Cheyenne were astride horses, other tribes astride horses gave chase. Provoked into intertribal conflict by American expansion west, competing tribes vied faster, farther, and often fiercely, for territory within the finite quantity of land just described, the High Plains.[7] To defend against the Sioux in the first years of the 1800s, the Cheyenne forged an alliance with the Arapaho, then situated here at the foot of the Rockies.[8]

Because European traders represented a market, the Cheyenne killed buffalo for trade as well as sustenance.[9] The tribe became the middlemen between the horse-rich tribes to the south and those with guns to the north. They traded at outposts such as Fort William (Laramie), Fort St. Vrain (a few miles from Big Bend Station), and Bent's Fort.[10] According to some sources, fur companies shipped around 130,000 buffalo robes through New Orleans between 1825 and 1830.[11]

The High Plains climate, land, and resources differed from those on the Missouri. Those horses that Plains Indians rode and the wild horses they traded, as well as the bison and smaller game they hunted—these animals competed for grassland and water sources too.[12] The tribes moved around a lot to make sure the horses could fatten on nutritious short grasses—the buffalo grass (*Buchloe dactyloides*) and blue grama (*Bouteloua gracilis*).[13] No wonder then that the Cheyenne, Arapaho, and other Plains tribes understood what pioneers did not, what most Americans still don't understand. Native Americans understood carrying capacity.

Yet, precipitation was ample on the Plains between 1815 and 1845.[14] It was a "time of plenty." All populations copulated and pollinated like crazy, and numbers of people, animals, and vegetation swelled within the boundaries. The Plains supported as many as 60 million buffalo, what Meriwether Lewis called a "moving multitude, which darkened the whole Plains."[15] At the same time, the Spanish moved up from the Southwest, the French and British down from the East and Northeast, and American pioneers poured in from the East. Human population on the High Plains *doubled* between 1820 and the mid-1850s.[16]

·········■··■·········

Who could have guessed that precipitation and economic expansion would bring about the demise of the American Indian and almost reduce *Bison bison* to extinction?

Times of plenty are deceptive. Abundance leads first to false expectations, second to imbalance. And what of the word *finite*? Because the area that these bigger populations depended on was finite (as it still is), additional numbers of people and animals became that much more competitive for space and resources. They were also that much harder on the space and resources. A few years in the lifetime of a single generation, my great-great-grandfather Ben Eaton's generation, would totally upend that carrying capacity. *Out* with thriving numbers of Plains Indians, buffalo, snakes, cactus, and antelope. *In* with farmers, cattle, and farms. Novel inhabitants, novel foods. New interactions with resources.

The year that Ben Eaton hit puberty in Ohio, 1845, drought hit the Plains. Just as our recent drought followed three decades of above-average precipitation, there was hardly any precipitation for over a decade, until 1856. Lack of rain and snowfall meant less grass. Now-inflated populations of buffalo and antelope moved eastward toward the Missouri River but were there restricted by increased human settlement. Prairie plants and animals dwindled, which stressed the tribes that relied upon them. Not surprisingly, the Native Americans' survival strategy was to hug the wetter, more fecund creek sides and river corridors. These wetlands were the Cheyenne's and Arapaho's versions of today's commissaries and malls, where supplies of food, clothing, and shelter could be had. Near water, the tribes could feed their horses and find game, since wildlife had the same clinging-to-wetlands survival strategy. Unfortunately, pioneers navigated along these corridors too, for the same reasons. *Trails followed water.* Had numbers of pioneers remained low, the prairie might have been able to recover . . . but they did not.

White folks had problems of their own. The Panic of 1857 hit in the East, and American railroads' speculative bubble burst. Loss of confidence in banks followed, and 5,000 businesses failed in a single year. How many more than 5,000 businesses were there in the country then? Unemployment led to protests.

Then, when things were grimmest, gold was discovered in Cherry Creek. My father's haunt, Cherry Creek, feeds the South Platte River, in what is today Denver.

A harkening! The July 1858 discovery in Colorado detonated a massive influx of westward-bound fortune hunters, most of them under age thirty, with their whole lives ahead of them. Benjamin Harrison Eaton was among them.

I wish I could write that Ben Eaton's trip from the Midwest was mindful of ecology and respectful of the Native Americans' prior claim. He was but one of 100,000 mostly heedless travelers. That many people and all their gear laid waste to the land along the Platte Trail. Between 1858 and 1861 a long and unending cloud of gritty alkaline dust hovered over the landscape, day and night. Pulverizing caravans of oxen, mules, horses, wagons, wheelbarrows, and scuffing plodders trampled in a queue that extended as far as the eye could see. As the prospectors progressed, they hunted indiscriminately and cut trees for fuel. Their animals decimated diminishing grasses. Jettisoning extra weight that they no longer needed, the westward bound left a path of detritus and filth. Rotting carcasses and bones lay bleaching in the sun. All the fortune hunters, whether feckless, reprehensible, or like my relative—simply seeking a new way of life— participated in the ransacking. From a distance, the Cheyenne, Arapaho, and other tribes watched the wetlands they depended upon for survival carelessly despoiled by strangers who believed they had left limitations behind. The Indians thought the white people were crazy.

Once to the Rockies, not everyone's get-rich quick scheme panned out. Disappointed, many turned on their heel, plundering the banks of the Platte all over again in reverse. Ben remained, though. He and a new friend, Jim Hill, pushed on to try their hand at prospecting farther south.[17] Seeing the San Luis Valley changed Ben's life forever.

Ben *knew* how to farm. He'd already made a go of it in Iowa and Ohio, where farming was the same as in northern Europe. It counted upon rain. He hadn't thought about farming recently, because weeks on the dry prairie didn't augur success. Ben's impression was the same as Major Long's: Great American Desert. For that reason, the San Luis Valley was a real jaw dropper. Crops spilled, *heaped* even, over the landscape. Herds of fine-looking cattle, sheep, and goats were everywhere. How did farmers accomplish such bounty with so little rainfall, Ben wondered?

The 100th Meridian

This line of longitude is 100 degrees west of Greenwich and runs through central Nebraska, figuratively represents the line between our country's moist East and its arid West. Roughly, the West gets less than half the rainfall that falls east of the meridian. In the east, with twenty inches or more a year, farmers need not rely so much on irrigation. The Union Pacific Railroad reached and marked the 100th Meridian in 1868.

Ingenuity in the San Luis Valley was the product of people who knew how to make do with less. Six hundred years earlier, the native Hohokam tribe had irrigated thousands of acres using dams and ditches in the Southwest. Later tribes such as the Pueblo and Tohono O'odham did likewise.[18] Spanish colonialists in the Americas brought similar irrigation methods passed down from the Alhambra and Extremadura, for which they in turn could thank resourceful Moors on the Iberian Peninsula. Such dams and ditches were perfected on New Mexican land grants. Applied in the San Luis Valley, they captured Ben Eaton's intellect and his ambition.

No more counting on rain as one would in Iowa and Ohio. Instead, farmers diverted from an existing water source—Culebra Creek in the San Luis Valley—via a "mother canal," called an *acequia madre*. Water flowed along the acequias, pulled by gravity. The acequia madre split into lateral branches called *sangrias*. This sangria is a short ditch constructed to a grade that insures flow to the fields. The

Acequia

Translated from the Spanish, acequia is an irrigation ditch. The Arab word for *acequia* is *assaquiya*.

Sangria

Before *sangria* meant "wine-laced punch," it meant "bloodletting."

results were so impressive that Ben and his amiable friend Jim determined to try them out farther south in the New Mexico Territory.

Only, faraway rancor between Northern and Southern states got in the way. Anticipating the South's secession, the US Congress was keen to get Colorado's minerals (its "inexhaustible" resources) under Union control, so it hastened to create the "Colorado Territory" on February 28, 1861. Fewer than six weeks later, Confederates fired on Fort Sumter and the Civil War began. The South needed resources. Confederates advanced through the Southwest.

Unionists scrambled to deter this incursion. Typical red-blooded young men, Ben Eaton and Jim Hill volunteered in the impromptu New Mexico Regulars led by Colonel Kit Carson. Untrained, bordering on insubordinate, and armed with dubious weapons, the Regulars were infamous as the militia of last resort. This may explain why only one Regular died.

Enter the miscreant, Colonel John Chivington, reputedly 6'7" tall and 250 pounds and decidedly not one of Carson's Regulars. Chivington's lone, lost phalanx stumbled upon the Confederates' supply stash on March 22, 1862, where he and his soldiers slaughtered 600 screaming animals with bayonets, then burned everything else. This brutality completely dismantled Johnny Rebel's supply train, and the Confederates were forced to retreat. Carnage elsewhere continued for three more years, but in the Southwest—game over.

This put Ben Eaton and his buddy Jim Hill again at loose ends. Ever since the Louisiana Purchase, the federal government had been trying to overcome its buyer's remorse, pushing to make good on its investment by luring citizens West with incentives. In 1862 Congress legislated such an enticement, the Homestead Act. All a settler had to do to gain title to 160 public acres was hunker down there for five years. With hunkering down in mind, Ben and Jim tied their squirrel

Cache la Poudre

Cache la Poudre means "hiding place for powder" in French. The river was so named because trappers secreted their gunpowder near the river in the 1820s.

guns behind their saddles and gravitated back to the South Platte basin. They paused where they had met three years before, where the Cache la Poudre River met the slow-moving Platte. Twelve miles west of the confluence, about fourteen miles from Big Bend Station, the determined pair laid claim to 160 acres. As security, Ben and Jim hastily pulled together a shack of cottonwood logs. That done, they rode back to the Midwest, to get provisions and, in Ben's case, a wife. With dispatch, Ben married Jim's sister Becky, about whom he'd already heard an earful.

·········■■··■■·········

Why would a young woman let herself be willingly dislodged from a large happy family in Iowa's safe, fertile farm country, then led off in a wagon with a couple of washtubs, to the lurid tune of gruesome Cheyenne attacks? It must've been love! No sooner did Ben, Becky, and Jim's wagon cross the Missouri River in summer 1864 than their journey ground to a halt. They could not continue along the Platte until enough armed men could be mustered to protect the caravan from Native American raids.

Native Americans were not reinventing themselves, as were Ben, Becky, and Jim. They were *desperate* to survive. Tribes had endured continual upheaval, betrayal, displacement, and starvation. Whooping cough, cholera, smallpox, and measles had reduced their numbers dramatically.[19] An 1851 treaty allotted the Arapaho and Cheyenne a region that is today southeastern Wyoming, most of eastern Colorado, western Kansas, and southwestern Nebraska. Ten years later, a new treaty signed at Fort Lyon reduced that reserve to one-thirteenth its size. With justifiable outrage, Cheyenne tribes went to war against the US Army.[20] Their retaliatory attacks were severe enough that they successfully closed many overland trails.

Coloradans, by then beating their chests over Union victories, wouldn't stop for "heathens," oh no! Soldiers back from the Civil War took up arms again, and the "Colorado War" officially began. As many times featured in cowboy and Indian classics, Plains tribes tried to maintain control of buffalo migration grounds in the upper river valleys, including the South Platte, which had adequate grazing land that the settlers wanted. Pioneers had turned the South Platte into a trail of trash and were cutting off water supplies by homesteading upon its banks. Distilled to its essence, the Colorado War was a fight over access to water. It also marked the final episode in prairie ecology that had sustained buffalo and Native Americans for millennia. In this finale, my great-great-grandparents were inadvertent players.

When Becky, Ben, and Jim finally reached the Poudre's cottonwoods and meadows, the groom tried to throw open the door on the love nest he and Jim had erected months before. It wouldn't budge, because cattle had taken refuge from a storm within and become trapped by snow. The poor animals had starved to death. Summer had sped up decomposition. So much for the honeymoon cottage.

On August 10, 1864, barely a month after Jim and the newlyweds arrived back in Colorado, a front-page editorial in the *Rocky Mountain News* written by the paper's founder, William Byers, exhorted: "Eastern humanitarians who believe in the superiority of the Indian race will raise a terrible toll over this policy, but it is no time to split hairs nor stand upon compunctions of conscience. Self-preservation demands decisive action, and the only way to secure it [is through] a few months of active extermination against the red devils." Many took Byers's call to arms to heart—Colonel John Chivington, whose pitiless mule-slaying had subverted the Confederate advance on the West's "inexhaustible" resources, for one. And Chivington had full support from Territorial Governor John Evans.

The Cheyenne kept an American flag hoisted over their camp at Sand Creek, as stipulated by the Fort Lyon Treaty. Nevertheless, there, on November 1864, Chivington's drunken minions conducted one of the most appalling acts against Native Americans on record. The Sand Creek Massacre was ghastly in its numbers and its details, which included murdering and mutilating approximately 200 mostly unarmed women, children, and old men. Soldiers adorned their saddles and persons with dismembered genitalia, which they carried back to Denver as trophies. The nation was in shock. After testimony against Chivington in Washington, the outraged US Congress turned down the US Army's request for war against Native American tribes. President Andrew Johnson demanded Territorial Governor Evan's resignation and got it. Congress refused to support Colorado's appeal for statehood. Worse, Colorado's "war on red men" intensified rage over water and land. Retaliatory Cheyenne and Arapaho raids on settlers brought more fatalities.

So, no sooner had the Eaton trio unloaded the wagon than a courier rode in yelling about an *end-to-life-as-you-know-it* warpath. In retaliation for Chivington and others like him, tribes were to strike the next day in fully a quarter of the territory. The three took refuge at a fortified ranch nearby. There, Jim and Ben ultimately left Becky for the winter. Badly in need of money, the friends took off to be "bullwhackers." This profession was that era's counterpart to the teamsters, and until the railroads found their way West, the only way to move freight, along waterways, of course.

Becky was a real trooper. Because her brother and husband were coaxing oxen with bullwhips, she did not move into her new cabin until late spring 1865. Once ensconced in her prairie home, Ben's wife got domestic. We Eaton cousins are used to hearing the story of Becky, who had made a pie, chasing after marauding braves with a broom. Ben and Jim rushed to help her during this episode, making a great show of cracking their bullwhips. Hear tell, the visiting braves thought this was wildly amusing. I wonder what sort of pie Becky, so briefly settled, might have made. Prairie turnip?

By then the parents of a newborn, Ben and Becky made a go of it as farmers. Ben dug a system of acequias and sangrias, emulating the direct-flow ditch system he and Jim had seen in the San Luis. Ben then plowed and tried his hand at small grains such as wheat, oats, and barley. Adjacent, Jim Hill staked his own claim and built another cabin. Other settlers were drawn to the Poudre, and farmland there slowly became a little oasis on the otherwise-forlorn expanse of prairie.

"Forlorn," though, wasn't how newspaperman Horace Greeley, editor of the *New York Tribune*, remembered Colorado from his visit to mining towns in 1859. The Rockies exhilarated him. Back in populous New York City, moods were susceptible to financial downturns. Within the city's tall, tightly packed brick walk-ups, the horizon began and ended across the street. By contrast, horizons in the West were wide open, and wide horizons suggested broad opportunities. To Greeley too, the illusion of "infinity" was scintillating. His July 13, 1865, editorial famously cajoled, "Go West, young man, go West, and grow up with the country."

One of Greeley's sidekicks was the *New York Tribune*'s agricultural editor, Father Nathan Meeker, by all descriptions a bit of a prig. Meeker and Greeley were high on *The Communist Manifesto* (published in 1848) and in thrall to the Utopia Movement. "Intentional communities" out West, they considered loftily, seemed a great panacea for down times in the East. Together, Greeley and Meeker cooked up and promoted such a community in Colorado. In late 1869 the *Tribune* posted a notice calling colonists to the "Union Colony," named in celebration of the northern win. The hitch was a vow of sobriety. From several thousand would-be abstemious applicants, Meeker and associates chose 700.

In 1870 Father Meeker and two others traveled to Colorado to pick the Union Colony site. This locating committee fell under my great-great-grandfather's spell, after Ben Eaton brought the gentlemen to his farm to show off the possibilities and perhaps to eat pie. Ben Eaton suggested that the land southeast of his place, at the confluence of the South Platte and Poudre, might be ideal. After all, it had water and, by then, rail. Ben Eaton promised to assist with the ditch construction that was critical to the colony's farms. Bankrolled by Horace Greeley, the Union Colonists secured 60,000 contiguous acres. On March 15, 1870, the executive committee named the town Greeley.

Soon after, the Denver Pacific Railroad engine clanged its heavy bell and debouched its first colonists. Right off the rails, bewildered newcomers paid a $155 fee and signed a covenant promising to abstain from alcohol and gambling. In exchange, they received a house site in town and a farm on the higher benchlands.[21] It had been a long trip. Colonists, who might have craved a drink, could only drink in a vastness absent trees for building houses. Had they really traded away the civilized world for an investment in a cactus landscape where any movement was probably a rattlesnake? The terrain seemed hopeless, unbearably so to some, who about-faced to return to civilization, calling Greeley "a delusion, a snare."[22]

Those who stayed got serious. Gauged by contemporary Greeley's array of malls and superstores and its population of almost 100,000, the colonists' circumstances are hard to imagine. For inspiration, many made the trip out to the Eaton's proto-farm to the immediate east. Its headstart of fields and a small grove of fruit trees proved instructive. My great-great-grandfather was not only honest, but a champion of the "can-do" attitude. He and a handful of settlers knuckled under to establish a means of irrigating the settlement's crops before fall of the next year. Ditchdigging was all the talk all the time.

Whereas chokecherries and milk vetch suited Native Americans, the colonists strove to grow grain. Unfortunately, their ditch had hitches. Canal No. 1 was continually thwarted by gophers, which thrived since water was directly delivered to them. With new gopher holes needing to be plugged every day, the first canal's volume was insufficient to turn the prickly pear thicket into waving grains, much less to turn a mill for grinding grain. Yet, the settlers doggedly dug on and patched their ditch under a blazing sun.

After a hard day of toil, no one could toss one back at the saloon or disport with card sharps. There were none. Nothing to be done except hit the sack and wake up to dig again. As *The New York Times* correspondent wrote of Greeley, "Don't stop in that town; you'll die of dullness in less than five hours."[23]

Bovidae

Buffalo (*Bison bison*) and cattle (*Bos taurus*) are cousins, both members of the Bovidae family. Bovidae also includes sheep, goats, antelope, and other ruminants.

According to Union Colony meeting minutes and lore, Ben Eaton *wouldn't give up*, wouldn't stop combating the gophers while widening the ditch. If New Mexicans could irrigate, so too could the colonists, he figured. Ben's business officially became irrigation contracting. Over the next few years, the thirty-five-mile long canal was enlarged many times and the river dammed. It took $87,000 in 1870s' dollars ($1.5 million in today's dollars) to irrigate a mere 2,000 acres.[24] That and one zealot.

Struggling crops faced an additional threat. All over the prairie, millions of newly arrived Longhorns chewed, mooed, and defecated. This incursion was largely the work of two enterprising cattlemen, Oliver Loving and Charlie Goodnight, who saw dollar signs in the form of hungry western miners. Loving and Goodnight reasoned that the prairie had supported enormous populations of ruminants for centuries. Weren't cattle just a less nappy version of buffalo? Move the buffalo out; move the cattle in: presto-beef-o.

Yet the differences between buffalo and cattle were many and affected prairie water supply. Any cowboy might have told you that buffalo aren't thirsty and are therefore less likely to overgraze. Such observations were evident, but obscured by the opportunity for profit . . . and by the many consumers who hankered for beef. Few recognized—maybe no one recognized—how much the buffalo's distinct diet and behaviors added to prairie ecology, making biodiversity and sustainability possible. Prairie grasses, which the cattle needed, flourished because the buffalo were there, and buffalo habits resulted in food, habitat, and water for other animals too.

Take wallowing. A buffalo's massive dark shape—conspicuous against muted prairie colors—slows, sniffs, stops. Suddenly, the animal heaves its ton of weight to the ground. Bam!

> ### Ruminant—A Mowing "Machine"
>
> A ruminant is a split-hoofed mammal with a series of digestive chambers that turn grass into high-quality protein. Food is first softened in the first two stomach chambers (known collectively as the *reticulorumen*) until it becomes a cud. Then the ruminant regurgitates the semidigested cud and chews it again. This ceaseless chewing is called *ruminating*. The food enters the third chamber (omasum), where its water and inorganic minerals flow into the bloodstream. The fourth chamber (abomasum) functions much the way human stomach functions. These chambers, helped along by microbes, break down plant fiber into the fatty acids, and protein and nonstructural carbohydrate become fermented.

Twisting and writhing, its back scratch and sometimes mud bath raise a swirling cloud of dust, as animated as a dust devil. Wallowing created depressions that collected standing water that other animals could drink. The water also irrigated surrounding foliage, such as the grasses and sedge cattlemen planned on feeding to the cattle.

But no one knew that. Cattlemen and everyone else perceived the prairie as totally separate from the animals it sustained. It was the United States' piece of land, bought and paid for, there to exploit. What was good for the buffalo would be good for the cattle, Loving and Goodnight decided. *Think about the dollar signs.* In 1865, one steer was worth three to four dollars in the West, but could be sold in the East for thirty to forty dollars.[25] Thus motivated, the pair blazed a trail 2,000 miles north from West Texas to Denver and eventually onward to Cheyenne. Over the Goodnight-Loving Trail, nearly 5 million head of Longhorn cattle moved between 1866 and 1884. And the prairie, which was mostly public land, *was* good for the cattle as long as its resources lasted.

Cattlemen made themselves at home on the public land. It afforded free feed, range, and water. They even began fencing it in, making illegal enclosures to contain their herds. Their animals blitzed the waterways and tore the hell out of the grasslands. Meanwhile, the cattle boom was driving the other prairie ecosystem assailants—the farmers—out of their gourds, because cattle were destroying crops. Greeley fenced itself off from the cattle and cowboys, with $20,000 worth of posts and wire. My ancestors fenced off their land too. Bear in mind, however, that these same people *ate* beef.

Native Americans depended on unimpeded migrations of buffalo, elk, deer, and antelope. Cattlemen turned prairielands into a range where other ruminants were unwelcome competitors. In response, Native Americans tore out fences. They burned ranches and drove off cattle, but it was hopeless. New railroad lines meant new markets, beyond the miners, and shipping cattle to eastern cities enlarged Colorado's cattle industry exponentially. To make it easier, cattlemen—in concert with railroaders, bankers, and the military—devised to purge the range of Native Americans.

In addition to hollow treaties and genocide, American industrialists' next most-effective method was to get rid of the food source: *Bison bison.* The military exhorted white hide hunters to "cut the heart from the Plains Indians economy."[26] Under Generals William T. Sherman and Philip Sheridan, the military routinely sponsored and outfitted hunts, clearing land for railroad expansion that could, in the interim, carry hides.[27] Between 1868 and 1881, an estimated 31 million buffalo were killed and transported by rail for bone and hide. That number does not include those that died from hunting or other causes. Cattle diseases such as bovine tuberculosis, brucellosis, Texas fever (anthrax), and Spanish itch (sarcoptic mange) decimated buffalo herds. By 1894, it was hard to find more than 500 buffalo within the United States.[28] Reduced from 60 million to 500, in a brief half-century, the American buffalo, whose genus had thrived for more than a million years, faced extinction.[29] Like everyone, I have always thought of this period with horror and shame, but not until writing "Thirst for the Known" did I recognize this extermination was rooted in pure consumerism.

Earlier versions of consumers like us supported a market for beef, and buffalo were in the way. At the time, American businessmen and settlers regarded the disappearance of the herds with jubilation, as "a triumph of civilization over savagery."[30] And in the process, those native peoples for whom living sustainably was the highest cultural value were subdued, their wisdom perceived as pathetic, laughable.

On the march toward civilization, Ben and his neighbors had ceaseless tribulations. The winter of 1871–72 was severe, blowing, and frozen with a cold that took bites from colonists' commitment. Ben sprang Becky and their growing family from exile at the Cache le Poudre and moved to a rented house in Greeley, so they could keep warm by proximity. There, he and a neighbor tested crops to ascertain the best species for scant water, seasonal conditions, and the lighter soil of the bluff lands, where settlers would soon plant. Such was the activity of honest plodders.

Despite the Union Colony's travails, the grand experiment—the drive to prosper on the prairie—continued. Other intentional communities sprang up, with more sodbusters arriving in northeastern Colorado monthly. That didn't mean that there was enough water, however. In the foothills and mountains, colonists cut timber to use for building, but the river didn't even have enough juice to float the cut downstream. Ben Eaton was much in demand as the go-to canal builder, constructing two additional acequias madres (direct-flow ditches) for the new Fort Collins Agricultural Colony. It rained little the following growing season. Downstream from Fort Collins, Greeley's canals dried and cracked. By July 1874 trees and crops withered. Greeley's farmers became panicky, and then livid when they discovered that Fort Collins's upstream canals were to blame. Yes, only four years into settlement and already there was too much demand. The water situation was desperate.

Tempers flared. At Greeley, former Union soldiers turned colonists organized to take water by gunfire if necessary. The welcome wagon for new colonists at Fort Collins wasn't friendly neighbors, but truculent cavalcades instead. Luckily, Honest Ben and a few others calmed the Greeley colonists with a commitment to divide the water according to need and a promise to deliver it. This wasn't ultimately necessary, that year at least, because it rained.

So without bloodshed, the subject of insufficient water moved to the back burner, remanding the one resource that no one could do without to whom? If not God, perhaps government might solve the problem of water allocations?

The territorial government *was* trying. Some thought statehood might make that difference, but Colorado's long wait for statehood was the least of the disaffected farmers' concerns.

July 1874 delivered yet another sign of calamitous environmental imbalance. Skies darkened midday with not just millions or billions but *trillions* of locusts. The Rocky Mountain locust (*Melanoplus spretus*) was the only grasshopper in North America that had a "locust phase," meaning that it *swarmed*. This swarm, extending from the Dakotas to Texas, was more like a long voracious siege.[31] One could hear the insects on approach—the whir of wings, the stridulating legs, and the chomping mandibles. Individually, the insects were round and thick as a cigar. Some were as much as six inches long. Shimmering accretions of bugs clung to fence posts, siding, to everything. Branches bent under their weight, only to snap back totally denuded. Farmers threw blankets over crops, but the grasshoppers ate the blankets, then gnawed through the crops, leaving fields looking burned. They ate the leather off saddles and the wool off sheep.[32] For days afterward, people's clothing crawled with grasshoppers. Oh, Becky Eaton—doesn't your heart ache for her?

Rocky Mountain Locust

Melanoplus spretus, in Latin, means "dreaded black mass."

This assault made the cutworm moths that had greeted our family at Big Bend Station in 1970 seem like a single fruit fly. Many orders of magnitude greater than any previous swarm seen in the United States, it repeated *four summers in succession*. The 1875 epidemic was 1,800 miles long and 110 miles wide.[33] Industrious farmers, never stopping behind the eight ball or taking a nip, devised all kinds of impediments. They doused their crops with kerosene. They fanned grasshoppers into vats of oil. Whole families such as the Eatons stood sentry, shaking their fruit trees while the insects ate their very clothes. "Hopperdozers" drawn by unfortunate animals, crushed hoppers, if the critters could be waved into harm's way.

The locusts bred in wetlands. There, females deposited eggs in dry, sandy soil. After undiscovered eggs hatched into the nymph phase, the insects went on the march in big clumps. These accumulations were so adhesive that nymph masses six inches thick could pontoon across streams and rivers. Once nymphs sprouted wings, the grasshopper plunder commenced. They could travel 200 miles a day. So, communities set a bounty on locust eggs and families set forth to find the crusty casings. Greeley families didn't have to search long since Greeley was *in* the river valley. The locusts were back in 1876 and 1877 too. As summer 1878 approached, tooth clenching mounted.

June passed without swarming, then July, then August. Amazingly, Rocky Mountain locusts were used up. How could a species that had swarmed for perhaps thousands of years so abruptly cease? Few wondered why. They were simply happy that prayer, fate, and egg hunts had worked. Much later, scientists determined that the cause of extinction was the same as that precipitating the record-breaking migrations to begin with—*destruction of wetlands*. First in their excursions west, pioneers had stomped the river valleys, cattle had stomped likewise, and farmers had planted there. Grasshoppers had nowhere left to breed. The species' last gasp still holds a place in *The Guinness Book of World Records* as "greatest concentration of animals" ever. *Melanoplus spretus* hasn't been spotted since 1902.

The years since gold materialized at Cherry Creek were but a blink in the thirteen millennia during which prairie carrying capacity had remained relatively stable, with little evident entropy. Yet those seventeen years effectively purged the region of its indigenous *Homo sapiens*, its *Bison bison, and its Melanoplus spretus. As settlers poured in, increasing demand for "the source," hundreds more species were driven close to or into extinction.* Despite nature's evident defiance, Coloradans persisted. In 1876, this insubordinate territory—with its ruined ecosystems, uncooperative resources, opportunistic vermin, pestilence, illegal enclosures, scarce water, and reactionary settlers with their despoiling livelihoods—became the "Centennial State," thirty-eighth in the United States of America.

The federal government, prodded by the railroads and still calling Major Stephen Harriman Long's bluff, kept up the enticements: the Desert Land Act of 1877 gave away 640 acres parcels for only $1.25 an acre, as long as it was irrigated. In answer, Ben Eaton considered the advantages of extending a *really* long canal, a manmade river that would deliver water to the bench areas at the farthest reaches. By then, he knew which land would best serve which crops. He knew which natural contours best carried water forward. He

Benchlands

In geomorphology, a bench or benchland is a long, narrow, level terrace, edged by steeper slopes. Benches can be of different origins, but along the Platte they usually define the former path of the river.

knew that buffalo wallows were hard enough for natural storage lakes to supply farmers when the river dropped later in summer. Ben put up his own funds in 1878 and got digging. His ten yokes of oxen ripped up a ribbon of raw earth, upending sagebrush and cactus eastward, while Ben talked up the farming opportunity in his quest for capital.

Dauntless plodder that Ben was, he at last convinced British capitalists to invest in the canal's construction and buy adjacent land as prospectors. The Larimer and Weld Irrigation Company was incorporated, the largest and longest canal of the epoch, irrigating 50,000 acres.

My forebear's toil paid off. The wasteland was no more. Subsequent irrigation projects transformed northeastern Colorado prairie and attracted thousands of late-arriving utopia seekers, most to propagate thirsty crops and thirsty children. "Carrying capacity" be damned, a long, rollicking dance on the grave of the Great American Desert ensued, a dance with ever more ambitious water diversions that continue today.

They told us on our fieldtrips, over and over, that diversion and irrigation had transformed the unyielding desert, not into a sea with barking seals as I'd imagined at the state capitol, but into a high-yielding agrarian economy. Yet, no one mentioned that the South Platte did not have adequate water to sustain that economy, not even in the nineteenth century.

Hindsight, though informative, is deeply disturbing. Ben Eaton was no gambler, not technically anyway. He was not sneaking off on Becky to play poker, but he *was* laying bets on the unknowable. Ben—whose forward momentum occurred in a time when plodding was a virtue, *a time very unlike today*—never guessed how much his exertions would catalyze population growth. There are 4.5 million people along the Front Range right now. Ben couldn't know that building canals, dams, reservoirs, and diversions would get out of control. He'd be thunderstruck to hear that Colorado's water has become owed to and owned by millions in nineteen states, more than a third of the United States. Shocked to learn that his early ingenuity inadvertently led to Rocky Mountain snowmelt becoming his great-great-granddaughter's water supply 1,200 miles away in San Diego, where contaminated wastewater flows unceremoniously into the Pacific Ocean with its barking seals! Ben didn't anticipate that the appropriation and upended ecosystems of which he was an early instigator would be reiterated *all over the West* and that only now, a century and a half later, the rollicking, wet dance seems over.

GROWING UP TO BE COWBOYS

The quality of owning freezes you forever in "I," and cuts you off forever from the "we."
—JOHN STEINBECK, *THE GRAPES OF WRATH*

One of Pop's first acts at the farm was to ditch his spurs in the tack room near the corral. We all saw the spurs there. I even reached through the cobwebs to twirl the rowels now and then, to make sure they still jangled. Outside, though, that rattle on gravel was *not* my father in his spurs. That's why events at the farm went as they did.

Bill earned his cowboy gear before moving to Big Bend Station. In Wyoming, and on ag land across Colorado and Nebraska, he was a "Charlie Goodnight" Revisited. During the 1960s, he managed hundreds of thousands of acres of rangeland for a big corporation and was responsible for grazing 20,000 head a year. He'd had no experience in ranching before he got the job, but he improvised as he had since adolescence—with inquiry and dare. Bill plied successful cattlemen for advice. He then acted on their answers, hiring seasoned foremen and cowboys and cattle brokers. Afterward, he leaned on corrals, drank lots of coffee, and traveled in helicopters and private jets—to monitor what was going on. Where special coaxing was required, Bill built relationships using skills he'd learned growing up at a country club. Sometimes it took a game of tennis or golf, or a day of hunting or fishing, to maneuver his way out of a corner. Operating thusly, Bill's rangeland management was a triumph. The spurs, with their hand-engraved silver shanks, were honorary.

Ranching in the 1960s was about growing great beef, or that's how it seemed, as my sister, brother, and I peered at successions of Herefords over our earlier summers spent in Wyoming. Calves were born in the fall and branded and then weaned at six months. After moseying in pastures and feeding in lots when the weather was bad, 550-pound weanlings arrived to forage in the sagebrush-dotted grasslands and aspen glens. Eating grass, as cattle's digestive system evolved to do, built good muscle, red meat.[1]

> **How Foraging Builds Muscle**
>
> Muscle = Red meat
> Grass is high in fiber and low to intermediate in energy. Tromping around to graze builds muscle.

Cowboys kept the cattle in perpetual proximity to a great green buffet. The most colorful cowboy was Joey Hatfield, an impressive talent who sang as well as Johnny Cash and called me Linda Lou. Linda Lou spent a lot of time contemplating cowboys as a child and teenager, sitting on fences at rodeos, learning how to whistle through blades of grass, ogling the foreman's son, stalking him at cattle drives.

Riding at a leisurely gait alongside or behind cattle, cowboys nudged the herds to new terrain. They didn't want the cattle to rush or run, or worse yet stampede. The goal was to move the lil' doggies along gently, so they didn't lose much weight. Once in a while, a steer or a group of steers would wander off and the cowboys had to coax them back to the herd. A seasoned hand such as Joey often trusted this procedure to his dog, to whom he'd casually say, "go git 'im," so he himself could continue to rock slowly forward in his saddle behind the cattle.

From my little twerp perspective, those were sublime months in breathtaking scenery, for steers, for cowboys, for all of us. Come late fall, the idyll ended. Cowboys herded bellowing animals out of the hills and into semitruck trailers. By then, the steers each weighed about 700 pounds. Off they went to the feedlots, some of them very near Big Bend Station, which Pop did not yet own. In the feedlots, the steers ate grain, to "marbleize" their muscle. When at last we cut a bite of steak or skewered a morsel of stew then, we were looking at nine months in the high prairie and forests eating blue grama and buffalo grass, "finished" with six or more months of high-roughage and grain rations in the pen. This feed comprised corn, corn silage, and alfalfa. The idea was to fatten the animals by 450 pounds. Frosty weather meant that weight gain took longer. Animals up to three years old were then trucked off to the nearby slaughterhouse. That was beef in the 1960s. "Nature's own," Bill called it. That was before he owned his own feedlots.

The weight gain in the feedlots in the 1960s was around two pounds per head per day. Sometime during the late 1960s, a salesman from the Midwest showed up along the Platte, to promote a feed supplement called "Doughboy." Overseeing a ranching operation that generated 20,000 head a year, my father seemed like a promising prospect. Like most businesspeople, Bill was often under siege by vendors and was inherently skeptical. This guy claimed that adding his "Doughboy" pellets to high-corn rations could increase steers' weight gain to three or more pounds a day—a 30 percent enhancement!

Transactional Activities

All transactions involve water, land, and energy

$
Seed and other inputs

$
Farming

$
Storage and sales

$
Dairies and meat production

$
Prep, packaging, and packing houses

$
Shipping and transportation

$
Wholesalers

$
Retailers

$
Consumers

Squinting at him, Bill proposed that they put Doughboy to the test, "We'll do one lot of traditional rations. Right next to it, we'll have your Doughboys." Rations in the latter lot were higher in corn and lower in roughage but Doughboy-fortified to produce high gain at low cost. The new technique worked. Sure enough, the cattle eating more corn, with pellets, gained almost an extra pound a day. This approach cost less and decreased time in the feedlots to four and half months . . . or a bit more if the weather was bad. Other folks in the industry got wind of this experiment. Other outfits formulated and manufactured such pellets too. This experiment was among those that changed the industry to the high-concentrate rations used today. Since there was greater demand for corn, struggling farmers grew more of it. By then, Bill had quit corporate ag and moved to the farm.

In plotting new business at Big Bend Station, one of Bill's moneymaking ideas was to quarter cattle there during those last months, an interval that Doughboy and other pelletized food supplements had reduced by at least a third. His property on the west side of the South Platte River came with several feedlots, sufficient for as many as 1,200 head of cattle at a time.

I can't gild the feedlots. They were no picnic for the animals, not after grazing in Wyoming. The steers' only activity was at the trough. Even so, Bill's feedlots were not like today's factory farms. His Herefords—russet brown steers with white bellies and markings—were not densely packed together, clomping around in their own excrement. Manure was shoveled daily. Water was fresh and cold. And the steers' internment was usually fewer than twenty-one weeks, not a lifetime.

Bill needed cowboys to tend the animals and feedlots. From Wyoming, he lured three young broncobusters, including Joey Hatfield, with a promise of a place to stay and a good salary at Big Bend Station.

Over the previous decade in Wyoming, "Linda Lou" had observed that cowboys like a routine in the wide, open range, a routine that includes alcohol, tobacco, and spitting, where they can exercise their aptitude for breaking the habits of wayward animals. Ideally, the range routine is punctuated with occasional women and occasional heroism. My impression was that good cowboys are gifted and even miraculous when it comes to horses, dogs, steers, and to some extent women, as long as women behave like horses, dogs, and cattle. Where cowboys break down, where they become less useful—both as employees and lovers—is when their activity is too tamed. Confinement, for a cowboy, is a prescription for disaster. I never tested these assumptions, but the cowboys' time at Big Bend Station would prove my hypotheses in its own clinical phase.

The bunkhouse Bill set up at the far end of the farm might as well have been Leavenworth. The cowboys weren't where the buffalo roam. Not anymore. Their job was tending 1,200 penned steers. What did the cowboys have to do really? Heave feed. Mound manure. That's what. They couldn't even use their spurs.

.... ▬ ▪ ▪ ▬ ....

Those three cowboys, and my father with them, were teetering on what amounted to a paradigm shift in food cultivation. At the time Bill left corporate ranching in 1970, the cattle industry was already on the road to what some perceive as hell. McDonald's had reached its "more than a million served" benchmark. Other fast-food chains followed suit, precipitating a demand for cheap beef of almost any quality. Fewer people gave a damn about grazing and cuts of great beef. Overnight, a steer became a short-lived burger-making factory, fed almost entirely corn (which required lots of water), lard, and subtherapeutic antibiotics, and with no time whatsoever on rangeland before he was dispatched to the stunner. So much for "nature's own."

And it took no soothsayer to *smell* the future. Breezes at the farm typically blow from the west, but when the wind shifted we knew we were near something very disagreeable. Down the road, fifteen minutes to the east, a rancher named Kenny Monfort began fattening a huge number of cattle at a time in a crowded purgatory where the fare was predominately high-energy flaked corn, plus Doughboy-like pellets to balance the ration and boost performance. Think of it: the world's first 100,000-head lot, just down the road! To his credit, Monfort tried to finish the cattle without antibiotics, but the experiment did not work.[2] Confinement and a diet at odds with cattle's digestive system increased the animals' susceptibility to infection.

> **Beef's Water Footprint**
>
> A one-third pound serving requires 615 gallons of water to create, twenty times greater than the water allotment for the same weight in grain. Remember, though, that the steer has turned the grains to protein and manure, both valuable resources.
>
> SOURCE: Calculated from waterfootprint.org.

This turbo weight-gain process culminated nearby at Monfort's abattoir north of Greeley, where innovations in slaughtering, packing, and distribution were integrated. Monfort's operation augured the consolidation that meat cultivation has become. It catalyzed agriculture and brought more jobs to Weld County—some higher paying, some minimum wage. The whole chain required a staggering amount of water, but the efficiencies of size and integration kept food prices low, prices beef consumers enjoyed . . . thus creating demand, a key element in the circle of shame and blame. More animals and more jobs registered as "growth" and seemed to boost Colorado's "carrying capacity"—the numbers of lives it could support. The "entropy" resulting from contaminated water, increased antibiotic resistance, and other problems went largely uncalculated. Those who spoke against cheap beef didn't speak as loudly as the consumers. The judgment and negativity about the industry that my father felt then—I feel it still.

With the Wyoming corporation's big herds, Bill had been in the game. Now as a family farmer, his luck changed. His feedlots, holding a mere 1,200 head, were so minor, not enough to become profitable, but enough to feel the heat of industrial upheaval. Bill had banked quite a lot of currency as the big boss in Wyoming, but as a small-timer he was spending money and influence faster than he could replenish them.

A cloud of cowboy discontent stretched from the bunkhouse to the feedlots. It was hard to watch my father look that direction, like watching an antacid commercial. Worse than one unhappy cowboy were three unhappy cowboys:

more drinking, more sleeping late and having to be roused by loud knocks on the door and deadlines prompted more broken promises. If those three had been Herefords instead of cowboys, high-voltage cattle prods would have been necessary.

Far away, but at the same time, a spate of federal environmental regulations passed—to protect everything from groundwater to endangered species. Legislation, though perceived as necessary, made ranch and farm life that much more arduous and expensive, and most unappealing of all—*different*—not just for my father, but for all ranchers and farmers . . . and cowboys.

Among the issues was regulators' concern that concentrations of feedlot manure might contaminate groundwater and surface water, fill it with nitrogen, phosphorous, and other rogue elements from the periodic table. Bill wasn't adverse to protecting groundwater, but he couldn't meet the regulations without willing employees. New regulations made the wayward cowboys' jobs even more distasteful. Even when they could be cajoled into agreeing to perform better manure collecting and hauling, it didn't mean they'd actually do it. Together, they were a passive-aggressive personality times three.

New Regulations

National Environmental Protection Act of 1969

Federal Water Pollution Control Amendments of 1972

Endangered Species Act of 1973

Federal Land Policy and Management Act of 1976

Clean Water Act of 1977

Public Rangelands Improvement Act of 1978

While on the topic of manure, Bill had told Gogo: "You'll have your own vegetable patch just behind the house." Yes, among the carrots he extended to her, to build enthusiasm for the farm, were carrots. Together, my parents converted what had been a corral into a vegetable garden, believing that long decades of manure there had enriched the soil. And then some! High nitrogen content scorched the carrots and other seedlings, making Gogo's adjustment to country life that much more challenging, that much more of a burn. By then in the third year, the vegetable yield still looked caramelized.

Gogo steered clear of the bunkhouse, because she was cute and Bill didn't really think the cowboys were reliably safe. Not that they were bad guys, but they were drinking a lot. More than once a week, the three faced off against my dad. There was no longer any "Yes, sir, Mr. Phelps, glad to oblige."

The taciturn two left the talking to the silver-tongued Joey Hatfield. Using his gift for lyricism and repetition, Joey might eventually agree to move more manure, but *only with provisions*—better trucks, better pay, and another day off . . . a paid day. We called them the "cowboy mafia."

I was by then living in Denver, trying to wring an income from my own independent streak. Visits to the farm suggested that Bill, in whom we all had infinite confidence, was doing as he'd always done—making it up as he went along. His vision of life in the country didn't include currying favor with regulators and being extorted by drunken cowboys, though. Besides which, as Gogo noted, the cowboys' bunkhouse looked like Dogpatch. Bill was forty years old. Nobody had helped him. He'd saved a million dollars and retired to his own farm. The hitch was *it was no fun.*

.........■■· ·■■.........

I had only the itinerant observer's sense of farm life, that is to say, no sense at all. Still, I did notice. Take, for example, farmers' nearly palpable fear that arrives with summer thunderclouds. In a city, we watch July and August's yeasty clouds expand upward, popping additional spheres of moisture-heavy marvel and think how lucky we are to live under such intensely lovely and changeable skies.

Not so over South Platte farmland. Summer thunderclouds don't arrive until farmers have signed over their lives to the banks for whopping farm loans; bought expensive additional machinery and seed; tilled, planted, fertilized, irrigated, weeded, then irrigated and weeded over and over again, up to and beyond sixteen hours a day, every day for weeks. By July and August their fields of healthy maturing crops are strapping, *full of promise.* And what is it that they are promising? They are promising a yield that will pay back the banks and sustain the farmer and his family through the winter . . . maybe. The whole thing is a gamble.

So, when thunderheads gather during summer afternoons, farmers, their wives, their children become tense. When I visited Big Bend Station during the summer, I watched the rippling heat radiating off the shiny dark green leaves. It made the distance vibrate. That radiating stopped when the sun disappeared under dense cloud cover. Even the animals became tense. The cattle might lie down. Business slowed in the little towns down the road. Merchants peered out to the southeast, and they too saw the anvil-shaped thunderclouds. They were tense too. The whole county was tense. No stretch to conclude that the shiny leaves registered the tension. The clouds got thicker, darker, and more menacing. The mountains clutched for the late afternoon light, pulling it under. Then the gloom was earnest.

At last the instability reached its Wagnerian climax. The thunderheads lit up from behind, their multiple coronas momentarily ablaze with lightning. There was a boom, like a pressing of massive defibrillators against the Earth's surface. By then we would have raced to the window to watch the clouds rent by terrible javelins of electricity, each bolt paired with an explosion of thunder.

We prayed for a nice rain, a rain that would soak the fields without carrying off topsoil, maybe save us a day of irrigating, then clear in time for a spectacular Colorado sunset over the Front Range.

The unspoken attitude at Big Bend Station's windows seemed to be pretending that we didn't care. The rest of them (my family) were a lot better than I at feigning indifference, no matter the stakes. Everyone's failure to register only increased my burden as the figurative lightning rod. I groped to hold hands with anyone, but no one ever took me up on it. Au contraire: they'd move farther away. Even the dog sensed that hanging near me would increase the atmospheric norepinephrine.

It was never just our crops that hung in the balance; it was the whole county, a whole county of farmers and merchants and by consequence bankers who made the farm loans, whose world was upended if it were not rain that fell from the burst clouds . . . but *hail*.

The pulverizing effect of icy grenades would take its victims, first by way of the shiny dark green leaves, plus tomatoes, squashes, melons, and corn—all that might have repaid the bank reduced in five minutes to ghastly pooled fields of "gazpacho."

Hail didn't happen often, but when it did the county pulled tightly into itself. Neighboring farmers felt more like neighbors, for the grimmest of reasons. An outsider, I knew nothing about farming, but didn't need to look farther than from the window to see ruin. Nor did anyone else. Pop called it "promise broken."

I had only to drive away, back to the city, to put this collective devastation behind me. What were the tribulations of growing food downstream to tribulations in Denver?

THE SOGGY VERGE

*From below, the river noise came up strongly, and a damp chill flowed around
her feet. She could not see the water, only a darker, inverted sky down there, with
nearly lost stars in it. For all her eyes could tell her, the bridge might lie on black
bedrock glinting with mica, or it might span bottomless space opening under the
bottom of the world.*

—WALLACE STEGNER, *ANGLE OF REPOSE*

Bill purchased a cattle brand shaped in a sinewy "U.S." We all regarded this as a
coup, a great source of pride, a sign that he'd managed to secure his own nation.
He had the "U.S." monogrammed on his Oxford-cloth shirt pockets (instead of
initials as his Denver buddies did) and designed a twenty-four-carat gold dinner ring with a brand on it for Gogo. She had US cocktail napkins printed. He
cut the brand off one of the branding irons and attached it as a handle to the
cabinet that held the Victrola. If there was bad news, and often if there wasn't,
he and Gogo rolled back the carpet after dinner, turned up the volume on the
Cole Porter records and foxtrotted away any blues that might otherwise keep
Bill from sleeping.

.... ▬▬·· ▬▬ ....

One Saturday morning, mid-May 1973, floodwaters overtook the farmland and
almost the house. I drove up from Denver before dawn and descended the quarter mile from the "bench" into the river valley where Big Bend Station is situated.

Even though the day was barely light, I could see that water had filled the farm's lower reaches. Two-thirds of Colorado's annual river flow occurs when the weather heats up in the late spring, and it seemed as if that whole two-thirds were right there at Big Bend. Melting snowpack from the mountains had swollen the river far beyond its banks. No longer 100 feet across, the river was twice as wide as a city block is long. It was *everywhere*. The house was an island. Its image reflected back in the glassy surfaces around it, the inundated fields. The vehicles were parked on the highway. I parked there too, pulled off my shoes, and waded in.

My brother, Will, and a few friends from his high school had spent the last three days sandbagging. A baby raccoon that they had rescued was living in a deep box in the laundry room. "I watched from the window," Gogo said. "This isn't like Denver, honey. Will's friends don't speak English. Will's given them Mohawk haircuts."

"Gogo want a burrito, Mom?" Will chimed in, goading her.

"What's the raccoon's name?" It was adorable, wanting to be picked up.

"Ralph."

"What if it's a girl?" Gogo asked.

"Don't lose your sense of humor now, sweetness," my father commented.

"I'm marooned!" Gogo sounded chipper, but you could tell that her worldview, largely observed through rose-colored outings and assorted ladies' groups, was flickering.

"Want to drive around the farm with us, Gogo?"

Her look said no. That little painting of Ben and Becky Eaton's love nest, the cabin where cattle had become trapped, perished, and putrefied, now hung in the kitchen.

Past it, Pop and I walked out, climbed to the highway and into his Volkswagen Thing, roof down, to drive south of the house along the bench. With a good chunk of the farm underwater, his tour could but skirt the perimeter. The huge mirror of still water below us reflected a garland of dawn clouds. Despite the quiet, the land's transformation screamed "verge," as if announcing that whatever had happened before would not happen again.

Bill gestured without saying anything toward the lower field, which had been planted in winter wheat the year before. Before us was an astonishing sight.

Mounting sunlight combed a thinning mist from the treetops, and small rainbows arced across the water. Beneath them *hundreds* of tall, white shapes hovered just above the deluge. The water below these specters rippled ceaselessly, making their stark forms seem to skitter across the surface, like ghosts blowing through low fog. I blinked with confusion.

44

"Wha . . . aaat? What are they?" I whispered, unable to see them clearly.

"White pelicans," Bill answered. The erect birds stretched above the surface, seeming to float, because it was not yet light enough to see their thin legs in the murky water. Intermittently pairs of wings opened in immense dihedrons, nine feet wide, reaching skyward, only to fold again in concord.

"They look like angels!"

"See the red beaks?" Bill asked. "The males have a knob on the top this time of year. Breeding season."

"They look as if they are moving fast . . . but they aren't moving at all, are they? What makes the water ripple so much?"

"Carp, washed in from the river. The carp are swimming underfoot. The movement is their dorsa. The water isn't very deep."

"Oh, the birds have come to eat. Gosh, what a feed!"

"You said it. But that field isn't going to be useful for a while."

We continued along the bench, the dry uplands high above the river. Inundation on the house side of the river meant inundation on the other side too, near the feedlots. Worse, we could see sheared shoreline, muddy and denuded of vegetation—a sign that water-heavy banks on both sides of the river had collapsed in several areas, carrying severed farm property downstream. I was far enough into adulthood to feel the kick to the gut. I peered over at him, worried. It was an expensive morning.

He didn't like his vulnerabilities being noticed. It was no good being compassionate, no good saying I was sorry. I'd regret it. He didn't want anyone noticing the cracks in his "grand plan," the move to the country. *Stiff upper lip*—a rule of men.

Anyway, what could we do? There was no climbing into the river, no spreading arms to hold up the shore. How many thousands of dollars, how many years of my father's work, his "dérive," had the floodwaters beaten away? He had let himself be drawn by the attractions of the terrain and the encounters he found there, but some part of "there" had turned to mud and washed downriver overnight. Worse, what part of his carefully crafted business plan had washed away too? What would it take to make his footprint on the Platte economically viable? What if viability were tied to stability?

There were many questions, as big and numerous as the pale specters on the lower field, but Bill said nothing. To us on the sidelines, his concealed feelings felt the same as power. His vulnerability was an unknown that others could navigate only as guesswork. It was without proportions. It contained his deliberations, but was big enough to hold the insecurities, hopes, and fears of everyone around him too. People had hung in there with him, for the same reason his family did, I expect, because he felt big.

He veered suddenly toward the south and drove the Thing silently toward the bunkhouse. Given the cigarette hanging from his lip, the soundtrack from "The Good, the Bad and the Ugly" was all but audible. He pulled up, set the brake, then walked over to the cowboys' trucks and removed the keys from the ignition before moving to the door. First stooping to grab two empty beer cans with one hand, he knocked loudly. I slumped down in the seat. As he started to rap a second time, the door opened a crack. I could hear a voice say, "Uh, yup?"

"You three are supposed to be at work."

"Yeah, yeah. We'll be there. We said we'd be there."

"No, you won't," Bill said evenly. I sank further in my seat. That unperturbed authority laid over anger and frustration was worth avoiding. "I've had enough," he continued without raising his voice, shoving the empties into Joey's hands. "Go wake up your buddies in there, the other two good-for-nothings and who-ever they have in bed with them. Then I want you to spend the day cleaning up this place. I'll be back later. If it's not cleaned up, I'll dock your paychecks. Your *last* paychecks. I'm sick of you."

Not wanting to become another finale in the morning's Acts of God, I kept mum as Pop drove back to the house, to my mother. Breakfast dishes done, she was ironing. Ralph the baby raccoon was asleep in her lap. To her, he said, "I fired the cowboys." My father had to feel lower than a scuffmark, but by then we all knew that my cute little mom was an adjunct at the farm, not a *force majeure*. He knew she couldn't fix the mayhem, just as she knew he wasn't going to iron. If circumstances were going to crumble, at least they'd be clean and pressed. When he got like this we were all afraid, not because he was mean or violent, but because without his happiness and big ideas, all seemed ruined. I went upstairs, leaving Gogo still ironing, ironing everything from bed linen to his boxers under an aerial photo of the farm.

.... ▄▄· · ▄▄ ....

The South Platte's course is evident in this photo. In the topography, you can see the river struggling, at a geologic pace, to wrinkle the land, to erode down-ward and outward along its northbound course, before heading east to join the North Platte and, eventually, the Missouri River. The river basin is within a topo-graphic depression called the "Colorado Piedmont." Not just lower in elevation than the mountains to the west, the Piedmont is also lower in elevation than the High Plains to the east. (*Pied* means "foot" and *mont* is, of course "mountain.") The land drops off noticeably along the Front Range, below 5,000 feet, as if it were scooped out. And indeed it *was* scooped out: The South Platte created the Colorado Piedmont landform, through erosion. Deflected from harder, less-erodible gravel deposits to the east, the South Platte dug an *erosional runnel* northbound through the softer bedrock there. Within the floodplain of the river itself, the soil shows eons of deposition, erosion, and compaction—indicators of occasional floodwaters, such as those then covering the farm.

The point is that the river must push northward until it reaches a low spot in the High Plains. Only then can it turn eastward and find its way to the Missouri, the Mississippi, and the Gulf of Mexico beyond. Big Bend Station is one such low spot. The behavior of the river in this valley, flanked by low hills of soft bedrock, is an uncertain and ever-changing exertion. These meanders are the normal business of rivers with a low gradient. Many rivers the world over look like and behave like this; most all of them have by now irrigated farms and many still do. A front-row seat on these eddies and swirls, though, is humbling. They mark the river's historic path as it pushes away from the mountains near my parents' house. Water doesn't stop for property rights and pipedreams. And the ever-changing exertion was happening right here under my dad's big idea.

Now join him at his desk: his wretchedness at this point was acute. None of us made a move; we were so used to his solving problems on his own. And he did. He dialed numbers until he'd sold the feedlots to someone who could stomach the hassle, to a family named Ehrlich, which owned lots in Windsor and Greeley.

That 1973 flood was the end of Bill the Rancher; *Goodnight, Charlie Goodnight*.

Then, using the money from the feedlot sales, my father did what humans have done throughout time: he moved with brute force to protect his property from water's ravages. The midsection of the farm became his sandbox. As the flood subsided, the earthmovers mobilized to manifest Bill's will. From the kitchen window, you could see them belching diesel as they gnawed by the shovelful. Next, flatbeds mounded with junked automobile bodies and broke concrete arrived, and crews jammed them in at the river's edge. The compressed metal stabilized the banks, but it wasn't pretty. Bulldozers recontoured the distance between the river and the house, reinforcing the banks and building a big scythe-shaped dike around the field where the pelicans had been. The dozers' handiwork truncated the Big Bend Ditch, which trickled north into a new seasonal wetland, known thereafter as the "Yacht Club," before rejoining the river. That dike, plus the completion of the capacious Chatfield Reservoir upstream at Denver, meant that yearly runoff no longer jeopardized the house. It didn't stop frogs, however.

Annzo telephoned. "Dad is calling himself Squire Phelps," she announced coolly. "Have you heard about the frogs?"

No, I hadn't, though I *had* heard the frogs themselves. High waters coincided with egg laying, over 5,000 eggs per female. That ushered in tadpoles. By summer, receding waters left an infestation of Northern Leopard Frogs (*Lithobates pipiens*) piping as robustly as the Royal Philharmonic's bass section. Their guttural hum made the meadows sound as though they were singing through rubber.

Gogo looked out on mowing day to find Bill sashaying across the grass with a bucket and a nine iron. She stopped to watch as "Squire Phelps" tipped the bucket, nestled the golf club behind the frog's spotted derrière, and tapped it into the bucket. Worry not: he was *not* thwacking frogs, only gently scooping, so they'd be out of the way of the mower. Then, noticing that Gogo was watching him, Bill turned around and grinned. With flourish, he pulled a bottle of her Christian Dior nail lacquer from his hip pocket and gave it a shake. Then, palming one frog at a time before freeing it in the meadow, he applied a small dot of red polish to its acid-green back. Inevitably, some frogs would hop back to the garden the next week. Any frog caught in the garden three times, with three dots of Christian Dior, no longer got a free ride to safety and would have to fend for itself against the whirring blades. Of this pastime, Bill said, "Everything is a game."

The frog game is my earliest memory of imbalance between my father's God-given strengths and his prospects. By acquiring the farm, he'd achieved his dream to live, not the life of continual obstacles and hard toil that Ben Eaton had lived, but as Ben Eaton's son (Bill's grandfather) had lived—as a gentleman farmer. What, besides frog relocation, now? And how to pay for it? The summer pressed on with the newly contoured fields now planted with acres of white corn and sugar beets. The river's flow abated, and it rained little. No matter, because the aquifer belowground was all but bursting with water. The six wells practically pumped themselves. Water meant thriving crops. Yet, as Gogo was already saying, "Something is always happening in the country."

········ ▬ · ▬ ········

What happened was a neighbor and desperado named Arne Johnson (name changed to protect the uninvolved) with a rifle strapped over his shoulder, working a spade. My father, out on the farm astride his VW Thing, caught Arne trespassing, feverishly digging a hole in the new dike. By the time Bill found Arne, Arne had made some progress. *Burble, burble, more burble.* His plan seemed to be to divert Big Bend Ditch water into an all but invisible gully that led off toward his property across the highway.

Numerous times before, Bill had spoken with Arne in town, at the Gilcrest Farm Supply, a sort of souped-up trading post where they, like other farmers, stopped to buy gopher bait and exchange clipped how-dos and g'byes. Having made Arne's acquaintance, my father had the wherewithal to address him by name when he came on him stealing water: "Arne," he said impassively, "get the hell off my property."

Arne looked at Bill—broad shouldered, 6'4", and still young, sporting Levis, a custom-made monogrammed shirt and clean nails. Kind of hard to take seriously someone so obviously "not from the country." Bill looked at Arne: not too tall and older, kind of stocky with a big belly, dirty ball cap, gray hair, and bad teeth. Arne, to my father's surprise and probably even to his own, lodged the spade in the irrigation gully, then took the rifle off his shoulder and said, "Make me."

Make me? Here was a dare Bill hadn't heard since childhood, minced out in a field waist-high with corn, by a haggard farmer toward a newbie farmer who thought he *owned* water.

Bill took measure of Arne. There was probably a means of making him get off the property. But a gunfight? Bill, like my brother, Will, was an excellent marksman. He had a shotgun in the Thing and everything but a missile launcher back at the house. Coming on someone else's property to steal water was surely a decision of last resort, though. Arne looked sort of coiled, scared, scared, and crazy, crazy like he'd as soon shoot as not, even shoot in the back.

What was this: the Old West?

Bill and Arne with their ordnance and their purchased rights to the little manmade canal called the Big Bend Ditch exemplify the challenges of owning water rights. Everything about water is dynamic. Put a little water in your hand. Think about owning it and preserving it. Water isn't easily contained. It moves around; it evaporates; it freezes. Its force moves other things around. In concert with sunlight, water makes weather, another untrammeled force. And, every living entity on the planet needs water critically.

The Big Bend Ditch came into existence and became a water right on September 26, 1873, a hundred years before this faceoff, when Colorado was still a federal territory and not yet a state, at the time my great-great-grandfather Ben Eaton was digging canals for Greeley fifteen miles north of Big Bend Station. Three other Colorado farmers—misters Mullin, Lovelady, and Albee—declared themselves trustees and managers of the new Big Bend Ditch Company, for the water's use in agriculture, milling, and draining surpluses. Then they got digging.

Bill's Big Bend Ditch Right

"An undivided one-fourth
interest in and to the Big Bend
Ditch Company No. 1, priority
no. 32 in Water District No.
2 in the State of Colorado,
which undivided one-fourth
interest is one-sixth portion
of said property decreed by
the District court of Arapahoe
County for 20.88 cubic feet
of water per second out of the
South Platte River; conveying
also the appurtenant one-
fourth interest in the river,
dam, and the structures
along the course of said
ditch, all rights under any
court decree relating thereto,
and all rights of way and
appurtenances to said ditch,
together with the right to
change the point of diversion
of the Grantee's share of said
priority appropriation from its
head gate on the South Platte
River to a pumping plant
upon the individual lands
of the Grantee herein along
the course of said ditch, and
within 100 feet therefrom;
provided, however, the use of
the Grantee herein and said
water right shall henceforth
be limited to irrigation of 80
acres of the lands of Grantee
in Section 18, Township
4 North, Range 66 West,
6 P.M., in Weld County,
Colorado."[1]

Using picks, shovels, and mules, the three farmers constructed a headgate on the East Channel of the South Platte River, at the point marked on the map showing the Eaton Cattle Company property boundary with a big, dark, circled dot.

The East Channel, a narrow slough, wiggles to the east across the horse pasture before being swallowed into the Hundred-Acre Wood. There, it passes under the cottonwoods and through the snowberry before the beavers' handiwork turns it into a small pond, after which it debouches into more farmland before reentering the Platte downstream. This is the thin gray line on the map. By the time Pop bought the farm and maybe before, the little slough had warm water in it. People suspected that the slough's water came from percolating springwater, agricultural waste irrigation, and storm runoff. Wild watercress and a little pink-flowered plant called lady's thumb grew in it. Ducks lingered in the slough almost year-round because it never froze, even when everything else was blanketed with snow.

If you own a property in New England, its boundaries are defined as a certain distance from a mountaintop, a creek, or another visible feature like Bill's East Channel. The property boundaries and topographic features are inseparable. However, legal definitions of property boundaries in most parts of the United States are defined in another way, as "sections," and sections are tied to latitudes and longitudes, not river courses or other topographic features. Sections make a big invisible grid over most of the United States; each little square is 640 acres (one square

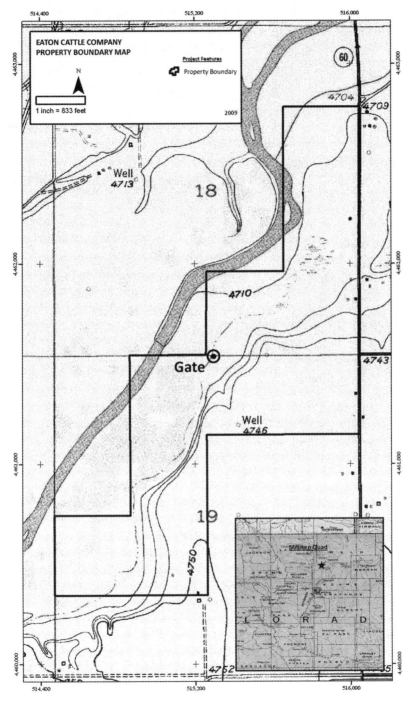

Eaton Cattle Company property boundary map.

mile) that informs surveyors and geographers and GIS paraphernalia. See the faint gridlines on the map of the Eaton Cattle Company property boundary? Those are the section lines. In 1873, the ditch diversion was made at the northeast quarter of the northwest quarter of Section 19. Importantly, whereas section lines remain constant relative to longitude and latitude, the course of rivers, creeks, and channels are not so reliable.

People bought or inherited property that was paired with water rights, but that pairing was based on original decrees. New owners such as Arne—whose family had indeed owned a right to the ditch—were required to keep the Big Bend Ditch open as a provision of their ownership. Arne didn't. Records show that in 1965 and 1969, flooding clogged the ditch with debris.

Water Rights

Without water, land has little value. Despite the value of water rights, they are little understood and expensive to protect. Their ownership is not maintained by any agency and is not easily traced. Water attorneys can research transfer of water rights on property transfers and give an opinion as to whether the water rights included in a title transfer are legitimate. However, title companies seldom research or insure title to the water, as they do the land.

Arne had not used the Big Bend Ditch water in a long time, and indeed the ditch, as I mentioned, had silted in north of our farmhouse, enough so that representatives of the court found it too "obliterated" to reach Arne's property. Arne's nonuse of his decreed right represented "abandonment of water rights" according to Colorado water law. That's why my dad saw Arne's actions as trespassing.

So Bill turned on his heel, his spurless heel. Neither hearing nor feeling bullets, he went back to the house. Purposefully seating himself in his old swivel chair, which is engraved with signatures of previous bosses who'd sat in it while making decisions grave and small, he telephoned a man who had been his friend since high school: his lawyer, Alex Lovewell in Denver.[2] Getting out his checkbook, Bill wrote a retainer to Alex Lovewell. Thus, Bill entered the labyrinth that is Colorado water litigation.

Lost in Colorado water litigation, Bill would grope blindly, not for months but for years. Putting his trust in Alex Lovewell, he occasionally thought he understood what was going on. There, he'd catch his breath alone in the darkness, remembering that he must defend his water right, that he must prove that Arne had abandoned his water right and therefore the right to come on Big Bend Station's property. Then the phone would ring or mail would arrive, and Bill stumbled painfully back into the obscurity where he might lose everything (as

Arne was losing) and put Gogo at risk, or an as-yet-unknown force would shove him off into additional dizzying mire.

This ordeal played out throughout the 1970s. There was no getting a handle on it. Arne kept riding onto the property with his gun and diverting water every summer. Bill didn't talk about this, except to Alex Lovewell and Alex Lovewell got nowhere. Alex Lovewell's pursuit was made more difficult by the fact that Arne had no legal representation, and talking with Arne didn't make sense.

Four years passed without resolution. There was no progress whatsoever. Finally, after giving Mr. Lovewell over $18,000 in legal fees (which might have been $180,000 in today's dollars and legal setting), Bill finally got a decision in his favor in 1977. Arne was disallowed from trespassing by a restraining order, which should have been the end of it. However, it wasn't.

One morning, Gogo walked back from the mailbox at the road with an envelope from Alex Lovewell. Bill and she eyed it hopefully, as if progress might finally occur. Astonishingly, though, the envelope contained an invoice for tens of thousands of dollars, for services supposedly rendered by Alex Lovewell. That was a kick to the gut considering there had been no further action; so even though it was a weekend, Bill was indignant enough, and knew Mr. Lovewell well enough, that he called him at home. Poised to say something like "Lovewell, what the hell is this?" he was astonished to hear his lawyer's wife's sobbing voice on the phone. Two nights before, her husband dispatched invoices and then locked himself in the bathroom and overdosed.

My brother and sister had moved away by then, but my parents weren't living alone. *Hatred* moved in. Bill made room for intense feelings in himself so Gogo wouldn't have to. He couldn't hate Lovewell; Lovewell was dead from sorrow and hopelessness. He couldn't hate Arne either, because Arne was unhinged and shit outta luck too. But Bill did indeed hate someone or something and that hatred was there at Big Bend Station, separating him from Gogo and everyone else. He was taciturn; he was in a stew. The stalemate needed an effort or an action that he couldn't identify. He couldn't charm his way out of the mess. The triple confrontation—the loss of his old friend, needing to avert unwarranted invoicing by Alex Lovewell's estate, and the still dissatisfactory legal proceedings with Arne Johnson—needed actions Bill didn't understand. So he hated it all instead.

Come summer, Arne again rode in, bold as bold can be, in contempt of the court order. Espying Arne, Bill called the sheriff's office, and then set out to head Arne off in the VW Thing. A police car was right behind Arne on the road. Afterward, Arne filed a written claim saying: "Phelps had his gun in his hand and pointed it at me and was going to shoot. When he saw the sheriff's car behind me, he put the gun in its holder." Reading this, the DA questioned the officers involved. They denied seeing the gun in my father's hand and reported that Arne didn't mention the gun when they were right there on the scene. The court refused to prosecute, and that was the end of trying to solve the Arne Johnson problem "among gentlemen." Bill telephoned the Weld County district attorney, who, practicing in a largely agricultural county, wore Colorado water law in his front pocket.

From the court's perspective, numerous incidents worked against Arne's claim to the ditchwater. My father wasn't the only neighbor who objected to Arne's tactics. Three other neighbors had testified against him in 1968, two years before our family moved to the farm; the Office of the State Engineer then denied Arne Johnson's request for a permit to divert Big Bend Ditch water to his farm across the highway. In 1970, Arne formally expressed his intent to abandon use of water from the channel of the South Platte River. In 1973, in his first trespass onto our property since we'd owned it, Arne excavated a portion of the dike as I mentioned, permitting flow to empty onto Bill's property but preventing it from reaching his. Further, Arne weirdly consented to let the Colorado Department of Highways fill in the culvert beneath the highway, which might otherwise deliver ditch flow to his land. There no longer existed a path for the ditchwater to return to the river, which was nearly a mile away from Arne's house, so the ditch could not recharge the river except on our property. Adjacent property owners were concerned that Arne's actions would lead to flooding. Given all this activity, it's impossible to divine Arne's logic. One thing for sure: he couldn't resist the water to the west, restraining order or not. In 1978, the court denied all Arne's motions and saddled him with a permanent injunction against trespass and an order to pay Bill's legal fees.

While Arne and Bill volleyed despair and harassment between them, and sugar beets and white corn grew with help from the water they fought over, I moved to Southern California, a region almost entirely dependent on water from Colorado snowmelt. I didn't have to buy a 410-gauge shotgun or hire an attorney or try to get my mind around water law. To get water, I didn't need a decree or an appropriation. Every month I wrote a little check and used an envelope.

Arne Johnson's wife left him, after which Arne hung up his spurs and shot himself. There was one fewer farmer and one fewer farm's worth of American vegetables and grain. No one in Southern California knew they should care because faucets still worked.

BANGING A GAVEL IN WATER

For all men believe in justice. Otherwise they would not be men.
But there is the world and there is the idea,
there are the flesh and the word,
there are the Old Court and the New.
—ROBERT PENN WARREN, *WORLD ENOUGH AND TIME*

Air at the farm is light, clean, with little mois-ture in it, so Pop followed moisture from dew to gutter spouts, from the soft slap of water against a snag, to patter off the wing of a heron overhead, and from groundwater's gush toward the furrows. Water was within him, the void that always asked for more.

Thirst is always there, for all of us. Dehydra-tion begins when we are born, the moment babies wiggle from the uterine sea. At birth body-water content is as high as 75 percent, more than it will ever be again. From then on, life is a long desiccating squeeze. Even so, humans manage to tank up, first from mama's breast, then with other liquids, and the water

> **Feel sick? You may be thirsty.**
>
> With dehydration, blood becomes thicker and loses volume. Thicker blood is harder for the heart to pump. It challenges circulation. Losing just 2 percent of one's body weight in water can impair physical performance by an average of 6.5 percent. A 2.5 to 5 percent loss of body weight in water may impair some cognitive function up to 17.5 percent.[1]

in all vegetables, fruits, and meats. Every choice we make can be said to involve H_2O because all bodily processes—circulation, respiration, metabolism, you-name-it—rely on water.

Choices Change the World.

Captivated by this water connection, consciously or unconsciously, some choose water as their profession. They become swim instructors, hydrologists, fishermen, divers, well drillers, or ditch riders. Or they might become water attorneys, water judges, or farmers. Of these choices, agriculture seems the oldest profession, doesn't it? With the possible exception of fishing? That's how I see it anyway, because food is humans' most pressing priority after drinking water. Farmers were first in time, first in numbers—the "backbone of democracy," as Thomas Jefferson called them—and first to rise, too!

Farmers awaken, not on a city schedule, but before early birds and worms. At around 5 a.m. every day, Bill leaned over in bed to rub his lips and nose against Gogo's head, in that easy way it is to claim someone deeply and without reservation, as long as she is asleep. Then he pulled his limbs from the loose skein of my mother and the bed linen, before pulling on his many-times-mended clothes.

"This is it!" he thought. Even in the dark, he was master of his domain. With the Rockies silhouetted against a still-starry sky, he made his way to the kitchen. Outside, a great-horned owl hooted in the oblivion. Bill turned on the radio farm report, to mainline that rural rap with coffee and a smoke. Listening to the radio before dawn was a habit from his corporate ag days, but made just as much sense at the farm. That fast-thumping radio voice, with its country-western twang, placed him in a land apart from the city. He loved it. He loved it a million times more than making someone else rich.

Wheat futures down, y'all.

Corn futures up.

We're gonna look at Denver's cash-tradin' bids, as events in the winter wheat pits heat up . . .

The announcer, whose consonants reverberated like a plucked banjo, came and went between commercials. Bill then listened to other twangy voices promoting seeds, or fertilizers, or varmint getters. He had another Camel. Most farmers in the county tuned to the same channel at the same time, while they ate heart-stopping breakfasts, before or after they fed their animals. Like other American small farmers, with sunrise gradually changing the scenery, Bill considered not what to grow or how to grow it. That was foregone, based on the market. Planting, irrigating, and harvesting were all consuming—physically and timewise—but relatively straightforward. It was mental puzzles that lit him up. The question he asked himself daily was how to step over the many and increasing obstacles to making a living.

He strategized possible maneuvers without minions, without a real assessment of potential markets or potential threats, or even so much as an aide-de-camp. The weight of his daily concerns seemed light but ubiquitous, like the cottonwood seed that piled in drifts against fences during late spring. Still, this was the life he had planned for. He was at last living his truth.

Gogo came to the kitchen around 6:30, but when she did it was as *a reason to farm* not as a farmer. She was still very much a "city girl." His unrequited feeling returned. He still wanted her, desperately even, but she was increasingly like a stranger. My parents' new phase, the "empty nest," left them both yearning for something, something that being awake and in the same room didn't supply. He was alone. And down the road in every farmhouse, it was mostly the same— middle-aged farmers alone—alone with their crops and their obstacles.

.... ▬ ▬ ....

Obstacles have always bent the "backbone of democracy." When farmers couldn't get what they needed or couldn't get along, other people, *people who could sway opinion*—usually not farmers themselves—were called in to arbitrate, so after farmers, "law" materialized as a profession. This happened throughout history, and it happened in Colorado's early days. When it did, the outcome of initial Coloradan arbitrations would eventually determine water law throughout the arid western United States, the fate of American-grown food, and a good measure of the urgency for this book.

During the Gold Rush, a young lawyer from Illinois named Moses Hallett came to Colorado to pan for gold, just as Bill's great-grandfather had. When Hallett's panning failed, he did not become a farmer like Ben Eaton. No, he set up a private law practice in Denver and, by 1866, had demonstrated such impressive powers of persuasion that he became chief justice of the Colorado Territorial Supreme Court. From itinerant prospector to chief justice in six short years! Hallett had sway.

Remember, things happened quickly then, as if overnight. Within fifteen years, Native Americans had been subjugated.

LEGEND

Water

Food cultivation

Cities

Flow to sea

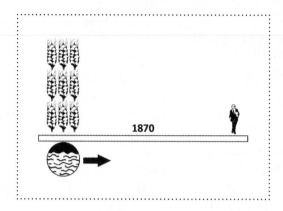

Buffalo were soon all but extirpated. The many-millennia-old prairie ecology capitulated to incoming settlers and ceaseless cattle drives. Let the inevitable water conflicts ensue.

Upstream at Bear Creek, a South Platte tributary southwest of Denver, two dogged settlers in canvas trousers, suspenders, and slouch hats rolled up their sleeves and dug a ditch together. Named Jason Yunker and Andrew Nichols, the settlers' goal was creating a "diversion"—a ditch or canal off the creek that would divert water to their homesteads. Nichols was nearer the headgate (the point of diversion from the creek); he cut off the ditch, so that not a trickle reached Yunker's place. It got contentious. In the territorial court, *Yunker v. Nichols* came before Judge Hallett in 1872.

Well, whose water was it? Isn't water like oxygen, a public resource to which we all have an essential right? No. This isn't true, not today, as paying rising water bills attests. And it wasn't true then either. Federal law had made land (such as the Louisiana Purchase, which included part of Colorado) and the water that occurred within it "public." As for regulating that water, Congress left setting and enforcing rules up to the territories and states, whose right it was to make the water available for use by local government and private entities through usufruct rights.

Hitherto in the States, regulations governing water had mimicked the English Law of the Commons, which adhered to "riparian" water rights. In riparian rights, whoever owns property that adjoins a waterway owns a use of the running water on a basis coequal to upstream and downstream property owners, and that ownership cannot be transferred to a property away from the waterway.

Riparian

Ripa means "bank" or "shore" in Latin.

Mr. Nichols, accustomed to riparian law, in which rights were inferred through proximity, felt he had the greater claim to the water because he was closer to Bear Creek. Trouble was, riparian water rights were impossible in the West, because there simply wasn't enough water. Few Colorado creeks or rivers were broad enough to navigate year-round, strong enough to turn a mill wheel, steady enough to sustain thick groves of trees, or even deep enough to float logs downstream. Riparian rights worked well in Europe and the eastern United States, where precipitation was abundant. Not so in Colorado, not for farmers, not for cities.

Weighing the acrimony between Yunker and Nichols, Judge Hallett considered a water appropriation system that miners had been using and came up with words now immortalized throughout the West:

> **Usufruct**
>
> PART OF SPEECH: Noun
>
> PRONUNCIATION: (YOO-zuh-fruhkt, -suh-)
>
> MEANING: The right to use and enjoy another's property without destroying it.
>
> ETYMOLOGY: From Latin *ususfructus*, from *usus et fructus* (use and enjoyment). Earliest documented use: 1646.
>
> SOURCE: *Merriam-Webster*, s.v. "usufruct."

> **Beneficial Use**
>
> Lawful appropriation employs reasonably efficient practices to place water to use. Uses deemed "beneficial" have evolved in response to changing economic and community values. In Colorado, the following uses are considered "beneficial":
>
> - Augmentation
> - In-stream flows and natural lake levels
> - Commercial
> - Domestic
> - Dust suppression
> - Evaporation from a gravel pit
> - Fire protection
> - Flood control
> - Industrial
> - Irrigation
> - Mined land reclamation
> - Municipal
> - Nature centers
> - Power generation
> - Produced water from Coal Bed Methane production
> - Recreation on reservoirs
> - Recreation in-channel diversions
> - Release from storage for boating and fishing
> - Snowmaking
> - Stock watering

In a dry and thirsty land it is necessary to divert the waters of the streams from the natural channels, in order to obtain the fruits of the soil, and this necessity is so universal and imperious that it claims recognition of the law.

Given his "recognition," the judge ruled that because Yunker and Nichols dug the same ditch together at the same time, they had an "appropriative" right to equal portions of the water that ran through the ditch. Hallett underscored that an *appropriative right* is very different from a *riparian right*. Water law in the dry and thirsty land could *not* rely on the proximity of the land to the water source. Even though Yunker's farm was farther away, because he appropriated the creek water at the same time as Nichols and from the same location on the creek (the same headgate), his "right" was equal, as long as he continued to use the water for "beneficial use." As an intervening property owner, Nichols had no right to intervene with the irrigation ditch needed to bring water to Yunker's farm.

Hallett's ruling was a radical agrarian rupture.[2] It differentiated Colorado from the English common law, which favored the private landowner on the bank of the stream. Instead of parceling water out generally and making it practically valueless to any, Colorado's early settlers adopted the only rule founded in equity that would control and limit water use.[3] We're still talking about Hallett's 1872 ruling today because it became the basis of the doctrine of "prior appropriation" water rights. "First in time, first in right," they said of Colorado's new approach to water sharing.

Colorado's provisions for governing water through prior appropriation were called the "Colorado Doctrine." However, to give an idea of how broadly Hallett's gavel was heard and still endures, eight other states—New Mexico, Arizona, Utah, Nevada, Wyoming, Montana, Oregon, and Texas—subsequently adopted the Colorado Doctrine and abide by it, no matter whether the appropriations are made for urban or rural use. The *California* Doctrine—a mix-

Diversion

A *diversion* (building a ditch or canal off a river or stream) does not create a prior appropriation water right, not until the water diverted is actually placed to a beneficial use. When the water court *decrees* the diversion, it determines the priority date, location of diversion, rate of diversion, and type of beneficial use, thereby officially recognizing the water right. The state engineer, seven water division engineers, and local water commissioners administer the decreed water rights. The decree date (officiated by the water courts) establishes its priority relative to other appropriations.

ture of riparian and prior appropriation rights—is adhered to by California, Oklahoma, Kansas, Nebraska, South Dakota, North Dakota, and Washington.

This Prior Appropriation Doctrine couldn't make everyone happy, but it established a legal means for divvying up the use of scarce water. People could acquire an appropriative right to transport water to new places for beneficial use. Unlike riparian rights, prior appropriation rights can be sold or transferred for use by a different person or for a different use—for example, ag to municipal, *even away from the point of diversion to an entirely different river basin provided that the transfer inflicts no injury to other water rights' holders and that there is no waste.*

The older the right, the more "senior" the claim. Rights filed more recently are junior. When water is insufficient, the senior right-holder's claim to her or his full cubic-feet-per-second (cfs) must be satisfied before any junior rights' owners can receive a drop.

The Big Bend Ditch (featured Spectacle 4, "The Soggy Verge"), for example, was "appropriated" in September 26, 1873; that's when the Big Bend Ditch water was first put to "beneficial use." It was decreed in 1883. This meant that the holder of that right had a priority senior to rights that were appropriated after September 26, 1873, *junior* to Yunker's and Nichols's rights. (The ditch right and its priority had been inherited and sold along with the farm's property, whose value the water right doubled, over the intervening century. Eventually Bill bought it.) An appropriative right does not come without restrictions. Rights owners must maintain their ditches, so they have physical access to the water and continue employing that water for beneficial purposes.[4] Bill's neighbor Arne's non-use and nonmaintenance of the Big Bend Ditch infrastructure influenced the court's decision against him.[5]

Four years after Hallett's decision, my farmer ancestor Ben Eaton's actions relative to water

Diverting Unappropriated Water, Priority Preferred Uses

"The right to divert the unappropriated waters of any natural stream to beneficial uses shall never be denied. Priority of appropriation shall give the better right as between those using the water for the same purpose; but when the waters of any natural stream are not sufficient for the service of all those desiring the use of the same, those using the water for domestic purposes shall have the preference over those claiming for any other purpose, and those using the water for agricultural purposes shall have preference over those using the same for manufacturing purposes."

SOURCE: Constitution of the State of Colorado, Article 16, Section 6.

disputes helped frame the articles that governed surface water use in the Colorado Constitution. As ratified in 1876, the Colorado Constitution codified Hallett's ruling. Prior appropriation was thereafter Colorado law, with a right of private condemnation, with payment of just compensation, across the lands of another in order to build and maintain ditches and canals for beneficial use. This agrarian antimonopoly, antispeculation doctrine was, by design, intended to assure that the finite public resource benefited many.

Hallett's decision institutionalized prior appropriation at a time when few people resided in the Colorado Territory, most of them farmers, yet his ruling has had lasting impact on development not only in Colorado, but throughout the arid West where the population now numbers almost 100 million people. If you live in the United States, you have a 1-in-3 chance that Judge Hallett's ruling influences your lifeline. Moreover, 46 percent of all US-farm sales are derived from crops grown in the seventeen westernmost states, where most irrigation occurs.[6] *That means that just under a half of all US-grown food sales are influenced by Judge Hallett's decision too.* And as water scarcity becomes a greater issue, the wake of banging a gavel in water seems not to subside but to grow.

Moses Hallett and Ben Eaton and the rest of the forefathers conceived methods and law that they thought would work, suited to the variables they knew in the 1870s and believed they could depend on. Those who drafted the Colorado Constitution strove for bedrock principles, with the understanding that the document would be amended as times changed. Through statutes, Colorado lawmakers too strove and strive to help the state's citizenry, industries, and resources adapt to changing standards and conditions. Yet, from Spectacle 2, "The Nuisance of Hindsight" we know that Colorado is a "cube" of finite size. Its resources expanded and contracted, as did its precipitation, *but its human population only increased.* And then, there was "entropy," slowly creating accumulations that were no longer available for productivity . . . though these were less

Surface Water

This water flows or is stored aboveground. Water in rivers, streams, creeks, ditches, canals, ponds, or reservoirs is surface water.*

Groundwater

This water is below the land surface, occurring in pore spaces and fracture in geologic formations, not just the water occurring in formations that yield usable or economic quantities of water (aquifers).

*For purposes of *California* law, surface water includes underflow of streams, underground streams, and any other subsurface flow that is identified with a defined bed, bank or channel.

evident in the beginning. Colorado, like the rest of the West, seemed resilient and enormous.

Citizens may believe that constitutions and laws will result in peace, but prior appropriation does not guarantee that everybody will get along. It's about "first come, first serve" or "finders keepers, losers weepers" or some similar version of acknowledged possession. Those who came first, found first, and used first got an early ("senior") water right, to use and transfer either through inheritance or sale to subsequent comers. In this scenario, keepers and weepers have frequently been at loggerheads. Therefore, it is truer that the Constitution and laws make no promise of peace, but rather assume conflict and establish rules of engagement. Moreover, money matters. Those who have the most money can buy the more senior rights. In a dry and thirsty land, *to which many insist on moving despite its scarce water*, people are asking for controversy.

This is why venerable geologist John Wesley Powell—the one-armed explorer who braved the Grand Canyon Colorado River's rapids in 1869—was convinced that the better part of the West was no place for settlement, no place to farm, except in those few pockets near adequate water. Later, in 1881, when named the second director of the US Geological Survey, Powell's directive was to characterize the agricultural and grazing potential of the arid West, based on an analysis of its rainfall. (Without agriculture, there could be no settlement.) His ultimate *Report on the Lands of the Arid Regions of the United States* ardently cautioned against settlement, because only 2 percent of the lands were near water sources.

Powell was dispatched again in 1888 to survey irrigable land and identify optimal sites for constructing reservoirs and canals.[7] His directive from the federal legislature was a reflection of a broad interest in transforming the warm, sunny regions of the arid West into thriving agricultural centers. Speculators dogged his survey process, jeopardizing the push for publicly (federal-government) owned reservoirs, and Powell's populist views ran afoul of Congress.[8] Nevertheless, the irrigation survey and the federal engine behind it augured the federal government's future role in irrigation and western development through US Bureau of Reclamation dam building.

As a scientist, Powell warned: "Gentlemen, you are piling up a heritage of conflict and litigation over water rights, for there is not sufficient water to supply the land."[9] Few listened. The capitalist dream—the confluence of moneymaking opportunity, of preexisting investment by the railroad companies that then owned over 183 million acres, of political will pushed by railroad companies, of baseless propaganda such as "Manifest Destiny" and "rain follows the plow"— promoted and sold agrarian settlement without relent. And pioneers themselves,

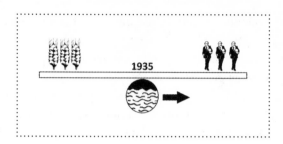

who had already risked everything to settle in Colorado, California, and else-where in the West—they too were determined to turn "not enough" to "plenty."

Those in authority scoffed at Powell's conclusions. His conclusions lost him his job. But they weren't predictions; they were observation! Diversions and irrigation proliferated in the South Platte River basin where summer surface-water flows were scant between 1880 and 1885. Colorado was not even ten years into statehood, and the Platte was already "over-appropriated."[10] In other words, there were already too many water-rights holders relative to the water supply.

As Powell warned, unceasing conflict and litigation over water rights did ensue. They cast the fate of rural food growers into the cities and into the courts. The tightening screw of urban versus rural is what gave Bill's predawn mornings with the radio farm report the feeling of strategy sessions, summoning the mul-titudes, but attended by one. Growing cities were far from immaterial to the task of farming, as my father well knew from his prior life of hanging out with power brokers, power brokers who understood farming hardly at all. His predawns were terrifying.

· · · · · · · · ■ · ·■ · · · · · · · ·

Meanwhile, midsummers at the farm arrived with their satisfactions and their worries. And their high-pitched bug life. The incessant hum was loud-est in the fields. On the ground, in the ground, on the corn, between the corn, above the corn, the buzzing hoard performed the business best known to bugs. Thunderous but invisible—except to killdeer, turkeys, and blackbirds—the insects set about their barbaric tasks. Bill moved among them along the irriga-tion ditch. Cornstalks high as his belt stretched out into the distance, the ears of corn formed but still small. As summer pushed to its conclusion, the ears climbed ladders of additional leaves, until its throbbing ceiling of insects and evapotranspiration rose past eight feet. Yet to get there, to sustain those leaves (destined to feed cattle) and the bigger ears (destined to feed humans), took water, lots of water.

Bill's "surface water" wasn't in the muddy Platte to his back. It was in the ditch right there at his feet, flowing toward him from its "point of diversion," the headgate where it left the river upstream. Getting water from the ditch into the fields, he used low-tech, gravity-fed *furrow irrigation*. Backbreaking and unrelenting,

Furrow irrigation with siphon tubes.

throughout the summer, furrow irrigation demanded the damming of the ditches at the tops of each field, and then moving curved irrigation siphon tubes into successions of furrows so water could flow downhill from the ditch between the crop rows. An important plus to furrow irrigation, often lost on detractors: whatever water that plants do not take up recharges the aquifer or returns to the river.

········ ▄▄· ·▄▄ ·········

Since Colorado's statehood, the Division of Water Resources had employed a succession of water commissioners, the state engineers' field staff. The commissioners' responsibility was to assure water's beneficial use and prevent injury to senior rights.[11] To achieve this, commissioners eyed the Platte's flow, and then considered the "calls" on the river, with a mind to satisfying those who had the senior-most surface-water rights and then working their way down to the junior rights holders. Afterward, the commissioners decided how much water to release into the ditches from the points of diversion in the river. Once the water was diverted into a particular ditch, a ditch rider prorated it along the whole ditch according to the proportionate number of shares each ditch stockholder held. This was prior appropriation, or the "Colorado Doctrine," in action, with the growth of that waist-high crop in the balance. (Municipalities buying surface-water rights are subject to the same rules.)

If no water remained in the ditch, never mind; Bill had only to lean toward one of his five pump houses and flip a switch. On went an irrigation well pump, whining and sucking from groundwater fifty to ninety feet below. All the water the fields needed, whenever he wanted, gushed from that enormous invisible bladder beneath the soil, the South Platte Aquifer. Using groundwater wells

Alluvial

This adjective is a geologic term meaning composed of sand, soil, and gravel, deposited by running water.

left time for the million other things that always need doing on a farm or ranch. Wells got around the possibility of the ditches being out of priority during the day, or needing to change the dams in the middle of the night to assure that the entire field got irrigated. For nearly seventy years, Colorado farmers had operated exactly like my father and profited, because—although *alluvial* groundwater and surface water were recognized as interdependent by the 1950s—irrigation wells remained unregulated. There were few restrictions on the supplemental water drawn from the aquifer.

········ ▄▄ ·▄▄ ········

The problem of overappropriated surface water—too many straws in streams, rivers, and ditches—was then of no consequence to farmers, not if they had wells. It didn't matter if ditches were empty in late summer, just when farmers most needed water. Growers simply used groundwater, another finite resource. They used groundwater because they could, because they owned rights, and because no laws or restrictions held them back. They leaned into pump houses and flicked a switch.

All because Hallett's gavel had missed a variable in the big cube called Colorado in 1872—groundwater—over 10 million acre-feet of the wet stuff in the South Platte Aquifer alone. Not until after the Colorado Constitution was forged was groundwater put to use. That is why groundwater wasn't regulated. In the early 1900s more dogged men in overalls and slouch hats dug wells, but by 1909 there were only seventy-nine wells in the entire Platte Valley.[12] (The first irrigation well of which there is any record was excavated by E. F. Hurdle, in 1886, northeast of Eaton not far from Wood's Lake where my great-grandfather lived.)[13] Farmers drilled and operated wells, to supplement undependable surface water supplies. Even the most senior surface-water right could benefit from having an irrigation well too. Population was low enough and pumping modest enough that no one thought one way or another about the wells.

Later, though, after development of the vertical-shaft turbine pump and mechanical drilling, well installation boomed in the South Platte River basin, and an additional 550 high-capacity wells were dug and in use by 1930 as insurance against drought.[14] During the Dust Bowl, more wells were developed, among them three with centrifugal pumps powered by gas engines at Big Bend Station. By 1940, 1,957 wells pumped 220,000 acre-feet.[15] Cooperative electrical associations gave farmers access to cheap, stable energy. Many high-capacity irrigation wells, including two of Bill's, were dug in the 1950s. Not until 1957 did one even need a permit to dig a well.[16] Much less an adjudication. The state government was all over farmers to develop wells and, in many cases, offered cost-share.[17] By 1960, an additional 1,900 high-capacity wells had been dug.[18] The drought of 1963–65 brought the number of wells up to around 10,000.[19] This "conjunctive use" of surface water and groundwater maximized the available water supply.[20]

Adjudication

This legal process is the formal issuing of a *decree*.

Thus encouraged during my childhood, Colorado's agrarian economy boomed. So too did its cities, and withdrawals of both surface and groundwater increased. In 1880, when the position of state engineer to administer water was first established, Denver's population was under 36,000. Today that metropolitan region is home to over 2.5 million. Other Front Range cities burgeoned too. Water sucking was a frenzy. Even water commissioners, charged with supervising withdrawals in certain segments of the rivers, were known to compete against each other for larger shares of the water.

Groundwater was like magic. You couldn't see it, yet you pumped and it appeared. The capacity of aquifers was difficult to fathom, as was quantifying whereby and how long it would take for pumping to impact the surface water, whether negatively or positively. More unanticipated and relatively incalculable variables missed by Hallett's gavel!

Don't forget that Colorado's river basins are alluvial—land primarily made up of decomposing granite and sediment that snowmelt pushed down the mountains over time. As a result, creeks

Conjunctive Use

This term describes the practice of using two water supplies—surface water from aboveground vessels and storage, plus groundwater from aquifers. In wet years, surface water is used and also recharges aquifers, from which it can be withdrawn and used in dry years.

and rivers on the Front Range aren't like concrete-lined ditches; they are like lines in a sandbox. Vegetables and fruits and alfalfa and grasses consumed part of the water that farmers pumped from the aquifer (between 30 and 50 percent). Some water evaporated from the soil surface; plants transpired water back to the atmosphere. (Together this is evapotranspiration.) The rest wiggled through the alluvial soil into the aquifer, and from there to the river in a process known as *return flow*. Water also soaked through the mud and gravel on the river bottom and eventually percolated into the aquifer. Only stretches and depths of sandy soil separated the river from the aquifer. And of all the sandy-bottomed riv-

Cone of Depression

Pumping groundwater from a well creates a "cone of depression" in the aquifer, an actual depression of the water level that takes time to manifest in the river. (The groundwater in the South Platte aquifer is "tributary," meaning that it connects to the river.) This time it takes for well pumping drawdown to reach and reduce the river flow is called "lag time."

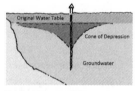

Well with cone of depression.

ers exiting the Rockies along the Front Range, the slow-moving South Platte was perhaps the sandiest. Clarence Kuiper, state engineer and head of the Colorado Division of Water Resources 1969–79, said that it was like the Platte "had a hole in it."[21]

Flows in Colorado's streams and rivers remained erratic, as Major Powell had divined. With population growth, demand on the rivers and aquifer increased. The Platte looked like a real river during snowmelt and rain events, but by late summer had barely enough to float an inner tube. Late summer was exactly when farmers most needed extra water, so that's when most groundwater pumping occurred. No wonder then that as the number of wells multiplied, and August rolled around every year, people in some places on the river observed that stream and river depletions coincided with well owners' drawing water from the aquifer. Even though no one could see belowground, Bill knew it wouldn't take a PhD to conclude that the water table and the river were conjoined. This observation was another of the many and maybe increasing obstacles to making a living.

THE INSCRUTABLE HITCH OF ABOVE AND BELOW

Keep a-movin', Dan,
Don't you listen to him, Dan
He's a devil not a man
And he spreads the burning sand with water.
Dan can you see that big green tree
Where the water's runnin' free
And it's waiting there for me and you
It's water
Cool, clear water
Cool, clear water
Cool, clear water.
—BOB NOLAN, "COOL WATER"

Earlier, in the years when Bill could but dream of buying the farm, divisiveness and competition over water escalated. It was like runs on banks or gas lines. Farmers came to feel that if they didn't nab the groundwater, their neighbors might. Surface-right owners, some of which were municipalities, saw the river empty in late summer while wells were pumping, and they pressed for regulation.[1] They wanted groundwater to be managed in priority with surface water, meaning in deference to senior rights. Their rights, some decreed in the nineteenth century before the earliest wells were dug, were "senior" to the groundwater rights. Municipal water districts needed to protect supplies for urban customers.

As the race for additional water heated up, a significant alliance began to fracture. Since the very beginning, our country had remained committed to growing its own food, but a feeling of us versus them (cities vs. farmers) began to take hold. This made sense to bureaucrats charged with finding water, because farmers owned and used a lot of water. The insanity was forgetting that farmers needed the water to grow food everyone eats.

Annually, the South Platte Aquifer's water level hadn't changed much, despite seasonal fluctuation. Groundwater was lowest in the spring and highest by mid-October after deep percolation of irrigation return flows. Pumping increased during drought years (1940, 1953–57, and 1963–65), but given the dynamics of an alluvial aquifer, the system stayed in balance. Hydrologists call this "steady state." For this reason, farmers whose products were literally made of water chafed at talk of regulation, Bill included. He didn't like being told what to do. Independence from all that was the idea behind buying and moving to Big Bend Station. Having no college degree himself, he was skeptical of those whose point of view came from books. On the other hand, he trusted people who actually worked the land, who kept a tidy productive farm. That was work he could see and emulate.

As my dad chewed this over with the owls before dawn and all day long by himself, building biases against "city show-offs," biases that were common over at the Gilcrest Farm Supply, biases that were the twanging undercurrent on each morning's farm report, he kept pumping every summer. Everyone did. Meanwhile, golfers played at overirrigated courses. Kids splashed around in pools. People installed hot tubs. New suburbs with new strip malls sealed off wetlands forever. Growth came to equal prosperity, though given its considerable downsides, growth was confederated recklessness too.

Most folks remained unaware that under the big, gold-leaf covered capitol dome, where Ben Eaton's stained glass portrait is, the Colorado Legislature was enduring a laborious and contentious process to draft legislation to govern groundwater. Passage, in 1965, of the Colorado Ground Water Management Act, prevented the drilling of new wells without augmenting depletions to avoid injury to senior rights holders.[2] Well owners (those who were paying attention) fought against groundwater regulation like wildcats. Given the rancor, State Engineer Clarence Kuiper worked hard with legislators to craft a bill he thought he could enforce.

Colorado's Water Right Determination and Administration Act finally passed in 1969. It was the most comprehensive water legislation ever enacted in the history of the state, perhaps in any state. Like it or not, farmers or not, the act formalized the indivisible relationship between aboveground and belowground. The new law integrated groundwater irrigation wells into the priority system and required that surface water and groundwater be administered together according to the same priority system: "first in time, first in right." Some legislators, later grasping the unintended consequences, claimed it was not their intent to impede Colorado agriculture. "Intent" or not, the groundwater-rights owners risked being last in time, last in right.

The act organized the state into seven water divisions, one for each major river basin in Colorado. To oversee water administration, the Colorado Legislature assigned the duty of confirming priority dates and amounts to seven district water courts. This assignation kept water matters separate from civil courts, giving rise to distinctly dual Colorado judiciary processes. Instead of going through the Court of Appeals, water matters would thereafter be appealed directly to the Colorado Supreme Court, by operation of the Colorado Constitution.

Water Judges

Colorado *water judges* exercise a civil law jurisdiction over water rights within their entire water division. (There are seven divisions in the state.) The Colorado Supreme Court chief justice annually appoints water judges from among the available district court judges in that district.

Bill and many other well owners understood little of this new legislation. Living their truth, they continued flipping their pump switches in late summer to make up for surface-water shortfalls. No one yet stopped them. As farmers clomped around in their rubberized boots swatting at deerflies, State Engineer Kuiper was back at his desk in Denver, trying to figure out how to keep agriculture, then Colorado's most lucrative industry and a source of national food, in business despite the act, how to cobble groundwater management that would increase beneficial use of water but prevent injury to water-rights holders.

A year after the act passed, I left for Paris. It was 1970, "The Year of the Environment." Today, the words *environmental movement* sound so yesterday, almost quaint, but then, in the beginning, the movement seemed unstoppable. Coloradans had noticed that their "cube" of land, air, and water was not as accommodating, not as resilient as the state's forefathers had hoped.[3] Our state—with its fine weather, breathtaking scenery, and abundant natural pleasures—became the environmental movement's epicenter. The University of

Colorado at Boulder was the nation's flagship institution, first to offer a degree in environmental studies. The counterculture was politically resolute, and Colorado's counterculture had sentries, men and women who saw peril ahead—peril in the form of pollution, overpopulation, inadequate water, and resource deprivation—peril that would lead to wars, to crime, to the end of life as we know it. One sentry was a lawyer and politician named Dick Lamm. In 1967, as a member in the Colorado House of Representatives, Lamm drafted and successfully passed the first abortion law in the United States. In 1972 Lamm rallied opposition to Denver's bid to host the 1976 Olympics and succeeded. Lamm's positions seem more radical today than they did then. They included restricted growth, legalized suicide, and anti-immigration too, all as aspects of zero-population growth, which at its core was an attempt to turn around or stop the runaway destruction of natural resources. Most voting Coloradans seemed to agree. Zealous Dick Lamm was elected governor in 1974 and served three terms. Being a democrat, Lamm drove most farmers and ranchers crazy. Small ag operators didn't want government messing in their business. That included my father.

The low grassland at the edge of our Hundred-Acre Wood contains not just a handful of prairie dogs, but a whole "Prairie Dog Town," as we refer to it. Black-tailed prairie dogs are highly gregarious. They keep families, kiss, groom, snuggle, show off, fight, murder. They thrive in clans, eating everything in sight, decimating one area, until they have to move on or kill each other in order to assure adequate resources. Sound familiar? Prairie dog towns have sentries, lone animals that stand alert above a hole observing the comings and goings of predators and frustrated farmers with varmint getters. When a threat presents itself, the sentry yips as excitedly as young Dick Lamm, and all their kin scamper willy-nilly for the nearest hole. Farmers are not like prairie dogs.

···········■■··■■···········

Near our Prairie Dog Town, a trail crosses the slough. There, industrious beavers chisel and haul willow and cottonwood branches, to maintain their watery retreat year-round. Through the Big Bend Ditch, the spillover from this little beaver pond inundates another wetland to the north, where, in all but the most frigid weather, cattails dangling over pintail and snipe make it seem as if the ducks had dropped in for tea at a palm court. It does get nippy though, sometimes far below zero as it was in the winter 1972. Prairie dogs stay in their burrows. Beavers eat underbark in their food piles. And ducks flee, lest they freeze into the water. The woods immobilize, white with frost.

I was visiting. At the table my siblings, Annzo and Will, hung limply over their pancakes. Eyeing the early morning apathy, Pop abruptly said, "Ready for Ice Capades?"

As heavy as icicles, we stared at him. "Are we going somewhere?"

"Got your skates?"

None of us had used ice skates for years, because we'd spent every weekend at the farm, not the country club. As skeptical and disgruntled as crew on the *Endurance*, the family dug out the thick socks and skates and set off for the cattail pond. Well muffled, we laced up. All but Gogo had outgrown their skates. We yanked them on anyway. There was grumbling. Thinking back on this now, I wonder at how obliging we were, Pop's marionette family, coming to life at his bidding. Unlike the country-club rink, the pond had plants growing through the ice, challenging the few figure-skating feats my sister and I remembered. Nothing complicated; bumps fraught even our simple spins, and we capsized. Pop grabbed Gogo for a dance number on ice. Skittering along the bumpy surface, our mother squealed and he hummed old tunes like "Me and My Shadow." Their footwork launched them into a thicket of reeds. Soon they emerged feathered in brown cattail fuzz.

Their feathered look inspired Will to cry out, "Let's play fox and geese!" then pointing at Gogo and Pop, "You're the geese . . . *obviously*." Out of our minds with cold, we fanned out in every direction, while Will—by then as agile as my father—made haste for the kill.

After lunch back at the house, I volunteered for the death-defying trip to the mail. The daily excursion across the highway to the mailbox meant grain trucks bearing down at seventy miles per hour. Managing a successful crossing, I then loped back through the lane—through a tunnel of snowy cottonwoods—around the juniper and into the kitchen, carrying what would prove to be a copy of a letter from a Denver law firm, addressed to the Colorado Cattle Feeders Association and forwarded to my father. This is the only evidence that my father was notified—by however chancy a means—that he might lose use of his irrigation wells. Because he'd paid for the right to pump from the wells, because he maintained the wells, because he used the water for beneficial use, Pop thought of them as his.

Come to find out they were only on loan.

According to the letter, the only way to maintain his groundwater rights was to file for "adjudication" for each of his five wells by July 1, 1972. Pumping from any well not reported to the court for adjudication would thereafter be illegal. Bill called a Denver friend and attorney and asked, "What is this?"

"The water court will quantify the water rights, telling you how much you can legally pump from each well. Then it will assign each right an official appropriation date and decree. The decree gives your wells a priority relative to other water-right holders."

Pop groaned.

State Engineer Clarence Kuiper, acting on the Water Right Determination and Administration Act, under orders from the legislature to develop rules for bringing groundwater wells into the priority system, asked that well owners comply with the new statute. Those who pumped from a well were obliged to register their right(s) in the water court, together with the amount they historically pumped. This adjudication would protect the wells at a certain volume of usage, but put them in a pecking order.

To comply was a scary move, because strictly applying the new legislation— in which older claims would be entitled to their full share of water before newer groundwater claims could pump so much as a drop—threatened to shut down most wells in the South Platte River Valley, as Kuiper well knew. Well users could not deprive senior rights owners of water, no matter what. Period. The word they used wasn't *deprive*, though; it was *injury*. No one was allowed to do anything that would cause injury to senior rights owners. Most surface water appropriators had higher pecking order (i.e., seniority) and therefore a greater priority. That meant that wells would be out of priority when the depletion caused by summer pumping manifested in the river. The lower river at that time would cause injury to a senior rights holder downstream. If the well was very near the river, then the depletion from pumping might hit the river right away. Yet, depending on the wells' locations and the soil types, the depletions from pumping might not actually show up in the form of low flow in the river until several months, or even years later. (Predicting these depletions was then unsophisticated, and even today's computerized hydrological modeling is subject to heated disagreement.)

Bottom line, come the dry months of July and August, when farmers ran out of ditchwater, they could no longer simply flick a switch. This signaled mayhem for Bill and for owners of over 10,000 Colorado irrigation wells. Pop's "truth" moved a little farther from the truth he'd hatched so long ago, back at his grandfather's place at Woods Lake. He poured himself a midday martini.

The farmers were hobbled. The legislature tried to keep them in business. And so did the state engineer.

Kuiper puzzled long and hard. The law allowed junior well owners to pump out of priority under only one stipulation: they had to *offset* the downstream river (surface water) depletions that their pumping would precipitate. How to do that? They had to find and purchase sufficient replacement water, then make sure that water got back in the river in time, place, and amount for senior vested surface rights to use it. Yes, the only way this out-of-priority pumping would be allowed was if they delivered additional water, "augmentation" water, to recharge the river basin.[4] It was a solution, but it certainly wasn't easily executed.

Wasn't driving tractors, combating weeds, and bucking bales enough?

In the United States, the "land of plenty," most of us live out our lives without testing the limitations of our rights. The majority takes its rights for granted year in year out, without pushing to see what they really are. This Water Right Determination and Administration Act of 1969 should have forced everyone who owned a water right to take a good, hard look at what they owned. The fact that a groundwater right was a "right" at all made it seem like the opposite of wrong, like something special, something worth paying for, something that couldn't be taken away.

However, buying a water right in the arid West, as it turns out, is not the same as owning something that you can do with as you please. A water right is more like free speech and the right to bear arms. Even though Americans can speak freely, they cannot falsely shout "fire" in a theater. Even though Americans can bear arms, they cannot lawfully shoot one another, except in justifiable self-defense. Owning a water right is like being issued a driver's license. You can only exercise a water right if you follow certain legal provisions, just as the right to drive a car hinges on following traffic regulations. Free speech and guns, and maybe even driving, come with more leeway than rights to use often-scarce water resources.

Big Bend Station's Five Groundwater Well Rights

Colorado Water District 1

Appropriation Date	Total Acre-Feet
1930	464
1933	267
1934	297
1954	580
1957	595

That said, sweaty, independent-minded farmers with worn jeans and dirt under their nails—particularly the small-time operators who couldn't afford to spend days with attorneys—were dumbfounded to learn that the water directly under their land, the water their families may have depended on for generations, wasn't really "theirs," had never been theirs, and now had all kinds of strings attached, strings farmers couldn't even begin to figure out how to pull. Not only that. They reasoned that they weren't using the water to indulge themselves. It wasn't as if they were committing a crime. They were using it to grow food for everybody else. Wasn't their profession a public service? What about the backbone of democracy?

Kuiper sympathized, not least because agricultural production was Colorado's biggest industry. Food had to come from somewhere; why not Colorado? As Bill learned when he went ahead and adjudicated five wells, Kuiper prodded well owners to form associations or conservancy districts that would develop plans to replace water for them. Farmers had little inclination. They didn't really like to talk with one another, much less join forces. Again, they weren't like prairie dogs. Bill had moved to the country to avoid associations. Augmentation was a headache, a huge headache.

..........▄▄··▄▄··········

Other people's headaches would become somewhat of a specialty for a man named Jack Odor, then a young engineer for Fort Morgan, a farm town about an hour east of Big Bend Station, also on the South Platte River.[5] Jack was keen, with a gift for math, thoroughness, and getting things done. As a reflection of his attention to detail, Jack was a meticulous collector. His butterfly archive boasted one of every species of the United States. His living room had dozens of mounted animal trophies in it, including one of every deer of North America. Jack Odor was that thorough. In 1971, his boss summoned him to a meeting at the Radisson Hotel in Denver. The new demands for augmentation had forced irrigation into a new era.

Soon after the meeting, Jack Odor found himself in charge of the newly spawned Groundwater Appropriators of the South Platte, known as G.A.S.P., possibly because it gave farmers such as my father and his neighbors the breathing room they so needed. G.A.S.P.'s directive was to borrow and lend water, to be used to recharge the South Platte River on behalf of well users.

Bill had adjudicated his wells with the water court, as the new law demanded, but to keep pumping during August and September, he needed to replace some percentage of the water he pumped. He and a lot of others too asked, "How can I do this?" Bill could have built an unlined recharge pond and hired an engineer to determine how fast water deposited there might recharge the river and how that compared to the rate at which he was depleting the river using his wells. He could have done that, but it was expensive, so he asked, "If I join G.A.S.P., will they find replacement water for me?" And the state said, "Yeah, that'd be fine."

Groundwater Appropriators of the South Platte was cheap. It only cost Bill twenty-five dollars a year to offset each *hundred* acre-feet of water or part thereof that he drew from a well. Bill signed up and paid his fee. Most farmers did this; well users for 3,000 wells put themselves in Jack Odor's hands, so they could pump during the summer without depriving water appropriators downstream of their senior right to the water. (Another organization, the Central Colorado Water Conservancy District's Ground Water Management Subdistrict, formed the next year for 1,000 additional wells.)

Jack Odor strove for minimum red tape. Sure, he had a choice to file an augmentation plan; that was certainly encouraged. An augmentation plan *must be judicially approved by the water court* in a grueling process that can be controversial, highly contested, expensive, and a pain in the tail. The applicant must establish the timing and location of the depletions caused by his or her out-of-priority use, as well as the availability of sufficient replacement water to prevent injury from those depletions. If another party wants that water, as another party always does, it can go badly for the applicant, particularly if the other party has an army of lawyers and hydrologists, as the other party often does.

Groundwater Appropriators of the South Platte got around these tribulations. Instead of filing for augmentation-plan approval, the meticulous Jack Odor, who got things done, engineered annual *substitute water supply plans* (SWSPs), sufficient to keep 3,000 wells pumping every year. A substitute water supply plan could then be approved annually by the state engineer, no water court required. This was the key to Jack Odor's success, this year-by-year basis. And every year was different.

Each year, Odor started by assessing snowfall and predictions to estimate the potential water supply. Afterward, he'd weigh that

Augmentation Plan

This court-approved plan allows a water user to divert water out of priority, so long as adequate replacement is made to the affected stream system and water rights in quantities and at times, so as to prevent injury to the water rights of other users.

SOURCE: Richard Stenzel and Tom Cech with contributors Hal Simpson and Dick Wolfe, *Water: Colorado's Real Gold* (Fort Collins, CO: Richard Stenzel, 2013).

Substitute Water Supply Plan (SWSP)

This water-replacement plan identifies sources of water that are either owned or leased and can be introduced into the same water body from which water is withdrawn, in a location that prevents more senior water-rights owners from being negatively affected by the out-of-priority withdrawal.

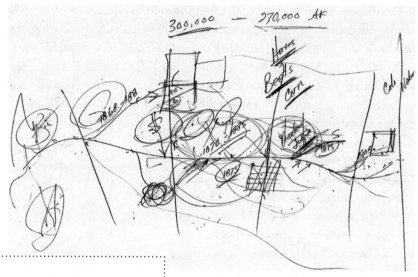

Jack Odor's Decision Making

Jack Odor explained his process to me using this drawing. In it, he needed to supply substitute water for 270,000–300,000 acre-feet of pumping. The circles are opportunities. The horizontal line that bends downward on the left is the South Platte River. That bend is the approximate location of Big Bend Station. The right margin represents the Colorado-Nebraska line.

amount against the anticipated uses, which were the quantity he had to offset. Throughout the watershed, Jack then used the fees my father and other well owners paid in order to identify, purchase, or rent water. Groundwater Appropriators of the South Platte provided replacement water using several methods, including (1) recharge ponds, (2) pumping groundwater into senior canals to lessen the impact of well pumping, and (3) permanent reservoir or ditch-company rights—water from which G.A.S.P. delivered directly to the South Platte. A description of these water supplies—some leased and others owned by G.A.S.P.—were turned in each year in different combos to the state engineer, who approved the company's replacement plans (SWSPs) for the ensuing twelve months.

That water, which was then leasable for about ten dollars an acre-foot, was delivered to the depleted river to augment its flow. So doing protected downstream senior diverters from injury by well pumping, thus allowing G.A.S.P. members, well users such as Bill who paid annual fees, to continue flicking a pump-house switch in late summer. Even though G.A.S.P. members were pumping out of priority, G.A.S.P. satisfied their "debt" to the river in advance. Downstream senior rights holders were happy. Bill was happy to have one less headache. Other farmers were happy too. Jack Odor, busy being thorough, was happy.

How much replacement was necessary? Everybody, including Pop, used furrow irrigation in those days. Furrow irrigation is said to be 50 percent efficient, meaning that crops consume approximately half the water applied. Sometimes less. The remainder of the water returns to the river and aquifer. So if you were pumping a hundred acre-feet for furrow irrigation, the *depletion* would be fifty acre-feet. The other half was *return flow.* Well users only had to replace their depletions when a downstream senior right made a call. Generally, river calls occurred during July and August (17 percent of the year). During dry years the pumpers replaced 10 percent of their consumptive use. The rest of the years, 5 percent was sufficient.

Why was the call so limited? For decades prior to 1969, a "Gentlemen's Agreement" between upstream and downstream reservoir owners, had minimized winter calls on the river caused by post-pumping depletions. Well owners might or might not have known about the Gentlemen's Agreement, which was a key reason that groundwater depletions in the river were low, but either way, all well owners soon became accustomed to paying for only modest replacement.[6] Resting on a handshake, this agreement masked well owners' depletions for many years. It also maximized use and worked great.

Bearing the Gentlemen's Agreement in mind at that Radisson meeting in 1971,

Consumptive Use

This water is removed from available supplies without returning to a water resources system. In farming, this is the amount of water that is taken up into the plants, together with the amount that evaporates from the soil surface and foliage. The portion of water consumed in crop production depends on many factors, especially the irrigation technology. *Consumptive use is the same as depletion.*

Depletion

Depletion

=

Consumptive use

=

Plant transpiration + soil evaporation

Irrigation Return Flow

Return flow is irrigation water that is neither consumed by the crop nor evaporated from the soil and is therefore available for other uses. Return flow may flow off the bottom of the field and/or percolate through the soil to the water table, and from there then flow to the river or remain in the aquifer.

The Gentlemen's Agreement

Since 1929, owners of the large senior reservoirs east of Kersey (much downstream from Big Bend Station) voluntarily waived their right to call water down to their reservoirs after irrigation season, thereby allowing upstream junior reservoirs to store water first.

Division engineers let the water be stored upstream, out of priority because downstream reservoirs did not call. With good return flows from agriculture and municipal discharge, the senior reservoirs downstream nearly always filled. Filling later in the year, they didn't suffer as many losses from evaporation and seepage. If downstream reservoirs needed more water, they placed a call during the runoff season.

Since the reservoirs placed fewer calls on the river, the groundwater appropriators had smaller depletions to replenish. This maximized use in Colorado and helped reduce the amount of water flowing out of Colorado to Nebraska.

Kuiper had floated the figure 5 percent of the consumptive use as the amount that might need to be replaced. That was the starting point. In drier years, more water would be needed.

"I put in whatever amount it took," Odor said. "Sometimes it was five, but some years no augmentation was necessary, when the river flowed all year long anyway. Everyone had enough water during those years. Why put something back? Why go to the additional expense? On years where water was harder to come by, maybe 20 percent was the right number, and we addressed that. I always had a little something in my hip pocket, a way to satisfy up to 30 percent. Another factor: Most pumping activity and irrigation occur from May to September. Why replace water during winter and spring? You're wasting your time. It's not necessary. So what I would do is to try to line up enough water to be reasonably covered for a bad but not catastrophic event."[7]

From the 1970s through the 1990s, the state engineer sometimes pressured G.A.S.P., saying, "We like this source and we like this source, but we don't have anything here." So, with the same enthusiasm Jack might use to net an elusive butterfly, he would hasten to find an additional recharge site. He'd then take his list of water sources and wells, a list of everybody's pumping activity, a list of everybody's crop patterns—my father's included— on and on and on, to the state engineer, who was at first Mr. Kuiper. Then he'd say, "I think you can see that I have satisfied the state's water augmentation requirements." And the state engineer would say, "You bet." Then he'd sign it and give G.A.S.P.'s permit slip for that year to Jack Odor. The same process occurred the next year, the year after that and so forth, always with the aquifer in a "steady state."

This is how, when my father and other South Platte farmers got a chance to learn that water rights are like drivers' licenses, deferring to Jack Odor and a succession of state engineers to achieve conjunctive use allowed them to forget. More than 100 years after Judge Hallett's decision, it should've been clear that the Colorado Doctrine was a doctrine of scarcity, that overappropriation meant too much demand to satisfy everybody. With ever-present dehydration sucking the juice out of every human, with unanticipated variables such as groundwater and population rise confounding predictions of water availability and challenging the effectiveness of law's ability to satisfy during periods of drought, this doctrine of scarcity should have been cautionary. No one in the West should have trusted others, should have moved any farther from our water sources than Bill was from Gogo during "Me and My Shadow." We should not have, but we did.

Nonetheless, Jack Odor continued to engineer SWSPs for the South Platte basin in twelve-month increments, and then to lay them in front of Clarence Kuiper and his successors, Jeris Danielson and Hal Simpson. These Colorado state engineers approved them for thirty long years—during which Big Bend Station thrived and other agribusinesses in the South Platte River Valley thrived too, all in a state of forgetfulness . . . until everything went kerflooey.

HYPOCRISY, IN A KERNEL

*If we are to really change the politics-as-usual debate on the Farm Bill every
five years and create a sustainable food system for the long term, it is critical for
progressives in the environmental and conservation movements to stop blaming
farmers for the food policies that agribusiness and the food industry have lobbied
for and achieved incrementally over the past eighty years. Scapegoating farmers
is not only unfair; it also will not help us build the farmer-eater coalition that we
need to advance enlightened agriculture and food policy.*
—WENONAH HAUTER, *FOODOPOLY*

Without confusing you, may I briefly buck chronology?

An eon later, in the new millennium, my brother, Will, and I would weave
after Gogo down a corridor in a cloud-piercing skyscraper. Attorney Anne
Castle was escorting my mother to a conference room at Holland & Hart, a
Denver firm with a specialty in water law. We watched Ms. Castle incline toward
Gogo, which seemed a solicitous and an almost protective posture. "It is not as
if the farmers are blameless," we heard Ms. Castle remark.

Considering all that we had gone through by then, this sentence should have
stopped us in our tracks. It didn't though. We just kept shuffling forward, inexorable yahoos from the country. All that Paris, all that Los Angeles, all that Buenos
Aires, all that claptrap and years of avoiding bumpkinhood, and I still had no
gumption! And Will, Will who had bested all manner of big mammals in the
woods? We never challenged her, never asked. Was it our naiveté? Intimidation?

Many times since I have wondered what Anne Castle meant. She would
become President Obama's "Water Czar" at the Department of the Interior.

What, in the view of a *czar*, did farmers do wrong? Where had my father gone amiss?

Grounded in all that a city dweller knows about farming, which isn't much, but informed by the popular spin against American agriculture, my best guess: Bill grew water-guzzling corn.

So what's wrong with corn? Corn itself isn't terrible. Nothing more delicious, nothing more innocent than freshly harvested sweet corn, shucked, roasted, or boiled, then slathered in butter with salt and pepper. Yet, in the last forty years, for better or worse, the crop's permutations have put corn at the center of the US food system and divided us from the very people with whom we should have a strong bond—our growers. Growers, there with corn at ground zero, have a story of their own that started even as the ink was drying on Bill's farm purchases.

Now, back to the 1970s.

.... ▬ · ▬ ....

Corn wasn't always at the farm. Bill first grew the dependable irrigated cash crop that originally put Weld County on the map—sugar beets (*Beta vulgaris*)—just as his grandfather and great-grandfather had. Though sugar beet processing was smelly, no one carried on as if growing the enormous root was a cardinal sin. Pies and sodas and cookies didn't have a bum rap. Not in the 1970s. Americans weren't fat. Our palate wasn't yet controversial. The region's good-draining soils, high daytime temperatures, and cool nights were ideal for sugar beets, which Big Bend Station for years delivered to the Great Western Sugar Company in nearby Windsor.

Meanwhile, as we Americans kept eating, a series of overlapping political, scientific, and business activities began to transform our food, and therefore to transform us.

This is where the Gilcrest Farm Supply reappears in the story. My parent's farm is oriented toward the west, toward the Rockies, toward "drama" and "opportunity." Yet, many mornings Bill got in his VW Thing and drove four miles in the opposite direction. On County Road 44—without windshield, without doors, without seatbelt—he could smoke as he marveled at the eastern orientation. It was endless, uniform, flat, and to Bill's way of thinking, "his people": American farmers and ranchers. Timed properly, he arrived at the Gilcrest Farm Supply with the old-timers. With them, he enjoyed a cup of joe and chewed the fat around the redoubt's big potbellied stove. Afterward, Bill might purchase gaskets, a toggle switch, or a new shovel. The owner, Bob Bruce, always had a big roll of cash. It was faster to bank with Bob than to drive to Greeley.

The eastern horizon also led to Omaha, Decatur, St. Louis, Minneapolis, and other ag cities of the Midwest where ConAgra, Cargill, Archer-Daniels-Midland, and a handful of other companies were poised to gobble and plot their way into the agriculture behemoths we now refer to as "Big Ag."

In Decatur, a medium-size operator of mills and grain elevators named Archer-Daniels-Midland (ADM) had appointed Dwayne Andreas CEO in 1970. The company began its ascent into a multinational powerhouse, taking many steps at a time. A gifted strategist, Dwayne Andreas was as cunning at leadership as he was at ingratiating politicians, even world leaders whose allegiance he was able to leverage to get his own way domestically. Not just shrewd management was involved, but also campaign financing, price fixing, and apparently donating ADM stock to a trust fund set up to benefit the children of one of Senator Hubert Humphrey's advisors![1] This advisor was appointed as a member of the Commodities Futures Trading Commission in 1978. The CFTC regulates many of ADM's market operations. And here's a watery detail from an old *Fortune* magazine article: Andreas rose every morning at 5:30 and dove into a long swimming pool equipped with extra powerful water jets. There, he swam against the current for twenty minutes.[2]

Ronald Reagan was elected. Reagan's swagger captivated my parents as it did most farmers and ranchers. Seemingly about rebuilding America's self-respect, Reagan rode into Washington on *laissez-faire capitalism*, with a mandate to loosen regulations, reduce taxation, and upend antitrust laws . . . much to the satisfaction of Andreas and others like him. The Federal Trade Commission, tasked with keeping competition alive, got a new director. His mission was not to prevent mergers but to *encourage* them. The talk was less government, but the substantive idea was *vertical integration*, a business model that acquired and stacked suppliers, producers, processors, and marketers under the same ownership. That, and much less regulation.

Under Andreas, who learned from water each morning, corn's utility evolved. It was still made into cornbread, tortillas, tamales, polenta, grits, hush puppies, corn pudding, and the flaked kernels ranchers used for finishing cattle. Yes, but then ADM launched high-fructose corn syrup, claiming that HFCS not only sweetened but also stabilized, preserved, inhibited spoilage, withstood temperature, did not crystalize, and was cheaper than conventional sugar made from cane or sugar beets.[3] Archer-Daniels-Midland made sure HFCS was cheaper, because ADM lobbied for a fierce sugar tariff, made restrictive by Reagan in 1982.[4] That's when the sugar beet really lost ground . . . literally.

·········· ▰▰·· ▰▰··········

Corn as sweetener was but the beginning. Corn as fuel (ethanol) soon followed. Today corn is ubiquitous. In an average supermarket, one-quarter of the products has corn-derived ingredients.[5] It's in plastics, packing materials, insulation, chemicals, explosives, paint, paste, abrasives, dyes, insecticides, pharmaceuticals, adhesive, organic acids, solvents, rayon, antifreeze, soap; the list goes on and on. Even vitamin C, made with sorbitol, has corn in it. Corn is also in feed for pigs, sheep, poultry, and—down the road from Big Bend Station—cattle. Soylent Green? Yes, it's corn.

By winnowing out or eliminating the competitors and putting multiple operations under single corporations with vertical integration, consolidation did for food cultivation what Henry Ford did for manufacturing. Food became industrialized. Efficiencies and economies of scale translated into more food and lower food prices for consumers, which sounded great, but it wasn't long before downsides were apparent. As consumers, we now know the hazards of fast food and junk food and processed food, but who was first to feel the hit? The producers. Farmers and ranchers, whose revenues had always been a small portion of the price that consumers pay, lost their autonomy and a feeling of direct contact with suppliers and processors. Regional buyers such as Great Western Sugar faltered. Grain elevators changed ownership or closed. Trusted seed vendors had new seeds or select seeds, or maybe they went out of business.

With fewer and fewer choices, both for suppliers and markets, family-owned agriculture operations had less autonomy. Banks only made loans for certain crops. Processors only bought certain crops. Decisions were made for producers: they grew corn. The word *chute*, made for livestock, works: my father and other small farmers and ranchers were in a chute.

My chute was different: Californian, more progressive than conservative, a reader, organic tendencies, friends who are academics, artists, and designers. I'm a known "type," everything but the yoga mat. Though concerned and well meaning, my general penchant for do-gooding was a high horse. By this, I mean that I believed that by reading both *The New York Times* and *The Wall Street Journal*, I was ingesting a balanced view of "the way things are." But I wasn't. My own father was inscrutable to me, masked by his Gary Cooper charisma, as well as his acquired profession, which was—to me anyway—arcane.

Just like the rest of the farmers around him, Bill grew corn guilelessly, yearly, and abundantly—as much as a 150 bushels an acre—for a buyer who was right down the road. That buyer, having been consolidated into an operation by ADM or another large corporation that employed many, was connected to transportation, processors, markets, and consumers in all over the world. Bill and neighboring farmers collected subsidies because they could, because why not? The farm still ran at a loss.

········ ■ ·■ ········

Agriculture Commodity Market

Commodities derived from raising crops and/ or animals may be direct products such as wheat, feed grains (such as maize or corn, sorghum, barley, and oats), cotton, milk, rice, peanuts, sugar, tobacco; oilseeds such as rapeseed; and meat products such as poultry, beef, pork, and lamb and mutton. Other ag commodities, such as high-fructose corn syrup and ethanol, are derived from direct products.

During the Middle Ages, trade of agricultural commodities gave rise to the first exchanges. Today, agricultural products are among the most important commodities and futures contracts traded.

The commodity market influences the price of physical goods and vice versa.

It took years to discern what was always obvious: for good reasons, my father wasn't growing rows of snap peas and salad greens with names from the romance languages. Big Bend Station occupies the westernmost portion of the vast agricultural middle of our country. Northeastern Colorado is sparsely populated with small farmers who have invested their money and their lifetime in learning how to plant, cultivate, harvest, and sell, not vegetables and fruits (produce), but *commodity crops* that must be processed or refined to become edible. Their generation and all the generations before them for 150 years did the same thing and were encouraged to keep at it by railroads, regulators, subsidies, water transfers, water administration, and—since laissez-faire—Big Ag and chemical companies.

Commodity growers sell crops that reenter the food system as a component of another food—as a grain, oil, starch, or sweetener, or as feed for animals. These are not a marginal part of our diet today. Oils alone make up 8 percent of average caloric intake.[6] Food is just the beginning of it. There are also myriad other products made of commodities, as I've already described about corn. Today, fewer than 800,000 farmers such as my dad grow all the American corn, soy, and wheat and other grains, for consumers and manufacturers the world over.[7]

To my mind, all this utility didn't necessarily make it right. Again and again over the years, I'd descend on the farm with the same questions and inferences about doing things differently.

Disgruntled with me, my father pushed down on the door handle. A gust grabbed the door. When he tightened his grip, the wind pulled him outside then fought him, the 200-pound man, as he shoved the door back into the jamb.

Wind made itself part of the argument. On the High Plains wind arrives unpredictably all year long. It doesn't feel like wind in a city, where hard surfaces interrupt its force. On the Plains air is uninhibited, wild, flattening grasses, tearing at crops, grabbing branches off trees, then shoving them to break fences. Wind quickly turns beauty into headaches and frays nerves. I followed my father out. The wind threw me around too, and I tumbled both with and against it to catch up with him.

"You don't know the first thing," he growled. "It's not as if we have an army of workers crouched here all day long. See anyone pulling weeds and plucking out caterpillars? We're using machinery, which takes gas."

"Pop . . ."

"I've explained this to you before," he shouted at me over the wind. A gust sucked saliva from his mouth out over his cheek. The conversation was like *On Golden Pond* in a cyclotron.

"What about organic?" I yelled.

"I don't want regulators on my back. Anyway, growing corn that way around here wouldn't work."

"Because of transportation . . ."

"And labor. And refrigeration. And markets. The corn itself. And weather, the damned weather!"

I flashed on what this wind might do to berries and baby greens. Grains, it doesn't bother. Prairie and grains are part of a piece, perfectly compatible.

"You eat bread. You eat meat. This is where it starts."

. . . . ▄▄ · ▄▄ . . . .

Consuming, readers, is everyone's piece of industrial agriculture. And it's a big piece! Even I, the impecunious epicure, am a player. According to the US Agriculture Census (most recent numbers are from 2014), when I buy organic US-grown food, I am among 1.3 percent of the total.[8] Imports include "organic" food, and consumers will pay more for organic. *Nutrition Business Journal* estimates organic is now over 4 percent of total food sales.[9]

Everyone else and me too—when we buy a loaf of non-organic bread or pasta or a container of oatmeal or food packaged in a biodegradable plastic-seeming container made of cornstarch—we are part of the other 96 percent.

Turning Crops and Animals to Food

In the most recent study from 2008, gross US farm receipts were $316.3 billion. Government payments were $12.2 billion. Of this total $328.5 billion, only $4.8 billion were direct sales to consumers and grocery stores that buy locally grown produce. The rest, 99.9 percent of the sales, went to packagers, processors, aggregators, brokers, marketers, and/or distributors. These transactions moved crops and animals through intermediaries where it became food.

SOURCES: *Farm Income and Wealth Statistics, 2008* (USDA Economic Research Service); Sarah A. Low and Stephen Vogel, "Direct and Intermediated Marketing of Local Foods in the United States," Economic Research Report No. 128 (USDA Economic Research Service, November 2011).

And on what do we rely for this 96 percent? On the "flyover states" or flyover parts of states, where easily overlooked people like my father and the farmers and ranchers around him—whose profession is making sure we have food to survive—must get things done rather than talk about them. Far from Denver, Bill and his ilk cannot sell produce directly. Theirs aren't those sorts of operations. Rural farm and ranch operations are part of a supply chain that sustains processors, aggregators, brokers, marketers, packagers, and distribution systems of products that end up on our plates.

Just as access to water is taken for granted, so too are these farmers and ranchers. Also common is thinking that if you were a farmer, you'd do it differently.

We don't have to try not to notice these folks. They're in a world apart, and they're holding on by their teeth. They're out there getting the life drained out of them by subverted antitrust laws, consolidation, and secret water deals, while getting farm loans to pay for suddenly proprietary seeds and inputs that may or may not contaminate soil and water and maybe them too, but will certainly enslave them to the few companies that they are obliged to buy from. And what do they have? They have each other.

Such was the demand, so Bill grew corn, as did many, even most growers in the South Platte basin, irrigating from their wells, irrigating from their ditches. From the beginning, my father had understood that a mutual ditch is an earthen invitation to get to know farmers up-ditch. It was as much Bill's obligation to maintain the Western Mutual Ditch as that of others who used it. The idea was to keep the ditch clear of obstructions so the maximum amount of water could flow to Big Bend Station. There might be weeds to burn, silt accumulations to remove. And he was sure to learn a thing or two, to make a study of the locals.

During these investigations, Bill saw and met two brothers named Varela who worked at the farm south of Big Bend Station. From Chihuahua, Mexico, a spot called Temósachic (that means "surrounded by water" in Tarahumara), both were hard workers. One spoke English, but Bill was most drawn to the brother who didn't: Ernesto Varela. Bill knew no Spanish, but he could spot a hard worker with a good attitude. He liked Ernesto's smile, the set of his shovel, the way he so often said, "Sí, por supuesto." Bill and Ernesto had an immediate rapport.

At the south end of the farm, where irrigation water from the Western Mutual Ditch first flows into Bill's property, is the little house where the cowboys had bunked. Several tenants had been there since Bill had jettisoned the cowboys, but that southern outpost was at the moment vacant. Bill told Gogo that he thought Ernesto would make a great sentry. And his wife, Erminia, could help Gogo with housework and garden, maybe.

"Don't you think I should meet her?"

"I'll ask." Bill somehow communicated this to Ernesto. Gogo set off alone to meet Erminia Varela, to see Erminia's impeccable housekeeping. As Ernesto tells the story—still in Spanish, not English, years later—Erminia and Gogo never needed words. They knew what one another was thinking from the beginning, because they communicate as plants communicate with each other, Ernesto says.

And the bond was forged: all outposts occupied. English speakers in the north. Spanish speakers in the south. Hardly any conversation, but the work got done.

. . . . ▬ ▪ ▬ . . . .

Apropos of gifts from the South, let's talk about corn as a species—this versatile, controversial, malleable grass that is a currency, a livelihood, and perhaps a curse.

Pre-Columbian Mesoamericans domesticated *Zea mays* as early as 8,700 years ago (the age of soil deposits in which milling tools were discovered).[10] The word *domesticated* implies selection, breeding, and cultivation—activities that were an early form of hybridization, genetic modification if you will. Indigenous people's triumph was to enlarge the size of corn ears. They achieved

Zea

This genus of true grasses is in the family Poaceae. Several species commonly known as teosintes are found in Central America. *Zea mays*, or corn, is the only domesticated taxon in the genus *Zea*.

this over time by virtue of corn's promiscuity, the easily dispersed male "inflorescence," its pollen, from the tassel. Most pollen falls within a few feet of the tassel, dusting the female silks that emerge from each whorl of husk leaves. This falling and dusting is what results in kernels (seeds). It can also bring about crossing and backcrossing, cross-pollination, and cross-contamination between varieties (which is why it is so difficult to keep varieties certifiably pure, as my father kept telling me).

Long ago, a man who would become first the secretary of agriculture and then vice president of the United States, Henry Wallace, spent his earlier years experimenting with corn varieties, enough to believe in hybridization as a way to improve taste, nutritional value, and yield, and also enough to learn how to get ahead in life. In 1925, with other Iowa pals, Wallace founded the seed company that soon became Pioneer Hi-Bred Corn Company. Later in public office, Wallace stated his lifelong mission to "make the world safe for corn breeders." By 1973 Pioneer had gone public. By 1981, when Bill began farming corn, it dominated corn seed sales, and soon, Weld County landscape.

Corn's shallow root depth made it ideal for flood irrigation, but weeds had to be controlled, because they outcompeted corn for water. No problem. Soon after the last frost, we'd hear the first thwacking propellers overhead at the farm. Crop dusters flew very low, scattering our fields and others in the valley with herbicide, insecticide, and fertilizer. Swear to God, we didn't think twice about the momentary clouding with petrochemical-derived confections designed to scorch broad-leafed weeds and arthropods, all the while delivering life-giving nutrients to corn. We trusted that Uncle Sam had the situation well under control. *Thwacking*—that happy sound of summer.

On the High Plains, modern agriculture continued to turn vast stretches of land into a blanket of human possibility, anew year after year, but it came at a cost. We'd all like to think that our food supply could be secured with minimal or no chemicals, yet only farmers and those who really garden—I mean on their knees several times a week year after year—notice correlations between soil, drainage, water, weather, weeds, and voracious predators. (If nematodes keep you awake, you know what I mean!) Figuring out what to do about weeds and pests required compromise in perpetuity.

·········■■··■■·········

Expansive acres of corn constituted a market into which additional businesses could insert themselves. New frontiers followed old frontiers. All crops have hundreds of years of experimentation in their past, perhaps corn most of all.

Ingenious engineering and science revved in the last quarter of the twentieth century. Enter legions of PhDs in lab coats, men and women who garner three and four times the earnings of the dungaree-clad farmers. Genetic engineering, plus the Supreme Court's surprising ruling that a life is patentable, put biotechnology in hyperdrive.[11] During the 1990s, Big Ag companies that had invested in biotech fell over themselves to snap up smaller seed companies of the type from which Bill used to buy seed, and to saturate the market with newly patented seed derived of gene splicing. Add Big Chem—Monsanto, DuPont, Dow, Syngenta, and so on—and whatever they could concoct from the periodic table to market as chemical inputs, often for corn.

Agricultural Inputs

Seeds

Fertilizers

Pesticides

Herbicides

Water

Take *Bacillus thuringiensis* ("Bt" for short), a spore-forming soil bacterium. Bt produces protein crystals that are toxic to many types of insects. Commercial forms of the bacterium have, since the 1920s, effectively defended crops from Lepidopteran caterpillar pests. Organic farmers use liquid sprays of Bt. Caterpillars starve after the bacterium paralyzes their digestive tract. Farming is not for the squeamish.

In 1996, traditional growers were introduced to corn seed that was genetically engineered to include a *Bacillus thuringiensis* gene. Bt corn itself produced pesticide. This "in the bag" prevention meant fewer inputs and greater yield, so the farmers around Bill were ready to try it. Farmers, more than anyone, knew that every crop plant had been "modified" many times over millennia. The difference here was that Bt corn wasn't just resistant to caterpillars; its chromosomes *contained* Bt genes.

That same year in corn history, 1996, Monsanto introduced their proprietary "Roundup Ready Corn" seed, which was genetically engineered to withstand regular dowsing with Monsanto's proprietary "Roundup" herbicide (glyphosate and surfactant). In fields, everything except the corn perished under this

Bt Corn

The use of Bt corn has led some pests (fall armyworm and African stem-borer) to become resistant to the bacterium. Another worry is the effect of the GMO on diminishing numbers of nontarget species such as Monarch butterflies (*Danaus plexippus*) and reducing food sources for other species. Should pollen-expressing Bt be determined a real concern, it can be addressed by modifying the corn not to express Bt toxin in the pollen.

Atrazine

In the United States, atrazine is one of the most widely used pesticides, on golf courses too. It was banned in Europe in 2004, because of water contamination, but as of 2016 the EPA is still analyzing it.

regime, which increased yields all the more. Farmers who bought the seed could no longer save some of the harvest to plant the next year, though, because the seed was proprietary. Good results and slim margins meant that every year farmers were obliged to buy more seed and more Roundup from Monsanto. Atrazine, a pesticide from Syngenta, was another product that almost everyone used on corn. And to redouble yields, the crops needed fertilizer. Like its relative turf-grass, GMO corn requires more nitrogen, potassium, and phosphorus than many other crops, not all of which are absorbed into the plant . . . and are thought to contribute to dead zones in gulf regions.[12]

Helped along by machinery, chemical farming, genetically engineered corn, and other technologies, an acre of American farmland now yields around 150 bushels, over seven times as many as a century ago. Such harvests make good rejoinders to questions about feeding rising populations, but they come at a price—to consumers, wildlife, water quality, the marine environment, and climate, as well as to farmers and ranchers.

Changes turned the food sector into an hourglass, with farmers and ranchers at one end and the rest of us at the other end. Separating food producers and consumers is a narrows of very profitable, consolidated, and interlocking corporations. Manufacturers of seed and inputs, those that purchase and process crops and animals, plus the smattering of big-brand food manufacturers—they occupy this pinch point, the *oligopsony*. With each passing year, its constituent corporations are fewer in number but with greater power and revenues. The oligopsony makes most of the money as well as controls regulation, pricing, acreages, exports, and . . . international affairs, plus what we eat.[13] It also does a good job of transferring blame to the growers. Don't we always hear farmers vilified for receiving subsidies?

Oligopsony

OLIGOI = "few" in Greek
OPSONIA = "purchase" in Greek

An oligopsony is a market where numerous suppliers and/or producers compete to sell their product to a few, often powerful, buyers.

Agriculture subsidies date from passage of the first Agricultural Adjustment Act in 1933, during the Depression, while Henry Wallace, defender of corn breeders, was secretary of agriculture. The government didn't do this out of largesse. The act's goal was to control, support, and stabilize commodity growing. Why? Commodities were and are tremendously important to national food security (and increasingly, to security in other sectors such as energy and health) and as international bargaining chips. Since 1933, the federal government had exercised a combination of subsidies, supply and price controls, acreage allotments, production quotas, tariffs, and export subsidies.

A lot of people believe that even small farmers and ranchers are getting fat on subsidies and other government payments. The situation is *not* one of greed, not for small- and medium-sized growers. They would go under without government support. And the problem isn't sloth either. It's that producing tightly controlled commodities—corn, for instance—costs more than the commodities are worth in the marketplace dominated by Big Ag. The price supports (whether subsidies or some other payment) are there to take care of this government-instituted shortfall.

Let's say it takes $3 to grow a bushel of corn, but the buyer/processor only pays $2.50. The oligopsony (buyer/processors)—be it Cargill, ADM, ConAgra, or another multinational corporation—wants costs low. Buyer/processors can afford to lobby Congress to keep up the price supports, to encourage farmers to overproduce corn, thereby depressing prices, lower prices of which consumers are beneficiaries. Thus, taxpayers, not these conglomerates, pay that extra fifty cents a bushel to reimburse the farmer for the difference between the cost to grow and the selling price.

While we're pointing fingers, we should note that American shoppers spend between 70 and 90 percent of their food budget on processed food (often derived from this corn), not the fresh food typically found in the refrigerated areas of the grocers. (Very little of that food budget actually goes to farmers.) Food in most supermarket aisles is commodity dependent. Check its labels. As I've already said, our other consumption habits—energy, pharmaceuticals, clothing, electronics, you name it—increasingly depend on commodities too.

This is the root of Pop's exasperation with me: on paper anyway, farmers have always had the choice of dropping out of the government-supported program and raising whatever they wanted, such as vegetables and fruit. The "why" was apparent. But how? As I've already said, market volatility and the lack of marketing infrastructure keep farmers from stepping outside their zone. The margins aren't wide enough to take chances. Loans, suppliers, processing, and transportation matter too. The next growing season arrives before you know it.

Let's say the odd Weld County farmer decides to grow quinoa. (This is the kind of idea that might occur to well-intended city folks.) He or she probably couldn't get a bank loan, might have problems getting seed due to Bolivian protectionism, and wouldn't have an easy way to process and transport the harvest. Also, the USDA wouldn't cough up subsidies. By whom and where would the inspection take place? And marketing? How would the harvest reach consumers? Challenges like this mean that farmers remain trapped in thrall to Big Ag, Big Chem, and Washington, who together decide what they can produce and on how many acres, in order to remain eligible for government income support. And over the last thirty years, corporation-promulgated subsidies made corn (grain, silage, sweet) the most profitable—more profitable than sugar beets, more profitable than wheat, more profitable than alfalfa. Is this a reason to put farmers in the crosshairs?

A farm bill known as "Freedom to Farm" passed in 1996, the Big Corn Year. Continuing subsidies as they were would have cost taxpayers $12.2 billion over the ensuing seven years. The new bill required taxpayers to pay $36.5 billion, that is, it *tripled* the supports. Some of these set-asides were invested in rural job development, conservation, and environmental protection. The bill also put an end to paying farmers to take land out of production. The bill *forbade* farmers in the "Freedom to Farm" program to grow fruits or vegetables on 85 percent of their acreage. If farmers grew alfalfa—a livestock feed that adds organic matter to soil—on more than 15 percent of their acres, they would forfeit government payment on each extra acre. Farmers could grow hay for livestock, or graze livestock on Freedom to Farm acres, but only under the same restrictions. These provisions seemed made to manifest hundreds of thousands of acres of corn.[14] And they assured that farmers would be purchasing inputs from Monsanto and Syngenta as well as supplying ADM, Cargill, and ConAgra with low-price grain. The cost! Ninety-eight percent of eligible farmers wound up receiving government support anyway, in the form of "deficiency payments" or "production flexibility contract payments."[15]

And where did all this corn go? Bill's grain harvest went either west to the grain elevator right next to the Union Pacific rail line, or down the road to the feedlots, neither any longer owned nor run by people he knew. He sold to whoever would pay more. Commodity market fluctuations and supply established the price, which was invariably less than the cost to grow it. The government paid Bill the shortfall. And the farmers to the south, west, north, and east of him did the same.

Big Ag companies profit greatly from the current system and have the political cachet to maintain the status quo, but mom-and-pop farmers and ranchers are foundering. Some say that our problem is not that we subsidize farmers and ranchers, but that we only subsidize certain crops and only enough to keep them barely afloat. A real commitment to American-grown food security and keeping food prices down would require making sure small ag operations have enough money to make a living growing healthy food sustainably. Otherwise, we should allow farmers to charge the actual market price for food, whereupon processed food might soon lose popularity.

· · · · · · · · · ▬ · ▬ · · · · · · · · ·

Individuals such as my father have wriggled under this system for decades now. Bill, a do-it-yourselfer, considered his options for diversifying and perhaps making more money. With several corrals, acres of pasture, and a woods full of meadow brome (*Bromus biebersteinii*), he had resources. He could do his own thing, couldn't he? The idea of growing a cattle herd appealed to him; it seemed manageable. Bill knew little about cow-calf operations, but he could start small, learn something, see what happened. Still raw from the cowboy chaos, Bill asked an older wrangler, Del Brewster, to come down from Wyoming, to help him figure it out. Confident he could buy promising livestock, Bill called a guy who knew a guy. And that guy called someone else. Next thing he knew, my father owned thirty-five Herefords.

The cow-calf operation seemed auspicious from the beginning, from that handful of long-eyelash cows—downright flirtatious in their ways—to the five strapping bulls. One of the bulls might have been a show bull, if it hadn't had close-set eyes, "like Muammar Gaddafi," Pop commented, but Bill had bought him cheaply on account of that shortfall. Still, that bull alone was $3,000.

Grasses

Brome is a "cool season grass," green in the spring and again in the fall in Colorado. Warm-season grasses are blue grama, buffalo grass, and bluestem.

Grass and Cattle Nutrition

Grass is between 7 and 10 percent protein, content that diminishes as the grass dries. Cattle, by virtue of their four stomachs, efficiently extract this protein. Cows turn that protein to milk. Cattle need to eat 3 percent of their body weight in feed per day (nice green grass in the growing season, and alfalfa / grass hay with some grass pasture in the winter and early spring). With a mineral supplement and a good water source, this diet keeps their digestive system very alkaline rather than acidic. While ruminating, cattle chew their cud and belch, or "eructate," as it's known.

Bill knew he was green to the business. The surrounding farmers and ranchers knew he was green too, but he was used to their sideways glances. He was going to try the cow-calf thing anyway and that Gaddafi bull gave him much confidence. "Building a herd"—that was Bill's next benchmark.

Part of that goal was about grazing, which Bill understood, inside and out. The herd had to have protein, plus a place and pace to digest it. The next step, breeding, seemed effortless. Surely, the cows and bulls were anatomically and hormonally equipped to pull it off, given a certain amount of togetherness. He'd just pasture them together and see what happened. It was the calving that worried Bill. Much could go wrong. Still, watching the cows, witnessing new lives, the nursing and the nibbling at the grass were a mostly gentle pleasure, especially compared to the rigmarole that was outside his gates, much of which concerned corn.

In the cavernous back drawers of my memory are a handful of "keepin' it real" moments with cowboys, squeeze chutes, and knives, where Bill's calves had their manhood snipped away, skinned, breaded, and fried. Unfathomably, the human menfolk seemed to enjoy this ritual. Off in the distance, the poor mother cows bawled and bellowed, begging someone, anyone, to relieve the agony of stretched-to-capacity udders, where even the little veins weaving over the thin skin screamed "help!" Because these rites of weaning were unspeakable, Gogo, Annzo, and I cowered elsewhere. I now look at that word *cower* with new eyes.

Once dismembered, Bill's steers were trucked off across the river to the feedlot. They were funneled into the backgrounding pen for a get-acquainted with corn. Skipping the grassland grazing of yore (described in sunny Spectacle 3) reduced the distance from sucking at teats to boxed beef from three years to fourteen months. From the backgrounding pen to the feedlot, the steers' lifespan collapsed like a nested travel cup.

The less you know, the easier it is to be a carnivore . . . though soy-product production is no picnic either. In the backgrounding pen, steers "transitioned" through hay (grass and/or alfalfa) and silage (cornstalks) to the flaked corn. Because cattle evolved to eat grass—not rich, starchy corn—this period had to be handled delicately. One of a steer's four stomachs is the rumen. On grass, the rumen has moderate pH, but corn acidifies it. To keep the rumen from bloating and/or worse, *abscessing*, backgrounders added antibiotics to the diet. (Here is where an additional phalanx of pharmaceutical manufacturers got into the mix.) Referred to as a "feed conversion efficiency," low concentrations of antibiotics became a staple for the steers' remaining months. They improved daily weight gain, aided digestion, and suppressed disease.

Once the tikes reached about 600 or 700 pounds, it was time to move them in with the big kids for "finishing" on a diet entirely without grass, a diet of corn made artificially cheap by legal bribery at the federal level, not by farmers and ranchers but by Big Ag.

For many years, the first cattle feedlot to fatten 100,000 head at once was down the road, Monfort, about which you've already read. During the 1980s, Monfort "integrated" beef with its "gate to plate" program. Monfort was the fifth-largest meat finisher, packer, and distributor in the world. Colossal as it was, Big Ag was bigger. Monfort fought a merger between Cargill/Excel and Spencer, but weakened antitrust laws and the courts allowed the buyout to go ahead. Consolidation increased, and the company sold to ConAgra. Several deals later, that expansive feedlot down the road is now "Five Rivers," part of the largest beef-feeding and -processing company in the world, a Brazilian company named JBS, S.A., which has its US headquarters fifteen minutes away in Greeley. Globalization comes home.

Each steer was once a calf like those born at Big Bend Station. Each eats twenty-five pounds of corn a day. A 100,000-head cattle operation requires about seventy tons of corn per hour. (For a visual, think of corn loads as big as ten elephants per hour.) Huge trucks go in and out of the feedlot all day long. Since bovine digestive systems are evolutionarily disposed to thrive on grass, why work at counterpurposes to nature? Well, corn is much more fattening, much more compact than grass, and puts weight on the animals faster. And—thanks to the monopolies just described—corn, though expensive to produce, is very cheap to buy (as long as taxpayers foot the difference). Put another way, economies of scale, time, and space make corn more economical, but only because the profit and loss statement omits the costs of price supports, environmental degradation, and antibiotic resistance, as well as the incalculable defrayed expenses of petroleum production.

> **Corn's Water Usage**
>
> Growing seventy tons (140,000 pounds) of corn requires 29.1 acre-feet of water.
>
> This water does not include water used to produce the inputs or fuel.
>
> Growing one acre of corn consumes 1.75 acre-feet of water.
>
> One acre yields 150 bushels of corn.
>
> (56 pounds per bushel × 150 bushels = 8,400 pounds or 4.2 tons)

Today, it's not all bleak. There's a glimmer. Tireless Temple Grandin has worked to make feedlot and slaughterhouse practices more humane. Calves that stay with their mothers through the summer before being shipped to a feedlot

Temple Grandin

In addition to being an autistic activist, doctor of animal science, and Colorado State University professor, Grandin consults to the livestock industry. Her tireless work toward humane livestock handling has improved standards in slaughterhouses, livestock conditions, and meat quality.

for finishing are marketed as "all natural" and do not receive any antibiotics (unless they are actually sick, and then those calves are pulled and sold separately). Thanks to food movements and other awareness building, some consumers buy grass-fed beef, and producers can get a premium for that beef. These improvements don't yet help feed the masses affordably, though perhaps they eventually will, as consumers themselves take responsibility.

I can't know if I guessed the water czar's meaning about farmers and blame. One thing for sure: Anne Castle got me thinking. Because I don't hunt, except at the grocers, I'm like most people—I outsource the "taking of lives" to food producers. Does that in some way absolve me? Researching and writing this, then staring at so astronomical a number on paper—ten elephants' weight worth of corn per hour, which took 66.6 acre-feet of water to grow—I find I can't blame small farmers and ranchers, not more than myself. The chutes that sort us into rural and urban, into "enviro" and farmer, into progressive and conservative—these chutes are worse than counterproductive. They're perilous,

Locavore

A person who favors food produced locally, not moved long distances to market.

because each of us can blame someone else and take no responsibility ourselves. No more chutes! Together, we must rally behind healthful, affordable food production *right now*, because—as you'll soon read—the additional question of whether water will still be available to grow food is grave and imminent.

MOVING AGAINST THE GRAIN

Evans had heard about the Platte. He had pictured it in his mind. He thought
he knew what he was going to see, but now that his horse stood on the sum-
mit, he couldn't believe. He couldn't believe that flat could be so flat or that
distance ran so far or that the sky lifted so dizzy-deep or that the world stood so
empty . . . He thought he never had seen the world before. He never had known
distance until now.

—A. B. GUTHRIE JR., *THE WAY WEST*

When early settlers such as Ben Eaton arrived, the South Platte was up to three
miles wide below Denver City. The river slowed to a trickle in late summer in its
lower reaches. Time and humankind have greatly changed the waterway, however. The South Platte River basin, which includes a half-dozen major tributaries—Cache la Poudre, Big Thompson, St. Vrain, Boulder, and Clear and Cherry
Creeks—is today home to the majority of Colorado's residents. In places it is ten
times narrower and five times deeper, due to regulation by upstream reservoirs
and importations of water from other basins.[1] Treated effluent from the cities
means the river, now a workhorse, never stops flowing.

So the years went by in a river of days, and Bill's days were made of river,
ditches, wetlands, and aquifer. He was busy, distracted, and imbedded in a culture of farmers and ranchers. With much to do at the farm, he could almost
forget population growth upriver and downriver, though Big Bend Station had
become a destination for our ancestor Ben Eaton's widely dispersed kin, prolific

enough to strain "carrying capacity" themselves and nearly all living in cities. For them farm life was a novelty!

Eaton children in my father's generation had been corralled together during obligatory visits to the ranch of their redoubtable grandfather, Bruce Grant Eaton. My father idolized his granddad, but few cousins felt the same. Each visit to Woods Lake put manners through their paces. No horsing around; the correct answer to any line of inquiry was "yes, sir." Everyone stood behind his or her chair when Granddad entered the dining room, and no child sat down until all adults were seated. Children vied to help women relatives into their seats, but otherwise were to be *seen but not heard*. No using the wrong spoon.

There's no overstating the severity of these earlier generations. Pop's Aunt Babyns was Bruce Eaton's youngest daughter and the granddaughter of the renowned ditch digger, farmer, and governor. At one midday dinner then, hearing a horrible squeal issue from one of her brood—each had been continually cautioned not to embarrass themselves or her—Aunt Babyns learned that one had bitten another. Not wanting her father to single her out for punishment, she motioned the perpetrator to come to her end of the table, a long way away.

"Did you bite your brother?"

The culpable party nodded.

"May I see your finger?"

Aunt Babyns took the little digit in her hand and then inserted it between her teeth, where she bit down hard. Everyone was very impressed that she drew blood.

.... ▄▄ ▄▄ ....

Shouldn't jolly times between characters that issued from this gene pool rekindle? Some of Ben Eaton's great great-grandchildren, those in my generation, had never met. Gogo suggested a first-ever reunion of the Eaton family. Bill chose July 4, 1982. Pretty much everyone accepted the invitation. My cousin Dana, who is a gifted artist, drove up with me early. To get to the farm, we decided to follow that fringe of willows that lined the Platte below "Denver City."

The journey north went first through perdition, manifest evidence of recklessness and downsides.

Like all cities, Denver's ability to sustain itself both required and generated considerable unpleasantness. From early on, Denver's unpleasantness moved outside city boundaries, and to the north Commerce City became a repository for whatever Denver needed but didn't want to look at—stockyards, sewage processing, oil refineries, junkyards, and worse. Passing through it, Dana quietly began sketching and I began apologizing.

Since 1942, Commerce City's ramparts of storefronts and chain-link-enclosed lots had obscured the Rocky Mountain Arsenal, 20,000 acres that the Army Chemical Corps used for "mad science." During World War II, scientists there conceived everything from mustard gas to sarin to napalm—the full complement of murderous biological and chemical weaponry used on the Japanese . . . as well as on the land, water, and air at Commerce City. During the Korean War, the army manufactured nerve-gas bombs at the arsenal. Shell Oil leased part of the land for pesticide development. More toxins. Wildlife died but the deaths, accidents, and disposal practices were shoved out of sight in ditches and unlined pits. The waste was even injected into the soil, and the injections triggered small earthquakes.[2] The Platte and its aquifer were immediately down gradient. *Trickle, trickle.* In 1962, when I was ten, Rachel Carson wrote of contamination witnessed nearby: "Farmers several miles from the plant began to report unexplained sickness among the livestock: they complained of extensive crop damage. Foliage turned yellow, plants failed to mature, and many crops were killed outright."[3]

No wonder journeys to the farm through that patch of hell had disquieted me as a child! By the time Dana and I drove north in the 1980s, arsenal operations had ceased, and the land had been declared a superfund site. An example of entropy (see Spectacle 2, "The Nuisance of Hindsight"), the arsenal was referred to as the "most toxic place on the Earth." The army planned to clean it up somehow and repurpose the expanse as a wildlife refuge.[4]

"Hard to understand how Americans could do this to our *own* land," Dana commented.

.... ▄▄ ·· ▄▄ ....

To the west of Commerce City and on the opposite side of the river, the city of Thornton's starter homes was within view. The city began in the 1950s the way many towns began: a man bought a square mile, not to farm but to subdivide. Incorporating under the name *Thornton* triggered the town's obligation to provide infrastructure, maintenance, and water. The costs fed the little municipality's escalating addiction to tax revenue. Thornton annexed land to increase revenues to pay for water. And neighboring landowners asked to be annexed so they could get water. Sewer connections and treatment needed financing too, which could only be offset by higher user rates and tax revenues from more housing. The loop repeated, with costs rising. Every city is the same, which explains why *development* and *growth* are promoted as synonymous.

As we continued north, Dana feverishly made thumbnail sketches of scenarios on either side of the Platte: the mountains hung in her backgrounds like a raised velvet curtain, the highway like a proscenium. The sets were uninspired housing, weeds, billboards, and for-sale signs, a willow here, a farm animal there. Amazingly, the view held hardly any people, though around that time Thornton—which was the physical size of the neighboring Rocky Mountain Arsenal and had 40,000-plus residents[5]—projected a fivefold population increase. To accommodate such a future, the city figured it was short some 60,000 acre-feet of water. The Clean Water Act's passage had awakened consumers to water quality. Directly downstream from Denver, Thornton didn't savor being stuck with used effluent from a crowded metropolis. What Thornton residents "deserved" was water freshly discharged from the Rocky Mountains. Indeed, Front Range municipalities such as Thornton had a supply plan, building the Two Forks Reservoir, but enviros would make sure that it didn't happen.

Water challenges emboldened the city. On the sly Thornton hired a realtor, a broker named Duane Rennels, according to *The Denver Post*.[6] Information about the broker was hush-hush. His mission? To scout for water rights up in that rolling countryside where my Eaton ancestor had settled on the Cache la Poudre River. Over fifty miles away! There was a lot of money to be made, in the millions, so the broker was relentless. He scoured for hard-up farmers, farmers in debt. The broker must have lit on those farmers like their best friend, like their savior, with an answer to all their troubles. *Just sell your water. Why worry about your land? Take a look around here, mister. Your land's gonna be housing.*

The broker's objective was different from G.A.S.P.'s, Jack Odor's organization that found water for well users like my father. Groundwater Appropriators of the South Platte *leased* water from diverse locations, taking advantage of the river's surpluses in any given season. The Thornton broker's objective was to *buy* many shares, if not a controlling interest, in a premium supply of mountain water. His target was one of Colorado's most venerable agricultural ditch companies. In operation since 1891, the Water Supply and Storage Company's network of ditches, laterals, reservoirs, and tunnels spanned over a hundred miles, though none reached as far south as Thornton.[7] The company had built the first transmountain diversion, the Grand River Ditch, which has diverted water from the western slopes of the Never Summer Range, east over the Continental Divide into the Platte basin since 1894. Expanded numerous times, the Grand River Ditch brought an additional 20,000 acre-feet of water annually to the South Platte basin. This water and the company's other holdings served farmers and ranchers.[8] To Thornton, the water sounded delicious.

The broker wouldn't divulge for whom he was buying. If he had, the sellers might have held out for more money.[9] He purchased 283 of the 600 shares in the oldest shareholder-owned agricultural ditch company around there. The Water Supply and Storage Company purchases affected over 100 agricultural operations and cost Thornton $50 million. The broker received a $3.6 million commission.

Thornton soon filed water-court applications for diversions from the Poudre for direct use and storage, river exchanges on the Poudre, and ditch exchanges within the Water Supply and Storage Company. Next the city applied to change its portion of ditch rights (almost half of the ditch company's rights!) from agricultural to municipal use, meaning away from food production and off to toilets and lawns.[10] Thornton expected the purchases and these additional actions to yield in excess of 50,000 acre-feet of water per year, just as it expected its population to increase fivefold, just as it expected to divest farmland of its water supply without consequences, just as it expected to be able to transport the water fifty-six miles away. It's easy to think of expectation as "speculation," but water speculation is illegal in Colorado. Thornton's water users hadn't seen the water, but their rates increased 37 percent in the next three years alone.[11]

As Dana and I progressed northward, leaving the Thornton behind, my cousin drew silos, tractors, and water towers. Under Dana's pen, the former Platte Trail became a corridor of roadside equipment dealerships and grain elevators—industrial farmland. Did the artistic rendition hide a presentiment of more Thorntons to come? How many Duane Rennelses shared the road with us? Dozens of other realtors, hundreds maybe, must have known farmers and ranchers in debt who were sitting on senior water rights. How many dealmakers could persuade people into selling the water out from under their land? With population mushrooming, it wasn't as if water were going to lose value (though no one talked about the degradation of water quality that might come from more use). Like people always say, "liquid gold." Change was at hand.

Economic growth is ridiculously selective in its metrics. Yes, housing and commercial development pay for infrastructure, create jobs, and encourage investment and commerce. That's why development registers as "growth." Nevertheless, there are often, even *always*, unacknowledged costs that are not on the spreadsheets. They may be "externalities" or "internalities," but whatever they are, someone eventually pays.

Externality

In economics, this cost is to a party who did not choose to incur that cost. Taxpayers' responsibility for pollution and financial bailouts are examples of externalities.

For instance, development sometimes relies on ill-collateralized lending schemes that can lead to very costly meltdowns. In another example, development makes resources but it also *depletes* resources. And once these developments are indelibly there, sustaining them requires more resources. If profit-loss analyses included these otherwise-defrayed externalities and internalities, "growth" might come across as unaffordable. The idea of *carrying capacity* might not go unexamined.

Thornton's bold move was in the vanguard of what would soon become many thirsty cities acquiring water that formerly *created food*. These transactions suggest countless externalities and internalities, to me anyway. What are the costs of eliminating US-grown food?

Internality

This cost is one a buyer incurs in the long run, which was not taken into account at the time of purchase. Foreclosure and disease caused by exposure to toxins are examples of internalities.

When I began writing this book, I heard ardent author and human-rights activist Maude Barlow speak about global water issues. She says that a supply-side mentality that delivers water to people who will pay, at any cost, fosters an unsustainable addiction to growth.[12] Even *smart growth*, the newer buzz word, models a life and business style that centers on *more*. More housing, more belongings, more shopping, more children, more consumption. Given this excess, ignoring the long-range mathematics seems not smart, but reckless. Most all of us participate in this kind of growth. I'm an environmental activist who recycles, eats organic, and drinks tap water. But I drive; I fly back and forth

Ecosystem Services

Conservationists had long been rankled about the unquantified monetary costs of perceived growth. The first moves to quantify occurred in the early 1980s, when the term *ecosystem services* was used in scientific literature. By calculating the cost of redressing pollution, disease, water quality, and other internalities and externalities that are the result of ecosystem destruction, actual dollar value can be ascribed to those ecosystems.

For instance, if a storm-water filtration system serving 16,000 developed acres is estimated to cost $1.4 billion, that means that a single undeveloped acre of wetland provides $87,500 in storm-water filtration. It makes sense to figure this amount into cost/benefit analyses prior to destroying wetland and/or moving water many miles away, since taxpayers will be hung with the $1.4 billion and additional, likewise astronomical, costs of air pollution control, water quality remediation, and so on.

between California and Colorado; I shop. I left home and then my son's father, so I have a separate dwelling. And my son? He's going to require a separate dwelling too. It's not as if someone else is causing growth; we all are.

.... ■■ · ■■ ....

When Dana and I at last turned at the sign that says "Big Bend Station" and drove up past Gogo's little rock garden to the house, Dana sighed happily. Eyeing the fence line, she immediately started drawing cows. The cows stared impassively. Were they captivated by us? No, Dana suggested, they were sending us subliminal messages.

Bill and Del Brewster had loosed the five bulls in the same pasture as the cowherd. As usual there was much admiration for the bulls, particularly Gaddafi, the one that might have been a show bull, had it not been for its close-set eyes. Add to that always-lively conjecture about sex. The cattle were beautiful, and it was nice to see them together, heads down in the grass, lying in the grass, chewing their cud. If a curiosity presented itself—a dog, a truck, or a bale of hay—the cattle interrupted their routine and meandered over together en masse to confer their subliminal messages.

Although we had a busy day ahead, it was still early. I helped Gogo pour her irresistible tea into frosted glasses that we carried to the screened-in porch overlooking the meadow.

As we sipped, Pop (who always had an activity in his pocket) said, "You know, girls, we could be having lobster dainties for dinner. You've got to be on your toes, though."

I stared at Pop as if at a madman, then rolled my eyes at Dana. It wasn't hunting season, thank God. Aside from acres of corn, the watercress, some wild asparagus, and maybe the mint, surely nothing remotely edible was to be found, except in the refrigerator. "Lobster dainties?" I asked, worried for the three or four frogs hopping across the porch underfoot.

"Oh, *you know*, love," Pop answered dismissively, waggling a long finger and a thumb to show just how dainty the lobsters might be.

Gogo's Signature Iced Tea

In a 2-gallon kettle, simmer the following for 1/2 hour:

1 gallon of water

12 black teabags

1 crushed cinnamon stick

1 bunch of wild mint

1 tablespoon freshly grated nutmeg

20 cloves

Strain.

Remove from heat and stir in

1 cup of honey

6 cups orange juice

juice from 4 lemons

Refrigerate until serving over ice, with a sprig of mint.

When I harrumphed, he unfolded himself from the chair with a slight groan (the creeping arthritis), beckoning Dana and me. We lumbered after him toward the shed, where he caught up a long-handled net, and then led us down past the pump house and along the cornfields to where his new wetlands drain to the river. The wetlands were doing a good job of intercepting ag runoff and giving birds a place to eat and breed.

Perched on a nearby snag, a belted kingfisher concentrated on the languid water as it moved in slow swirls over the sandy bottom. A hatch of gnats hovered inches above the wet banks where cottonwood seeds mounded in drifts. Dana giggled with pleasure. It *was* paradise.

I still thought that Pop was bluffing, that the excursion couldn't lead anywhere except hip deep in slime. Leaning over, he eyed the shallow algae-edged shore. "See the bubbles?" There, he sank the net into the muck and came up with blackened glop. Within squirmed what looked like a large shrimp.

"A crawdad!" cried Dana, making a grab for the net.

"Crawdad?" I cried with horror, "We can't eat those! They're bottom feeders."

Like Thornton's masterminds who, by planning to remove water from land, would also be destroying many thousands of acres of habitat and water infiltration, I was oblivious that the wetlands' inscrutable depths were a "food web."

Crawdads

Crawdads, "crawdaddies," or crawfish look like miniature lobsters, to which they are taxonomically related (Astacoidea and Parastacoidea families). The animal is also called *crayfish*, a word that comes from the French *écrevisse*. These freshwater crustaceans live in slow-moving water that does not freeze. They breathe through gills and eat plants and animals, dead or alive.

Nor did I yet know that the food web was also cleaning water of excess nitrogen and contaminants. Algae is phytoplankton, single-celled photosynthetic organisms. Phytoplankton is food for zooplankton, teensy members of the animal kingdom such as rotifers and copepods. Larger invertebrates such as snails, fingernail clams, worms, leeches, insects, and crawdads consume the zooplankton. Who knew we were eyeing a circle of predation? Birds did. Mammals too, among them Dana.

"But they're delicious," my cousin objected. She'd always been far more game than I was. "Let's get as many as we can . . . for appetizers! We can boil them in salt and cayenne."

"That's the spirit, Dana!" Pop said with approval. "Serve them with garlic butter. Living off the land, girls."

Preparing for the reunion, my parents had gone all out. The driveway burst with red and white petunias. Its midsection was reserved for the fireworks setup. A roving barbecuer named Chef Phil pulled his chuck wagon—a Conestoga lookalike fitted out to grill and serve juicy brisket—into the far stretch behind the garden. In the garden, Pop erected, with some huffing and puffing, a huge white canvas tent. Dana and I moved in the tables. Gogo added gingham cloths and more petunias. A small dance quartet warmed up on the rented dance floor. Providentially, the breeze from the west blew feedlot fumes the other way. The stage was set, for what would soon go down like a Robert Altman movie. I wore what I call my "aloha" dress.

As cars began to pull in, so did the subversive twists. An electrifying cry suddenly went up from the Conestoga. Chef Phil had (by accident of course) set his hand on fire. He was rushed away to Greeley, leaving food-for-seventy very iffy. Pop made to baste the brisket, until alternative help could be summoned. The youngest Eatons of Pop's generation, twins, arranged and prioritized fireworks. (One was an operator licensor for the Nuclear Regulatory Commission.) Particularly among male relatives, opinions about fireworks flowed freely.

So did drinks. There seemed little point in quashing any addictive tendencies that coursed through our DNA. Those assembled turned on as did the party lights. And it was fun to meet the second cousins—marvelous even. Many photographs later, people carried their food to tables and sat down around the reigning matriarch, Aunt Babyns, who was by then very old.

We couldn't help but notice that Aunt Babyns was increasingly tiny in the way of the elderly. Her little head with those illustrious pearlies was barely as high as the table. We all loved her, and no one wanted her to disappear. Sitting near her, relatives wondered whether the wind had shifted, because the tent had a distinctly foul whiff. Somebody, and I don't know who, looked down. As it happened, Aunt Babyns's chair was sinking, not just into the lawn but into the septic tank, which had—under siege from seventy flushers—overtopped. Just as Pop put down his potholder, better to pry Aunt Babyns from the family wastewater while the crowds shuffled to higher ground, an ill wind arrived. Really more of a chinook, it snatched the enormous tent from its tethers and hurled it against the house, where it crumpled in a heap.

Never mind. The twilight's last gleaming meant fireworks! And with that, any electrons that remained paired parted ways. Clicked Bic lighters flitted across the darkness like fireflies. Red rockets flared, pyrotechnics burst through the air, while—at the same time—people arranged more rockets in empty coke bottles, an activity often undertaken but never wisely. Distinctions between children and men blurred, as the dominant prankster strain unleashed. In ecstasy, everyone competed to light the array. The soberest of those Eatons in the driveway shoved lit sparklers at the smaller kids, then yelled: "Not here!"

"On the lawn!"

"Back off!"

"Dammit!"

Gogo arrived with a tiny tube of Neosporin. One aunt located a fire extinguisher. Another two carried an ice chest. Someone thought to bring blankets, in case of stop-drop-and-roll. In the end, only three people were burned, none badly except for Chef Phil, though there was a big scorch hole in someone's skirt.

Which left the dancing. The final blasting agents spent, the quartet started up with "Smoke Gets in Your Eyes." Most people had only a spin or two. Some couldn't be pulled off the floor. The Eatons are excellent dancers, more so by then sloughed their manners. "Cheek-to-Cheek," of course, the "Red River Valley," "Fascination," "Blue Moon," and even "I Can't Get No Satisfaction" for us whippersnappers, quite a few of whom either felt or were stoned. One rising star, a little blonde niece who had recently been in a Hollywood production of lil orphan "Annie," performed "hang on till tomorrow, come what may" flawlessly.

The next day, only dwindling numbers of Eatons remained. As we bumped around the kitchen, the cattle were a couple hundred feet away, out the window. It was usual to admire them globally, not identifying individual animals. That morning, however, one bull had problems, clear problems. And it wasn't just a bull; it was *the* bull that might have been a champion. The rest of the herd grazed. Gaddafi didn't. He tried haltingly, but he couldn't keep his head down. His penis, looking like a long pink carrot, was dragging along the ground, not retracted discreetly into its sheath as it should've been.

Abruptly, Pop pushed back a chair and moved to call Del. "We have a problem." Del called the veterinarian, who ruled the stinger done for. The conclusion was that a cow hadn't taken to the bull's advances, that she had kicked or bolted, maybe both, probably to the side, badly lacerating the prepuce (front part of the penis), enough so that it wouldn't retract. I blamed the fireworks. A farm is no playground. Before lunchtime, Gaddafi, the $3,000, and Pop's incalculable ambitions too were hauled off to Greeley to meet the stun gun. Somberly, we referred to this as the "trip to town."

Pop took this broken penis badly, an additional cost, an additional setback that reflected his limitations, which attached to his manhood too. He didn't say this, of course. I'm the nosy daughter, the one whose head Pop might have wanted to hood at a time like this. I left my observations unspoken. But I'll tell you, the next few days at the farm were the shits.

.... ▄▄▄·▄▄▄ ....

Bill never took long to *wade back in*, though. Pairs of swim trunks and his waders cycled through, always with tears and patches. His dent-worn aluminum boat screamed "dinghy." Gogo, on the other hand, was strictly terrestrial. She hated to swim. She liked to feel the earth firmly under foot. So, when the amphibious vehicle appeared in the driveway not long after Gaddafi had been hauled off, she was miffed.

"You told me that we'd each have a horse . . . that we'd ride every morning."

"This will be more fun. We can cross the river."

"Horses cross rivers," she thought, though not out loud because she'd never liked crossing rivers on horses. She'd seen the movies. Her first memory, as a tike with her nose pressed against steamy windows, was watching drowning dairy cows wash down Cherry Creek in the Castlewood Dam flood. Water was for fish, also crocodiles.

"We can even *float* the river," Bill added with enthusiasm. "It's eighteen-horsepower. That's sixteen more horses than we'd have if were riding."

Unimpressed, Gogo frowned slightly.

A murky green, the "Coot" was a proto all-terrain vehicle. Its body frame was articulated, meaning that the front and back ends canted separate directions, which—to my father anyway—seemed like a real plus. The oversize inflatable rubber tires were squishy, to make rocky terrain feel smoother. The wheels also "paddled." My brother remembers that it had a roll bar. Annzo and my mother are trying to forget. A killjoy, I noted that the Coot epitomized military-industrial contributions to recreation. Who needs a monument to plastic injection molding? "How about a test drive, Gogo!" Bill jubilantly proposed. "Just a sec . . ."

"Bring your camera!"

So, with a Hasselblad camera around her neck, they articulated on out over the ditch, over the cattle guard, onto the Dike Road, past the cornfields still planted with pre-GMO corn, and soon made the Old Picnic Ground, where my father "drove" from the path right into the middle of the Beaver Pond, seamlessly. Drifting there in the watercress, Bill pitched woo and then broke out a thermos of coffee with two cups and donut holes he'd bought her in Gilcrest. Laughing, Gogo took a couple of photos of Bill popping holes. This giddy interlude took place without either of them without setting foot outside the Coot, without their knowing that Thornton had just made off with almost half of the water from one of Colorado's most venerable ditch companies.

"It's really like picnic furniture," Bill noted. "More comfortable than the ground, isn't it, sweetness?"

Gogo nodded indulgingly, still skeptical.

"And if you don't like this setting, we can try another!" he offered, sculling slowly forward to the bank. The Coot heaved onto solid ground as if from the Mekong. Then unexpectedly the machine lurched toward the moving water, the Platte.

"Bill!" Gogo screamed, already scooting backward for better or worse.

Too late. The Coot nosedived into the Platte, irrespective its used urban effluent . . . just like a real coot. Hood first, the Coot sank, the water closing around the steering wheel. Not wanting to lose his mount or his wife to the deep, Bill never let go. He threw his legs into the air like a cowboy doing "spin the horn," then vaulted sideways to land outside the alleged amphibian. Though his shirt-tails were out and his legs were in the river, he kept his grip on the wheel, straining to keep it from disappearing forever. My father peered over his shoulder. Gogo, no cowgirl, was crawling away, up over the rear of the vehicle like Jackie Kennedy.

BROKERS OF THE APOCALYPSE

Until fairly recently in the United States, a variety of federal and state laws and regulations inhibited farmers from selling their water. Under the "use it or lose it" rule, for example, irrigators could lose water rights that they did not put to some use considered "beneficial." As legislatures and courts gradually sweep away these restrictions, markets are opening up. The State of Colorado, for instance, has one of the best institutional support networks for water markets of any state, and trading has flourished there—both within irrigation districts and between cities and farms.

—SANDRA POSTEL, *PILLAR OF SAND*

A change for the worse can feel abrupt to those of us on the receiving end, can't it—as if the spell of the tranquil past was broken all at once in one big whammy? Blindsided, we register the change with shock. Though, now writing about "water" on the Platte, I observe that our shock must have been an error of awareness. Why weren't we paying attention?

Eyeing changes in the river basin as they arrived one by one over the past decades, we might have recognized that each was a harbinger. A careful inventory would have revealed those incremental adjustments that *always* tug at tomorrows, like the sweaty six-hitch horses that long ago pulled into Big Bend Station, team after team, hauling travelers and freight and news, novel cargo that altered events at the frontier. I've read that healthy stagecoach horses then set off as eager and fresh as new ideas, only to arrive at relays along the Platte so exhausted that they often had to be shot! I've read that *horses* couldn't make the stretch of river between Fort Morgan and Fort Lupton, because the way was so gravelly and sometimes muddy that only *mules* could conquer it.[1] And that's how it is with events that presage collapse. Conquest, competition, scarcity, and death are almost always involved. They seem separate, but they ride together.

·········■■··■■·········

The battle between the ditch companies north of us and those who wanted their water continued. The Water Supply and Storage Company, plus a few dozen more objectors took the City of Thornton to the water court. A whole decade passed, but finally the water court imposed restrictions on Thornton's grand 50,000 acre-foot plan. Thornton wound up buying not just the water rights but the farms themselves, irrigation equipment, and tractors too, 21,000-acres' worth. The water court ruled that Thornton could divert 33,000 acre-feet of irrigation water. Of the 21,000 acres of farmland that Thornton bought, 18,000 would be dried up.[2] The water court required that Thornton recharge the aquifer in the vicinity of the historic irrigation rather than returning it to the river.[3] Thornton's purchase was becoming more and more expensive, both in terms of its actual bill and its externalities.

The case continued to the Colorado Supreme Court, which cost more and took two additional years to sort out. The Supreme Court affirmed Thornton's right to purchase the ditch shares, no matter how covertly. It went on at some length to explain why Thornton's actions were *not* speculative: The city had population-growth forecast. Those numbers seemed to demonstrate the city's *proven need* for the water. "It is not but the highest prudence on the part of the city to obtain appropriations of water that will satisfy the needs resulting from a normal increase in population within a reasonable period of time," stated the opinion.[4] This statement seemed to afford municipalities the right to prospect, if not speculate, in accordance with the doctrine of "great and growing cities," in place since 1939.[5]

Speculation

1. To enter into a venture, the profits from which are subject to chance.
2. To buy or sell with the expectation of profiting from fluctuations.

The Prior Appropriation Doctrine is widely considered a wedge against speculation. Beneficial use, forfeiture, and waste are its "holy trinity" protecting water from wheeler-dealers.[6] A water right has a "basis, measure and limit," meaning that the need for the water, its quantity, and the location where it can be used are legally defined. There can be no waste. If a water-rights owner can't use a right according to these terms, he or she must sell or forfeit.

As part of the speculation proofing, no one can obtain or change a water-rights decree without demonstrating an actual ability to use the water at a specified place. From the beginning, this aspect of the Colorado Doctrine was designed to prevent wealthy speculators from marauding and monopolizing the development of Colorado's water resources.[7]

Thornton couldn't get around the "specified place" requirement. The court affirmed Thornton's right to transfer water, but with numerous conditions to prevent injury to other water rights and to return to the court every six years to prove its continued need for the water based on real population numbers in the future, what the court called "reality checks."[8] By statute, the applicant for a change of water right bears the initial burden of establishing the absence of injurious results from the proposed change.[9] The court insisted that Thornton kick-start native revegetation on farms it was drying up, as another cost of removing water to the city. As if restoring busted-up prairie grassland were easy . . .

What would "claiming the water" mean, if Thornton couldn't pipe it to its ratepayers? It would mean trading that Poudre River ditchwater for water closer to Thornton, that's what. And those trades? What was to prevent Thornton from trading to the highest bidder? And would such trading not be speculative?

While the City of Thornton maneuvered for more and better rights within the structures of authority, so did my mother. Thirty years into marriage my parents had their long-established habits, their own micromaze of protocols promulgated around Bill's position as the governing body and Gogo's as the seemingly governed constituent. Every morning for years at breakfast, operating according to protocol, Bill put the big honey pot in the middle of the table, because Gogo claimed to prefer honey on her cereal. Every morning, he laid the wooden honey drizzler beside the pot too. In this small way, he was trying to put pounds on her, weight she didn't want.

My mother epitomizes positive thinking in action. She has always managed, despite the challenges set before her, to be happy and usually to get her own way. Gogo's role as the weaker sex was largely for appearances. To do what she wanted without confrontation, Gogo had a simple approach: she went through the motions.

Once, sitting there with the two of them at honey-drizzling hour, with Gogo's slender arm hovering over her cereal, I heard Pop announce, "You'll note that there is no honey on your mother's honey drizzler." Gogo froze over her cereal, drizzler in hand. Pop kept eating. I looked at the drizzler. Sure enough, it was bone dry. It had not been dipped in the honey.

"Gogo!" I cried incredulously, "You're drizzling without dipping?"

"Yes," she said guiltily, then turning to Pop and narrowing her eyes. "How long have you known?"

"I've always known."

"But you've moved the honey pot to the table . . ."

". . . for years," he said, finishing her sentence.

As to where this story fits with the authority and outcomes of Colorado Water Law, suffice to say that both Thornton and Gogo conformed to protocols, though not without consequences. Coincidentally, when the honey pot stopped coming to breakfast, actual honeybees began swarming, returning to the farm in football-sized swarms to establish new hives.

························

While unfettered water prospectors, representing municipalities and districts, not individuals, sniffed along the South Platte downstream, wild turkeys migrated upstream.

Big Bend Station's fields plateau about thirty feet above the Wood. This is the "bench," the former banks of a wider, earlier Platte. There on the bench's edge, with a view of the lazy slough and the birdlife, Bill built a little cabin he called the "Office," though it had no desk and no phone. The Office's features included two rocking chairs, a toaster oven, binoculars, and a screened-in porch. For Gogo, he stocked ginger ale, for other guests, bourbon. This aerie was where Bill indulged his independence and took his meetings. The farm's natural bounty attracted more visitors.

Late one afternoon in the 1980s, the wildlife manager for what was then the Colorado Division of Wildlife (now *Parks* and Wildlife), sat with Bill in the Office watching mallards skid feet first into the slough. It wasn't unusual to spot white-tailed deer that time of day too.

"These woods could use some turkeys," the game warden mused. "Rio Grande Wild Turkeys. There's enough cover here. The birds could nest in the snowberry (*Symphoricarpos occidentalis*). And you have that corn. They need "hot grain" like that to sustain them during winter."

Hot Grain

This feed is a combination of corn and moist-soil grasses. It provides high energy and may also include invertebrates.

"I'm game."

The other man peered at him for hidden meaning.

"What I'm saying, warden, is that we like turkeys."

"You wouldn't be able to hunt them, Bill. The state would introduce here with the hope that they'd increase in numbers. And I don't want you goading me about hunting them either."

"No recipes for stuffing?"

"No."

"Fine."

Some weeks later the patter of tires on gravel signaled the turkeys' arrival.

One hundred thirty miles downstream at the Tamarack Ranch State Wildlife Area, state crews had baited the birds, drawing them to one place with corn—though turkeys like each other's company and the "rafter will move as a group" anyway, the game warden told Bill. As the turkeys pecked at the corn, a big cannon net shot out over them. So they wouldn't be injured, the ranger crew scrambled to lift the birds into individual boxes. Two hours later, two trucks, carrying four toms (cocks) and eleven hens, arrived at the slough.

Though native peoples of the central Plains certainly locked eyes with the big birds over millennia, English-speaking settlers first recorded the Rio Grande Wild Turkey (*Meleagris gallopavo intermedia*) in 1879. The population was soon decimated by hunting and habitat loss, part of the witless plunder of the prairie. There had been no historic sightings of turkeys near our farm, Big Bend Station, but the Division of Wildlife initiated an introduction anyway. The eleven birds' new longitude had much in common with their old longitude downriver. Wildlife rangers thought they'd be fine.

One by one and carefully, the rangers opened the boxes to release the birds. From the truck, the turkeys moved forward tentatively, as if from time machines, their dinosaur-like heads bobbing on long knobby necks. Their body feathers were a green so dark and shiny they looked chiseled of anthracite. The lighter tail and lower back feathers were almost coppery. With longer legs than their eastern cousins, these Rio Grande birds were better adapted to the prairie. Some were almost four feet tall.

Without turkey chick survival, the introduction would fail. The rangers left them in the Wood, near the Platte. Water-fed shrubbery there would obscure nests and brooding when the beige-dusted chicks were small. According to the biologists, turkeys thrived where the understory—the tangle of lower shrubs and fallen branches—is high and the canopy dense, as it is in some places at the farm.

These large birds perch in trees as an escape, or for rest, or to roost. That's why the Wood had such appeal for them. *Whoosh*, the rafter rose together, each fifteen- to twenty-five-pound bird finding its perch in concert. In the cottonwoods above the insect buffet that buzzed below in the grass, they could stay clear of the coyotes. Stacked there in the trees, they seemed stationary, like so many totem poles.

"I wish you'd stop letting the cows graze the Wood, Pop," I mentioned, not for the first time. "And stop burning the downed branches too."

"The birds'll be fine, love." That was the word from the farm's "governing body."
The idea was that transplanted turkeys would thrive, that their numbers would
increase . . . and they did.

As did people in Colorado.

·········■··■·········

During the 1970s, three-quarters of a million people moved to the state, over
200 people a day![10] It seemed like a lot then, but the pace would soon quicken.
Why this influx? Middle East tumult during the 1970s (OPEC's oil embargo, the
Yom Kippur War, and Iranian Revolution) catalyzed oil and natural gas exploration in Colorado. Boom! Almost overnight sensational skyscrapers transformed
Denver's downtown skyline, and the new Denver Tech Center invited tenants
to conduct business with a glitzy panorama of the Rockies too. Suddenly everyone's business was oil and gas. My brother, Will, signed on as a roustabout. My
sister stopped modeling and went to work as a landman. She and her husband
(who also got into the oil business) bought a jaw-dropping house that resembled
that of the Denver oil magnate portrayed in the TV show *Dynasty*. While mag-
nates, brokers, and municipalities angled to increase revenues, so too did my
father. With no revenue from the feedlots; the costs of flood reparations; and the
long, costly litigation with Arne Johnson; plus the bull's trip to town, and so on,
Bill's balance sheets needed an infusion. The number of oil wells drilled in Weld
County in the 1980s was 4,634, five of them at Big Bend Station.[11]

The cost of water ballooned even faster than population. Consider that G.A.S.P.
had been trading water for no more than ten dollars an acre-foot, as Jack Odor
negotiated leases to fulfill annual SWSPs. True, G.A.S.P.'s transactions involved
readily available water, water that didn't have to be transported, didn't have to be
litigated, didn't have to buy farms, didn't have to remake prairie grasslands, and
didn't have to be guaranteed for perpetuity. The City of Thornton's transactions,
though, were purchases, *not* leases. Estimates put the per-acre-foot cost of buying water from its "Northern Project" somewhere between $4,000 and $9,000.[12]
Maybe more. The phrase *all over the map* seemed made for the price of water.

Where oh where did they find enough water around which to shape such
elaborate deals? Major Stephen Long had described the High Plains as the "dry
and arid land" 170 years before, when there were only trappers and tribes. In the
1870s the South Platte River was so empty that rankled people went after each
other with guns. So what had happened since then?

As years passed, it was clear that most of the state's precipitation (as much as
80 percent) fell on Colorado's Western Slope; the bulk of the humans, though,

were accumulating on the eastern flank, on the Front Range.[13] Acting on the success of the Water Supply and Storage Company's Grand River Ditch, Front Range Coloradans at last leveraged a US Bureau of Reclamation opportunity to import over 200,000 acre-feet of Colorado River basin water annually from the Western Slope through the Continental Divide.

They named this project, authorized by Congress on the heels of the drought in 1937 and completed in 1957, the Colorado–Big Thompson (or the C-BT) because the water disgorged into the foothills through the Big Thompson River, just downstream of Big Bend Station, near Spomer Bison Ranch, where we buy our buffalo. The primary purpose of the C-BT project was to shore up water-short farms in the seven northeastern Colorado counties. The C-BT encouraged a flourishing agricultural industry along the Platte between the Big Thompson and the state line.[14] To make maximum use of this influx of water, government pushed farmers to dig groundwater wells by offering cost-share, as already mentioned.[15]

A Strasberg, Colorado, farmer named Frank Zybach had invented center-pivot irrigation in 1948, but not until the late 1990s did circular cropland and fields irrigated by linear-move sprinklers proliferate noticeably. As I've said, flood irrigation was at best 50 percent efficient, but 80 percent of whatever sprinklers used was consumed. Farmers could grow more, but efficiency meant lower return flows to the river, less water for others downstream. Within the Northern Colorado Water Conservancy District—Fort Collins, Greeley, Loveland, Longmont, Boulder, Louisville, Lafayette, many small towns, rural and domestic water districts, and local industries soon bought C-BT allocations as direct supply too.

In 1989, not long after Thornton deployed its broker to buy up ditch shares, Broomfield—a community whose settlers made brooms—did likewise. Panicked about water contamination from yet *another* weapons-production facility in the South Platte watershed (the US Department of Energy's Rocky Flats Nuclear Weapons Plant), the City of Broomfield bought C-BT water for the parts of the city area in Boulder County and in Weld Counties and took advantage of another transbasin diversion called the Windy Gap. The Windy Gap (completed in 1985) now brings water to Broomfield, Boulder, Estes Park, Fort Collins, Greeley, Longmont, Loveland, and other municipalities.

> **Colorado–Big Thompson (C-BT)**
>
> When the Colorado–Big Thompson (C-BT) first came on line during the 1950s, two-thirds of the allotments went to farms and one-third to cities in the Northern district. Today, it is vice versa.

Add to this the transbasin diversion and storage projects that Front Range cities built themselves.[16] Today, over 500,000 acre-feet each year move from the west over the Continental Divide to the east.[17] Nearly half of Denver's water is transbasin diversion from the Colorado to the South Platte Rivers. These additional flows recharged the Platte and raised the water level, and for many years alleviated the South Platte's overappropriation, diminished calls on the river, and built a thriving agricultural industry.

Large transbasin diversions typically move massive amounts of water into the darkness. Swallowed by gargantuan pipes, the conduits travel through granite, rationalized by flurries of paperwork across tabletops and now across the Internet. Each enterprise is its own epic, leaving anxiety in one basin and hubris in the other. Viewed this way, as water moves away from the land and into darkness, sub*basin* diversions are hardly less dramatic.

Diversions

Transbasin diversions move water west to east, from the Colorado River basin to the South Platte basin, or from the South Platte and Arkansas River basins to another basin.

Subbasin diversions move water around within basins, for instance, from one place to another along the Platte.

I believe that all this almost invisible "forcing" of water in contrived directions separated and separates individual people—you and me—from our firsthand knowledge of water, and not just in Colorado. Between 1960 and 1990, domestic withdrawals of water in the West more than doubled.[18] We, who gestated in water, who were aware, *born geniuses*, toddlers who navigated complex terrain and knew the difference between up and down, between wet and dry, turned into folks who abdicated their know-how of water, except to know it came from the faucet and now from plastic bottles. So much for *psychogeography*.

We were no longer the children who ran along and even in creeks, who fished and swam in pools. We were passive, expectant, and progressively thirstier. Meanwhile the enterprises requiring engineering, construction, management, monitoring, and legal costs made our wet stuff, which used to be as affordable as air, increasingly expensive. The enterprises commodified water, giving brokers an unregulated market for transactions, transactions that also inflated water's cost.

Water's rising cost across Colorado was out of reach of small ag businesses and increasingly problematic for municipalities, but to water brokers, entrepreneurs, and water privatizers, it was irresistible.

Somewhere in his past Colorado-born Bob Lembke, who has both a master's in taxation and a law degree, must have slapped his forehead and said, "Why spend my time helping others grow their assets when I could be growing my own?" This entrepreneurial life-plan may or may not have coincided with the collapse of the thrift market. Either way, the savings and loan crisis of the 1980s and '90s helped. Mr. Lembke began buying inexpensive property in Elbert, Adams, and Weld Counties.

Bob Lembke's mind moves, as does water, toward opportunity. Now reading about "special districts" yourself, you may imagine how the special-district idea must have tickled such a mind. A tax-exempt enterprise that can borrow at extremely favorable terms and even condemn property? With what you will soon appreciate as Mr. Lembke's almost preternatural gift for discerning inroads that are invisible to others, he eyed an empty one-acre parcel in Elbert County with the goal of establishing the "United Water and Sanitation District." The name

Special Districts

Special districts, which are quasi-governmental, maintain public services. They date back to mining camps in early Colorado, though not until 1949 did the Colorado General Assembly authorize their legal structure. These agencies might offer public improvements and services such as water, sewer, streets, drainage systems, landscaping, traffic-related safety enhancements, park and recreation facilities and services, fire protection, mosquito control, and/or transportation improvements. Special districts are required to submit a number of filings to various state agencies throughout the year. These filings are primarily financial, but also include election results and lists of boards of directors.

Special districts are not accountable in the same sense as traditional government. They are accountable to their boards of directors, drawn from taxpayers within their district, whose members may or may not have a financial interest in their activities. That is the "quasi" part.

According to Colorado legislation, creation of these special districts must be authorized by a government entity. With public notice, the boards of directors must meet and act in public session. The quasi-governmental agencies can obtain financing on a tax-exempt basis, at lower interest rates and on more favorable terms than the private sector. Special districts can purchase goods and services tax-free. They can participate in intergovernmental agreements. They can exercise eminent domain, issue bonds, and levy property taxes. According to the State of Colorado website, special districts make up a "third level of government" in the United States. They are "quasi-municipal" public entities engineered to advance subdivision growth promoted by the housing industry.[19]

sounded helpful and patriotic. The lot had no occupants, no offices, no infrastructure, not so much as a bucket on it. Seeking governmental approval of his special district, Mr. Lembke had only to convince Elbert County commissioners.

The Denver Post reported that the United Water and Sanitation District proposal to the commissioners did not identify that the district's services were needed, whom it would serve, or a water source.[20] The proposal did meet the legal requirement that special districts have defined boundaries. The Elbert County commissioners approved the special district's formation in 2003. Mr. Lembke then picked his new district's board and announced that United's service plan was to provide a water network serving future development not just in Elbert County but *throughout the Front Range.*

Quasi

According to the *Oxford Dictionary*, this prefix means "seemingly; apparently but not really."

If United Water and Sanitation were private, buying water rights for customers it didn't yet have would have been illegal, according to the antispeculation doctrine. But it isn't private; it is "quasi-governmental." So it stood to reason that, like Thornton, United could buy water rights for customers it anticipated having. Transaction by transaction, Mr. Lembke began to grow United's reputation for buying and selling water. And it wasn't long before other entrepreneurs copied his model, setting up their own special districts, sometimes on thumbnail-sized parcels distinct from the communities they planned to serve.

Hadn't John Wesley Powell declaimed the divorce of water from land, saying that: "If . . . the practical control of agriculture shall fall into the hands of water companies, evils will result therefrom that generations may not be able to correct"?[21]

With the great and growing cities' doctrine at their back, upstream special districts and municipalities—with money and proven need for water (i.e., "pro-

Water Rights Condemnation Act of 1975

Under Colorado law cities may condemn and pay just compensation for water rights. The political furor surrounding Thornton's proposed condemnation of water rights in the Clear Creek watershed led to passage of the Water Rights Condemnation Act of 1975. The act's purpose was to make sure that condemnation would not occur unless a city had no other reasonable alternative to serve its needs. The act reaffirmed and narrowed the prior statutes that authorized and implemented municipal condemnation of agricultural water rights.

jected growth," a growth that they required to pay for more growth), continued to stalk nether-river water rights that they might purchase or even condemn. Additional businesspeople branded themselves as water brokers, to enable transactions of millions of dollars of water rights, water storage, and farm and ranch transactions. Water reliability, location, and quality affected cost. The ultimate qualifier was what the market (in this state where speculation was illegal) would bear.

.... ▬ ▪ ▬ ....

These activities seemed like predation to farmers and ranchers. It couldn't help but disenfranchise them, make them paranoid. At Big Bend Station nighttime fog off the river pulled in around the house, separating it from all beyond. Within this opaque vapor, Bill considered his small herd and hugged his ditch rights, as ancient as the slouch hats and suspenders on the men that made them. Further, he told himself, even his groundwater rights were senior to most cities' reservoirs. Out there on the other side of the fog, where not even owls could see movement, the cities held their burgeoning tax bases, giving them what most farmers and ranchers didn't have—revenue to protect those rights. Bill made no mention of this to Gogo. If he didn't know what to do about it neither would she, he reasoned. The farmers and ranchers in their fog.

As the sun came up and warmed this setting, the fog inched away. The effect was the house first, then the farmyard as an expanding island that soon became as big as the fields. The days got longer during the spring. The grass got greener. The work got harder.

The pace quickened with warmth, and with quickening, warmed. I visited at the same time as my brother, Will, the gifted tracker. By then living on forty acres in Montana, much more at home in woods than at strip malls or in highrises that were separate from the soil, Will noticed the stories written on the water and land, like Pop, like most small farmers and ranchers. Walking through the cottonwoods or sometimes even across the fields, Will had spotted earth under our feet that looked as if it had been swept. He explained that courting male turkeys arc their wings, as if to take flight. But the toms don't take off. This is their pageant of arousal. Air flows under their wings, stirring secondary feathers and arousing them more. The toms drag the tips along the ground as they strut forward, their chests puffed. Their wing tips leave signs of sweeping in the dust. *Take that, you jakes.* ("Jakes" are immature males.)

Will and I then quietly indulged in turkey porn, an activity for only the very patient. The toms were all tail, their feathers fanning in the sunlight like card tricks. A hen acknowledged the toms' awesomeness. She lay on the ground in a submissive posture, scrunching back and forth to get comfortable, and then she coyly glanced around to see what would come of her invitation. A tom approached from behind and climbed onto her back where he walked back and forth for a few minutes. I wanted to cry out, "Hey, lighten up. You're crushing her!" Thusly massaged though, the hen at last lifted her tail and for a few seconds love was requited. Once the tom dismounted, the two sauntered off in different directions while rearranging their plumage.[22]

And Gogo too sauntered off. New communities seemed to spring under her wheels, even from under the wheels of the increasing traffic passing in front of the farm. It was all trucks and tractors before; now there were cars. Former ranches and farms subdivided and subdivided some more. As interest rates fell, housing and malls proliferated. Towns that had only a post office got planning departments. As long as there was an initial water supply, developers worried little about where additional water would come from. That was the job of the special districts.

Growth was unfurling south of Denver too, way upstream in the South Platte basin. Food wasn't growing—no grains, peaches, or cantaloupes—but housing developments were. A Southern California company, Mission Viejo, flush from turning thousands of acres of coastal chaparral into subdivisions, had bought the 22,000-acre Highlands Ranch in Douglas County in 1979. Those acres, which would never graze cattle again, were among the *1.5 million acres* of ranchland Colorado lost to development in the last twenty years of the century.[23] By 1997 Highlands Ranch had a population of 39,000 (which would more than double in the subsequent decade).[24] Come to find out, Highlands Ranch's three aquifers did not recharge at a pace consistent with growth. Highlands Ranch's water provider—the Centennial Water and Sanitation District—joined the rampage for additional sources of water.[25]

The word *rurbanism* was coined to describe residents who live on former rural terrain but commute to midlevel urban jobs. Rurbanism's popularity, plus Highlands Ranch's planned neighborhoods, put Douglas County on the map. Known as the second-fastest growing county in the nation during the 1990s, the county itself stayed the same size. It just got more crowded. In 2000, Douglas County had the highest median household income in the nation.[26] Advertised as the most affluent county, Douglas County still didn't have enough water. And the water it needed was in the South Platte basin.

And so what author George Orwell called the "invincible green suburbs" advanced. Between 1970 and 2000, Colorado's population doubled.[27] Willows were bulldozed away. Ephemeral streams and topography that had taken millennia to form and recharge groundwater were wiped out, sealed off under asphalt and concrete, and with them species macro and micro were pushed closer to extinction. Air became browner, water became dirtier, carbon emissions multiplied, and incidents of cancer increased. The costs of these ever-more-chronic problems accrued. And still no one had a better idea for raising money than to build more invincible suburbs, which required more water to remain green.

Observe the incremental yet major novelties steadily arriving on the Platte, just as did the sweaty coach-pulling teams in the 1800s, changes crossing the Plains that could be, that *were*, harbingers.

VAGARIES OF BASINS

As the psalmist says: "These are my Father's things. These hills, their gurgling rills, the majestic trees and the fleecy clouds that float above them in an azure sky, are my Father's things. Yes, these and the fields, the growing crops, the soil in which they grow, and all that feed thereon. We use them only through sufferance. If future generations are to be permitted to live and enjoy a general state of wellbeing, no generations must destroy these things.
—MICHAEL CREED HINDERLIDER, QUOTED IN RICHARD STENZEL
AND TOM CECH, *WATER: COLORADO'S REAL GOLD*

Ten minutes away over the river is a now-abandoned grain elevator where farmers and ranchers used to buy feed before "vertical integration." Each small town in northeastern Colorado had at least one grain elevator, plus colorful characters who frequented it. Back in the 1960s when my father owned but a few acres in Weld County and everybody still knew everybody, a young cowboy named Ron Ehrlich sauntered into the then-thriving mill. There greeted him a compact man in slacks and a sweater vest.

"Hello, I am Arnaldo Einaudi,"[1] the man said, extending his hand. His eyes fluttered weirdly. These mannerisms puzzled Ron, the son of a local rancher, with whom Bill did business when he was still in corporate ranching. Ron asked Arnaldo, "What's going on?"

"But your family is going to own all this!" Arnaldo announced with a smile.

And indeed, the name "Ehrlich" was soon emblazoned on the high, white grain elevator. Corn prices rose; winter wheat didn't. And most other predictions emanating from the grain elevator manager came true. Rumors of Arnaldo

Einaudi's psychic powers grew. When anyone wanted to divine an outcome, Arnaldo brought out his crystal ball.

Time passed. Maybe the mail lady, maybe conversation over at the Gilcrest Farm Supply, or maybe just Arnaldo's prodigious instincts told him that my father watched the future too. Bill's approach though was reading financial publications like *The Wall Street Journal* and *Fortune* magazine. Bill had never had a real conversation with Arnaldo, but was familiar with his weathered face, which was in keeping with the grain elevator, and his natty attire, which was not. So when Arnaldo pulled into Big Bend Station in his used but very shiny black Buick, Bill greeted him warmly.

"How you doing, Arnaldo? Good to see you."

"Hello, Mr. Phelps, good day." Arnaldo's English was quite good but bore a distinct accent. He tipped his felt hat. He buttoned the suit jacket over his vest. "Mr. Phelps, I hope I am not inconveniencing you."

"Not at all, Arnaldo. Do you want to come in?"

"No, Mr. Phelps, I do not. I am interested in your used newspapers and magazines. Do you throw them out?"

"Sure."

"Would you be willing to give them to me instead? I could come by once a week."

"That'd be fine. I'll save them for you. Do you want *Time* magazine too?"

"Yes, please."

So the news handoff began. If Gogo or Bill went to town, they left the news at the grain elevator. Other times, Arnaldo pulled into Big Bend Station. Before too many weeks had passed, my mother spotted a book on palmistry on the backseat of Arnaldo's Buick. "Arnaldo! I hope you'll pardon my prying," she asked. "Do you know how to tell fortunes?"

"Yes, Mrs. Phelps, I do."

Gogo involuntarily pulled back her hands. She was apprehensive. Bill was aging; she wasn't. She sometimes thought of being marooned out at the farm. Just as often, she thought she might be stuck in Denver unable to get back to him. Though fearful of learning the meaning of the grooves and smaller tributaries in her palms, particularly while standing there near the drama-prone Platte, Gogo thrilled to make the acquaintance of an actual seer. Chatting with Arnaldo, she soon extracted his extraordinary provenance. Born in Turin, Arnaldo said that he had been abducted as a little boy by gypsies! A gypsy woman ultimately returned Arnaldo to his birth family in exchange for living with them. When Arnaldo's family emigrated to the Rocky Mountain region, the gypsy came with them and so did the crystal ball.

125

When Gogo told Bill that Arnaldo traveled with a fortune-telling book, my father said he wasn't surprised. "Everyone who knows Arnaldo believes him."

·········■· ·■·········

Like Arnaldo Einaudi's family, people from the world over are drawn to Colorado's scenery, scenery that is a family of its own. The state has 637 peaks higher than 13,000 feet above sea level and fifty-some over 14,000 feet. Groupings of ranges in every direction. These Rocky Mountains make Colorado a mother of rivers—the South Platte, the Rio Grande, the Colorado, the Arkansas, and numerous others. The South Platte's headwaters are in the "Mosquito" Range, which has five peaks over 14,000 feet. Rainfall and snowmelt on one side of the Mosquito Range drain to the Platte basin, but precipitation on the other side of the range drains to an entirely separate river basin, the Arkansas River.[2] As the years inched forward, this proved an ever-more drastic difference.

Picture yourself as a water droplet up in a cloud, a big puffy cumulus bumping against the Mosquito Range. It's freezing! Cold, blowy, inhospitable, and above timberline, the skies darken, ready to shed a few snowflakes. Are you ready to fall? Down, down, down you drift. Below, you see the town of Fairplay, the town depicted as "South Park" in the television show of the same name. You see your future playing out. Perhaps you'll be skied on! Then in April you'll melt into the South Platte to join other water chasing down the hills past Big Bend Station toward Nebraska. As you contemplate this future, a gust from the southeast zips you and a few other snowflakes up over the range. You're still drifting downward, but now Leadville is below. As snowmelt, you'll no longer wind up in Nebraska. You're headed first for the Arkansas River, then *Kansas*.

Fate twisted greatly in the early years of the twenty-first century, such that a mere gust like that would determine the Colorado's state engineer's authority. Like a chess tournament played by the masters, so knotty and cutthroat that only psychics like Arnaldo could foresee checkmate, litigation in one river basin would dramatically alter fortunes in an entirely different basin, including Bill's.

·······■· ·■■·······

The Difference between a River Basin and a Watershed

Both watersheds and river basins are areas of land that drain to a particular water body. In a river basin, all the water drains to a large river. Watersheds are smaller areas of land that drain to streams, lakes or wetlands. There are many smaller watersheds within a river basin.

The complexity began a century ago, when multiple states vied for irrigation water, during the US Bureau of Reclamation's first years. Because our United States are *united*, because Rocky Mountain water is a common resource, other states, other citizens, other organisms lay claim to it too. In the early 1900s, adjacent states filed their first lawsuits over water in the US Supreme Court. Another relative through marriage, Greeley lawyer Delph Carpenter, worked toward settling interstate water issues through the treaty-making powers available to the states.[3] Not for a couple of decades did the states start using the Compact Clause of the US Constitution to negotiate how to share water resources. (We forget now, with *cities* jockeying for water, with food sources from all over the world, that the United States was then fiercely committed to agriculture within its borders, and one of decision makers' greatest priorities was making sure regions that could grow abundant crops received plenty of water.) Nine interstate water compacts with Colorado, the mother of rivers, resulted.[4] These constitutionally binding agreements assure that Colorado delivers water over its state lines. Each compact was negotiated during periods with more precipitation than there is now.

US Bureau of Reclamation

Within the US Department of the Interior, this entity oversees interstate water resource management, which includes operation of water diversion, delivery, and storage projects that the agency built throughout the western states. The water supply serves irrigation, municipalities, and other uses including hydroelectric energy.

With importance that will eventually be evident to our story about the South Platte, the Arkansas River Compact, signed by Kansas and Colorado in 1948, remained problematic. Kansas sued Colorado a third time in 1985, claiming that Colorado well pumping diverted more than its share. The difficulty was in measuring groundwater. Representing Colorado in this case were special assistant attorneys general Dennis Montgomery and David Robbins. Resolute and revered, both veterans of Colorado's natural resources legal conflicts of the 1970s, the mustachioed pair seemed like characters of the Old West.

Interstate Compacts

Colorado River Compact

Arkansas River Compact

South Platte River Compact

La Plata River Compact

Rio Grande River Compact

Animas–La Plata Project Compact

Republican River Compact

Costilla Creek Compact

Upper Colorado River Compact

Ten years later, this suit was still undecided. Indeed as in watching chess, the impression that nothing was happening masked myriad calculations and strategies. Called to testify before the state Supreme Court's special master was Hal Simpson, a career engineer at the Colorado Division of Water Resources who had been promoted to state engineer three years before. State Engineer Simpson was careful about what he said, careful about what he did. Like most engineers, his basis of judgment was rooted in quantification, though tempered by the "wild card"—*climate*. As a state employee, Simpson was also sworn to follow the letter of the law.

In 1995, the Colorado Supreme Court made an interim determination that Colorado's newer wells *were* impacting Kansas.[5] Mr. Simpson must have been persuasive, because the highest judiciary body in the country underscored the Colorado state engineer's authority to prevent such depletions in the Arkansas. (Not until 2008 was a final report on this case filed with the US Supreme Court and a judgment and decree negotiated between state representatives.)

Bill read that the US Supreme Court's 1995 decision had prompted the Colorado state engineer to promulgate the "Arkansas River Basin Rules" down in Denver and thought, "phew!" Thank heaven these additional rules weren't for the South Platte. Courts and legislatures, from Bill's perspective, were a lot like classrooms. They had disciplined seating, established hierarchies, and people who were educated in ivory towers. The people within were apt to exhibit ruthlessness, a quality he'd never cultivated because my father had enough charm that he hadn't needed cunning.

When Bill Phelps was a high-school student during World War II, the country-club chef packed his sack lunches. After all, the teenager bunked in a garret that didn't have a kitchen, and his parents were in Washington, DC, for the war's duration. Young Bill

Out-of-Priority Water Use

As a provision of the prior appropriation system, Colorado's junior water-rights owners (those whose decrees were filed more recently) are approved to use water out of priority only if they have sufficient additional water to reintroduce into the system such that senior water-rights owners are not "injured" (deprived of water). A *replacement plan* (sometimes known as a Substitute Water Supply Plan or a SWSP) identifies annual sources of additional water. By contrast, an *augmentation plan* requires the purchase of additional water supplies for perpetuity. Whereas replacement plans (SWSPs) may be approved a year at a time by the state engineer, augmentation plans are long term and must be adjudicated by a water court.

relished the lunch, but only rarely went to school. Instead he played snooker in a smoky dive not far from East Denver High School. Many times truant, *constantly truant*—especially after a lunch that was likely to contain roast beef during war-rationing years, and was therefore as much of a stigma as a meal— he was occasionally called to the principal's office. "Phelps," the principal would say, "you've been mostly truant."

"Yes, sir, I have."

The principal's office reminded young Bill of the Front Range view where his attorney father had practiced before the war. Bill loathed his father, who had betrayed his mother. She followed him to Washington because she didn't trust him.

"Your attendance record shows that you've been absent more than present in almost all your classes," the principal resumed. "What do you have to say for yourself?"

"Yes, sir, I have."

"Phelps, it isn't so much the absences. It's your total disregard for school regulations. It's the fact that they're *unexcused* absences, that you've made no effort to inform school personnel of your whereabouts."

"Yes, sir."

"Other kids conform to this protocol, Phelps."

"Yes, sir."

"Okay, that'll be all, Phelps."

"Thank you, sir."

Not long after, my father stopped in at the principal's office on his own.

"Phelps?"

"Yes, sir."

"What do you want, Phelps? I'm busy."

"I'm letting you know, sir, that I'm going down to the Spotlight this afternoon."

"The Spotlight?"

"It's where I play pool. You said to let you know, so I'm letting you know."

"Phelps!"

"Nice to see you, sir," young Bill added as he slipped out the door.

My father had a problem with authority, because authority had often let him down. Abandoned, even at a country club, he had few boundaries and no one to count on but himself. A truant and a dropout, he only knew what he'd learned by doing and, like most of us, he hadn't learned enough. The Arne Johnson lawsuit had left him cowed by the legal system. For him the legal system represented "the other side," an Achilles heel, the force that couldn't be bested. Bill's true north was being an Eaton, being honest. "Veritas Alles Vincit"—*Truth Conquers All.*

Whereas small farming was struggling to grow something as necessary as food, he reasoned, an astonishingly big and growing cadre of politicians, lawyers, and other water professionals seemed all about making and bending rules that aimed to hem him in . . . like the principal at East Denver High School.

So, my father shoved the Arkansas basin hubbub to the back of his mind, like most farmers and ranchers around him, who had their own aversions to being hemming in. The hubbub didn't much bother Arnaldo's old grain-elevator customers. The corn market was good. If Colorado well pumpers in the Arkansas had challenges, well, that was "down south," not in the South Platte. Turning a blind eye to the Arkansas was common. This disregard would turn out to be foolish, but for the time being disregard found persuasion in numbers. Anyway, these "1996 Rules" seemed to strengthen the Colorado state engineer's enforcement powers, on which G.A.S.P. members relied. Hadn't the US Supreme Court just acknowledged these powers?

Well shutdowns were still up to the state engineer. Any water user who violated ever-more-stringent guidelines and/or failed to replace out-of-priority depletions couldn't pump. The interstate compact stipulations had to be met, period. The 1996 Rules demanded that junior rights owners have (1) a decreed plan for augmentation approved by the water judge, or (2) a plan approved by the state and division engineers in accordance with these rules, or (3) a substitute water supply plan (a SWSP) approved by the state engineer. This last stipulation is what G.A.S.P. used, another fact reinforcing the reliability of practices in the South Platte, making it seem as if the state engineer had the same authority in the South Platte as in the Arkansas, that snowflakes landing in Fairplay would be governed the same as those snowflakes that fell on Leadville.

There was a legislative rationale for making decisions of this gravity. Since 1974, Hal Simpson and two men who preceded him as state engineers had used the Colorado Revised Statutes (CRS 37-92-501) to promulgate rules for the administration of groundwater. Another statute, 37-80-120, was their basis for annual SWSP approvals such as those that G.A.S.P. members relied upon year after year. On the one hand, the state engineer's annual approval of SWSPs was averting "injury" to senior water-rights owners, and on the other, making sure that any quantity that could be used beneficially was used beneficially. That was his job—maximize beneficial use, minimize waste. Meanwhile, the climate cooperated. Precipitation was ample, crops aplenty since the 1980s.

Let's talk about the weather, the wild card. Dynamic, unpredictable precipitation inspired dynamic replacement strategies for water depletion. Flows fluctuate all over the place. Even urban early-morning showers and toilet flushing lower flows noticeably. "In Colorado stream flow changes daily," State Engineer Simpson explained. "It is not constant. Diurnal effects can be significant. During snowmelt runoff in particular, daily stream flow can fluctuate hundreds of cubic feet per second. So with that daily change or the change resulting from a thunderstorm, which we have a lot, rivers are never constant. Sometimes we get a slug of water and the demand is satisfied, and then the call can shift to another right. How we do that is through our water commissioners and through an evolving process."[6]

Call on the River

In times of water shortage, the owner of a decreed water right will call for water. Colorado Division of Water Resources administrators then issue shutdown orders against undecreed water uses and decreed junior water rights upstream of the call as necessary. These shutdowns allow the senior water-right owner downstream, whose water right has greater priority (decreed earlier) and is more valuable, to fulfill its beneficial use.

Decades ago, water commissioners might have advocated for their section of river, even stealing water and covering it up. No one was the wiser because the data weren't available. By the 1990s, to keep track of the rivers' vicissitudes, the Colorado Division of Water Resources monitored data at 400 gauging stations and canals throughout the state every fifteen minutes, then that information was transmitted back to the office by satellite. Everyone, commissioners and the public alike, could access the data: rafters, fishermen, farmers, hydrologists, lawyers, my father . . . *everybody*. The automated system put an end to the petty larcenies and meant that the state engineer made ever-more-considered decisions.

And so, during the 1990s, Hal Simpson used those improved data to negotiate and approve G.A.S.P.'s SWSPs presented by Jack Odor, just as the state engineer's office had done in the South Platte basin for over two decades. Bill and other farmers only pumped out-of-priority groundwater during July and August. About half the water they pumped was unconsumed; it seeped below the roots into the ground, and water that returned to the river later becoming available to reservoir owners and others downstream. The 1929 Gentlemen's Agreement (see Spectacle 6, "The Inscrutable Hitch of Above and Below")," the handshake between South Platte main-stem reservoir owners, assured that junior and senior reservoirs filled during the winter and spring runoff, so senior calls were confined to the peak of the irrigation season during those years. Precipitation and good runoff made SWSP approvals relatively easy. Taking his clues from the long view like my father, and uneasy about what that long view seemed to augur, Arnaldo said less and less.

·········· ▄▄ ··▄▄ ··········

Times were changing. Remember how early nineteenth-century precipitation increased populations? Conditions repeated in the late twentieth century. A million people, an average of 275 a day, moved to Colorado in the 1990s. A greater population couldn't help but tip the equilibrium. Who in Colorado didn't feel that way? Rush hours, crowded intersections, malls galore! All manner of construction projects. The Ehrlichs, who had run the granary, diversified. They became developers!

The growing demand for water increased the number of junior appropriators. And when water districts and others appropriated out of priority, they needed to augment supplies to prevent injury to senior rights. Artificial recharge projects for augmentation plans filled during "free river" periods when there were no calls. Problem was that that free river was also when reservoirs filled under the Gentlemen's Agreement, and the Gentlemen's Agreement was what kept the farmers going. In other words, the agreement occurred, but there were many more users than existed in 1929.

At the same time, municipal and industrial users reclaimed water, which reduced return flows from upstream. The demand for artificial recharge water exceeded the supply.[7] Nevertheless, the appropriators obtained decrees and appropriation dates. The river, erstwhile under call only in the summer, was more and more under call during fall and winter, which increased the depletions owed back to the river system by well users (farmers).[8] Impinged opportunities to fill the reservoirs strained the Gentlemen's Agreement.

Mr. Simpson always warned appropriators that a drought would impair his ability to approve SWSPs. In every letter of approval was his stern warning: they had better be looking for and purchasing additional water rights. And G.A.S.P. too: Jack Odor said, "We put those letters in our plan every year and mentioned the issue at every meeting."

Artificial Recharge Ponds

Unlined, human-made ponds created to recharge a water system, an aquifer, a river, or some combination. The idea is that water in an unlined pond will reach an aquifer or river in time to prevent "injury" to other water-rights holders. Augmentation water must be purchased and transported to the pond.

At the time, water conservancies had significantly fewer wells than G.A.S.P. (which had around 3,000) and much more revenue, since they exercised mill levies, but G.A.S.P. couldn't afford to acquire great quantities of water. The association relied solely on annual assessments, affordable to small farmers like Bill year to year. This meant that every July and August, the ears of corn laddered upward on a dare . . .

. . . while Pop wound down. He'd always been limber and inventive. We thought he was invincible. Seeing his long frame wobble was shocking, and it got worse. He relinquished the farming to another neighboring family that paid him half the yield. Fine by him; his knees were going. Dean Ackerman and his nephew Ronnie Ackerman had everything you'd expect in farmers: the twang; the matter-of-factness; the absence of pretense; the boots, hats, and jeans; the shovels and perspiration. Neither was idle, ever. Bill might find them out on the farm; other times they'd meet him up at the Office. While talking, the Ackermans coaxed out a weed, mentioned a new seed, mended a fence. Bill felt lucky to have gifted farmers, Gogo too. Arnaldo had passed away, clouds filling his crystal ball.

Too ornery to get his knees fixed, Pop began using a cane. Anyway, anticipating this eventuality, he'd accumulated a collection—canes with handles of tooled ivory, a brass goose head, a flask, a built-in blade, and secret compartments. Hobbling on over to his trusted VW Thing, he tossed in a cane next to the shotgun and shovel, then climbed in and lit up a Camel, "Ready for the tour, love?"

I was making an infrequent visit. The farm then grew around 200 acres' worth of corn. The late-summer fields were lush and cool, like eight-foot-thick lawns. "Wow, Pop. It must take tons of water."

He winced, not much impressed with the topic. "Most of the water falls right through the soil, love. You may find you don't know what you think you know."

"What do you mean?"

"The soil isn't so much soil as . . ."

"Sand?"

"More like gravel. Here," he said, pulling to a stop. "Grab that shovel and dig just a little. See for yourself."

While I worked the shovel into the ground, Pop's Labrador jumped from the VW Thing to hurtle toward the river. The "soil" didn't hold together. Its grains were the size of peppercorns, only heavier.

Alluvial soil has little organic matter or clay, so the water seeps quickly through it. Irrigating an acre of corn, Pop said, might require pumping as much as 4 acre-feet per season, depending on summer rains. But of that 4 acre-feet of

Consumptive Use

Consumptive use is water removed from available supplies without returning to a water-resources system, such as a river or aquifer. In farming, this is the amount of water that is taken up into the plants, together with the amount that evaporates from the soil surface and foliage. From the total water diverted from a water-resources system, the portion of water consumed in crop production depends on many factors, especially the irrigation technology. The common amount is 50–60 percent for furrow irrigation and 85 percent for sprinkler irrigation. Consumptive use is the same amount as *depletion*.

water, the corn only consumes around 1.75 acre-feet. The rest seeps instantly into the soil and makes its way back to the aquifer then the river. "This is why some people turn their farms into gravel quarries?"

"Sure."

"Why didn't you do that?"

"I didn't want the mess. We'd rather have ducks and critters. Keeping the trees alive, love. Improving the soil. Hunky dory for the birds . . . and my friend there," he said, gesturing toward his dog, who had returned wagging and wet to shake water all over us.

Clearly, not all irrigation water at the farm is "consumed." Because the soils are so coarse and permeable, around 60 percent finds its way back to the aquifer immediately below-ground and the river, a few dozen feet to the west. There, someone or something else can then use it, and it can continue on to Nebraska, to fulfill the interstate compact. Sure, some water moves past our heads into the sky as evapotranspiration. And crops store water too, water content that gets hauled away inside the harvest. The amount that does *not* return to the aquifer or river as "return flow," that 40 percent, is called the "consumptive use" or "depletion."

Figuring the consumptive use at a well and the length of time for the impact of this consumptive use to reach the river is mind-bending, but instrumental in calculating the amount and timing of water that needs replacing in order to prevent injury to senior water rights. Those variables are key to the state engineer office's calculations, to hydrologists pulling together SWSPs and augmentation plans, and to the water court—to all those tasked with making sure Colorado's creeks, rivers, and aquifers continue to function healthfully for the benefit of all . . . including adjacent states such as Nebraska, Kansas, Wyoming, New Mexico, and Utah, and over to the southwest and southeast toward the Mississippi, including wildlife for heaven's sake, on and on here on the watery planet. In the days when the interstate compacts were first forged for Colorado's various river basins, few thought of wildlife, though it was then more obvious that humans weren't here alone.

Just Measure of Agricultural Water Use

Diversion *minus* Return Flow

=

Depletion to the river from a surface or ground water diversion

=

CONSUMPTIVE USE

Whether irrigation is diverted from surface water via ditches or pipes, or from groundwater via well pumping, consumptive use is the same, and the return flow is the same. Irrigation's return flow mostly percolates through the ground to the aquifer. From the cropland, some tailwater can flow down gradient over the ground.

Surface-water diversions, being immediately drawn from the river, impact the river immediately. Groundwater diversions create a cone of depression in the aquifer belowground, but that effect on the river is delayed. The lowered water table within the cone of depression propagates outward from a pumping well as pumping continues, potentially reaching directly beneath a river. The cone of depression induces flow to the pumping well. The radius that the cone of depression attains is a function of the duration of pumping, the transmissivity, and storage potential in the aquifer.

Only wells located close to the river withdraw from the river. Farther away from the river, pumping intercepts groundwater return flows that would otherwise flow down gradient by gravity to reach the river, thereby diminishing river flow.

Concerned that people might be forgetting, I indulged my rebel streak during the late 1990s. And yes, the urge was prompted by watching Big Bend Station with my father, marveling at insects and wildlife drawn to water, and by my own hopes for the future. As he began to let go, I took hold. My San Diego neighborhood, supported by water from the Rockies, is underserved with no parks. On a manic tear, neighbors and I saved a blighted nearby coastal canyon from being paved, raised half a million, mobilized kids to plant native plants, and won a bunch of environmental awards. One upshot was that I began to understand stuff like disenfranchisement, watersheds, water quality, soil conservation, ecology, regulation, and government intransigence. The other upshot was a willingness to question out loud.

THE PERFECT DROUGHT

You can plan all you want to. You can lie in your morning bed and fill whole note-books with schemes and intentions. But within a single afternoon, within hours or minutes, everything you plan and everything you have fought to make yourself can be undone as a slug is undone when salt is poured on him. And right up to the moment when you find yourself dissolving into foam you can still believe you are doing fine.

—WALLACE STEGNER, *CROSSING TO SAFETY*

All boys and some girls of my father's generation, and to a lesser extent mine, had more than a passing interest in fishing. Fishing cultivates awareness, pre-cision, and patience . . . qualities that used to be in big demand. Creeks, ponds, and lakes were close, often within walking distance. Everyone had a relative or a friend who could demonstrate how to read the life in the water, how to bait a hook, and where to cast. In Colorado anyway, trout were the fish to fish. And almost all Colorado boys and men either were, or wished they were, trout fish-ermen. Some girls and women too.

The Rockies had excellent fishing. Tasty, delicate trout spent entire lives idling in eelgrass ponds or darting between gnats, mosquitoes, and larva in small cold stretches of creeks. In those days, there were fewer people.

As additional people sought recreation and getaways in the mountains, they didn't go to the trout. The trout were made to come to them, and sometimes the water too was made to order. Resorts began to stock ponds and even create ponds, for purposes of satisfying that God-given yearning to cast, catch, and throw back, but sometimes to clobber and eat. Nothing is as delicious as freshly caught trout.

One such case of intentional fishing holes occurred in the Arkansas River watershed. At the time, the trout-pond incident seemed of little moment, with scant effect except on those immediately involved. Astonishingly, as you'll read, its ramifications jumped a watershed, right over the Mosquito Range, to undermine existing protocols in the entire South Platte River valley hundreds of miles away.

The incident began at Empire Lodge, a mountain getaway near Empire Creek, a tributary to the Arkansas River. Again the Arkansas basin. To attract buyers to its residential subdivision in a rugged setting, the lodge developer dug two basins, filled them with water from a ditch off Empire Creek, threw in some trout, and called the basins Beaver Lakes, to give the impression that beaver had done the handiwork. Access to the subdivision was over an easement on ranch property owned by Anne and Russell Moyers just downstream. The Moyers also owned an adjudicated 1871 water right, a senior water right. The Moyers' seniority meant that filling the Beaver Lakes would require out-of-priority diversions. The state engineer made it clear to the Empire Lodge Homeowners' Association that they needed an augmentation plan, but he granted annual diversions subject to providing water back into the system.

This went on for ten years, but between 1987 and 1997 the Empire Lodge Homeowners' Association never filed for an augmentation plan with the water court. Unfortunately, the substitute water supplies that the Empire Lodge purchased went into the Arkansas tributary *below* the Moyers's point of diversion. When the Moyers placed a call on the creek, Empire Lodge retorted by filing for a "futile" determination, accusing the Moyers of asking for water they didn't need. The rising cost of water brought out the tooth and nail.

The Moyers then counterclaimed over the aforementioned injury—remember that depriving a senior right holder of water is called *injury*—and sought an injunction prohibiting Empire Lodge's out-of-priority diversions to its ponds, until an adjudicated augmentation plan was in place. The water court ruled in favor of the Moyers and put an end to Empire Lodge's out-of-priority diversions. The homeowners' association was forbidden to fill their trout ponds even during free-river conditions. "No Fishing."

Staring at their emptying Beaver Lakes, Empire Lodge Homeowners' Association appealed the decision to the Colorado Supreme Court in 2001.

A few years prior, Governor Roy Romer had appointed gifted attorney, history buff, writer, and poet Gregory J. Hobbs Jr. as a state Supreme Court justice.

Justice Hobbs had started his career under Governor Dick Lamm as first assistant attorney general for natural resources in the 1970s, the same job held by David Robbins and Dennis Montgomery (the special assistant attorneys mentioned earlier). Known as a man who required little sleep, whose passions were Colorado's water and its history, the Honorable Hobbs arrived at the bench with an originalist's confidence in the Prior Appropriation Doctrine and a mission to uphold and promote the doctrine by every means. Justice Hobbs and the other six justices heard *Empire Lodge Homeowners' Association v. Anne Moyer and Russell Moyer.*

Present at the trial was attorney Ronni Sperling, there representing the City of Boulder. Tim Buchanan, representing the City of Sterling, was there too. What were attorneys from cities and reservoirs along the South Platte River, *a whole different water basin*, doing there at a state Supreme Court session concerning the Arkansas? They were the amici curiae, the "friends of the court."

Amici Curiae

Such "friends of the court" may attend trials, oral arguments, hearings, and proceedings—not as party to a case, but to offer unsolicited information and argument in the form of a brief, which bears on the judiciary decision. Whether to admit the amici briefs is up to the court.

Somewhere during and after law school at the University of Colorado, Ronni Sperling must have noticed that the lion's share of Colorado's alluvial groundwater rights were in the South Platte basin. She may have noticed the water court's Empire Lodge decision's relevance to the South Platte farmers. Their summer pumping continued by dint of SWSPs approved annually by the state engineer. According to the water court judge's interpretation, statutory rationale was insufficient to support these approvals.

To guarantee water for their residents and businesses, Colorado's surface-rights owners had court-approved augmentation plans for any out-of-priority diversions. G.A.S.P. did not. This double standard chafed.

If groundwater pumping could be curtailed in the South Platte basin, senior storage rights downstream would be less apt to put a call on the river, and junior storage-rights reservoirs such as Boulder's Barker Reservoir could have more water. Attorneys from G.A.S.P. might have suspected that Ronni Sperling had reasoned this through, so they appeared at the *Empire Lodge* trial as amici curiae too. The attorneys from G.A.S.P. were the same gentlemen who had represented Colorado in the *Kansas v. Colorado* case, Dennis Montgomery and David Robbins, who were in private practice together. These opposing attorneys would continue to appear as "friends of the court" at landmark decisions of ensuing years.

Weighing *Empire Lodge v. Moyers*, the Colorado Supreme Court allowed that whereas approving SWSPs through 37-80-120 might be "legal," the Colorado Legislature had passed the statute to accommodate out-of-priority diversions in situations specifically authorized by the General Assembly. These situations were very unlike fabricated recreational trout ponds . . . and unlike SWSPs for irrigation wells, some of those present may have thought. Even writing about this all these years later, I can feel the tension and groans this must have generated among some in the court.

On December 17, 2001, under huge chandeliers and against deep drapery the color of the soil after which Colorado was named, the state Supreme Court upheld the water judge's ruling, but on different grounds. Justice Hobbs delivered the opinion. His exhaustive knowledge of the Prior Appropriation Doctrine gave the opinion a dramatic twist: Empire Lodge did not have the right to sue in the first place, the justices ruled unanimously. Why? Because Empire Lodge did not have an *adjudicated* water right. And as the amici curiae position had pointed out, the General Assembly gave the state engineer the authority to approve out-of-priority diversions but the assembly had never said, "Sure, go ahead with trout ponds." From the raised dais, the justices rejected the State Engineer Hal Simpson's interpretation of the statute that he and his predecessors had been using to keep farmers going for almost thirty years![1]

The effects of the trout ponds incident didn't stop there.

Justice Hobbs reminds those who question judiciary decisions that the courts do not make the laws; they only interpret and uphold them. His *Empire Lodge* decision included suggestions that the General Assembly clarify the state engineer's authority to approve SWSPs.

Even as Justice Hobbs's gavel fell, a very dry winter was at hand. With so little snowfall, Colorado ski areas had to exercise their water rights to manufacture snow. (Recreation is a "beneficial" use.) Hadn't the state engineer been warning agencies that in the event of a drought, his ability to approve SWSPs would be hampered? Well, the drought had arrived. And with it the *Empire Lodge* decision. Add to that: smart, unrelenting attorneys from thirsty municipalities. It was like *Dune*. In a Front Range without water, would wet tears have value? Well, the tears were going to come.

In 2002, the legislature passed a bill (HB02-1414), which gave the state engineer authority to approve a SWSP, provided only that an augmentation plan was pending in water court.[2] The bill included a requirement that interested parties be notified of a request to approve a substitute water supply plan.[3] The munici-palities and reservoir companies would always be interested. That was the "new normal."

⸻

Empire Lodge's potential for catastrophic impact to farmers hadn't yet occurred to most Weld County farmers, not Bill certainly. Putt-putting around the quiet winter farm in the VW Thing with his Labrador, Bill felt lonely, parched.

Licking his lips, he felt every crevice of him deepening, pulling down, back to the ground. On his mind was Gogo. Bill always thought of her as he did the farm: as *his*. Even though he had earned her, caught her, bought her, and cared for her like the land, she had her own yearnings. He had never considered that marriage would get so out of his control. This didn't used to be the case. He used to be able to put his arms around her and around several ideas at the same time. Working together, the two of them could bring the ideas along. It was gratifying.

As he drove past the stark furrows, Bill saw the dark mounds of turkeys forag-ing for corn at the field's periphery. Gogo had recently counted 85 birds, but Fish and Wildlife's official count was 105. He was surprised and pleased to see them himself, because Gogo had thought maybe they'd moved across the river to the west by then. The quiet was so complete that he could even hear the weight of their steps on the crusty frozen soil. They were in a group . . . *what was it called? Not a clutch. Not a murder. A rafter! A rafter of turkeys.* Bill's own courting rituals had created a rafter with three offspring; but now, like us kids, his hen was busy elsewhere. Despite his established pecking order, Gogo and he now had separate hierarchies—a his and a hers.[4] She'd never bought into rustication. Her women's groups, speaker's forum, hiking, skiing, ballet lessons, whatever it was—her stimulation was in Denver or the mountains. Complicit, he'd bought Gogo fancy cars; not stopping there, he'd given her her own gas tank! He didn't like it. Every time she left home, he imagined her in a car crash. He had tried begrudging, indulgence, commands, and sulking. Nothing worked. Finally he had resorted to letting his body fall apart. The farm, on the other hand, filled him with joy. God, he loved it. He did.

⸻

From Front Range cities, Bill and the neighboring small farmers and ranchers remained a world apart. No skiing or ballet for them. Dependent on G.A.S.P., which the state had urged them to join, which had cosseted them all these years, they didn't know they were on borrowed time. Many of them had never heard of the Gentlemen's Agreement; they weren't aware that it had long masked the effect of their well-pumping depletions in the river. State Engineer Hal Simpson was plenty worried, though. During the annual interval when farmers would need to replace their consumptive use, May through September in such a dry year, replacement water might be very hard to come by . . . and unaffordable.

At the time, the price of *purchasing* senior water rights was about $5,000 an acre-foot, and slightly less downstream, farther away from Front Range cities. For its SWSPs, G.A.S.P. was still paying five to ten dollars an acre-foot to *lease* water from reservoirs and recharge projects year by year. The organization had had a beat on enough water to take care of the whole summer depending on the snowmelt. Acting fast and economizing, consistent with the Prior Appropriation Doctrine, G.A.S.P. only replaced consumptive use when there was a call on the river. (This had been but 5 percent of water pumped in wet years and never more than 25 percent when there had been less precipitation.)

Each year G.A.S.P. came up with around 300,000 acre-feet of water to cover its 3,000 wells' out-of-priority pumping during the growing season. At ten dollars an acre-foot, it was doable on a year-by-year basis. That's $3 million. But consider buying that 300,000 at $5,000 an acre-foot; that's $15 million, or $500,000 per well. True, it's a lifetime purchase, not a rental. But not in a lifetime would a farmer raise enough on an acre to cover that half-million dollars. Not unless food were 100 times as expensive or more. Plus, banking water would mean that on all but the lean years, he'd be paying for water he couldn't use—that is, wasting water—in defiance of prior appropriation tenets.

With the drought, with municipalities jockeying to buy more senior water rights, calls on the river might go on all year. And the only way out of this—going to court and paying the legal expenditures associated with adjudication, and then paying several thousand

Additional Demands and Fewer Return Flows

1. Farmers who converted to sprinkler irrigation used existing allocations but increased their consumptive use. Less water flowed back to the river in these cases.

2. Larger numbers of junior recharge rights drew from the river and aquifer.

3. Reuse of treated municipal and industrial effluent, reuse of lawn irrigation return flows from reusable sources, watering restrictions, and water conservation reduced return flows to the river.

4. Downstream senior reservoirs began to need more water than was returning to the river, so they placed their calls to fulfill demands for direct irrigation or for well augmentation.

dollars an acre-foot—would be prohibitive for most farmers. Hundreds of well owners might be tempted or obliged to sell their water rights and/or their land. At stake was not just Colorado's ag yield, but all the industries associated with agriculture, as well as economic well-being in the state's northeastern cities and towns. Also hanging in the balance was the land itself, the land that might become desiccated and devoid of wildlife.

Outside, the winter without snowfall continued. As the state contemplated meteorological disaster, State Engineer Simpson hastened to draft rules for the Platte basin. His mission? To define those circumstances in which the state engineer could approve out-of-priority depletions to maximize use of the state's water resources without the approval of the water judge. The 1996 Rules for the Arkansas River basin were working really well. Why not use those? Mr. Simpson proposed rules that were nearly identical—the "Amended Rules and Regulations Governing the Diversion and Use of Tributary Ground Water in the South Platte River Basin, Colorado." This was the state engineer's idea for preserving what was then one of Colorado's most fruitful economies.

Even as the proposed rules were taking shape, it was obvious that 2002 was not just dry; it was catastrophically dry. Colorado's *average* annual stream flow is 16 million acre-feet, of which two-thirds is due for delivery to neighboring states. The year 2002 only yielded 4 million. Now suffering the worst drought in a half century, Colorado crept within a half-million acre-feet of exhausting its stored water assets. Calls on the river, which usually didn't occur until late July and August, commenced in June. The Division of Water Resources curtailed surface-water rights in the South Platte, all the way back to the most senior. Even those who owned rights decreed in the 1860s were restricted.

Yet, as Jack Odor said, "The farmers' state of denial remained a strong emotional component. They figured no one would dare deprive them of water. The farmers' position was: *They don't have the manpower to stop us.*"

········■·■········

While Mr. Simpson toiled, in April the Colorado Supreme Court heard another case appealed from the water court in Greeley. Concerning the upper reaches of the South Platte River, the parties were the *Board of County Commissioners of County of Park, James B. Gardner, and Amanda Woodbury v. Park County Sportsmen's Ranch (PCSR)*.[5] The contested property was up in the mountains in South Park, but the beneficiary was a Front Range municipality over a hundred miles away. At issue was the City of Aurora's plan for augmenting groundwater, what the water court characterized as "a scheme to augment out-of-priority depletions with additional out-of-priority pumping" that would "exacerbate depletions to the aquifer and the river system."[6]

Despite the plan's schemelike nature, and despite the fact that PCSR had not so much as a conditional decree, the issue became whether an aquifer was a public storage vessel that no property owner could "own" and whether property owners above an aquifer had any rights relative to the use of the aquifer as a storage vessel, if neither drilling nor structures were to be on their property. In a majority led by Justice Hobbs, the court decided that this was a threshold issue, that it needed sorting out, and the *Park County* case was as good a place as any to make a declaratory judgment.

Drawing comparisons with surface-water vessels, drawing science from University of Arizona hydrologists, and drawing on legal history, the court built its opinion, which Justice Hobbs authored. Artificially moving water into, from, or through aquifers that underlie surface lands other than one's own does not constitute trespass, he wrote. The *public* owns Colorado's tributary groundwater and surface water, and those waters are subject to the constitutional Prior Appropriation Doctrine for creation of water use rights by public entities and private persons. Those wishing to use tributary aquifers, through which water moves freely as storage vessels, need not condemn property, need not seek consent from landowners, and need not compensate landowners. Why? Because a tributary aquifer is not only hydrologically connected to its creeks, streams and rivers. It too is a public resource, five justices decided.

Two justices saw the case differently. Justice Rebecca Kourlis wrote the dissent, and Justice Nathan Coats joined her. Their position was, first of all, that the case was moot because there was no decree. They cautioned against addressing "a question of this magnitude without real interests at stake and without full factual development." Justice Kourlis also noted that whereas the contents of the aquifer—the water—was a public resource, the land under a property "carries with it all that lies beneath the surface down to the center of the earth" according to some legal history. The two justices agreed, though, that tributary groundwater and surface water are indeed hitched and that artificially moving water into, from, or through aquifers that underlie surface lands other than one's own does not constitute trespass.

·········■·■·········

This decision shouldered its way onto the field already crowded with "friends of the court" objectors, additional thirsty municipalities, water attorneys, and water brokers. According to this ruling, it was official: tributary aquifers under anywhere in Colorado were essentially everyone's storage areas, unconnected with the land above them, and unlike the land above, could not be other than public property. Never mind the living assets above that relied upon the aquifers' water. Never mind that higher water tables might increase salinity, might disturb infrastructure and crops. Never mind that higher water tables might damage dwellings.

On the other side of the line were the farmers and ranchers whose livelihoods and assets were married to the aquifers and who had, through the exertions of G.A.S.P. and the state engineer, become trustful. The odds—which began years before in a whole other water basin, the Arkansas—were severely stacked against the South Platte well owners.

After discussing the proposed rules with the South Platte water users, Hal Simpson filed them with the water court in May 2002. The rules were to become effective on December 31, 2002.

Meanwhile, because G.A.S.P.'s substitute water supply plan was approved, the farmers sowed their crops and kept pumping from their wells as they always had. Their state of denial persisted. Summer pressed on. Corn prices were great. Bill, though counting the profits, was uneasy. Something, and it wasn't *The Wall Street Journal* or *Fortune* magazine, filled him with grave concern.

The drought.

For the water-stressed municipalities and ditch companies, seeing vigorous crops burgeoning around wells that summer was galling in the extreme. My father might have anticipated Anne Castle's statement: "It's not as if the farmers are blameless." But by nature and necessity, small-ag operators *live in the now*. When they have an opportunity to grow more, from experience, they fear that the opportunity won't soon present itself. So they take it. Their lives aren't year to year or even season to season. Their survival measures are hour to hour. So is the bold use of groundwater, despite the drought, when ditch rights around them were curtailed, *to be blamed*? Were Bill and other well owners, in this sense, authors of their own demise? "Take the current when it serves, or lose our ventures . . ."[7]

Thirty-seven objectors lined up to oppose the state engineer's attempt to save the day for small ag. The case was named *Simpson v. Bijou Irrigation Co., et al.* Most of the appellees were cities such as Boulder and Highlands Ranch or senior irrigation water users (ditch companies) that relied primarily on surface water. For *them* water-court approved augmentation plans were de rigueur. Why not for the well users?

Filing protests to the rules with the water court in Greeley at the end of September 2002, the appellees (objectors) alleged that the state engineer lacked the requisite statutory authority to adopt the rules as proposed. A number subsequently moved for summary judgment on the same basis. Even though irrigation season had ended, calls on the South Platte persisted, a sign of high stress on supplies. Because senior reservoirs downstream didn't have enough water, the Gentlemen's Agreement risked turning from a positive cooperative tool into a doomsday device. This fanned objectors into demanding that all protests be heard before the water judge issued a final ruling. The water court obliged. Judge Roger Klein ruled that annual approvals of replacement plans (i.e., SWSPs) were not allowed by statute. To defend the state engineer's position, the state immediately appealed the case to the Colorado Supreme Court.

Colorado attorney General Ken Salazar would become President Barack Obama's secretary of the Interior in 2009, but for the moment he appealed the state engineer's case, *Simpson v. Bijou Irrigation Company, et al.*, to the Colorado Supreme Court in late 2002, asking for a *speedy judgment.*

.... ▬ · ▬ ....

As the cold locked Big Bend Station in winter torpor, Pop learned what ailed him. The emphysema diagnosis made his physical and emotional struggles real. With less air, his naps were frequent and longer, narrowing his view from 400 acres to a single gooseberry patch. Outside the bedroom window the gooseberry's rangy fountain of green put its thorns, waxy leaves, flowers, and fruit through their seasonal paces.

"This bush is a fascinating business, love," he said. He stopped to catch his breath. I waited for the full thought to follow. "There's as much to watch right here on this darned gooseberry as there is on the whole farm, love. Have a look." Sparrows, Cassin's sparrows (*Peucaea cassinii*) we guessed, bobbed on the tangled branches. Even in Pop's quietude a light opera played out in his head and around him, the sparrows as supernumeraries, while Gilbert and Sullivan played on the Victrola. His relationship with land was still psychogeographic, still a "dérive" of his own invention.

"You missed the climax . . ." he added breathlessly. " . . . berries. Robins didn't eat them. There were enough, even after the larks had their way, for a gooseberry fool . . . with ice cream."

In the interim, there had been little precipitation for the second consecutive winter, next to no snow for my mother to ski on or for the turkeys to scratch through, and the Colorado General Assembly had risen to panic about the drought too.

.... ▬ · ▬ ....

The legislators directed their legislative attorneys to work with proponents to draft a bill that might afterward be debated, revised, and finally approved or killed.

Therefore, it fell to a cabal of attorneys, facilitated by the Colorado Water Congress State Affairs Committee, to cobble together a bill. Ken Salazar was involved in commissioning this committee to create compromise legislation.[8] The primary drafters were attorneys for the objectors—Ronni Sperling representing Boulder and Mike Shimmin representing Bijou Irrigation, plus Steve Sims from Attorney General Salazar's office.[9] Mike Shimmin did the writing. Andy Jones, representing Central Colorado Water Conservancy District (also an objector), weighed in. The state engineer, and G.A.S.P.'s attorneys, Robbins and Montgomery, played a role too. Jack Odor was nervous.

The Colorado Water Congress

The CWC, founded in 1958 by statute, includes members from municipalities, irrigation companies, water conservancy districts, consultants, and attorneys. The CWC's State Affairs Committee considers all water-related legislation and votes on the position, then recommending that the CWC board take that position on the legislation. The CWC has a lobbyist and an office near the capitol.

Mr. Odor found little point in removing his muffler. He could traverse Civic Center between the Courthouse, the Capitol, the Colorado Water Congress, and back again to measure progress or lack thereof. As the appellants and defense aired their positions to the Supreme Court, the general feeling about *Simpson v. Bijou Irrigation Co., et al.* was somber. People expected the court to uphold the water court's decision against G.A.S.P.'s year-by-year replacement-plan approvals for its 3,000 wells. (These included Big Bend Station's five wells.) To Jack Odor, the court seemed to be dragging its heels, waiting to see what the legislature would do.

Down on the Platte, dry conditions and low stream flow continued to increase senior calls by the reservoirs. North Sterling and Prewitt Reservoirs were obliged to call out Boulder's Barker Reservoir, for which Ronni Sperling was attorney. The impression was that the attorney for North Sterling Reservoir, Tim Buchanan, knew that without the Gentlemen's Agreement, wells would have to be curtailed and that this would leave more water in the basin. Ronni Sperling and Tim Buchanan would soon start a law practice together.

Jack Odor ran into a City of Boulder water manager. Trying to be sympathetic, she said something to the effect of "None of this would've happened had Hal

Simpson not run water-rights up the creek, hampering us from putting water in Barker [Reservoir]."

Odor was incredulous, he said. "Why shouldn't he? Are you telling me that there were times he hadn't done this?" Why wouldn't priority apply to cities?

Mr. Odor wasn't the only one moving between one governmental body and the other. Ronni Sperling and her lawyer colleague Tim Buchanan could take the same path. Bill and the rest of the groundwater appropriators of the South Platte had chums they'd never met—Hal Simpson, Jack Odor, and G.A.S.P.'s attorneys—defenders of agriculture who doggedly pleaded with the legislature to loosen these shackles on the state engineer's authority, who fought to get G.A.S.P. the most time possible to get a plan for augmentation ready to file, and who pleaded likewise with the Colorado Supreme Court. No one needed galoshes, because it just wouldn't snow. The legislative session would end on April 30, and the clock was ticking.

.... ▄▄▄ · ▄▄▄ ....

For many cadres of closely aligned professionals on whose livelihoods outcomes hinge, there is after-hours discussion. Some felt, particularly those on the short end, that such late-day elbow rubbing took place—a meeting of minds about the final form of the legislation, a form that would force G.A.S.P.'s demise. The "Thursday Night Massacre" they called it. As to whether or not this massacre occurred? The outcome was the outcome.

Draft legislation delivered to the legislature for debate "pulled the teeth out of the state engineer," Jack Odor said. For a start, it imposed a requirement for *permanent ownership* of water used in a plan for augmentation. No more leases. Groundwater Appropriators of the South Platte didn't have the revenue to buy a bunch of water rights. Neither did most individual farmers. There was that big difference between $10 and $5,000 dollars an acre-foot. The legislation demanded that the full consumptive use, 100 percent, be replaced, whether that season required it or not. Moreover, the drafters added a notification process that would so prolong SWSP approvals that most available water sources would, by the time the many weeks allocated for approval transpired, be unavailable and/or unusable.

The approach of G.A.S.P., which had worked so well for thirty years, was one of minimizing waste. It worked with economy and speed, within limitations—scarcity of money, scarcity of water, and brevity of need—by waiting for intermittent water to be available, then leasing it quickly. Was that over? The Division of Water Resources, too, had managed great efficiencies and maximum use along the river in the absence of well-owner augmentation plans, with help from the Gentlemen's Agreement. That teetered as well.

The Colorado Supreme Court always issues its decisions on Monday, but Monday April 28 came and went without a decision. Meanwhile, the legislature debated over the draft bill. The court's lagging, Jack Odor felt, seemed to reinforce the direction the legislation was headed: no more seasonal water leases. Across Civic Center at the Capitol, where Ben Eaton's portrait hung under the gold dome, at four o'clock in the afternoon the next day, near the end of the session, legislators finished debating the new legislation.

Sure enough, should any appropriator not supply proof that they had applied to water court to adjudicate an augmentation plan and were operating under an approved SWSP in the interim by January 2006, his or her wells would be curtailed. Giving the well owners two and a half years to get court-decreed augmentation plans was put forward as a reprieve, yet the grace period seemed gratuitous, even cruel.

"The new statutes were passed without any detailed analyses of how those changes would truly affect water use and availability," wrote retired assistant state engineer Robert Longenbaugh, who had severe doubts that the conjunctive use of groundwater and surface water could be achieved under those statutes.[10] The statutes seemed to cripple the state's administrative requirement to maximize beneficial use of both water sources. They also undermined tens of thousands of acres of cropland, cropland that also supported wildlife, possibly forever.

Governor Bill Owens signed Senate Bill 03-073 on the morning of April 30, 2003.

Then the other shoe dropped. At noon the same day the Colorado Supreme Court issued its decision on *Simpson v. Bijou Irrigation Co., et al.* The court sided with the water court, restricting the state engineer's authority to approve SWSPs in the South Platte unless an augmentation plan had been filed with the water court. For those other water droplets—those that fell into the Arkansas River basin on Leadville's side of the range—SWSP approval could continue, but not in the waterway leading to Nebraska. Rules applicable to one aquifer are not applicable to another, the court noted. Moreover, they pointed out that the Arkansas Rules were never appealed and had not been before the Supreme Court.

.... ▬ ▬ ....

All this was a deathblow: Given the lack of water—G.A.S.P. members couldn't even meet the criteria for the upcoming 2003 irrigation season. Jack Odor, who liked to make things work, who had masterminded these calculations year after year for thirty years, hit this wall of litigation and legislation and time constraints. Groundwater Appropriators of the South Platte was done for. What water G.A.S.P. had went to cover post-pumping depletions. There was none left to support pumping that summer.

Over the thirty years that G.A.S.P. had been in business, Bill had paid an accumulated $3,000. In the end, when G.A.S.P. dissolved its assets—the permanent water supplies Jack Odor had collected the way he collected butterflies—the organization had enough money to reimburse its members for almost all their investment. Bill got close to $3,000 back. So did the other appropriators.

Groundwater Appropriators of the South Platte went out of business and Jack Odor retired, leaving 3,000 wells either without coverage or scrambling for coverage, including Bill's. Bill joined the South Platte Well Owners, a new group of 380 wells that filed applications for augmentation plans with the water court and received approval of a SWSP in the interim.

His wells weren't metered, but there were rumors of well curtailment. The fields were sown. There'd been some spring rain. The tenant farmers, Ronnie and Dean, occasionally showed up to chew over events with my father. They had already talked about the possibility of joining Central Colorado Water Conservancy District. Lately, they met not in the kitchen, not up at the Office on the hill, but in Bill's new place of business with its view of the gooseberry patch—the bedroom.

Bill lay on the bed. He pulled the oxygen cannula from his nostrils. "Adjusting my mixture," he nodded with a half smile at the farmers he admired so much. "How you two old showoffs doing?"

Ronnie nodded back. Dean took off his hat and smoothing back his damp hair said, "I reckon we're all right." And then, "We're wondering what you want us to do about the wells?"

Bill leveled a stare at them. "Well, the pumps still have switches, don't they?"

"Yep."

"Go ahead and flip the switches, then."

Dean and Ronnie looked at him, saying nothing, so Bill continued, "If anyone wants to know about it, tell them I did it. And . . . well . . . if anyone asks me, I'm gonna tell them you two did it."

Then he inserted the cannula and its snaffle and added, "Thanks for dropping by, guys. Nice to see you."

POSEIDON REVISITS THE PLATTE

Suddenly it is so clear: the world is running out of fresh water.
—MAUDE BARLOW, *BLUE GOLD*

As much as Bill loved his family, he was dreading Thanksgiving. Emphysema had by then reamed his lungs, breaking down connective tissue and clogging bronchial tubes, robbing him of breaths-in, breaths-out.

Bill had done what he could on the Platte, with the "source." He had pressed down until he couldn't any longer. An imprint. Now he and his ideas began to levitate. The land and the river folded around him, both a womb and a tomb, but they didn't demand anything else from him, not the way the dining room did. It seemed leagues away. His aversion, though, couldn't stop the Thanksgiving holiday, and numerous loved ones descended on him anyway.

We were happy to see our father and also sad because he lay on the bed gasping, a fish out of water.

We were vectors. As commonly happens with Thanksgiving visitors, we arrived with our winter pathogens. Germs mean nothing to the young. We could cough, sneeze, cook, and do the dishes, no problem; but whatever we bore bore down on Pop. Within a few days, pneumonia had lodged in what was left of his lungs, reducing him to a combination of infection, inflammation, and poster boy for Camels. We hugged him gently then left. Pop had been poorly for long enough that we took for granted that he would continue in this pattern, the invalid, until the next winter holiday and the one after that. But he didn't. "Pop's dying," Annzo said over the phone.

"You sure?"

"Whatever he has, the doctor can't fix it. He said Pop's lungs are done for."

"I'll come. Will'l want to come too."

"I don't think you'll make it. That's what the doctor says anyway."

"What's Gogo doing?"

"She's just sitting here. Hospice is here."

"Shit."

"They're showing us what to do. He wants them to go away." Annzo's voice cracked, and she passed the phone to Gogo.

"Gogo?"

"I didn't think he was ready."

"You okay?"

"I'm fine, precious. You should see him. He looks so young. The wrinkles in his face . . . it's all smooth."

"Can you get rid of the hospice?"

"No."

"Can he hear me?"

"I'll hold the phone up."

What was there to say? He couldn't answer. Or at least I couldn't understand what he said. Probably cursing strangers in the house. I decided, in vain, to sing a few bars of a song he liked: "As Time Goes By."

I hung up and closed my eyes, picturing Gogo and Annzo, gentle angels on the bed with him. Being city girls, they found peace inside, inside the moment, inside the house. His sibilant breaths evinced from those drowning lungs were still in my ears, though. I conjured his exhausted gaze, imagining him looking past Gogo and Annzo out onto his belvedere, forever to absorb the enormity of the horizon, the gooseberry bush, stumps of corn stalks in the snowy field, and the river striving to make the bend, reminding him that water is to be reckoned with. Beyond that, if the sky were clear, he could see Long's Peak surging across the skyline daring men to be bold, maybe even daring them to cultivate such a land.

When next the phone rang, it was to tell me that the man who thought he owned water was gone. Weirdly, with death at hand, I thought of pregnancy.

Despite our father's disappointments, he felt like a lifelong pregnancy, the biggest, most consuming presence in the room. Pregnancy—by occupying so much space, physically and emotionally—shoves both body organs and unrelated sentiments out of the way. Pop was like that, reducing the rest of us to inconsequentiality. Some of the grandkids called him "Big." The others called him "Boss." So when he died, the sentiments that had occurred to me after my son's birth recurred. It was: "Wow! *Feel* this vacuum. The firmament too high. The abyss too wide, too deep. No handholds. What a hole!"

We bit players awakened the next morning, entirely clueless about our responsibility. The day lurked there with its hollow questions. His farm was under the snow. His cottonwoods and willows stood stiffly in crystal sheaths. His ice girded the river, and his mallards hunkered down in the slough. Every once in a while, a quack interrupted the silence. Someone needed to keep everything trundling. So Gogo, Annzo, Will, and I groped in grief's corners for pieces of Pop we could carry forward. Nothing wants filling like a void.

········· ▬··▬ ·········

And life went on. What had been Bill's was now "ours"; however, only Gogo paid attention. Under cover of my father's illness and death, my mother's relative ignorance, and a distrust of government that was the invisible tenant on our farm and all around us, there thrived an assumption that everything was going to be fine—despite the drought that summoned us all to address water differently.

Finally, when Bill had been dead for three and a half years, the farm looked primed, *full of promise*, thanks to our farmers. Quiet Ronnie Ackerman and his uncle, big blustery Dean Ackerman, had prepared, tilled, and seeded 200 acres, using piles of machinery they'd accumulated with industrious opportunism. Though no longer Bill's cows and calves, their animals enjoyed the greening meadow. Farming Big Bend Station, the Ackermans had distinguished themselves as the real thing, as I've said, a hardworking family that honors water with frugality and loves farming. Before dawn they leave their houses, and they don't go home until it's too dark to work anymore. They live, literally, *in* the land. You never see them except in muddy boots and carrying a tool. By May 2006 long stretches of irrigation pipe, anchored to five wells, were laid out over the fields. That's when my mother telephoned with urgency. She's not one for outbursts, but her news came without preamble: "It's pandemonium here. We can't use the wells."

"What! What do you mean, Gogo?"

Knowing nothing of the legislation or Supreme Court decisions, she was shocked: "Our wells have been turned off . . . on all the farms around here. They say 30,000 acres are dry. The State of Colorado reneged on our water rights. They say they are going to lock meters on the wells and have disallowed all of us from pumping."

"What? But we own the water rights." I knew nothing of the legislation or Supreme Court decisions either. Talking to her from San Diego, I stared at my faucet, a Judas, across the room.

"Right, even though we own the rights. Everyone is in shock."

Shocking too to hear my mother—whom Pop had insulated against business for a half century—talk about water rights. And Gogo said "everyone." She meant the growing circle of rural neighbors whom her attention had charmed since he was gathered.

My mother is unlike most farmers and ranchers. They are cagey, self-reliant. With none of the obligatory bonhomie of neighbors in cities, rural people get by with an infrequent nod. Their idea of personal space is no less than fifty acres. Yet that spring in northeastern Colorado, there was enough outrage, enough helplessness, and enough stupefaction to create its own tropism. Wretched well owners turned toward each other.

And because nothing drastic happened except to farmers and ranchers (there was still food in the grocery stores), the 30,000 acres were just the beginning. The Colorado South Platte well lockdown soon ballooned to 100,000 acres until 2,400 wells were shut off, and the remaining wells were greatly curtailed, by approximately 50 percent. Half the wells in the basin, half the wells on the river's 270 linear-mile course between the headwater near Fairplay and the state line at Julesburg were out of commission. Those 270 linear miles are the same stretch that Front Range municipalities access for water. The ongoing drought, the worst in 200 years—back when only the Arapaho were looking—had the municipalities in a panic too, as you've read. The cities were on high alert.

Those farmers and ranchers who now included my suddenly on-task mother were not. They were isolated, breathing pollen, swatting flies, minding what they thought was their own business. Few realized how much water-right prospecting, brokering, and manipulating had been going on in Denver's high-rises. They'd been cushioned by very affordable annual SWSPs for thirty mostly wet years. They'd filed for augmentation plans. That there'd been continual calls on the river since 2003 hadn't mattered because the state had given them the go-ahead to pump. *Drought had happened before*, they reasoned, still in denial. *So what? There's always the aquifer.*

········ ▪▪ ·· ▪▪ ········

Now, the stunned well owners got their heads out of the alluvium and into the hands of what few water professionals weren't already making money taking water away from them. There, they found a flood of inscrutable complication. Grappling to figure out what hit them, these would-be appropriators finally got wind of the *Empire Lodge* decision—the "trout pond incident" in the Arkansas basin—and the ensuing legislation (House Bill 02-1414 and Senate Bill 03-073) that had made ongoing annual approvals impossible in the South Platte. They began to understand. Not only were all water-rights holders (or their representatives) frantically buying and stashing what replacement water they could afford, thus reducing the amount of available acre-feet. The growing cities (fearful of being outdistanced by other cities) had a pressing interest in recharge ponds and protecting their water supplies. In a single year, competition had driven up the cost of an acre-foot of Colorado water, from $2,000 to as high as $20,000 for some blocks of C-BT water.

Justice Hobbs, Judge Klein, State Engineer Simpson. The battery of objecting attorneys. As always happens, it was easier to identify the players than the explanation.

Jack Odor's yearly water-leasing approach for replacing out-of-priority depletions), in place for thirty years, ceased shortly after the *Simpson v. Bijou Irrigation Co., et al.* decision three years before. When that happened, ag operations including Big Bend Station hastened to buy into adjudicated augmentation plans (which again, are outright purchases of water that would be used to replace out-of-priority pumping when it occurs). With this objective, Big Bend Station and many other former-G.A.S.P. groundwater appropriators had transferred their wells to the Central Colorado Water Conservancy District in 2004, as people in authority had recommended. After all, "Central" was quasi-governmental, wasn't it? That gave people confidence ... in vain, as it turned out.

Central Colorado Water Conservancy District (Central) put these appropriators into the Well Augmentation Subdistrict (WAS) and then initiated a two-pronged hunt. WAS needed enough yearly augmentation

Calls on the River

CALL: The demand for use of water by a decreed water user

FREE RIVER: When the supply of water in the river exceeds the demand for water by all decreed water users

VALID CALL: The water commissioner's determination of the most junior right holder that may divert when the supply of water in the river is less than the demand. Also known as "the Call," this is a curtailment of junior rights in deference to senior rights.

water to keep 449 wells pumping during growing seasons, and it needed places to store and to recharge that water. What constituted "enough" augmentation water was tremendously different from the 5 percent of the wells' depletions that had sufficed for thirty years. Since 2003, strict enforcement required having enough water to replace *100 percent* of the depletions in perpetuity. The storage needed to be both near enough and far enough that the released water would find its way back to the river when senior water-rights holders made calls.

In the meantime, WAS well owners needed to operate, so Central had applied for annual SWSPs in 2004 and 2005. State Engineer Simpson had approved them—in keeping with Senate Bill 03-073's provisions—only because Central had already filed WAS's augmentation plan with the water court. This augmentation plan's court date loomed, also in May 2006, attracting a big wad of objectors. The Front Range water community had assumed that WAS's augmentation plan would follow Central's existing Groundwater Management Subdistrict (GMS) model, but Central informed everyone that it did not like the terms of the GMS plan and that it would not agree to an augmentation plan under those terms. So the rout ensued.

Who were these objectors? Municipalities, reservoirs, and ditch companies—with junior and senior surface-water rights—all along the Platte from the headwaters to the state line. Cities with deep pockets, or at least deepening pockets, could afford to hire gifted, well-connected water attorneys, in no short supply in Colorado. Cities' junior in-basin water rights are subject to being called out by more senior South Platte basin water rights, so they were prone to placing the blame on well pumping, whose effect on supplies was less understood. To make sure they *were* believed, municipal water interests, Front Range developers, privately held water districts, and attorneys and their hydrologists consolidated into a powerful cluster, helped along by expensive computerized hydrological models. From the *Empire Lodge* decision forward, the same interval as the drought, those attorneys had raced each other to the water courts like scouring Valkyries. Apprehensive about being bested by cities, ditch companies followed along even though they represented some farmers and ranchers who also had groundwater rights, so their objections pitted these ag operations against themselves! Their ditch rights were senior to their well rights.

Throughout those years, people in suits jockeyed for much larger volumes of replacement water that was both rarer and dearer. At the same time, people in dungarees had remained against all odds confident that their payments to Central would issue good results as G.A.S.P. had. All this would sort itself out, they thought, and production would continue as normal, because no one would let Colorado's ag economy falter. Sorting out the replacement water was Central's business. Attorneys' business was in the courts. Their business was producing food, so the country people secured their farm loans. They ripped their fields.

Meanwhile, Central's engineers had figured WAS wells' consumptive use at around 25,000 acre-feet each year.[1] Central's attorneys were Lind, Lawrence & Ottenhoff. Coming up on the May 2006 deadline, the attorneys had managed to cobble together a plan they thought would augment anticipated pumping, but the plan (crafted in the middle of a water-feeding frenzy) left no margin for bad luck. And there *was* bad luck, at the nth hour. The gravel pit where WAS intended to store replacement water was some 800 acre-feet short of space. Moreover, the plan relied entirely on a water source that was good for only one year and would not be forthcoming in subsequent years. Central and its attorneys' strategy had some real problems. They petitioned for a delay for the augmentation plan trial.

At the same time, attorneys from Boulder, Centennial, Sterling, Henrylyn Irrigation District, and a mining operation near Leadville pounced. Boulder's then legal representative and other opposition attorneys opposed the postponement, arguing that the replacement water that the subdistrict had identified was inadequate, that agricultural pumping was taking water away from cities. They appealed the already-approved 2003 and 2004 SWSPs to the water court. The feeling was that Ms. Sperling was insatiable. The water judge, Judge Klein, agreed to postpone the WAS augmentation plan trial, but only after allowing the objectors to demonstrate just how the SWSPs had so injured their water rights.[2] Out came the numerical hydrologic models.

·········■■··■■·········

Everyone, as usual, was waiting on the weather. Would there or would there not be late-season snow? (Snow might mean reprieve.) By May, the additional storm hadn't materialized and the melt began. Snowpack was so meager, so much less than average, that Central's already uncertain means of providing a SWSP for the 2006 irrigation season, the season they were already in, evaporated. Literally and figuratively.

On May 5, the state engineer, dear Hal Simpson, who had approved farmers' temporary replacement plans for so many years, called Central's director to tell him what he already knew, that the state just couldn't approve the subdistrict's 2006 plan, due to its shortcomings, not after the *Empire Lodge* decision. Simpson felt terrible for the well owners. At that moment, he knew better than they did what was at stake. He added that the subdistrict might want to appeal his decision at water court. But no.

In Greeley with a phalanx of objectors circling, Central decided to withdraw the 2006 SWSP request that would have allowed the farmers to pump their wells. In exchange, the objectors agreed to withdraw their appeal of the 2003 and 2004 SWSPs. This stipulation was incorporated into a water-court order that Judge Klein issued on May 8, 2006. The order stated that the WAS wells could not pump at all until the water court approved an augmentation plan. So that was it: barely a month into the 2006 irrigation season, the Central WAS wells were ordered curtailed until further notice . . . as Senate Bill 03-073 had regulated three years before.

The certified-mail notification arrived. Gogo called Ronnie Ackerman. Ronnie explained. Gogo called Annzo, Will, and me. She didn't want to go through this alone. We had no idea what to do, except listen. Division staff posted notices on the wells and collected meter information to verify compliance. Helplessly, farmers watched seedlings that were only just breaching the soil droop without irrigation—the seedlings that were going to repay the bank loans. Land that had grown crops for seventy or more years was abruptly dry as a bone.

The pumping wasn't going to resume, not until well owners could locate, pay for, and acquire enough replacement water, not just 5 percent but 100 percent, not just for that summer but for summers forever. And they had to pay an attorney to maneuver their plan through water court, past many well-financed objections. That had been the idea behind joining WAS, but Central was failing. And that additional hitch: the cost of replacement water was astronomical. No one had confidence that Central would succeed. Not anymore.

Incredulity grew. The well owners had bought and paid for the water rights. They *owned* the water rights. They could pick up and hold the titles in their chafed hands, many for wells deeded before the Dust Bowl. When they bought their land, when their parents and grandparents and great-grandparents bought their land, they bought the water rights too. It was there on the deeds in black and white, the right to pump from that great aquifer, with its recharging water.

Colorado has some safety nets for water-stressed farmers, like the option for rotational crop fallowing. Farmers whose water rights are purchased can sometimes lease back the water, to continue production. Since there was no transaction in this case, only curtailment despite having paid their dues, the well owners had no safety nets. And because they had little inkling, neither of the Gentlemen's Agreement that could no longer protect them, nor of the history behind the now-strict enforcement of augmentation plans in the South Platte only, most well owners felt blindsided.

Well owners appealed for mercy, and there was an offer of mercy in the form of Colorado–Big Thompson (C-BT) and Windy Gap water, but the objectors wouldn't be satisfied, and Judge Klein concurred, unless the WAS had secured enough water to meet a call on the river, 365 days a year, for three consecutive years. Poseidon's trident, the one that mythical Amymone had uncorked to liberate groundwater for the struggling farmers, was back in place. The aquifer was sealed off.

········· ▬ ▬ ·········

My sister, who lives in Denver, summarized matter-of-factly: "There's a drought."

"Yeah, but is the state rationing everyone? It's shutting down the farmers completely. And our wells are older than Boulder's reservoir!"

"Well, farmers use a lot more water than the cities," she answered.

And there it was, I thought with a lump in my throat—*the mindset*—and straight from my own dear kin, another shareholder in our great-great-grandfather's legacy. *Cities need water.* Apart from everyone in cities consuming products that require water to produce, cities use less water than farmers, therefore farmers should not grow?

This paradox jarred me greatly. Our nonchalance put the source in crisis. Climate changes, drought, pollution, and extinctions are but some of water's way of summoning us to change our ways, to avert almost certain peril . . . or so it seems to me.

Worldwide, agriculture uses approximately 70 percent of all freshwater withdrawals.[3] In Colorado, about 86 percent of water diversions go to agriculture. The distribution of water rights to farmers reflects what had been, from the beginning of settlement and prior to globalization, a commitment to growing food within our country and a universal understanding that food couldn't be cultivated without water.

Thinking in percentages is easy. We can picture the freshwater pie chart, but we can't see nuances. Percentages don't show that freshwater is drawn and redrawn as many as seven times within Colorado's border. Never mind that between 20 and 60 percent of ag's water flows back into the aquifer or recharges the surface water. Easy to overlook that over 50 percent of domestic water allocations are used outdoors. And what about the fact that the amount of H_2O on the planet has remained constant for eons?

It struck me that metropolitans like Annzo—like me, like most of us—are like squawking baby birds, nesting in cities with our mouths open, waiting for water and food to arrive—the more ready-to-swallow the better. We have little concept of food's "water footprints" or the water cycle, not to mention the yearly and hair-raising stakes that I am only beginning to learn about, the unpampered 24/7s that go into every mouthful.

In May 2006, not just our mouths were open. Our spigots were too, while just downriver our food producers, defeated and desolate, stared at shriveling seedlings. It was as if our mother, and the farmers and ranchers around her, had received a transmission: *the End of Everything*. Even though, by pertaining to food, the End of Everything pertained to all of us—urban and rural, American and international—the lines of communication were so buffered that no one could hear.

I was beginning to hear, though, and wanted to screech: "Farmers aren't using water on lawns and Jacuzzis and theme parks. They're using it on food! Cities need food as badly as farmers do. Water actually flows into cities in the form of food."

What I didn't yet know was everything you've now read and some that you haven't. And what wasn't fair about my hysteria was that my sister's view was everyone's view and it had been carefully hewn, not just by media but by globalization, by the corporatocracy, by reprioritization about water over time, by those changes I've already described as tugging at tomorrows. By shopping!

Scarcity doesn't pull people and agencies together. It pulls them apart.

AT THE NOT-O.K. CORRAL

Someone feeling wronged is like someone feeling thirsty.
Don't tell them they aren't. Sit with them and have a drink.
—LEMONY SNICKET

Compared to the 3.7 million city dwellers who proliferated across the developing Front Range, ag families of Adams, Weld, and Morgan Counties were hardly a sizeable constituency; they were a shrinking demographic.

Circumstances called upon well owners to react, individually and en masse, in a way for which none was prepared—not mentally, not emotionally, not politically, not financially. Ag land without water at least halved in price. What followed was sell-offs. Well owners were obliged to pay their creditors with assets that had instantly depreciated.

At auctions after May 2006, farmers found each other, often to say goodbye while their livelihoods were pieced out. Auctioneers such Chuck Miller were there at the piecing, at the end of farm lives, talking at a pitch, to bidders, whose money the defeated men and women would use to fund their nonfarming remaining days. Chuck's business seemed a kind of hell, grim reaping. Yet, he seemed to love farmers and ranchers. His job was to get them as much of their due as auctiongoers would muster, he told me on the phone. About the well shutdown, he was indignant and generous with information, all with an auctioneer's voice that anyone would oblige. He'd always start with: "There are two ways to get lynched in the West: Steal a man's cattle or steal his water." Chuck had a plan.

In the fall, to meet Chuck, to see Gogo, to attend a meeting about the well shutdown, I flew back to Colorado. Descending over the mountains, I was struck by the abundant reservoirs and recharge ponds below. All over the foothills and spilling into Denver and off to the east, like shiny coins cast on the landscape were hundreds of manmade ponds that weren't there when I was a child. Hoarding all this water aboveground while crops withered seemed crazy, profligate. (Water doesn't evaporate from aquifers.) On the other hand, the reservoirs were but iterations of those Ben Eaton had developed in the late nineteenth century. If Ben Eaton had only known. . . .

> **Irrigated Cropland vs. Dryland in Dollars**
>
> A 2012 report by the National Agricultural Statistics Service cites that an acre of irrigated cropland in Colorado was worth an average of $3,160 in real estate value alone, while an acre of nonirrigated cropland was worth $800, on average.
>
> SOURCE: Caitlin Coleman, "Grown in Colorado," *Headwaters Magazine*, Colorado Foundation for Water Education (fall 2012): 18.

I drove up the Platte on the same highway Bill and Gogo had taken to the Eaton place at Woods Lake as teenagers sixty years before. I passed the aged cottonwood at Brighton, the one right next to the road. Like my parents, it no longer had two trunks, but was now reduced to one. At the farmhouse, I left my bags at the top of the sunken stairs. Then I ran toward the river. It's an old habit. I found myself crying, for our ravaged, rotating orb, but mostly I wept in frustration. I didn't want to let go as Pop had let go.

> **Reservoir Evaporation**
>
> The average annual evaporation rate from Colorado's reservoirs and retention basins east of the mountains is 12 percent.

That sphinxlike bend in the Platte looked as it always looks in the fall—placid, lined with heart-shaped leaves ablaze. By the time I'd trod back to the clapboard house, my face was puffy, but I took off for town anyway.

In Platteville, at a watering hole called, ironically, the Double Tree, I waited in the entry in the company of mannequins dressed as Dale Evans and Roy Rogers. Many farmers and ranchers walked by me, into dinner and the meeting. Finally, a forceful man strode in, in a cowboy hat. I didn't have to wonder if he were Chuck Miller. Without asking whether I wanted whiskey, he ordered us both a double.

We shared the restaurant with close to a hundred farmers and ranchers. Unlike Chuck, the well owners were reduced. You've never seen such a beaten-down bunch, deprived of what alpha tendencies they might ever have had by the very system that had urged them along, that plus the drought. Not a smile among them, they looked, as Gogo had described them, like abject characters from *The Grapes of Wrath*. They had come together to talk, to strategize. The Ackermans were there. Also Jan and Gene Kammerzell, neighbors who own a tree farm to the north of Big Bend Station. Beforehand, we had dinner, not the pricey mini-portions on big plates I'd get in California, but vasoconstricting arrays of liver, bacon, and onions, spread out aside baked potatoes with sour cream and butter, plus a salad bar loaded with creamy dressings, for $12.95. Farm fare.

Taking a long draw of bourbon, Chuck said, "I had some terrible news today. Helen was killed." Exchanging looks, he explained.

"Farm Fare" Water Content	
Lettuce	94%
Cooked Liver	66%
Potato	79%
Sour Cream	62%
Tomato	94%
Carrots	88%
Cooked Bacon	64%
Onions	90%
Butter	18%
Whiskey	51%

Helen Chenoweth-Hage was the impetus behind Chuck's plan. Helen had made a legend of herself in the West. She was a congresswoman and a rabid property-rights advocate. Environmentalists like me made her blood boil. In defiance of the federal listing of Idaho salmon, she served canned salmon at fundraisers. In response, Green Idahoans printed bumper stickers and T-shirts that read "Can Helen, Not Salmon." Because feisty Helen refused to submit to search by airport security, she always chose to drive instead of fly. During her final term limit, in 1999, she married Nevada rancher and fellow firebrand Wayne Hage, whose legal ordeal some found relevant to the Colorado well shutdown. The case pertained to government restrictions potentially being placed on the water supplies that are crucial to the West's $156 billion irrigated agricultural economy.[1]

At the time Hage married Chenoweth, he had an outstanding lawsuit against the federal government over water rights, a suit with its basis not in water law, but in property rights assured through the Fifth Amendment. Proceedings were already so protracted that they'd ushered his first wife, Jean, into her grave. The new Ms. Chenoweth-Hage fell into the fight lockstep where she and Wayne Hage were ready heroes in the "sagebrush rebellion" against the federal government.

Hage had purchased the Pine Creek Ranch twenty-one years before, in 1978 for $2 million. In the western rangeland tradition, the price included 7,000 acres of his own land as well as water and grazing rights on 752,000 adjoining acres of federally administered US Forest Service and Bureau of Land Management (BLM) property. This isn't unusual. Lots of western ranch operations operate thusly, as my father had done on public land in Wyoming.

Wayne Hage was damned surprised in 1979, the year after he bought the ranch, when he and his hands came upon Forest Service personnel—not the usual faces but complete strangers from Austin, Texas. They told him that the federal government was laying claim to the water, *all the water rights* in public land in those parts, 160 of Hage's vested water rights among them, without compensation. Their position? Overgrazing was damaging the high-desert range. The Forest Service said that Hage abused his land and repeatedly broke agency rules.

> **Act of US Congress, July 26, 1866**
>
> Whenever, by priority of possession, rights to the use of water for mining, agriculture, manufacturing, or other purposes, have vested and accrued, and the same are recognized and acknowledged by the local customs, laws and decisions of courts, the possessors and owners of such vested rights shall be maintained and protected in the same."

Wasn't divestiture of property rights "un-American"? In 1981 Hage petitioned the state of Nevada for a determination of rights. Ten years later there was still no determination. In the meantime, the federal government tightened its hold on rangeland resources. Ranchers all over the West faced similar reversals. The relationship between ranchers and the feds had changed. Or, as Jim Nelson, then supervisor of two national forests in Nevada, told the county commissioners: "The days are gone when you'll come in here and pound on the district ranger's table and he'll piss in his pants and you'll get your way."[2] By spring 1991, Pine Creek Ranch was spending more time and money defensively than it was operationally, the kind of defense Colorado well owners might contemplate all these years later.

Property that is appropriated without compensation is a "taking," in violation of the Fifth Amendment. Federal appropriation of Hage's water rights represented such a taking according to his San Francisco–based attorney, Ladd Bedford. With help from other ranchers, in 1991 Ladd Bedford filed a takings suit for Wayne Hage in the US Court of Federal Claims.[3] They sought $28.4 million in damages. The National Wildlife Federation and Natural Resources Defense Council's legal counsel represented the government.[4] Those pesky enviros.

In the meantime, Hage's wife died and his daughter Margaret introduced him to Helen Chenoweth. Three years following their marriage and after ten long years in court, Judge Loren Smith issued his final decision on the determination of property rights on January 29, 2002. He concluded that plaintiffs owned extensive property rights on public land, including water rights. The federal government withdrew its appeal. Word was that the feds wanted to avoid a binding decision from the Supreme Court, one that would enforce a precedent that ranchers actually do own the water rights they had paid for on federal lands. There was still no settlement.

Wayne Hage didn't live to enjoy his victory; he died in June 2006. Four months later, on October 2, the night before I met Chuck Miller at the Double Tree, Helen Chenoweth-Hage, not wearing her seatbelt, was thrown from an automobile while holding her five-month-old granddaughter in her lap. The baby was uninjured but Helen, unrestrained to the end, was dead, as Chuck had just told us. But she had already passed the nugget of Hage's success—*property rights law*—to the Colorado well owners, via auctioneer. Chuck's point? That if farmers and ranchers were to be vindicated, it would not be in water court. (Colorado and Montana are the only states in the union to have a water court.)

Chuck reached to clink glasses. Bottoms up? I wondered. Ben Eaton's great-great-granddaughter's environmental-activist hands wrapped around a big, fat bourbon in a room full of devastated men and women who hated environmentalists: whiskey is for drinking; water is for fighting.

.... ■■ ■■ ....

"It's those birds." "Them plovers," I heard people mutter. These comments were but overture to an additional act in the drama: Nebraska was getting what might otherwise be Colorado farm water.

Preexisting in the South Platte River Compact, the interstate agreement approved by the US Congress is a legal stipulation that kicks in during summer drought. Colorado must deliver at least 120 cubic-feet-per-second of flow over the state line. Since precipitation had been adequate for years, many well owners didn't know that Western Canal, just over the Nebraska state line, had an 1897 water right for that amount. When Western Canal had a call on the river, rights junior to 1897 east of the Balzac gauge had to shut off diversions.

Moreover, come to find out that there was a new and additional demand, a federal demand, to push higher peak flows into Nebraska. This boost of water, the feds said, would force sand downstream to supply nesting conditions for a small fluffy shorebird called the piping plover, which is threatened with extinction.

In the mid-1990s, biologists could only find ninety-one breeding pairs of piping plovers on the Nebraska stretch of the Platte downstream. The problem was insufficient sandbars, which is where plovers breed, and least terns too. The largest bird in the United States, the whooping crane, is another habitué along the shallow lower Platte, and the crane is *endangered*, even worse off than the plover. The US Fish & Wildlife Service aimed to increase the breeding pairs of piping plovers there in Nebraska to 140. And they wanted to see those ninety-eight additional birds not just once, but for fifteen years. It didn't seem like much to ask. After analyzing the river's shortfall, it was decided that an additional 417,000 acre-feet of water yearly from the South and North Platte should do the trick.[5]

Whoa! That's a load of water, many times the amount that the WAS lands "consumed" in a season. An indignant administrator from Central Colorado Water Conservancy District had demanded: "Since they need sand, why don't they use bulldozers? Why expensive water?" That they wanted water, not dozers, fed the impression of a federal water grab.

You already know about the Platte's transmogrification. Narrower, deeper, and lined with more brush, it no longer has those wide sandbars that struck pioneers dumb and gave shorebirds shores. Nebraska, Wyoming, and Colorado were obliged to comply with the Endangered Species Act (ESA) and flush new sand into the lower Platte. This wasn't optional. And in case anyone thought it was, the feds could point to federal holdings in Colorado. The US government owned 36.6 percent of Colorado.[6] Many of the cities' high-mountain reservoirs were federally financed and on federal land. The cities would need permit renewals and additional reservoirs. And in trying to construct their own reservoirs, the cities had been bruised by the ESA before. Whatever the feds wanted, the feds were going to get. And they wouldn't be satisfied with dozers; they wanted water.

Therefore, on July 1, 1997, the three governors and the US secretary of the Interior signed a cooperative agreement for a "recovery implementation program"

Conservation Status

- **DELISTED**: removed from any of the at-risk statuses below.

- **SPECIES OF CONCERN**: not yet given status but have been identified as important to monitor.

- **THREATENED**: population in danger of falling below a sustainable threshold, likely to become an endangered species in the foreseeable future throughout all or a significant portion of its range.

- **ENDANGERED**: population numbers low enough and habitat insufficient to meet needs, such that the species is thought to be approaching extinction.

- **EXTINCT**: none of the species remains.

in the Central and Lower Platte Basins. That's when the money began to flow. To pay for contractors, the federal government allocated $2.2 million and the State of Colorado $1.35 million.[7] Greatly simplified, the goal was to figure out how to generate more sandbars along a 10,000-acre stretch by increasing the peak flow in the river. Gearing up for this project took thirteen years. Not for three years did anyone think to mention that Wyoming's Kingsley Dam and the Central Nebraska Public Power and Irrigation District's canal system were sediment traps that were going to prevent sand from reaching the restoration site.[8] That took some sorting out.

I have a rancher friend, a former Colorado agriculture commissioner, who harbors his own irritations with ESA protections. At Recovery Implementation Project meetings he attended during his tenure in the 1990s, his impression was that decision makers' responsibility for caching water for the birds was, even early on, going to be foisted on groundwater-rights owners in the lower reaches of the state. Another participant told me that as more federal money was allocated, more people came to the table and the project became a "taffy pull." Certainly, municipal reservoirs were going to allocate water. On the surface of it, stakeholders at the meetings spoke with a "warm, fuzzy kindness" for the ag well owners, according to these participants. But whatever was going on in the Lower Platte, "that's a farmer problem," they said. "We don't have to mess with that." And the legislature? Same thing: "That's the farmers' problem. Let them take care of it."

Not until the fed's final Environmental Impact Statement and Biological Opinion were issued in 2006 did WAS members really get wind of the "Three-State Agreement" that had been in the works for twelve years already. With the paperwork coinciding as it did with the well shutdowns, the agreement did *seem* like the farmers' problem.

Reinforced by Hage's plight and other horror stories they'd heard, the well owners' suspicion was that government was using the ESA to manipulate water administration for reasons beyond ninety-eight extra plovers. Riled northeastern Coloradans deduced that Nebraska's new peak flows were going to come from right under their land. Minus summer pumping of the groundwater wells, downstream reservoirs would fill more easily, they reasoned. That's how it was that night at the Double Tree gathering.

The premise of the ESA is to stop, or at least slow, extinctions of species such as the whooping crane, piping plover, least tern, and pallid sturgeon, all named in the Recovery Implementation Program. When the ESA passed in 1973, its preamble stated that endangered species of fish, wildlife, and plants "are of esthetic, ecological, educational, historical, recreational, and scientific value to the Nation and its people." Bottom line is that the ESA requires all federal agencies to use their authority to conserve threatened and endangered species.

The ESA often pits environmentalists against agriculture, because endangered species are more common on undeveloped land than in cities, where they've already been driven out or wiped out. The question of whether sustaining a struggling insect, bird, fish, or mammal population is worth incapacitating farm and ranch operations is common. Those who eat most of the food, those in cities, are fairly well insulated from the divisiveness. Some advocacy groups, such as the Family Farm Alliance, are committed to changing this lack of awareness. It can be easier for environmentalists who live in cities, like me, to object to farmers' and ranchers' positions about endangered species, because our urban property rights are not imperiled.

I believe in the impetus behind the Endangered Species Act, believe that the mass extinctions visited upon our time are a bad omen, not just for nature but for all of us. Extinctions caused by or coinciding with the apotheosis of Homo sapiens are abundant enough that the Stratigraphy Commission of the Geological Society of London announced that the Holocene is over. They gave our epoch a new name, the "Anthropocene." We, the eponyms of this freshly coined geologic eon, have nothing to be bigheaded about. In somber prose, wrote observant author Mike Davis, the society warned that the effects of the distinctive contemporary biostratigraphic signal are "permanent, as future evolution will take place from surviving (and frequently anthropogenically relocated) stocks."[9] In other words, one species, our species, has forced evolution into a new trajectory. The Stratigraphical Commission mentioned agricultural monocultures, as well as construction, erosion, denudation, and damming, with the result of creating sedimentation that now "exceeds natural sediment production by an order of magnitude."[10]

So stratigraphers too are sobered by the boundless tectonic upsurge of pressboard, drywall, rebar, and stucco, fastened to impervious concrete slabs that muffle our connection to the Earth's outer layer. Despite best intentions and cutting-edge engineering, that outer layer has been shoved into landforms that distort waterways, generate flooding, and defy healthful breathing and breeding by many species. Meanwhile, the consumptive habits of people living many multipliers away from what any interpretation of "psychogeography" would say is sane, are draining rivers and aquifers, storing water in full sunlight, contaminating and depleting land and ocean resources . . . on and on. Some impacts are from raising food; others precipitate from mitotic urbanism. Development here in San Diego, where I live, rendered the region the hottest "biodiversity hot spot" in the country. What this means is that San Diego has been documented as having both more species and the greatest extinction rate of any county in the continental United States.[11] Twelve hundred miles to the east, Colorado's population is projected to nearly double to between 8.6 and 10 million people by 2050.[12] The region could take a tip from San Diego if it cared to. San Diego doesn't have enough water either.

·········▬·▬·········

However, such thoughts are a luxury, the province of those who are not losing their livelihood, so that night at the Double Tree they occurred to me uselessly. For me, the well shutdown put the shoe on the other foot. I could but slump unhappily in my "progressive" mindset, while Chuck Miller told his Wayne Hage story to the dejected well owners. No one could look forward to leaving their place to expectant heirs or leveraging their water rights into a retirement plan, because population growth, legislation, and court cases of the previous six years—plus weather—had rendered those rights unusable. And like Wayne Hage, no one had been reimbursed, so the well shutdown either felt like or was a "taking," the well owners believed.

At the Double Tree, Dave Knievel, a farmer from Wiggins, many miles east of Big Bend Station, spoke. He and neighboring farmers named Kobobel were beside themselves. They'd received post-pumping depletion schedules, for pumping that the state had approved, that would take years to repay. He held up the kick-to-the-gut list so folks could see it.

As property owners, Knievel and Kobobel had committed, they said, to bring an "inverse condemnation" claim against the state.[13] Hadn't the state's actions deprived of them of their use of rights they had paid for? Wasn't this a 'taking'?"

That was their plan, Dave Knievel said. "And we'd welcome any of you who want to join us," he added as other well owners stirred nervously. "So think about it." (A ruling on the Kobobel-Knievel case would be several years away.)

"A taking may happen through regulation?" someone asked.

"Yeah, regulations that deprive you of your vested rights."

"Land isn't worth a damn if you can't use your wells."

"Water rights are the most valuable part of the property."

"So the water's just there in the ground doing nothing."

"How's that for beneficial?"

"And waste. How about the waste?

Waving an arm so old and brittle that it looked as if it might break off, one old farmer railed, "It was the government that got us them wells in the first place! If y'all 'll remember, most of them was installed with cost-share."

Near Brighton, Colorado, the Frank family, which used to farm 1,200 acres, was reduced to only 600 acres. They had twelve wells shut down. Lauri Frank said she'd take a hailstorm any day over the legal quagmire they had now.

Ronnie Ackerman added, "Colorado water courts have their own standard. It's 'guilty until proven innocent.' That's contrary to one of the foundations of American law, isn't it? In every other circumstance *guilt has to be proven.* Presumption of guilt isn't punishable."

"What you sayin', Ronnie?"

"Shouldn't the entity with the injured right have to *prove* injury? Just saying that it could happen is like saying we're going to take away your driver's license because, well, you might potentially, maybe kill someone. That's what this requirement to replace 100 percent ahead of time does to us. We have to buy water, even for depletions that might occur *when we're in priority.*"

Well owners hadn't been there at water court in May to hear and see Central's proposal for WAS, to hear and see the numerical models the objectors had used as evidence against them. Their trust in Central destroyed, the well users had only their own experience in and on the land, as well as the state's annual approvals all those years. No one had proven, to the farmers' and ranchers' satisfaction, that the well users had actually injured anyone.

Ronnie's other observation was that the State of Colorado had reneged on what should've been its responsibility. When the wells came into the priority system in 1969 (with the passage of the Water Rights Determination and Administration Act), the state might have moved to administer groundwater *in priority,* as it does with surface water. Water commissioners allow and disallow surface-rights holders like ditch companies from diverting, in priority and in accordance with calls on the river. Surface-rights holders make calls on the river. Well owners can't. He asked, "Why doesn't that same administration apply to groundwater? They forced us into the system. Since the depletion shows up in the river later, couldn't the state base its priority administration around that?"

"Good point!"

"And if they can't do that, then compensate us . . ."

"Yeah, why the discrimination?"

Neighboring farmers had heard that although Central's attorney had failed to secure their SWSP, he was rumored to have a new car and a new house. His house was appreciating. The farmers' land, agricultural land with limited or no water, continued to depreciate. It dropped 12 percent in a single year (and that was before the mortgage crisis).[14] Not only had water interests successfully parleyed their way through Colorado's inveigled water law to put an end to the pumping, but developers could now buy former farmland at bargain-basement prices.

·········· ▪▪ ··▪▪ ··········

If you want to lose confidence in government, hang out with farmers and ranchers. It was as if the groundwater-rights holders were bobbing on mechanical tracks, trying to muddle forward through legal and financial responsibilities unaided while being shot at. Gogo received another unwelcome letter, saying there was no way the quasi-governmental Central could come up with sufficient augmentation water for all the WAS wells, so it demanded Big Bend Station and other well owners keep only one well in the program. Choosing one meant condemning the others. Gogo isn't a blasphemer, but her response was, "Are you kidding me?" "What the hell?"

With Ronnie's help, Gogo chose the southernmost well, the well below Ernesto and Erminia's house. First knocking off an additional sixty-two acre-feet from the decreed water right for that single well, water to be derived from our ditch right, Central allocated "Ernesto's" well 102.45 acre-feet of consumptive use annually, to irrigate 105 acres. Other such forfeitures diminished WAS's wells from 449 to 219 and their consumptive use from 25,000 to around 15,000 acre-feet. The trial regarding the augmentation plan for Well Augmentation Subdistrict took place between February 5, 2007, and May 3, 2007.

At the trial, attorneys for the senior ditch companies were incredulous with what Central put forward for the augmentation plan. Their thoughts too were, "Are you kidding me?" "What the hell?" Flows on the Platte were so low that the gross inadequacy of the plan had them wondering whether Central's attorneys had actually ever gone back to the board to express the severity of the situation. Many objecting attorneys felt that WAS well owners were the victims of poor advice.

A ruling from the water judge was not expected for several months.[15] Until then, Ernesto's well was like the rest of them—on *lock down*.

In the meantime, the governors of Nebraska, Colorado, and Wyoming signed the final Three-State Agreement for revitalizing sandbar habitat. The cost of so doing—at the time of the well shutdown—was to be $317.33 million dollars for the first thirteen years.[16] The states were engaging in an effort to "retime" water that would eventually flow into Nebraska anyway. Flows were to be "banked" in augmentation recharge ponds at the turkeys' old digs, Tamarack Ranch, to reach the river from March through June.[17] Finally, from Colorado, the Platte River Recovery Implementation Program would require not hundreds of thousands of additional acre-feet, but 10,000 acre-feet of water yearly over the state line at Julesburg. Well Augmentation Subdistrict well owners still felt it was their 10,000 acre-feet.

At last, on June 6, 2008, seventeen long years after Wayne Hage first sued, the US Court of Federal Claims decided that his estate was due $4.2 million from the defendant, the United States of America. With interest and attorney's fees, the total bill to taxpayers will be several times that amount.[18]

Around this time, a fancy new sign with the evocative words "Two Rivers Parkway" appeared a few miles north of Big Bend Station. Not just a new sign but a *bad* sign from our now very-paranoid perspective. After the scene at the Double Tree, I was biting my nails. The new name for an old road seemed to entice urban development from all sides. Apprehensive, Gogo and I made an appointment with the mayor of Milliken, the little town five minutes away. We crossed Two Rivers Parkway to get there. We wanted to know about Milliken's plans to expand.

"There's no plan," then-mayor, Linda Measner said, though she made clear that Milliken was eager to expand. "We certainly don't want to end up like Berthoud," she hastened to add. Mayor Measner said "Berthoud" as though it were a dirty word. We pressed for explanation: Berthoud, to the west of Milliken, had instituted a growth cap a few years before in order to curtail development and preserve its small-town charm, its "quality of life." But with no one moving in, the lack of tax revenues was crippling it. The mayor said that water bills in Berthoud were three times as high as in neighboring towns.

Requirements for building and maintaining infrastructure, much of it related to water, are hot-breath-on-necks in little farm communities such as Berthoud and Milliken. Around there, words like *berthoudize* and *berthoudification* turn up in conversation as admonitions. As we drove back to the farm, my mother turned to me: "We never saw this coming."

The next morning, for me to catch a plane leaving for California at dawn, Gogo and I drove south in the dark. The car windows were open, and the breeze shifted by us in soft sheets. We passed along the boxed edges of Aurora, near Denver International Airport (DIA). Aurora is no Berthoud. By the time air moves over the mountains and hits Aurora's prairie location, it is wrung dry. Low humidity, high winds, and recurring cycles of drought are routine there. Aurora is lucky to get a dozen inches of precipitation annually. In 1891, far from the Platte and its aquifer, a real estate prospector named Donald Fletcher settled the town. Two years later Fletcher slunk away, leaving his neighbors with bond payments for water that hadn't been located. Ever since, Aurora has been serious about securing water, so serious it contested WAS's augmentation plan.

Aurora was the fastest-growing city in America during Colorado's oil boom in the early 1980s. It still promoted itself as the third-largest city in Colorado. That metropolises boast about size is a reflection on American priorities. Why not heart-stoppingly lovely parks named after heroes and poets? Shaded avenues on which to stroll with your lover? Even antigrowth measures? No, instead, we focus on *quantity*. Berthoud's emphasis on quality led to *berthoudification*.

So Aurora tentaculates outward, its unfurling subdivisions reaching to fill in and flatten such prairie farmland as remains between its historic beginnings and DIA. I spotted coyotes, shadowy outlines with eyes lit up by Aurora's lights, moving over the crest of a prairie rise. These prairie rises are really something. Too broad and rolling to be called hills, the graceful undulations presage the Rockies' enormous upwelling . . . until an earthmoving machine blunts them. As the sun struggled to light up this lost paradise, rabbits in the hues of prairie short-grasses moved over remnant nature as if navigating through landmines. *Slow, stop, immobilize, feign invisibility, prepare for the worst*: rabbit wisdom.

The unsuspecting well-owners might as well have been rabbits, so removed were they from control over their destiny. Not even the most badass, take-no-prisoners water shark wearing a custom Brioni suit and Ferragamo shoes could possibly want hundreds of rural families obliterated. Not really. However, drought and population growth had turned water procurement from an addiction into a "secure your acre-feet before someone else gets them." Unfortunately, everyone—the baleful profit mongers, the ingenious attorneys, the proud courts, the bureaucrats, Big Ag with its water-thirsty corn, and mostly complacent city dwellers—*everyone* was driving backward and forward over the future. By flickers and blinks, the lights were going out.

LET THEM EAT TURF

"That doesn't matter to me," Camille [Desmoulins] said. "I just like to see these people falling out amongst themselves, because the more they do that the quicker everything will collapse and the quicker we shall have the republic. If I take sides meanwhile, it's only to help the conflict along."
—HILARY MANTEL, *FROM A PLACE OF GREATER SAFETY*

Custom clothing, maître d's, elegant revelries. No one said that these indulgences, to which my mother was wholly accustomed, would disappear when she and my father moved to Big Bend Station. And, for the most part, they didn't, but urban ties became stakes whenever my parents quibbled. The more invitations Gogo accepted, the frostier Bill became.

"You don't know anything about the farm," he always said.

"You don't tell me anything about the farm," she'd answer.

And that was the end of the discussion, a mostly tacit agreement to divided allegiances, because he wouldn't relinquish control over the business and she wouldn't miss a party. My parents personified the dichotomy between cities and farms, a stubborn refusal to acknowledge their interdependence. Like many city people, Gogo thought farmers were hayseeds. Like many farmers, Bill decided city people were clueless. Between them, the line marking the differences between ag and urban was drawn and redrawn many times, over the forty years since they had moved to Weld County. To the extent that there was tension between them, that was it.

Like a setting from Edith Wharton, their house at Big Bend Station diffused the controversy because they both loved its carpets, its sconces and chandeliers, its leather-bound books, its Chinese pottery, pretty shuttle-woven brocades, and array of sterling . . . its civility. And every night, every night without fail, Gogo dressed for dinner, first pulling on girdle and stockings, right up until the night Bill passed away.

Without him, Gogo could have moved back to Denver, but she didn't. Instead she took to being a widow with the same oomph she had shown long before as a city wife. She let slip the girdle and the woman who had never worked, knew nothing about her assets, and had few responsibilities. In the hollow of a manless house, out came a new Gogo who opened Bill's file cabinets, hired an accountant by the hour, revamped the office and computer system, and asked a lot of questions. Just in time.

. . . . ▬ · · ▬ . . . .

Our wells and the others remained off limits. A hundred thousand acres' worth of food cultivation was out of business. Since the well shutdown two years before, Big Bend Station had paid Central quadruple the amount my father had paid G.A.S.P. over thirty years. (Remember that G.A.S.P. kept Bill's five wells pumping with methods that sufficed until the drought and population growth, and Central was trying to get only one well pumping.) Where was this augmentation that well owners had paid Central Colorado Water Conservancy District and its attorneys to secure?

Not until 2008, two years after the well shutdown, did the water court at last approve the WAS augmentation plan for our one well and 218 others. The ruling was one of the largest and most complicated water-court cases in Colorado history. Trying to track the following paragraphs, you'll believe me.

As the punitive 2003 legislation required, the approval demanded that WAS purchase enough water to replace all the consumptive use in the event of a continuous year-round call. (No other appropriator has this requirement.) Being 75 percent more than the well owners had ever replaced, the obligation effectively decommissioned many wells, as the objectors had intended.

Even that requirement came with big hitches. The objectors had convinced Judge Klein that very old depletions, from way back when G.A.S.P. started in 1974, continued to "injure" them, convinced the water court that the amount of replacement water well owners had provided over thirty years (and state engineers had approved) was inadequate.[1]

"Those objectors used flawed technology that is so complex that no one can understand it . . . and they got away with it!" declared Dr. Chuck Leaf, a longtime hydrologist and expert witness on whom many well owners pinned their hopes. Dr. Leaf cited a report by Robert E. Glover, F. ASCE, the author of the "Glover Method": "Glover stated that "even with pumping the aquifer still recharges every few years, so that a new regimen is established. Well depletions that took place in years past have only minor importance today."[2] The Central Colorado Water Conservancy District's groundwater measurements too reflected this "steady state."

> **Glover Method**
>
> This analytical model, also known as the Glover-Balmer method, has been used to assess the impact of field-based water management of interactions between groundwater and surface water.

Former assistant state engineer Robert Longenbaugh, the one-man force in defense of conjunctive use, stressed that the current augmentation accounting, the Glover and stream depletion factor (SDF) methods, use a number of hydrologic and physical assumptions, which do not match how "Mother Nature" actually controls groundwater return flow to the river. "Assumptions such as flat land, horizontal aquifers of consistent depth and thickness, no rainfall, no deep percolation of irrigation water, and so forth are obviously inconsistent with actual events and conditions. Such faulty assumptions can cause dramatic errors in augmentation accounting. The WAS augmentation decree is suspected never to have been field calibrated, and it is therefore likely that the accounting is seriously in error, not matching Mother Nature," he said.[3]

What of Colorado's 400 gauging stations and canals sending data back to the office by satellite every fifteen minutes? What of state engineers using observations, data, and the history of calls to negotiate G.A.S.P.'s SWSPs presented by Jack Odor for over three decades? The state had approved this pumping.

> **Stream Depletion Factor**
>
> Also known as the SDF, this is a semianalytical method for quantifying stream depletion caused by groundwater withdrawals in alluvial aquifers. Used by the Colorado Division of Water Resources and derived from the Glover method, SDF models account partially for variable transmissivity and nearby aquifer boundaries. They are thought to be accurate only at depletions of 18 percent.

Inexplicably (from the well owners' point of view), the water court did not put the burden of responsibility on the state.

Surely, low flows weren't entirely the well owners depletions! What of the burgeoning populations and the accompanying recharge projects that also depleted the river? What of sprinkler-irrigation efficiencies, conservation, urban reclamation, and reuse, which meant sending less water back to the river?

Before Big Bend Station and other WAS well owners could pump even one well, we, under Central, *first* had to replace 100 percent of the consumptive use that the state had approved us to pump those decades.[4] The farther the well owner was from the river, the more crippling the replacement. Big Bend Station was lucky to be *right on the river*, but our well's depletions wouldn't be replaced for four years! And even then Central might not have secured enough replacement water for us to pump.

To well owners—who had adjudicated their wells to integrate them into the priority system after 1969 at the government's bidding, who had enrolled in G.A.S.P. at the government's bidding, who had switched to the quasi-governmental WAS at the government's bidding, who had winnowed their wells to one. . . likewise at the same bidding—the decision was an astounding travesty. Well Augmentation Subdistrict well owners were being punished for outcomes the government had approved. Moreover, the rules had changed yet again!

There was no dispute that well pumping causes delayed impacts to the river and that the impacts might take weeks, months, and even years to be evident in the river. *The major controversy was the best way to calculate the amount and timing of pumping's actual lagged impacts to the river.*

Unknowns about Aquifers

Aquifer heterogeneity, complex stream geometry, streambed hydraulic conductivity, and finite-width aquifers with complex geometry can have substantial effects on stream-flow depletion that limit the reliability of analytical solutions for many practical applications, particularly basinwide analyses in which multiple wells pump simultaneously.

Computerized numerical-modeling methods can provide more accurate simulation where adequate data is available. It has not been proven that widespread adoption of this method would result in better management of the South Platte system.

SOURCE: Report to the Colorado Legislature, HB12–1278 Study of the South Platte River Alluvial Aquifer, December 31, 2013, 66–67.

Recall, the Central board decided not to "settle," as it had in its other groundwater management plan. The well owners were adamant that 100 percent replacement was much more than their due. Central's attorneys demonstrated that impacts were much less than the objectors' models showed, nowhere more than 5 percent in most years and 25 percent in very dry years, as Glover, Leaf too demonstrated.

Central lit on the idea that Ronnie promoted, that groundwater appropriations should be administered in priority with a *right to call*, as surface rights are. Central's Well Augmentation Subdistrict pointed out that alluvial wells were installed and put to beneficial use prior to Centennial's McClellan Reservoir and Boulder's Barker Reservoir, and much senior to alluvial recharge projects filed in the 1970s (Bijou, Fort Morgan Ditch, etc.). Why couldn't the wells operate ahead of McClellan and Barker when the calling right was the junior downstream reservoirs and recharge projects? The call could be administered as a "bypass" to the calling reservoir in the winter, and would be senior to recharge projects.[5] This idea seemed so reasonable. And just.

Well Augmentation Subdistrict called this concept, which would more closely administer the groundwater appropriations, a "well call." The well call was designed to satisfy the calling right in priority, gauged not on when the well is pumped, but when the pumping depletion arrives at the senior calling-right's headgate on the river. The calling well's depletions would then be in priority, and only junior well depletions would be replaced to satisfy the senior right holder. There was considerable debate and testimony. Objectors protested that well calls would injure vested rights. What about the well owners' vested rights?

Unfortunately, the state's division engineer was uncertain as to how much water the well call would actually provide to the senior right holder. Again that problem of how to calculate the *amount* and *timing* of those impacts. Plus the unknowable weather that might leave very different flow in the river from year to year, season to season, and day to day. Instead of clarifying how well calls might work, testimony and discussion compounded uncertainty as to how well calls would be reliably administered. Finally, Judge Klein ruled that a "well call" could not be decreed.[6]

Some talked as if Judge Klein's long-awaited decision would become landmark. Not WAS well owners. If the division engineer couldn't quantify existing return flows with enough accuracy to administer groundwater well calls in priority, well owners wondered, how could the objectors successfully convince the court that depletions from well owners' pumping thirty years before in the South Platte could be computed? The well owners felt scapegoated. Their actual priority, which in many cases was senior, remained immaterial because unlike other vested rights holders, they didn't have the right to call.

Well Augmentation Subdistrict wells could not pump, even when they were in priority, until that consumptive-use replacement water had been purchased and stored. This so-called Projection Requirement was another double standard, from the well owners' perspective. The only advantage for the WAS wells from the priority system occurs during the daily accounting process of replacement of depletions. If the call on the South Platte River is junior to the 1950s era well decree, on that day or days, the WAS augmentation plan does not have to make replacements.

The slender lifeline built into the WAS decree was its ability to approach the court with evidence that the decree was too strict and that WAS members could pump more and still prevent injury. Not until the tenth year would Central have the opportunity to go back to court to show the court that the projections are overly restrictive.

.... ▬ · ▬ ....

With no farm for miles around pumping from the South Platte Aquifer, tens of thousands of acre-feet of water were unutilized. Flow in the river should have been up, but it wasn't, not at Big Bend Station anyway. The South Platte was lower than ever. Farmers pondered this in the evenings, when they gathered to discuss their options. Gogo was among them, steno pad in hand, and with every event felt herself becoming more at one with the life she had eschewed for so many years.

At the meetings, hydrologists acknowledged that even though flows were low in the immediate vicinity, they were much higher both thirty miles upstream and even thirty miles downstream. "And have you noticed the temperature?" one farmer asked.

"Yes," another answered. "The river water isn't cold anymore."

"Weird kind of drought, isn't it?"

Gogo took notes and I, albeit confused, became her touchstone for rebellion.

Bell peppers, *Capsicum annuum grossum*, had been among Weld County's top vegetable crops. Soon after the well shutdown, my mother paused to scrutinize a bell pepper she had just purchased. Its smooth mounds and valleys felt like a handshake in her palm. Out of curiosity, she got out her magnifying glass and eyed the little sticky country-of-origin label (C.O.O.L.), which vegetables and fruits have these days. "Product of Canada," it said. Canada? My spirited, seventy-six-year-old mother climbed back in her car and, fueled by newfound indignation, returned to her grocer in Greeley, where she upbraided the manager while asking for bell peppers from the United States. There were none.

State restrictions on groundwater pumping did not affect domestic use of water in nearby Greeley, only agriculture. No surprise then that Gogo drove home from Greeley through new subdivisions, which were erupting so vigorously from former farmland that it was as if they too had been sown. And, in a sense, they had. The conversion from farmland to subdivisions was long planned. Narrow rural highways were simply numbered: Highway 60, County Road 532, and so on. More recently, Gogo had watched new signs with new names such as "Traildust Trail" and "School House Drive" gradually replace the county road signs. At first, she was enchanted to find storybook titles attributed to county roads where grain trucks, tractors, and machinery were more common than cars, though it didn't take long to realize that the new names referred to vistas that were to be obscured by developments. Everywhere, new housing, strip malls, and commercial parks repeated as regularly as a pattern on wallpaper. "I'm glad Bill doesn't have to see this," she muttered.

Gogo noted that no matter which development theme she passed—whether Spanish Colonial, Cape Cod, or Tudor—all housing was bracketed, front, back, and sides, *in lawn*. Bell peppers weren't thriving there anymore, but lawn was . . . and in places that were never previously irrigated.

Watching automatic lawn sprinklers chugging around in circles between Greeley and Big Bend Station on land that had historically been prairie—and during the hottest part of the day, when much of the water evaporates, no less— Gogo got madder and madder. She and her hardworking farmer neighbors could no longer grow edible crops, but new housing would have wet grass when their owners returned from workplaces . . . workplaces that were likely skirted in spongy lawn too.

While my mother hunted for US-grown bell peppers and Weld County was being turfed, an Italian scientist named Cristina Milesi tallied American turfgrass. Dr. Milesi found 40 million acres of lawn in the United States.[7] That figure included residential gardens; industrial, commercial, and municipal landscape; golf courses; athletic fields; parks; and over 9,000 acres of sod farms.[8] More than a third of our country's urbanized area was turfgrass.[9] Of this grass, three-quarters was in the arid West, where up to 75 percent of municipal water is used outdoors, most of it for lawn.[10]

America's obsession with lawn dates from the 1800s, when American landscapers began creating English-style estates for the wealthy. Lawn soon became a signature of affluence, the outdoor equivalent of a billiards room and a butler.

Let's Look at Lawn

A 1,000 square-foot lawn requires an average of 120 gallons of irrigation daily. There are 31 million–plus acres of irrigated lawn in the United States. The math looks like this:

5,227.2 gallons per acre / day × 85 days of summer = 444,312 gallons per acre per summer

444,312 gallons × 31 million acres (irrigated US turf) = 13,773,672 million gallons

13,773,672 million divided by 326,000 (gallons in an acre-foot)

= 42,140,522 acre-feet of water expended on lawns each summer in the United States

This makes turfgrass America's largest irrigated crop! A member of the Grass Family (*Poaceae*), whose short roots direct very little water back into groundwater, is taking up that much land and that much water, yet we do not eat it. How nutty is that?

As Gogo reflected, "Even before World War II, nearly everyone who was anyone had lawn in both their front yard and backyard. Parkways had lawn too. The wealthier people were, the more lawn they had." Never mind that England with its lords and ladies gets almost forty inches of rain a year, about four times the precipitation of most land west of Nebraska. Thing was, diverting Colorado snowmelt made lawn affordable when fewer people lived in the West, so lawning spread to the masses, literally a grassroots movement. Soon, even fast-food restaurants had lawns.

At the same time, the chemical industry beguiled consumers with turf builders—mostly petroleum-based inputs. Advertising campaigns featuring "lawn envy" turned yard work into a neighborhood pissing match. Nitrogenous compounds left over from World War I were rebranded as fertilizers. Organophosphates used as nerve gas in World War II made swell insecticides. Clouds of DDT (dichlorodiphenyltrichloroethane) puffed over gardens, parks, and golf courses when I was a child. Sometimes they'd even dust our bodies with DDT where mosquitoes and lawns coexisted. And although DDT was eventually outlawed, the neat fit between the chemical industry and lawnaholics continued to take new forms, right up to the development of today's genetically modified herbicide-resistant turf grasses that withstand and even require regular applications of weed-killing chemical additives. Of course, farmers employ these chemicals on crops, but "lawn-love" gave chemical industries an urban market too.

Gogo wasn't the first person to recognize that Weld County's lawns were a sign of badly skewed priorities. After World War II, the Egyptian government sent a man named Sayyid Qutb to northern Colorado to observe the American educational system. As a devout Muslim, Qutb was appalled by the uncovered women, what he called the "animal-like" intermixing of the sexes, and just as bad, Greeley's "decadent" obsession with lawns. Lawns symbolized America's materialism and selfishness, Qutb wrote in his letters to Egypt.[11] Hailing from an arid land, Qutb must have seen wasting life-giving water as a crime on a satanic scale. Outraged by Western culture of conspicuous consumption, Qutb returned to Egypt, quit civil service, and joined the Muslim Brotherhood, where he quickly rose in the Brotherhood's vaulted Guidance Council. He was eventually executed in 1966. Even dead, Qutb, the man who hated Americans' love of lawns, remains one of the most influential catalysts behind radical Islamic terrorism. Qutb's disciple Ayman al-Zawahiri is now regarded as the leader of Al Qaeda. My mom doesn't know the first thing about terrorism, but Qutb's experience shows that outrage over turf grass can run deep.

.... ▆▆ ·▆▆ ....

The decadent grass that Gogo drove past did not deplete the river near our house, not directly anyway, because Greeley's water supply comes not from the South Platte, but from the Cache la Poudre, Big Thompson, and Colorado Rivers northwest of there, as well as the Laramie River basin. So, why was there so little water in the Platte? Trying to help my mother, I stared hard at the names of municipalities that had prevented farmers from securing augmentation water, as explained in the just visited Spectacle 13. The City of Centennial, a city I'd never heard of, was one. A few revelations proved how much foresight and opportunism it takes to reduce a river's flow and dry up thousands of acres of farms legally.

Centennial, Colorado, called the "sudden city," invented itself at the beginning of the millennium. It incorporated from a hodgepodge of unincorporated developments south of Denver, a place that had been dryland farms and unirrigated pastures when we were children. We'd gone out there to "visit the cows" when Pop was a milkman. The region is more than an hour away from Big Bend Station. Founders named Centennial after James Michener's novel and Colorado's 1876 statehood. The sudden city's immediate goal soon became water.

Much of Centennial is served by Denver Water, but its far eastern portion is served by an entity called the East Cherry Creek Valley Water & Sanitation

District (ECCV). As the drought intensified, ECCV informed its customers that existing groundwater supplies would not last, not at the pace of development. East Cherry Creek Valley Water & Sanitation District had discovered, as Highlands Ranch and other suburbs had, that it was depleting its nonrenewable groundwater supplies. (I want to throw back my head and howl. Surely, developers and permitting agencies anticipated this.) All municipalities, including Centennial, had to commit resources to securing the water their customers actually use—plus an additional portion for augmentation to recharge the river if they used the water out of priority. Every city in the "Denver Metroplex" pursued their double-dip of water, with the goal of securing an allotment before other municipalities beat them to it. As the perfect drought persisted, the quest for new water rights tapped and retapped the South Platte River and aquifer. And it employed a lot of water attorneys.

To the east of the farm, where the South Platte River makes its right-hand turn toward Nebraska, is a wet expanse known as the Beebe Draw . . . wet because for millennia the river's untrammeled flow meandered through the draw, broadening the aquifer. The words *Beebe Draw* are still uttered in hushed tones; it's that hallowed. These wetlands were the Cheyenne's sacred hunting ground. More recently they became sacred hunting ground for large-property owners. In the past, when Gogo and Bill were invited to the Beebe Draw as guests, the take-away feeling was of reverie for a very special place, a "Shangri-La," she said. One of the best birding areas in Colorado, the area's vast marshes attract waders like whimbrels and short-billed dowitchers. They provide an oasis for western grebes and less common dabbling ducks such as Eurasian wigeons, and even harbor upland sandpipers—the "shorebird of the prairie." Ponds at the northern end are called the "70 Lakes," not because there are seventy of them, but because they are strewn around a 25,500-acre spread called the 70 Ranch, itself located on the north side of the Platte and so named because it is seventy miles from Denver, seventy miles from Cheyenne, and seventy miles from Rocky Mountain National Park. In 1992, the sacredness was broken by billionaire Texans, whose historic purpose, seemingly, has been what some would call sacrilege. Sid and Lee Bass bought the 70 Ranch and began developing it as a hog farm.

Years before, when I was still a little girl, my father downed a couple of drinks with members of the Bass family, that same Fort Worth oil family that is one of the largest property owners in the United States. Like crafty predators, the Basses had dropped in on Colorado to perch near Granddad Eaton's large farm at Woods Lake until the heirs stopped squabbling. Pop was the realtor. Over drinks with Pop, the Basses admitted that for them, squabbling heirs signaled opportunity. Like it or not, their business savvy impressed my father, and when the Bass brothers bought the 70 Ranch more than thirty years later, he figured nothing would stop them.

Figuring differently were two wealthy Coloradans, Peter Coors and Philip Anschutz, who owned adjacent property. They hadn't bought tens of thousands of acres of Shangri-La to end up downwind or down gradient from a massive, smelly factory farm that belched methane and leached antibiotic-laced nitrates. The pair mobilized to put the hog farm out of business and, with considerable effort, succeeded. The Bass brothers then off-loaded the 70 Ranch.

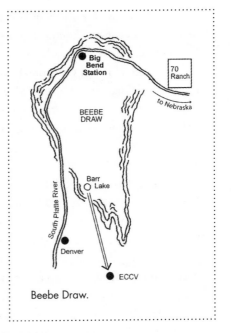

Beebe Draw.

Thirteen years later water speculator Bob Lembke, a suggested "broker of the apocalypse" who showed his nose for water in Spectacle 9, turned up. For $16.75 million, Lembke bought water that the Bass Brothers acquired for augmenting wells on the 70 Ranch, then immediately sold those rights to ECCV for $45 million. Mr. Lembke wasn't the only player. This deal and others like it continued to drive up the per-acre cost of water, making it more and more difficult for anyone, particularly small farmers, to afford augmentation supplies. Several transactions later, his company United Water and Sanitation District owned water rights closer to ECCV customers too.[12] This enabled him to negotiate to pump over a billion gallons a year from the aquifer at the south end of the Beebe Draw, near yet another nature sanctuary, Barr Lake State Park, a sleight of hand that cut forty-five miles off the distance between customers and the 70 Ranch, whence he'd purchased water rights for ECCV from the Bass brothers. Once siphoned from the aquifer, ECCV's appropriated water then travels in pipes an additional thirty miles south to its customers. There, residents and businesses of eastern Centennial and some unincorporated Arapahoe County communities can use it for drink and for lawns.[13] This is ECCV's Northern Project pipeline.

Even deals negotiated by the smart and shrewd Bob Lembke can require recharging the Platte with augmentation water when senior water-rights owners want the water. The Colorado water court did not let ECCV off the hook for replacing water in the South Platte system to satisfy such "calls" on the river. The court approved Mr. Lembke's request to release water back into the Platte seventy miles north of Centennial, way around the corner downstream from Big Bend Station, only when the call was downstream on the river, east of the 70 Ranch. Sometimes, though, calls were upstream, on the segment from Barr Lake right on down past Big Bend Station on the South Platte.

·········■■··■■·········

So, that's it: fast-growing urban areas like those directly east of the Rocky Mountains need water security and can afford to pay ever-more-stratospheric prices for supplies and augmentation, as well as for attorneys. Farmers can't. When those ag shares are bought and transferred to municipal use, dowitchers, grebes, and wigeons are out of luck, not part of the decision making. And by default, small operations such as Gogo's and her neighbors' end up in the same category as the water birds, despite having what may be senior groundwater rights. All the artificial recharge structures are junior in priority to the decreed irrigation wells, yet the recharging persisted, while the irrigation wells were curtailed.[14] City dwellers remand most of the water to lawns (up to 70 percent of domestic freshwater goes to landscape), without realizing that the water deals hurt them too. Letting them know became Gogo's mission.

"The whole time Bill was sick, global warming and water shortages were all over the news, but I didn't pay much attention, because they didn't affect me . . ." my mother corrected herself, " . . . or rather, they didn't *seem* to affect me. The issues were still murky to me. I was taking ballet lessons, for heaven's sake."

"They talk about 'injury' to senior rights' holders. To my mind, the true injury is trading food for golf courses and exotic landscape," Gogo added. "What is the more 'beneficial' use?"

Gogo was so horrified at what was happening—to her neighbors, to the farms, to the food supplies, to the United States (which news of other states' water problems easily conflated)—that she told one person after another. She had more access to Denver and Greeley residents than most farmers. People she had loved her whole life listened to her describe the farmers, the way they looked as beaten down as the Joads. But her friends' sympathy seemed merely polite, even patronizing: "Why don't you just move to Denver, Gogo dear?" they said.

"It felt like a slap in the face," my mother told me.

Had Pop still been alive, she would not have felt the well shutdown so keenly. He wouldn't have let her. That she did despair, that she began speaking out, made her a sudden player in events that have replayed themselves over and over again throughout history. Water scarcity has always been a prescription for upheaval, sometimes revolt. Take late eighteenth century in my breakaway country, France. Drought and poor grain harvests left French peasants without bread. They starved. And they revolted. This same scenario occurred more recently in Somalia, Egypt, and Syria. Farmers lost crops, herds, and ultimately their land to drought. Famine, displacement, and poverty helped push inhabitants into what has become revolt and war.[15] People mock Marie Antoinette's blithe suggestion, "Let them eat cake," because it made her seem out of touch and blind to reality. No more so than we.

Gogo couldn't infect her city friends with the fury that she felt. "*No one* pays attention until something happens to them," she noted.

THE TASTE OF PLUNDER

*Evil is like a shadow—it has no real substance of its own; it is simply a lack of
light. You cannot cause a shadow to disappear by trying to fight it, stamp on it, by
railing against it, or any other form of emotional or physical resistance. In order
to cause a shadow to disappear, you must shine light on it.*
—SHAKTI GAWAIN, *CREATIVE VISUALIZATIONS*

Few register water scarcity as a source of panic in urban areas, for a simple reason: water still pours from the tap. This obliviousness now terrifies me.

Municipalities' quests for water are based on projected population increases.
Colorado, in thrall to its "great and growing cities doctrine," anticipates that
Coloradans will double in number by 2050.[1] Important to consider, Colorado's
population projections (like other state forecasts) are partially predicated by economic forecasts.[2] Before births, deaths, and migrations, these forecasts predict
how many residents are likely given the current forecast of the US and Colorado
economic growth. (Remember that "growth" brings measured benefits without
measuring economic downsides such as pollution, water scarcity, diminished
wildlife, and less food cultivation, among many others.) These official population forecasts legitimize municipalities' pursuit of additional water.

Purchasing water from farmers in what are referred to as "ag-to-urban water
transfers" keeps water flowing to cities and city residents complacent. Without
dramatic changes, Colorado's increase will dry up to one-third of agriculture

and associated wetlands in the South Platte basin, with losses almost as big in the Colorado and Arkansas river basins.[3]

This is only the Colorado example. Other states—with less water, involvement, and debate—may be even worse off.

The transfers work like this: unlike rural communities, municipalities have a huge tax base, plus ratepayer revenues and the opportunity to issue bonds. Cities charge as much for water as they need in order to buy and manage the water utility. Cities take that significant financial advantage, remand some funds to water attorneys, and end up with ag-to-urban solutions, as Centennial did, as Aurora did, as many cities across the United States do. (This process differs from the events and actions that prevent Colorado well users from using their groundwater on 100,000 acres, because there, no purchase occurred.) A clever short-term strategy, such transfers quench the thirst of the voting majority—municipal consumers—but those 14 million acre-feet of water a month that Americans allot to lawn come at the cost of good American-grown food. Problem is that few except farmers and ranchers presently know it. Ag-to-urban water transfers don't prevent discord. Instead, like deficit spending, they add to the eventual toll of an outraged uprising by deferring it.

Gogo recognized that her neighboring farmers represent a diminishing demographic of hardworking, phobic loners who do not have the time, money, or expertise to organize a resistance. (The economy of their operations makes our food affordable.) Smaller farm and ranch families operating at a narrow margin, with big input costs, economize in every way. They don't have the money to compete with cities, to hire lawyers. What farmers have had is *water*. Globally, agriculture accounts for 80 percent of water consumed by humans.[4] Knee-

> **Water Footprint**
>
> The average person in the United States might use 150 gallons a day from his or her municipal water provider for cooking, drinking, bathing, flushing, and landscape. This amount is not all inclusive, because it omits that water that goes into making our food, clothes, energy, and miscellaneous possessions. Producing a glass of milk requires about 100 gallons of water, an apple requires about 28 gallons, and so forth. Packaging requires more water. For example, it takes six or seven times as much water as a bottle of water holds to create the bottle. So average American's "water footprint" rises dramatically from 150 gallons a day to 2,060 gallons a day! The global average is less than half that.
>
> SOURCES: Footprint Network at waterfootprint.org. See also M. M. Mekonnen and A. Y. Hoekstra, "Water Footprint of Nations," May 2011.

jerk reactions to the plights of suddenly waterless farmers are always the same: "Farmers use too much water."

People who comment thusly eat.

Most people are convinced that farmers waste water, water that should rightfully be sent to cities, because this is the spin. Further, most people miss the point that just as humans have high water content, so too does our food. It takes lots of water to raise produce and livestock. Gogo's bell pepper is 87 percent water; a potato is 79 percent water, lettuce 94 percent, beef 78 percent, and so forth. Even this is abstract. Producing a quarter-pound of beef requires an average of 450 gallons of water, three times the average daily amount municipal water providers supply to individual US consumers for drinking, bathing, and irrigation.

Farmers and ranchers aren't *stealing* water from us; they're using it to create commodities we can't live without. And the irrigation water that crops do not consume sinks back into the water table, replenishing groundwater, as the South Platte aquifer studies make evident. Small farmers' methods aren't perfect, but most are not deliberately wasteful. Gogo's neighbors don't have time for long showers or golf. No one is dancing under irrigation equipment in their skivvies, after which they sink into hot tubs. No; they're growing our food.

········ ▄ ▪▄ ········

Encouraged by other farmers, Gogo was swept up in the cause as the "widow of Ben Eaton's great-grandson." This left far less time for keeping up appearances. No ballet. Big Bend Station hemorrhaged to-do lists. Phones rang all the time. There were stacks of paper, newspaper clippings, and Post-its everywhere. Gogo's bed had as many papers on it as her desk.

Maybe Pop would've been proud of her, but it's just as likely that he would have gone ballistic. Approaching eighty years old, she'd let her hair go crazy and was spending little time in girdle and stockings. She lived in khakis, one of Annzo's torn ski parkas from the 1970s, and Rockports, perfect for walking around the farm, which she did regularly, except when there was wind. Windy days whipped over fallowed fields at Big Bend and other farms, blowing away topsoil. Dust storms obscured visibility and left dirt drifts in the roads and up against barns and houses. (These dust storms were evident over northeastern Colorado from the air, a Natural Resources Conservation Service staff person told me.)

"It's never been like this," she told me, gesturing at an old lawn chair out on the road. She'd dragged it to the halfway distance on one of her walks, so she could rest if needed. Running her finger through the deep dirty residue on it, she said, "This is since yesterday. Dust is smothering everything. Air pollution police should see what shutting down wells does to the countryside. Our topsoil! Oh, honey, this makes me so mad. I just can't believe this could happen in our country."

The farm's features had always represented challenges and successes, things to do and things done. The South Platte River remained a reminder of water's tie with wildlife. However, something was gravely wrong; I could see it myself when I visited at Christmastime.

"Where are all the ducks?" I asked. As it warmed up, the landscape was quieter, absent large numbers of songbirds, which had relied on the veil of dense vegetation and relative peace of agricultural open space. Would songbirds' melodies be replaced by the cacophony of starlings and crows that taunt us in cities?

Great blue herons and eagles nest in the Platte's cottonwoods; however, their numbers dwindled too. These birds feed on fish, but with water up in temperature and down in volume, the whole ecosystem went bonkers. "Treated municipal water doesn't seem to be the birds' cup of tea," Gogo said in understatement. Because these birds are usually in pairs, she thinks of them as symbols of partnership. When she sees an eagle, she invariably raises her hand and sends a sparkly-eyed greeting to her husband who adored the wildlife, even from his sickbed. "If he hadn't died, the well shutdown would have killed him," she said over and over again.

Farmers under prey for their water is an age-old story, in which the appropriating of ag water is a recurring theme. From the semifictional 1974 movie *Chinatown*, everyone knows the tragedy of California's Owens Valley, whose farm-irrigation water Los Angeles nabbed in the early twentieth century. Owens Valley is now parched, while L.A. sustains its lawns, even with average rainfall of less than fourteen inches. Las Vegas, once a small agricultural oasis, didn't become a city until 1911 but now has a population around 600,000 thanks to water diversions. Farmers on Arizona's Santa Cruz River capitulated to development in Tucson. Orange County, California, was filled with citrus groves fifty years ago. Now it's all hard surfaces that water slides off and, of course, lawn. You don't have to be old to have watched food sources turn to sprawl all over the West.

In addition to forfeiting food sources, incremental but unceasing development undermines water infiltration and carbon storage. More urbanization means more "heat islands" (heat radiating off roofs, asphalt, and other hard, impermeable surfaces). These changes affect temperatures and weather patterns.[5]

Around the time that the Bass brothers bought the 70 Ranch, I heard that the Basses were also acquiring farmland in California's Imperial Valley, east of where I live in San Diego. Pop had commented, "Watch out."

In the Imperial Valley, a highly productive 500,000 acres, agribusiness is a billion-dollar industry. Sunny year-round, Imperial Valley supplies fruits, vegetables and animal fodder across the United States and abroad. The valley's productivity was a motivator for the 4.4 million acre-feet allocated to California in the 1922 Colorado River Compact (Decision makers during those years were committed to maintaining US-grown food supplies.) The river disgorges whatever is left—less and less these days—into the delta south of the valley.

Eventually, the Bass brothers acquired over 40,000 acres for less than $100 million.[6] Western Farms, they called it. The Texans didn't buy the land to farm, though. Instead, their grand plan was to sell its water rights to San Diego. Here where I live in San Diego—at the tail end of the straw that begins in Colorado— we followed the drama as it unfolded, all the while blithely watering our lawns and filling our swimming pools. San Diego was almost totally dependent on Los Angeles' Metropolitan Water District, which has Colorado River water too, but at a lower priority than the Imperial Irrigation District (IID). Members of the IID board launched a resistance against the Basses, and it was decided that individual farmers could not sell their water, only the IID could. Foiled, as they had been in Colorado, the Bass brothers sold their land in 1997 for an amount then worth $350 million to US. Filter, a private utility that then claimed to be the largest provider of water and wastewater treatment.[7] A multinational private water company named Vivendi Environment bought US. Filter in 1999.[8]

Yet, Pop was right. The equilibrium had been disturbed. By then water supplies had tightened, and the IID board had members who thought selling water

Differences between Imperial Valley and South Platte Water Rights Owners

Unlike Imperial Valley farmers and ranchers, Colorado well owners received no options or remuneration, because another entity did not buy their water rights. Rather, the terms of complying with use of their water rights abruptly went from "usually 5 percent and never greater than 25 percent augmentation on an annual basis" to 100 percent in perpetuity, plus thirty years' worth of repaying post-pumping depletions that were greater than those the well owners understood to be occurring. These terms are so severe and costly that many and even most wells may be out of business permanently. Because the wells are not pumping, more water is available to other users, many of them junior to the wells.

to San Diego made sense. In 2003, the board made a deal to deliver 200,000 acre-feet to San Diego annually for seventy-five years, for $50 million a year. The payout was a historic enormity, the largest ag-to-urban water transfer in history. Imperial Valley farmers got an option to fallow their fields in exchange for money. In the first year, though, barely enough farmers took the option. Nervous about securing future annual allotments with strictly voluntary options, the IID bought Western Farms from Vivendi (now named Veolia).

The next year Los Angeles' big cash-rich water heavy, Metropolitan Water District (MWD) turned up at the threshold to lean on the IID. Recognizing that the deal would dry up the last US stop on the Pacific flyway, the Salton Sea, birders and environmentalists went ballistic, but few cared that ornithologists anticipated major die-offs. The numbers who cared about food crop losses were outmaneuvered too. Metropolitan Water District negotiated a deal—to buy up to 110,000 acre-feet annually. The agency offered such a high price for fallowing that many farmers found it irresistible. Metropolitan Water District made a similar deal in the likewise high-yielding Palo Verde Irrigation District and continued sniffing out ag-to-urban transfers all over Central and Southern California. By the time my father passed away, a now crisis-level asthma epidemic from the shrinking Salton Sea's airborne lakebed contaminants had begun.

Beggaring vs. Buying

In Colorado, when ag land is dried up by sale of the water, sometimes cities lease water back to the farmers and ranchers. If the water is gone for good, the decree must provide for revegetation of the land. However, the well owners' land did not benefit from these provisions, because the dry-up did not result from purchases. No other entity bought the water rights. Rather, the terms of complying with use of the water rights became prohibitive, leaving the possibility of desertification.

In the last twenty-five years, almost 107,000 square miles of American farmland have gone out of business.[9] New housing is *erupting* from former agricultural land (which in its time replaced prairie). Three-quarters of a million acres of farms disappeared in Colorado between 1997 and 2012.[10] Adding in the 2009 crisis in California's San Joaquin Valley made that an area about the size of Colorado that was no longer growing food. As small ag operations sell out, or even before they sell out, they sell their water too . . . or have it shanghaied.

Yes, down-on-their-luck farmers and ranchers, a burgeoning demographic, sell their water rights right out from under their land. This "unbundling," as it is known, doesn't lead back to prairie; it leads to "desertification." Decoupling land from its water sources kills the plants, animals, and even microbes that depend on the water, potentially rendering the land sterile. Desertification removes the carbon fixing, air-purifying open space, and it creates other costly environmental problems. It makes Earth hotter. Hence, farmers and ranchers themselves participate in the growing transfer of agricultural water rights to use for long showers, lawns, swimming pools, and golf courses.

By securing water supplies, municipalities buy time, irrespective of the fact that so doing plots biological, environmental, and *eventual human health hazards*, first by desiccating so much land. This practice, which is rampant in the West, has enough unconnected dots that it can be overlooked, except by its immediate victims: the farmers. This isn't an exaggeration; check out the air pollution problems promulgated by the receding Salton Sea, which is dreadful enough to be on the radar of the nation's then water czar: Anne Castle. Some attribute blowing pollution impacts affecting residents 150 miles in Los Angeles to the receding sea, with proposed remediation in the billions of dollars.

Eight out of ten water sales in the western United States are by individual farmers or their irrigation districts to municipalities.[11] Thanks to ingenious propaganda, this leaves the impression that farmers *want* to sell their water, that they're eager for deals. Not if the farmers at Weld County meetings are any indication! They don't want to sell anything except crops. They don't want to live, except to farm. You've never seen such a beaten-down bunch. Not a smile among them, their bodies are so wrung with sorrow that I thought that they would be lucky to keep the shells a careful distance from their shotguns.

It may sound as if I'm overdramatizing, but I'm not; it was awful. It is awful. Driving out to the farm, one feels the anguish of that shallow stretch, a life force being drained. The collective immobilizing weight of thousands in crisis hangs over the South Platte. If one includes the panic of farm animals and wildlife, those numbers balloon to millions, to billions, and even trillions when considering collapsing systems of plants and microorganisms.

One day Gogo learned that just up the road, at the next farm south, her neighbor, a woman just her age, was dead. (I omit her name, to protect her family.) That morning, this neighbor had seen her husband off to whatever was left of his daily regime, since he could no longer pump water. In her husband's absence, an itinerant farmworker, by then unemployed and deranged, did his worst.

Horror spread across the countryside and grew as the story was retold. The murder was very close to Big Bend Station. Gogo went up to see her friend, the farmer widower and his children, not knowing what to say, then visited him again days later, still at a loss for words. Barely able to speak, he mumbled, "This shouldn't happen to anyone, Gogo."

Grief and fear found what irrigation could no longer find—new depths. The death didn't make sense. None of it made sense. *All northeastern Colorado farmers were trying to do was raise crops that would be made into food for the masses.* No one could look at their homes the same. No longer refuges, not even as safe as prisons, their farms both wounded and exposed them. Farmers were, as if impaled on their farms, impaled to the life they loved. Ag-to-urban water transfers that are unwanted can as much as vivisect people who have given their lives to farming.

One of Gogo's friends sent me a *Denver Post* article reporting that between 2004 and 2009, fifty-three Colorado farmers committed suicide.[12] Data were not correlated to community or causes. After reading this, I spoke with a prevention specialist in northeastern Colorado, where she is a native with family-farming ties.

She explained that for most farmers, farming is not a career choice, an 8-to-5 job that can shift to another 8-to-5 job when they run into problems. Farming is in their blood. Their fathers were farmers, previous generations too. They aren't going to retire from farming, because there is nothing else that they aspire to do. Single events such as drought compound common constraints, such as more calls on the river, rising feed costs and lower dairy prices. These can coincide and/or domino with other tragedies such as foreclosures and failed banks. That's when suicides can happen.

The culture demands pulling yourself up by your bootstraps. Mental illness is not "real" out here, she said. Emotions equal weakness. So when times are hard, as since the shutdown, no one suggests: "Why don't you get some counseling?" Despite the difficult lifestyle, despite the growing evidence that pesticide exposures can increase vulnerability to depression, there are few health providers in the country.[13] Even if you are struggling, you don't want your vehicle spotted at the mental health clinic. Passersby would recognize the truck and think you were weak. People are tough. Many don't have health insurance. They tend to self-medicate, to take fate into their own hands.

Bottom line, for farmers, farming defines them and is their legacy for their children and generations to come. And shells don't always stay separate from the guns. That leaves the rest of us, the other 305 million Americans, still here, bumper-to-bumper on the drought-drying road to nowhere . . . only we don't know it.

Fruit and Vegetable Imports Exceed Exports

United States fruit and vegetable exports totaled more than $7 billion in 2011, but US imports of fruits and vegetables exceeded $18 billion (excludes nuts and processed nut products). This trade deficit is widening.

SOURCE: Renée Johnson, *The U.S. Trade Situation for Fruit and Vegetable Products*, Congressional Research Service, January 15, 2014.

Whether farmland water is bought, as it was in Imperial Valley, or beggared for want of water, as it was in northeastern Colorado, the results are the same. Ag-to-urban water transfers eliminate biodiversity, degrade air and water quality, and erode US citizens' access to American-grown food—which grows best in the sunny West. (In the early years of the millennium, over 46 percent of our country's crop value was grown on irrigated western farms, which accounted for 10 percent of US cropland.[14])

No one is telling municipal residents that their water comes at the expense of healthy, secure food supplies for the whole nation. No one is protecting consumers. Not really. The deprivation isn't apparent, because grocery aisles are still jammed with food. It is not as if this is accidental. Multinational food companies such as ADM, Cargill, ConAgra, and others spent the Uruguay Round of GATT (Global Agreement on Trade and Tariffs from 1986 to 94) eviscerating national protections for domestic agriculture worldwide. The document, entitled the Agriculture Agreement, was the hub around which turned the newly established World Trade Organization (WTO), which replaced the GATT in 1995. Member governments of WTO agreed, or were forced to agree, to improve market access and reduce ag subsidies.

Where Refinement Becomes a Wall

Growers and ranchers who operate close to cities are increasingly selling directly to grocers or at farmers' markets. This opportunity is not practical for farmers who grow grains, as explained in Spectacle 7, "Hypocrisy, in a Kernel." Their commodities are not comestible until they are refined. Since growing grain usually requires more land, these farmers are located in more remote areas and, unfortunately, are more easily forgotten.

It all seems so beneficent, but the multinationals' agenda was to eliminate barriers to farming where cheap labor is abundant, regulation nonexistent, and water easily commandeered. That agenda was realized. The WTO became a passport to food production abroad. In those foreign countries, these giant corporations have displaced domestic food production and ravaged the environment. Every container

194

full of grain, vegetables, fruits and meat, and dairy products to enter the United States represents both a depletion of some other country's water as well as a lost opportunity for American farmers and ranchers. And lest you think this outsourcing is only conservatives' doing, note that the North American Free Trade Agreement was signed into being in 1994. (NAFTA explains Gogo's red pepper from Canada.) The Clinton administration had a strong relationship with Ernest Micek, then Cargill's CEO, with whom President Clinton traveled to Africa to promote free trade there.[15]

Since the WTO creation in 1995, US agricultural exports have increased by only one-half of a percent.[16] Meanwhile, between 2003 and 2013 US food imports doubled.[17] Between 1982 and 2007, annual US imports of fresh fruit and vegetables have almost tripled.[18] And globalists are still at it today, with the push for the Trans-Pacific Partnership, for which Cargill and other multinationals want a fast track that gives presidential administrations the ability to make trade deals, bypassing Congress.[19] In May 2015, the WTO rejected US meat labeling, removing another layer of consumer and grower protections.[20]

"Why can't people see and taste that this is not the same food?" Gogo wanted to know. Not long after, my son bought filet mignon from Mexico!

Fruit and vegetables harvested abroad weeks before arriving here are comestible versions of smoke and mirrors. Sure, science has made food more cosmetically perfect. But as anyone who eats tomatoes knows, looks say nothing about taste. Nutrient value either. Foods are harvested before they ripen, limiting nutritional value. More nutrients are lost in the interval between harvest and tabletop.[21] Storing and processing imports in megafacilities contribute to contamination. Then there's the fumigation and irradiation. The greater the distance between farm and plate, the greater the carbon debt as measured in fuel. So yes, faucets still gush, but every time we turn them on we are sacrificing safer, more nutritious food. At the same time, we're accelerating global warming and absconding with other countries' precious water. Sorry to harangue, but I'm worried.

"Maybe people are too weakened from eating crummy food to act, Gogo," I speculated.

"Yes, maybe that explains complacency," she agreed. "Oh, it makes me so sad. And mad!"

.... ▬ ▬ ....

My mother isn't a whiner. If anything, she's a Pollyanna. Expecting an unwieldy bureaucracy, charged with inspecting and authorizing edibles from all over the world—grown, harvested, stored, transported, and processed in myriad places and ways and for differing time periods—to keep us eating healthily, is a lot to ask. Yes, it is worth asking, but with the margins for error growing, it makes sense to assume some responsibility for food security ourselves. As Gogo did.

Retrenching, she installed security gates, so the ravaged unemployed couldn't get *her*. She made a conscientious effort to eat American and eat well. She planted and mulched her little vegetable garden, which she irrigated with domestic, not agricultural, water. Her dog Pluck, who had numerous times torn into unsuspecting visitors, became part of Gogo's resistance. Pluck was suddenly the beneficiary of acupressure, laboriously cooked food with added vitamins, and extra walks, the goal being to keep the cur barking as long as possible. Refusing to sell Big Bend Station's access to the aquifer—a death sentence for the land and wildlife—Gogo left crop selection to the Ackermans' discretion. This gave us time to rethink Big Bend Station's moneymaking.

Gogo still knew little of farming. What she had learned was the topic of *responsibility*, because she hadn't left the farm when Bill died and was determined to make the inheritance work, not just for herself but for consumers. And Gogo decided—though perhaps not in so many words—that responsibility for what we eat mimics a kind of love, a topic about which she knew something. A relationship with food can begin with attraction and progress through phases of inquiry, interaction, and experimentation, just like a love affair, until we actually know our food better and commit to it. And the closer the food is grown to home, she thought, the greater the accountability of the grower, making it easier to build a commitment. Then she sat down to correspond with the governor.

She wrote that America's farmers are its sustenance, its very foundation, that everyone's health requires commitment to these hardworking people who are so much a part of what has made America great. She wrote that the well shutdown baffled her because it revealed an unrecognizable America that did not honor hard work but would undermine farmers so that cities might have lawns.

When Colorado governor Bill Ritter didn't respond, Gogo smoothed down her hair, climbed into her city clothes and drove to Denver for a rally at the capitol steps. She stood with her neighbors, people who, unlike her, had no safety net, who had little except loans collateralized by their land and water rights, which were now useless. At the podium, my tiny mom was too nervous to speak, so another farmer read Gogo's letter aloud, until near the end, when she put her hand on his arm, then spoke for herself:

"People in cities think farm life is some kind of escape, a rural idyll. That's what my husband and I thought when we moved to the country forty years ago, that we'd have cows and chickens and raise beautiful vegetables, for ourselves and for profit. But we learned that farm life is not fun and games. Growing delicious food is backbreaking work with constant risk and grave downsides. Unlike a lot of professions, though, *it is essential.* Essential. People in cities don't understand that they cannot live without farmers, don't understand and don't seem to care. Food is not a right. It is an agreement between growers and consumers. When farmers lose water—whether by being outmaneuvered by government or water wholesalers—*everyone* loses. By the time people in cities understand that their American-grown food supplies are cut off, it may be too late."

Then looking out over the small group of urbanites who had gathered, she said, "My husband used to say that we needed a revolution. What he didn't say was who or what would spark the revolution. Most Americans don't yet know the answer."

Pausing, she looked down. Gogo ran her thumb back and forth over her wedding band, almost conspiratorially, then added, "But *I do.*"

NEAR-DEATH EXPERIENCE

That's where life begins . . . marshes, sloughs, tide-pools . . . he was fascinated by them . . . you know when we first came out here he figured that if you dumped water onto desert sand it would percolate down into the bedrock and stay there, instead of evaporating the way it does in most reservoirs. You'd lose only twenty percent instead of seventy or eighty. He made this city.
—NOAH CROSS CHARACTER, *CHINATOWN*

My yearning to tell the story is racing against change, into the time without frogs. The yearning and the change are far apart, to either side of me, like two roads. They seem as if they will eventually converge in the distance, on a horizon. Yet as I move forward, the yearning and the change remain at my flanks, far apart.

"You should hear the croaking!" Gogo used to announce.

"All night long?"

"Yes, the usual serenade. Frogs announce spring . . . time to plant."

Frogs at the farm seemed inexorable, a yearly tide that couldn't be stopped. Remember Pop with his bucket and the nail polish? Their numbers were epic, but no one thought of them as a plague, because their croaking was such a pleasure. Plus, they kept the bugs down.

So removed from nature was I in those days that I thought of Big Bend Station's frogs as belonging only to the farm. In my mind, tadpoles appeared there through spontaneous generation every spring like clockwork, matured into adult frogs by summer then wisely dematerialized before the first frost—poof!—according to some Manifesto of Frogdom that kept them from freezing to death. I recognized no other acquaintance with these finger-length, green-brown characters with their blackish spots. Not until much later did it dawn on me that I had met this very species of frog, the Northern Leopard Frog (*Lithobates pipiens*), earlier and under different circumstances, when my ghoulish junior high school biology teacher apportioned me one. There were that many Northern Leopard Frogs—enough to pith in biology classes across America.

If pressed, I might have guessed, "yes, frogs eat insects," but my thoughts went no further. I didn't consider a buffet of mosquitos, beetles, worms, and gnats that might only occur in a certain wet, green setting. Nor did I know that because frogs' mouths open so very wide, they can make a meal of birds, little snakes, and other frogs, even bats! And this contemplation never extended higher up the food chain, to what preys upon frogs, other than biology students.

As it happens, great blue herons eat frogs. Raccoons, hawks, and eagles too. Today's discovery that herons eat frogs is hitting me particularly hard, because, in a not-altogether-soulful way I recognized the heron as my "watch bird" a few years ago, when I at last *went outside*. With long limbs and a beak I resemble a heron, so the idea of having a watch bird isn't a primal communion so much as solipsism. Nonetheless, I am now worried that "my" herons at the farm have nothing to eat.

I am stewing about all this now and at last, because the ineluctable yearly tide has stopped. There are now no frogs.

Where did they go? And could we entice them to return? I decided first to study our erstwhile frogs' habits.

.... ▬ · ▬ ....

Unlike most carnivores, who must be cunning to eat, frogs simply hang out. When a meal flits into view, the frogs' mandibles unhinge and their long, sticky tongues unfurl. Snap! Down the gullet the meal goes. Frogs find plenty to eat in and around water. Like us, holed up in a deli. Neither did frogs evolve to evade. If pathogens appear in their water, evasive measures don't occur to them. Frogs' entire world is linked to water. Today, their world is shrinking and less livable.

The Manifesto of Frogdom decrees that Northern Leopard Frogs hibernated beneath oxygen-rich water, as long as it didn't freeze. The farm has many suitable wintering opportunities—under the ice-crusted Beaver Pond, or on the leeside of a rock at the hardly there Yacht Club that is smaller than a dinghy, and, best of all, the never-freezes slough. The frogs didn't seem to burrow, but instead settled on top of the substrate. Overwintering there, lightly dusted in silt, the frogs lowered their heartbeat, their breath, their temperature, their appetite, and their sex drive, to wait out the winter.

Let's talk about frog sex. Amplexus, which is frog talk for breeding posture, occurs in ponds and slow-moving pools. The Yacht Club was ideal. As the weather warmed from mid-March until mid-May, adult frogs shook off their silt and found, like the rest of us, that they felt lusty. Males uttered their deep-throated call, often in water four to five inches deep, and grasped at somewhat larger females or anything similar in size, including other males. Male leopard frogs mounted females from behind, tightly grasping under their shapely fore-legs in amplexus, which lasted up to several hours. When females at last laid their eggs, usually attached to plants, males roundly fertilized them with sperm-filled fluid.

Colorado herpetologist, Dr. Lauren Livo figured that she'd experience species reductions in her lifetime. What she didn't figure was that she'd watch Northern Leopard Frog egg masses in a pond reduced by half one year, then reduced again by half the next year, and again the year after, until suddenly there were no more egg masses. Much of what I am now describing is thanks to Dr. Livo's descriptions.[1]

Providing eggs made it through the egg-mass phase at the farm, four days to two weeks later, depending on temperature, tadpoles hatched. Vulnerable at this point, they clung to the disintegrating gelatin of the egg mass, incorporating the remaining egg yolk into their elongated bodies. After about a week, the tadpoles started swimming around, their tiny rows of teeth gnawing at algae, bacteria, and detritus. Over eight to twelve weeks, limb buds near their tails began developing into rear legs. As the tadpoles grew in size, under the skin, the forelegs took shape. Then suddenly, in "metamorphosis," the forelegs popped out, the tail was absorbed, the gut changed in length, and the mouth grew and grew, to allow the transition from herbivore to predator. In late fall, frogs, including the year's crop of froglets, followed the retreating water back to the farm's wettest places, to wait out winter in torpor.

All seemed dandy for our Northern Leopard Frogs after my parents took possession of Big Bend Station, what with the slough and Pop's sending the water back to the river through the Yacht Club and wetland. The curtailed wells, though, afforded less water to the wetland.

Yet in the last fifteen years, frog populations have tanked, not just at the farm, not just all over the West, *but all over the world*. In Colorado, the Northern Leopard Frog is today a "species of concern." Globally, roughly *40 percent* of amphibian species are dwindling. More than 200 species have gone extinct since the 1970s! Some feel the rapid decline is part a great mass extinction event.[2] Most people, when they hear about this, are sad, feeling nostalgic for "the time of frogs." *Cute little things.* Sympathy is not enough! The trend is worse than that—really shocking—not least because it reveals important information about the wet stuff upon which we depend. Frog losses *may* presage grave effects to humankind and turn the frogs into Cassandras. (I include the word "may" only because conversations with scientists have taught me to pad my hysteric claims.)

According to Dr. Livo, "The reasons for abnormalities and dramatically reduced populations are varied, complex and not definitively studied, even though declines in amphibian populations are common the world over. The tools we needed to study declines were developed well after the declines had already occurred."[3]

> **Etiology**
>
> An etiology is a cause or the study of causes. The possible etiologies of Northern Leopard Frog losses in Colorado include
>
> - Habitat destruction
> - Water pollution
> - Competitive species
> - Emerging diseases
> - Solar ultraviolet radiation

Suspect causes of frog disappearance, however inconclusive and challenging to separate from one another, constitute their own glimpse of the past fifty years on the South Platte River.

Front Range prairies used to be strewn with ephemeral creeks and ponds that although adding little to river flow, nevertheless recharged aquifers. These prairie sinks entertained a large number of incremental exchanges between water and land. How beautiful that the ephemeral wetlands provided the momentary inundation that Northern Leopard Frogs required for breeding![4] A hundred years ago (1915) leopard frogs were "reported as very abundant near all of the ponds and lakes in eastern Colorado."[5] Not all wetlands were natural. Rural settlers constructed some too, increasing favorable habitat. Tragically, Front Range development—by scraping, filling, and building over these depressions—dealt what many biologists including Dr. Livo believe is a major blow to the species, especially in urban and suburban areas.[6]

Think of it. Water has fewer and fewer means of getting *into* the earth, because concrete, asphalt, and roofing cut it off. Construction patterns in Colorado are like everywhere: flattened, heavily hardscape, lots of commercial strip malls. Between 1986 and 1998, in the same dozen years that the frog numbers were tanking, impervious surfaces between Denver and Greeley increased by almost

Impervious Surfaces

These impermeable areas prevent precipitation from soaking into the land. Examples are roofs, parking lots, streets, driveways, sidewalks, malls, and freeways.

a third. Irrigated cropland too declined by a third. Often, raw ranch and farmland—hitherto pervious—was subdivided and largely covered in roofs, concrete, and shallow-rooted lawns—hardscape or relative hardscape through which water does not percolate. And wetlands declined by 65 percent![7]

A catastrophic enormity, "65 percent" leaves me faint. Wetlands are our planet's most efficient means of recharging terrestrial water supplies. Put another way, wetlands keep freshwater from flooding, from sliding into oceans . . .

Humans are woefully unacquainted with wetlands (that's why the sidebar). The reasons are many.[8] People tend to associate fens, sloughs, and marshes with the worst that the planet has to offer. Bogs, estuaries, and swamps too = bad mojo. Indeed, as low spots in the topography, they do tend to accumulate unpleasantness that we'd prefer to ignore, even though much (and ever more) of it is our doing. As a "place to be," though, wetlands are the province of species other than human. Rich repositories of microorganisms and slippery, squiggly denizens, they provide nurseries and food for birds, fish, and frogs. Recall the crawdads! Wetlands are difficult to know because to slog through them is to injure them. Navigating wetland is also strenuous. That does not, however, mean that they aren't valuable. As I've said, we can't live without wetlands and their rapid destruction is at the core of everything wrong in the world—from frog decline to climate change to famine, and from famine to war.

Wetland

This distinct ecosystem is saturated with water, either seasonally or permanently. It is characterized by hydrophytic soils and plants, plus periodic inundation.

Wetlands are considered:

• carbon sinks,
• the most productive ecosystems in terms of mobilizing nutrients,
• only 2 percent of the state of Colorado's surface but supporting 75 percent of its species,
• a natural means of cleansing and filtering pollutants, and
• the most biodiverse ecosystems on the planet.

So, inspired by my friend Jim Peugh, whose adage is "save another wetland and then you die," I thought one thing we might do to recuperate frogdom at the farm would be to get the wetland wet again . . . except we had no real clue what our legal water rights were, or which water source we could use.

We consulted an attorney. She advised us to get our oldest, most senior water right, the Big Bend Ditch, in play.

"Though repairing its headgate may be a considerable expense," she added.

Looking at the Arne Johnson court records made me paranoid. If my father hadn't maintained the headgate, there might be some question about our ownership. All of us assumed the headgate was not on our property but upstream where the slough split from the river.

So we set off to investigate. On foot, Annzo, Will, Gogo, and I followed the ditch, which turns into the slough, toward Bennie Guterson's place. At Bennie's farm, the cattails were as dense as a heart of darkness. The water converged from all directions. Based on cattail growth, we deduced that water seeping from the bluff and water flowing from the river dovetailed in the slough. The court documents from Arne and Pop's suit in the 1970s mentioned the seep. This was agricultural runoff, unused irrigation water from up-gradient farms worming its way back to the Platte. It didn't seem as if we could possibly make our way through the sharp cattails to the Platte and the headgate, not without machetes.

> **The Slough of Despond**
>
> In John Bunyan's allegory *The Pilgrim's Progress*, published in 1678, the Slough of Despond is a deep bog into which his character "Christian" sinks. Christian is burdened by his sins and his sense of guilt for them. Humanity's "sins" find their way to wetlands in the form of pollution and decay. That Bunyan's character passes "from This World to That Which is to Come" is also apt since wetlands transform pollution and decay into new life.

"Maintaining the headgate is part of proving your water right," the attorney had told us. It was dispiriting. That's when we called Bennie.

Bennie Guterson is the oldest man I have ever met. And any man would be happy to be as with it and fit as Bennie in his golden years. When a cow kicked Bennie, he made himself famous by crawling home across several football-fields lengths with a broken arm and fractured pelvis. At the time, he was into his nineties. Bennie's farm abuts ours at the southwest corner. Sometimes his cows wander, and when that happens Bennie ambles in pursuit, a pith helmet on his head and a stick in his hand, prepared to herd them home. His family has farmed here for several generations, way back when the well digging first occurred. When it comes to historical records, Bennie's memory is more reliable than any.

"Bennie, we're looking for the Big Bend Ditch headgate."

"Nah, yer in the wrong place," he answered, gesturing. "Up here, that ain' the headgate. That here is part o' the river. It's the East Channel, a meander."

We stared at Bennie with bafflement. "We thought the headgate was over there on the river," Will said pointing to the west.

Bennie flapped a hand toward the river with disinterest. "Nah, there's nothing down there but what you see, that mess o' cattails."

"Then, Bennie," Annzo asked, "Do you know where the headgate is?"

"Sure," Bennie nodded. And it was a relief to see him smile since we were worried. "The Big Bend don' divert until down there on yer property. It's at the other end of the cottonwoods there. That's the headgate."

"Where?" Will asked.

"By that li'l pond."

We were surprised . . . and jubilant. Bennie's words confirmed our right's standing, because my father had always maintained that headgate. Because Bennie's recollection saved us a few $100,000 we didn't have, Annzo, Gogo, and I all but kissed Bennie. Will shook his hand.

.... ▬ ▪▬ ....

Pop had used the Big Bend Ditch for his Yacht Club pond (only big enough to float a few decoys) and for the wetland, though those amenities had almost created themselves because the water table is so high there. It never occurred to Pop that the usage might require adjudication because he applied the ditchwater on fields where it had always been used. Flowing off the slough, the water just meandered there on its way back to the river.

The well shutdown suddenly made renewing this use an issue. I wasn't sure it was legal. Annzo was busy sorting out a property-boundary rights issue and left the water rights up to Will and me. Will likes to keep things simple. He told me not to worry. Gogo agreed with whatever Will said. And I, the innate stewer, stewed about losing 3.48 cubic feet a second—either by bringing it to the water commissioner's attention or by failing to bring it to the water commissioner's attention.

"All we have to do is divert the water like Pop did," Will said matter-of-factly.

"But like Ronnie [Ackerman] said, Will, we don't want to get reported to the water commissioner." Anymore, when land greened up, neighbors wanted to know where the water came from.

"What's your idea then?"

Up river at the Aquatic and Wetland Company, the nursery owners told us good things about Ducks Unlimited's Matt Reddy, the biologist for a restoration at Chestnut Slough just east of Big Bend Station. Ducks Unlimited, which has been around for almost eighty years, is helpful to hunters, but the organization's real focus is improving and increasing wildfowl abundance. And that means wetlands.

So observant Matt Reddy, part of whose job is to envision wetlands, showed up in his boots. With him, we clomped along the Dike Road then scrambled down the revetment and over the stile to the dry wetland with its mounds of brown sedge. Already he was optimistic about conditions, dry as they were. Matt explained that ducks forage on aquatic vegetation and small aquatic species. This builds fat and calcium reserves (for eggs), before they fly north to the "Prairie Pothole" in eastern Montana, Saskatchewan, and Alberta, to breed and nest. (Will already knew this but I didn't.)

A flock of small marsh birds called soras were plucking their way through the muddier patches that day, their thick bills as yellow as bananas. Matt pointed out lady's thumb (*Persicaria maculosa*) from the "Smartweed" family. The pink flowers give way to black seeds that the ducks love. Snails and other aquatic species fatten on the lady's thumb leaves. Another plant here, called lamb's-quarters (*Chenopodium album*), is one even humans might like. Tastes like spinach. (Lady's thumb and lamb's-quarters are naturalized, not native. We'd have to replant natives.)

"And look at that," Matt cried. "There's a Northern Leopard Frog! Got many?"

"That's the problem," Will said, scouting in vain for more frogs.

"Not nearly as many as we used to. Will ducks eat the frogs?"

"Occasionally, but they usually have their eye on other—smaller—bits. Herons, on the other hand . . . "

"Oh! The herons."

Matt explained that shallow-water complexes (such as our wetland if it were intermittently wet) functionally mimic the seasonal overbanking that occurred before the Platte was dammed and tightly controlled. Being temporary, wetlands benefit leopard frogs as well as waders like the soras. And, as I've already said, these fecund sanctuaries help keep water *in the land*, not in the Gulf of Mexico.

From the wetlands, we drove down to the Woods. Matt was excited about its proximity to the river and the warm-water slough—the ideal "thermal cover" for wildfowl in cold weather.

"Have you noticed fewer ducks here in the last few years, Matt?"

"Surveys are inadequate because wildlife agencies are underfunded," he answered. "But populations are definitely shifting. Sandbars and point bars are shrubbier because there are fewer peak flows to scour them. The river is also incised and deeper, because bank stabilization keeps it from being dynamic, as you know."

Remaking the wetlands wouldn't be difficult or expensive, Matt explained, if we used a system called "moist soil management." The method encourages growth of seed-producing wetland plants by mimicking the seasonal wet and dry cycles of natural wetlands.

"Which brings us to the status of your water rights."

The thorny topic. We groaned.

"You have decreed surface water rights, right?

"Yes, ditch shares in the Western Mutual and Big Bend."

"You're using the Western on row-crops. I believe I read that 3.48 cfs (cubic feet per second) is still allocated to the Big Bend Ditch, and that the wetland conservation area was irrigable with Big Bend shares in 1956."

"Does it use the word *conservation*?" I was skeptical.

"You'd have to take a closer look at the decree to determine its utility for the wetland."

"Okay sure, Matt, but we need to be careful, because obviously the water rights are valuable and under siege. That . . . and we don't know what we're doing."

Matt warned us that the economic recession had Ducks Unlimited in a pinch, but said he'd get back to us. He left. Will went back to Montana; I went back to California.

And Gogo went back to the incessant yanking that goes with running 400 acres, a more deeply complicated place that was now in her hands. She also hired a consultant to do an exhaustive title search, so we'd have every deed and

---

Moist Soil Management

1. Gradually draw water off wetlands in the spring.
2. When summer arrives, disk, mow, burn, or crop to eliminate undesirable vegetation.
3. Gradually flood moist-soil habitat in the fall, to create shallow mudflats and boost seed production in water-loving plants such as smartweeds and millet.

Water depths ranging from less than 1 inch to 18 inches will support the greatest diversity.

Every site is unique, so it may take some experimentation to determine the optimal timing and depth of flooding in the area. To obtain desired plant communities and wildlife habitat, sometimes drain-lines, water-control structures, and low terraces improve the hydrology. Wetlands are dynamic, so moist-soil management changes year to year.

---

legal description for our water rights, plus their location and how much water we might legally use. It may seem weird that Pop had left her without this water information. On the other hand, he'd never guessed that something so plentiful on the farm would turn into a war.

·········■··■·········

Here we were trying to figure out if we could reapply our surface-water rights to the wetlands, when additional *problems cropped up*, just as veteran hydrologist Chuck Leaf predicted. Now with some 2,400 wells curtailed, water tables rose. Five minutes to the east, up on the bench by the Gilcrest Farm Supply, farmers had water in their basements! Five minutes north of there, in La Salle, it was the same. The "source" again—such emergencies summoned us to reexamine assumptions about population and water demand, about economic growth, and about water administration. Oddly, only those adversely affected—not the water administrators themselves—seemed agitated.

Dr. Leaf liked to say that the "river forgets." Maybe so, but the aquifer seemed to be doing all the remembering. No sign of historic cones of depression in sight, former assistant state engineer Robert Longenbaugh reminded his peers of the state engineer's responsibility to *maximize beneficial use*. "Overaugmentation injures senior well rights owners and causes property damage. The state engineer ought to be evoking "retained jurisdiction" to manage and to prevent injury," Mr. Longenbaugh told me.[9] The WAS augmentation-plan decree had *invited* evidence that the decree was too strict, hadn't it? The aquifer overflowing into fields and basements was evidentiary. Many water professionals, farmers and ranchers were in agreement that curtailed WAS wells and overaugmentation were responsible, yet the state engineer made no move.

In response, the state legislature announced, *not* that the well owners could pump or even use the water, *not* that those with property damages would receive restitution, but that the state would fund a $780,000 South Platte River and Alluvial Aquifer Study (HB 1278) through Colorado State University.[10]

·········■··■·········

Trying to be positive, I dug deeper into plausible causes for the frogs' disappearance and what it would take to encourage a reappearance, I chatted with the scientists from government agencies, universities, and nonprofits. Whether they attributed frog troubles to "multifactorial etiologies" or untrammelled urbanization, they all said more or less the same thing. "In any of these situations where you have massive land-use change, it's tough to tease apart which elements are the major contributors to changes in a species status," said Harry Crockett, a Colorado Parks and Wildlife biologist.

Habitat destruction began to feel like only the most obvious and uncontroversial culprit. Whereas I had no luck getting employed herpetologists to finger chemical manufacturers (because none had conducted the studies themselves), the Internet is full of stories of scientists who have spoken out against various substances only to be smacked down with ceaseless seemingly corporate espionage, lab break-ins, discrediting, and sometimes dismissal. Another hurdle: grant funding tends to follow commerce. Because wetlands and rivers contain ever-fewer human food species, funding to study them is limited and unlikely to support attacks on business.

It's not that amphibian woes have no human ramifications; au contraire. Like amphibians, birds and other mammals, our stomach enzymes work on whatever we swallow, but topical contact and breathing expose us too. We're not invincible. We store contaminants and might eventually exhibit health problems. They just take longer to beleaguer or kill us. Like any species, we are also vulnerable to slow, generational impacts to our immune, reproductive, and other systems that ultimately affect population numbers.

Living in the water, frogs and other aquatic species do not share our luxury of time. Cold-blooded amphibians metabolize even slower than humans, but they cannot discriminate between what to drink and not to drink, because they drink through their skin. Substances go directly into their bloodstream with immediate effect. As such, frogs function as an early-warning system for other species, including us. It's not unlikely that if we want to learn how disregard for water will eventually get to us, the frog story will tell us. *I am spending a lot of time on frogs, readers, because the situation represents costly downsides that are too poorly reflected in the official water-administration dialogue.*

These sentinels' alarming decline suggests, as one cause among many, *foul water.*

The August 1, 1969, issue of *Time* magazine described Ohio's Cuyahoga River catching fire. Public pressure over a river that "oozes rather than flows" in which a person "does not drown but decays" prompted President Richard Nixon to propose water-quality protections. Nixon strove to quiet the disquiet, not necessarily to prompt far-reaching legislation. Nonetheless, in 1972, Congress passed the bill that was later officially named the Clean Water Act. Such is the power of airing disquietude.

The Clean Water Act's broad goal is to restore and maintain the chemical, physical, and biological integrity of the nation's waters so that they can support "the protection and propagation of fish, shellfish, and wildlife and recreation in and on the water." All surface waters are supposed to be safe enough to be fishable and swimmable, and they cannot carry untreated waste.

These objectives are not easily achieved. As Barb Horn, Colorado Parks and Wildlife biologist and founder of Colorado's River Watch, says, "Even though we act like we know 110 percent of what's in water, we don't know even 10 percent."[11]

In Europe, Barb Horn explained, environmental regulation is based on an assumption of damage. Still have fears? No permits. Most European countries ban fracking, for example, because its safety has not been reliably proven there. In the United States, by contrast, the Clean Water Act is based on *probability risk assessment*. Like most US environmental regulation, the Clean Water Act is "reactive." Only proven harm generates enforcement. The profusion of chemicals and microbes complicates determinations. Which pollutant is to blame? Once the pollutant is isolated, the agency must establish how much can be tolerated before agents even begin to enforce thresholds. As we know from *Erin Brockovich*, this can take years and sometimes mortalities.

So contaminants can enter the water in a few drops or in great abundance before alarms sound. And after the grim reaper arrives, it can take many more years of studies and counterstudies before action is taken. More than 80,000 chemicals available in the United States have never been fully tested for their toxic effects on our health and environment. Dangerously, subsequent legislation called the Toxic Substances Control Act makes it nearly impossible for the EPA to take regulatory action against dangerous chemicals, even those known to cause cancer or other serious health defects. Since the mid-1970s, the EPA has only required comprehensive testing for about 200 chemicals, and has partially regulated just 5![12]

That said, the EPA has established maximum contaminant levels (MCLs) in human drinking water for some ninety organic and inorganic chemicals, and has used these MCLs to require remediation of sources before they reach groundwater and surface water.

The Clean Water Act's enforcement is only as strong as the monitoring that ascertains contaminant levels, both in drinking water and at its sources. Monitoring is not well funded. The EPA can require chemical manufacturers to monitor and to report releases of these chemicals, after which the manufacturers submit their data to federal officials.[13] Reports submitted to EPA are signed and stamped by registered professional engineers, attesting to the reports' accuracy under penalty of perjury. Officers of corporations operating the facilities are required to do likewise. What can happen, though, according to an April

2014 article in *The New Yorker*: "Industries have a greater role in the American regulatory process—they may sue regulators if there are errors in the scientific record—and cost-benefit analyses are integral to decisions: a monetary value is assigned to disease, impairments, and shortened lives and weighed against the benefits of keeping a chemical in use."[14]

Atrazine is a high-profile example. After Monsanto's glyphosate products, atrazine is the second most popular weed-killer in the United States. Patented by Syngenta and now off-patent, the broadleaf-weed herbicide is widely used on golf courses and lawns, as well as corn and other crops. Sales in the United States are estimated at about $300 million a year.[15] In 2001, atrazine was the most commonly detected pesticide contaminating surface and groundwater in the United States.[16] In 2003, the EPA calculated that the total national economic impact resulting from withdrawing the use of atrazine to control grass and broadleaf weeds in corn, sorghum, and sugarcane would be in excess of $2 billion per year.[17] Two billion dollars—there's that monetary benchmark that the cost of disease and impairments must outdistance. However, the assessment did not quantify the difficult-to-quantify externalities (the third-party costs) of keeping atrazine on the market, because the veracity of those externalities was still in question. Atrazine was banned in Europe in 2004 but not in the United States.

The EPA polices atrazine levels in drinking water but an investigation by *The New York Times* found that atrazine concentrations in drinking water spiked following seasonal periods of application and hydrological events, sometimes for longer than a month. The reports produced by local water systems often fail to reflect those higher concentrations.[18]

Atrazine's presence in frogs' medium (surface water) is unabated. Published laboratory investigations demonstrated that atrazine is a teratogen, a substance that causes birth defects. It appears to act through endocrine disruption, rendering the reproductive systems of male amphibians and fish an uneasy mixture of male and female reproductive tissues. In some studies of Northern Leopard Frogs, the rate of "hermaphroditism" (as the effect is referred to) was as high as 92 percent.[19] However, the EPA (in concert with Syngenta, according to *The New Yorker* article) was unable to replicate these results.[20] Whether atrazine is or isn't part of the cause, amphibians and fish throughout the world continue to manifest hermaphroditism, and endocrine disruption is rampant.

Endocrine systems regulate hormones. Hormones are the body's messengers. Some chemicals mimic natural hormones, fooling the body into responding to the stimulus. Some chemicals block the effects of a hormone from certain receptors (e.g., growth hormones required for normal development). Still others directly stimulate or inhibit the endocrine system, causing overproduction or underproduction of hormones. A dozen years ago, the crosshairs were trained on pesticides and antibiotics in the water. Despite the public's implication as consumers, as usual the buzz blamed agriculture. Targeting popular pharmaceuticals and other consumer products touches more of a nerve.

Downstream of municipal effluent, in two locations, scientists found antidepressants (Effexor and fluoxetine) in the brains of native white suckerfish (*Catostomus commersoni*).[21] Talk about depressing! In a follow-up lab study, they examined the behavioral effects of exposed larval fathead minnows (*Pimephales promelas*). The animals were slow to evade predators.[22] Scientists speculate that in the long term, these subtle behavioral effects could lead to population reductions. Had frog instincts too been blunted by mood elevators?

> ### Endocrine Disruptors
>
> Like atrazine, chemicals such as 17β-estradiol, estrone, steroidal hormones, nonylphenol, phthalates, boron, bismuth, gadolinium, and ethylenediaminetetraacetic acid are ubiquitous and are used in pharmaceuticals, personal care products, cleaning agents, diagnostics, thermal receipts, packaging, plastics, electronics, or other products and processes that are usually more concentrated in urban settings.

When I told Gogo about the fathead minnows as a potential indicator species, she remarked, "I bet the canaries are happy this isn't on them."

In 2009, my then teenage son Diego read of "endocrine disruptors" affecting frogs and fish. Increasingly, "up to 7 percent of boys are now born with undescended testicles and malformed genitalia," the article said![23] Diego dialed up our municipal water supplier about this. The representative copped to endocrine disruptors in the municipal water supply, and explained that the EPA hadn't yet told the municipalities what to do. Then, she asked him, "Are you hairy?"

"Yes, why?" my son asked.

"If you have a lot of facial and body hair, you don't have to worry about this."

Shocked, Diego wanted us to get a water purifier.

Seven years later, as of 2016, the EPA is *still* evaluating selected chemicals as potential endocrine disrupters and implementing policies and procedures for screening over a multiyear process.[24] Meanwhile, contaminants of emerging concern (pharmaceuticals, hormones, personal care products, etc.) are not currently part of the regulatory requirements for drinking water quality or for wastewater treatment plant discharge.

What about our sentinels!

Suckers are notoriously tolerant of poor water conditions, but scientists at the University of Colorado found gender-blurred white suckerfish below municipal outflows at Boulder Creek. Males were carrying eggs.[25] In the absence of federal action, the City of Boulder went to work to reduce the endocrine disruptors in its effluent. The wastewater treatment facility improved the removal efficiency, particularly reducing the 17β-estradiol and estrone. The white suckers went back to normal.[26] Well, that's a relief, but it doesn't mean every other city on the Platte (or in the United States) is doing likewise.

Dr. Livo, who has spent her professional life nose-to-nose with the frog topic, referred to a study on intersexed frogs across a range of contexts. It concerned not leopard frogs but green frogs and found that both suburban and urban land covers increased the presence of abnormal sexual development. There was no evidence associating agricultural land cover with abnormalities. This examination suggests that cities are the hotspots for abnormal sexual development.[27]

Focused on reversing Big Bend Station's froglessness, I had help from pragmatic, hardworking men: I was very lucky to make the acquaintance of by-then-retired state engineer Hal Simpson, with his lifetime's understanding of water administration. As a consultant, he urged us to put aside our apprehension and broach the use of the Big Bend Ditch with the water commissioner. Bill Schneider, then with the Colorado Division of Water Resources, arrived to review our plan for the wetland and to determine whether an additional water right was necessary. And Ronnie Ackerman was on hand too, all 6'5" of him.

Carbon in Wetlands

In addition to intercepting nitrogen and phosphorous, constructed agricultural wetlands can also accumulate approximately a ton of soil carbon per acre yearly. Carbon in wetland soil can remain there for hundreds to thousands of years because water-logged conditions inhibit microbial decomposition. Wetlands can store carbon more effectively than rainforests!

Higher carbon dioxide in the atmosphere helps decrease objectionable methane emissions from wetlands. Methane emitted into the atmosphere decreased by 80 percent in areas of doubled carbon dioxide levels.

SOURCES: "Farming Carbon: Study Reveals Potent Carbon Storage Potential of Man-Made Wetlands" (American Society of Agronomy, June 24, 2013); Jill L. Bubier and Tim R. Moore, "An Ecological Perspective on Methane Emissions from Northern Wetlands" (McGill University, Montreal, December 1994).

At first Bill Schneider thought we were off our nut—you want to irrigate not crops but wetlands?—but luckily Hal was there to build confidence. The plan was to funnel our ditchwater through the wetlands when there is no call, as in winter. We wouldn't be storing water and wouldn't be growing crops. The water will soak back into the aquifer and/or return to the river. In the interim, it'll sequester carbon and provide habitat for shorebirds, ducks, and maybe frogs.

I scampered after the three guys toward the minuscule Yacht Club with its decrepit headgate. From behind his Fu Manchu, the then water commissioner asked, "This pond hold water?"

"Not really," Ronnie said.

"But it could. Seems like you should file a new conditional right. [Meaning that the priority date, if granted, would be in the year we filed.] As long as you're filing, you could get a storage right," said Bill Schneider.

"You're going to need to repair the headgate, install some staff gauges so you know what you're diverting," Hal added.

"I think you're going to need a survey," Bill Schneider said, "so you know what the area holds now and what it could hold."

"Well, it doesn't hold much. Water disappears right through it," Ronnie said.

Chatting out there, we got around to water quality. On his phone Ronnie flashed us a recent photo of wastewater discharge at a town near the farm. The stomach-turning chunks of green-brown could've been frogs from a blender. "How can that be legal?" I asked.

"Yep, that's what I wondered," Ronnie said.

"They factor in that the effluent will be diluted in the river," Bill Schneider explained.

"But there are so many cities doing it . . . " I said with incredulity.

All Colorado cities must meet municipal wastewater discharge requirements imposed by the Colorado Department of Public Health and Environment. All treatment facilities are in compliance. Some cities release more volume than others, of course. Metropolitan Wastewater Reclamation District (MWRD) serves Denver, Arvada, Aurora, Brighton,

> **Conditional Water Rights**
>
> An applicant may file for a conditional water right, obtain a priority date, and then put the money into the development of the right—such that ultimately, the entity can file to have the conditional right made absolute. This legally permissible form of speculation is applicable only when the beneficial use of a water right demands expenditure and time. The applicant can be assured that the investment of time and money will lead to the right being made absolute with the earlier priority date.

Lakewood, Thornton, and Westminster. Its effluent makes up at least 60 percent of the flow of the South Platte River directly downstream, and during the summer the river's flow below MWRD is almost entirely the facility's discharge.[28] Otherwise the river would be nearly empty.

Discharging many times the effluent of any other municipal treatment plant on the South Platte, MWRD is held to ever-stricter compliance. Through multiple complex mechanisms, wastewater treatment sifts and diminishes the guck from water before discharging the effluent into the river. The effluent looks and is cleaner than it was before treatment, but—remembering those as-yet unregulated "contaminants of emerging concern"—still contains a complex mixture of chemicals. Then there is the "leave behind." Whatever is not discharged doesn't just demolecularize. Most goes into biosolids that are then used as fertilizer.

In biosolids, the EPA admits the presence of metals, steroids, hormones, pharmaceuticals, and semivolatile or polycyclic aromatic hydrocarbons.[29] This stuff isn't necessarily inert; nor does it necessarily degrade quickly. Once the biosolids are land-applied as fertilizer on turf and crop fields, their constituents can take different environmental pathways into water, into soil, into food, into wildlife, into us. Contaminants of emerging concern in biosolids are sufficiently persistent and mobile to move vertically into the soil column, even in semiarid regions.[30] At the time of my writing, the EPA is not yet at the phase of protecting the frogs or us from biosolids. As posted on the EPA website, the agency is working to "fill the knowledge gaps."[31] The reason for mentioning this isn't to finger the facilities or regulators, as much to point out that turning human consumptive habits into someone else's problem downstream is exploitative, irresponsible, and unsustainable. We might improve water quality each of us by foregoing, switching brands, and so on. Or putting municipal intake downstream from the outfall . . .

As distinguished from wastewater, in runoff and storm water, humanity's unpleasantness travels the fast-moving superhighways of city infrastructure. The more developed the land, the more hardscape and the higher the concentrations of nitrate, phosphorous, dissolved solids, and suspended sediment in the water downstream.[32] Plus heavy metals, plus the insistent pharmacopeia. Much of this slurry finds its way back to the Platte (and other rivers worldwide, all of which lead to oceans). Agriculture causes pollution too, of course, but the widening slab of impervious surfaces and the concentration of nitrogen in urban areas have made urban runoff the leading source of water-quality impairment of surface waters in the United States.[33] "Surface waters" are the frogs' living room, dining room, bedroom, and nursery.

The time-honored defense against this cauldron bubble is soil and vegetation. Plants have no problem recognizing excrement as "nutrients," converting them to robust growth. This system has worked well for millions of years, but the last century has delivered chemical and microbial anomalies that are both mixed with sewage and hard to get rid of. Moreover, excrement (not just ours, but from the animals we eat) has burgeoned, even as porous, irrigable land has shrunk. Plants still "grow clean water" (sometimes at constructed municipal wetlands), but with less irrigable land they can't keep up with the load. We need more wetlands! Not just here and there and in sanctuaries, but everywhere.

"Eutrophication" is a sometimes outcome of elevated nutrient concentration, less common in running water than in reservoirs. In Greek, a *eutrophia* is a place with lots to eat. Like a buffet line, the profusion of nutrients in still water can get out of hand. The greedy push to the front, elbowing out the less aggressive. Organisms stampede the food sources, and suffocation can ensue. Fertilizers and sewage aren't everyone's dish, but phytoplankton such as algae *love* them. Perhaps you've seen vivid chlorophyll-green algae blooms, in the chaos in Toledo over Lake Erie, or even gotten a whiff of the unpleasant smell from a distance. You may even have felt how slimy they are. This is eutrophication. The gunk costs the water its oxygen, leaving it in a state of hypoxia (depletion of oxygen in the water, as a result of decomposers eating a huge amount of algae). So frogs, down there in the water, are unable to do what frogs do—exchange oxygen through their skin.

> **Sewage = Nutrients**
>
> Organic waste (excrement) is high in nitrogen and phosphorus, the same ingredients in chemical fertilizer.

Salt and Aquatic Life

A consistent and favorable level of salinity is important to aquatic life, because it keeps cell density in balance. Distilled or deionized water flows into the organism's cells causing them to swell. Low salinity causes them to float. High salinity causes cells to shrink, changing the organism's ability to move in the water column, so they sink in the water beyond their normal range. Amphibians, as a result of their semipermeable skin, cannot tolerate water with salinity higher than their own body fluids (below 2,000 parts per million).

Salinity is another suspect affecting frogs in the negative. Egg development may be especially affected by salinity. Kicking southward along the Dike Road with the dog, I see what Ronnie is talking about in the pasture. The verdant mat of meadow sedge thins and becomes patchy at the top of the field. Most of it is brown. The soil is moist, so the problem isn't drought. Ronnie says the water table is salty right there. Farmers had been noticing that waterlogged soils from high groundwater levels and using surface water for drip irrigation were together increasing soil salinization. Salinity reduces plants' water and nutrient uptake.

Historically, if you really wanted to undermine an enemy you salted his fields. Now we're doing it to ourselves and not just at our farm. Salinity is the measure of salts such as sodium chloride, calcium bicarbonate, and calcium sulfate dissolved in water. Saline springs and erosion of saline geologic formations can make water salty. The rest of the problem is anthropogenic. Water evaporates with use, leaving that which remains more concentrated, so each reuse issues water of higher salinity, a consideration in water reclamation. When water is stored in reservoirs, it evaporates, thickening the brew. Chemicals used in industry add to salinity. Transbasin diversions add to salinity. According to wetland scientist Laurie Gilligan of the Colorado Natural Heritage Program, its researchers hardly ever see wetlands of salinity less than 1,000 parts per million anymore. Oh, don't let the farm be possessed by nettles in perpetual salty desolation![34]

Get the drift of those "multifactorial etiologies" that are behind species declines?

Over twenty years ago, when the Ebola virus first burst from the jungle and began ravaging humans, Richard Preston's book *The Hot Zone* changed my life. At the time, my quotidian was strictly urban. From the fusty recesses of my subconscious, I could acknowledge that biodiversity was good and that habitat destruction was bad, but such issues were someone else's problem, not mine. And anyway, civilization had Manolo Blahnik and Mark Rothko and the "Tennessee Waltz" to sustain us. Preston's book, however, explained how habitat destruction can lead to infectious disease with the simple observation that for any organism, it's in the best interest to keep the host alive. When we destroy ecosystems where viruses, bacteria, and parasites can thrive without killing their hosts, dislodged species find new hosts. And with fewer immunological defenses, these new hosts may become ill, may even die. "For any organism, it's in the best interest to keep the host alive." Here was a truism that has broad applicability. I could even apply it to parenthood.

So two decades later, I was excited to read that the Johnson Lab at the University of Colorado focuses on biodiversity's relationship with diseases, including human diseases. The question of what amphibian mortalities mean to human health spurs scientist Dr. Pieter Johnson and his collaborators, who write: "To date . . . surprisingly few studies have explored the joint effects of host and parasite richness on disease risk, despite growing interest in the diversity-disease relationship."[35] Even modest extrapolation suggests that humans should not be cavalier about mass extinctions, not if we value our well-being.

Dr. Johnson's team examines conditions that fan epidemics into species losses. *At question is whether, and how, greater biodiversity reduces parasite transmission.* The researchers study these questions through a flatworm, the trematode—uninviting from human perspective but delicious to some freshwater snails. Trematodes are the causative agents behind schistosomiasis, a common disease that affects 210 million people annually and has a negative economic impact second only to malaria.[36]

Similarly, the trematode ribeiroia afflicts amphibians, causing webbing abnormalities and extra limbs that may, by impeding feeding and breeding, lead to early mortality and population reduction. The flatworms can be ingested by *a kind of snail that* hawks, herons, ducks, and even badgers might then gobble. (Herons again.) And note the large food web. The ribeiroia doesn't kill these other animals. More diverse communities dilute the impact of these parasites because less-competent hosts such as herons act as decoys, distracting trematodes and other infectious parasites away from more competent hosts (competency as measured by the parasite's success in colonizing within it). Sure, the flatworms may survive the journey through these large animals' intestines and through their excrement be delivered back into the water, where they may burrow into a frog's developing limb buds. However, a larger food web (biodiversity) reduces the parasites and incidents of infection can decrease.[37] In sum, diversity reduces the odds of disease.

The problem is that as water quality worsens, aquatic communities simplify. There is less biodiversity. With die-off at every level—from larger animals and plants down to the microorganisms—fewer, more tolerant species remain. These are the generalists: "bulletproof" fish such as channel catfish, suckers, small-mouthed bass, carp, fathead minnows, and bluegills remain, plus crawdads and bullfrogs. The American Bullfrog (*Rana catesbeiana*), whose natural range is not Colorado, has become established here in Colorado, possibly because permanent wetlands (such as the now very plentiful reservoirs) that allow the completion of bullfrogs' two-year larval development have become more widespread.[38] Not nearly as charming as its cousin, the bullfrog is however one up on the leopard frog in stamina. Although bullfrogs might be infected with the amphibian chytrid fungus *Batrachochytrium dendrobatidis* (Bd), they rarely become ill. Instead bullfrogs serve as "hosts," shuttling Bd to new environments where it infects other amphibians, including the leopard frog. We've seen bullfrogs at the farm, though not in huge number, thank heaven. By discouraging fish and bullfrogs, ephemeral wetlands like ours are more likely to reassemble Gogo's night choruses of leopard frogs.

Evidently, I have not bothered to disassemble these etiologies. I have dragged you, dear readers, into this swamp of interconnectedness that includes water quality, disease, invasive species, pharmacopeia, ag runoff, impervious surfaces, and us. Our urban-ag medley is a melee, a teetering ecology. Even if the smear of nasty conditions contributing to the frogs' plight turns out to be inexact, unrelated, and irreversible—even if the frogs' breakaway from Planet Earth is not the fault of humans—their mortalities still close around us as tightly as a tunnel. The only glimmer of which I am remotely capable is that of remaking wetlands.

Agriculture-Dependent Wetlands Add Financial Value

Studies in northeastern Colorado found wetlands add an average of $2,200 per acre to property value, both for environmental and recreational benefits. Vegetation provides habitat and forage for wildlife and filters water before it is discharged to surface waters.

SOURCE: The article by Caitlin Coleman, "Grow in Colorado," in Colorado Foundation for Water Education's *Headwaters Magazine*, quoted agricultural agronomist Chris Goemans: "We need to consider what impacts moving water out of agriculture will have and how it will affect us" (fall 2012: 19).

Have I sufficiently explained why? And who do I think I am? What does it take to retool land to adapt to water scarcity and dramatic, even catastrophic events? The audacity of me—to meddle with Big Bend Station's water when our wells were down, amidst people whose priority is cultivating crops, the common good. So I asked Ronnie and Dean if they were too staggeringly miffed to irrigate the wetlands.

"Why?" They stared as if taking the measure of an alien. "It's not as if it'll beggar any crops."

Where go frogs, there goes the planet.

AMERICAN GOTHIC

Hardly are those words out
When a vast image out of Spiritus Mundi
Troubles my sight: a waste of desert sand.
—WILLIAM YEATS, "THE SECOND COMING"

Few find their footing more quickly than those on a high wire. And don't let anyone tell you that tending crops and animals year-round is other than death defying. What do such men and women know of safety nets? At all times, with newborns on their watch, farmers' and ranchers' futures toss around on the weather, global trade, ravenous bugs, grasping conglomerates, and the nutty idea that agriculture is expendable. When the going gets rough, they think on their feet, grab a pitchfork, and dig in.

The well shutdowns petrified Gogo, Annzo, Will, and me. We had no idea how the farm would farm minus those 1,000-plus acre-feet that had been drawn from the aquifer every summer for seventy years. The Ackermans, though, didn't pause for self-pity. Dean was a talker, unwaveringly confident, and occasionally hot under the collar, sometimes at me. His circumspect nephew Ronnie anticipated Dean's thrust and then anchored their course. Decisions between them seemed to happen imperceptibly.

Neoagrarianism

Previous agrarian movements established the social, political, environmental, and economic significance of agriculture.

Concerns stemming from climate, toxicity, extinctions, social and environmental justice, and other contemporary issues have entered the fray. Agriculture's demand for labor, and usually fuel and machinery, continues to challenge solutions to feeding large, diverse populations.

Many diverse people the world over are reexamining the import of sustainability, rural communities, modest scale, and traditional rather than industrial farming. These values echo in cities with surges of community gardens, urban farming, "homesteading," and "spin-farming." Though not always affordable, farmers' markets and community-supported agriculture are other manifestations of neoagrarianism.

A thing is right when it tends to preserve the integrity, stability, and beauty of the biotic community. It is wrong when it tends otherwise.—Aldo Leopold, *A Sand County Almanac* (Oxford, UK: Oxford University Press, 1949)

Soon and in the spirit of simpler times, the Ackermans reverted to "hayers"—men who grew hay—the farmer equivalent of riding a bicycle. Not missing a beat, they quickly covered the benchlands in a seed mix of bluestem and buffalo grass—native species that would eventually establish a dense, matted turf without irrigation. Then they sowed Big Bend Station's lower fields with a flowering member of the pea family, a plant so ubiquitous and unassuming that I'd never given it a second thought—back-to-the-basics alfalfa (*Medicago sativa*).

Alfalfa is one of the planet's oldest crops, its documented use dating from ancient Persia, like much at our latitude. This "queen of forages" is a legume, a nitrogen-fixing cousin of clover that transmutes atmospheric nitrogen into proteins. Without fertilizer! Scientists have recently proven that the plant family's symbiotic relationship with bacteria and fungi dates to the disappearance of the dinosaurs 60 million years ago.[1] That was the last cataclysm, recall, though not so catastrophic as the one we anthropocenes witness today . . . when we so much as dare to look.

In the meantime, alfalfa persists. Now grown throughout the world, the crop can yield the greatest amount of protein per acre of any livestock feed.[2] The plant's protein content is 12 to 20 percent. Palatable and nutritious, alfalfa is grazed, harvested as hay, made into silage, or eaten by us as sprouts. Because global civilizations rely on ruminants for transportation, labor, dairy products, and meat, not for nothing did Middle Eastern horsemen call alfalfa the "father of all foods."

Alfalfa is part poetry but mostly business. The no-till perennial's long roots wriggle a good twelve feet into the soil, and because our lower fields are close to the water table, the crop hasn't required as much irrigation as the corn. It increases organic matter in our otherwise gravelly soil. This, in turn, improves the soil's water-holding capacity, beckoning earthworms and other tiny chompers and burrowers. The alfalfa will be in the ground for seven to twelve years, reducing erosion and compaction. The grasses and alfalfa won't yield as much income as corn, but they put the farm in transition.

The hayers monitored the alfalfa's progress. Had they used fertilizer, a surge of greenery wouldn't necessarily reflect good root growth. But the Ackermans didn't use chemicals, so the robust mounds were an honest reflection of strong plants. Once the alfalfa reached the bud-to early-bloom phase—that's when it has the

Nitrogen Fixation

Nitrogen is critical to biosynthesizing nucleotides for DNA and amino acids for proteins—the building blocks of life. Atmospheric nitrogen is relatively inert, but nitrogen fixation frees the atoms, which are essential for food cultivation.

Protein in Food

Like humans, animals require protein in order to sustain metabolism, cell growth, stimuli response, molecular transport and other crucial body functions. Ergo, feed with higher protein content is valuable.

most protein and the crop is most valuable—it was time to cut. First we waited out a storm, then Ronnie climbed into his swather. The two-armed monster mower moved down the field like Godzilla, spewing arcs of hay. The cut settled in shallow windrows that striped the field. From the house we could track the machine's progress by its buzz, rising as it came closer and subsiding as it returned north. The unfamiliar scent filled the afternoon. It wasn't gardenias. It was the beginning of everything.

For a handful of days the sun and breeze worked the cut, heating and weaving through the fibers to remove moisture. Then Ronnie was back again, first with an outfit to merge the rows and then with a baler. He hoped to get three cuttings before October. He kept some hay for the cattle and sold the rest to nearby dairies.

After a few years the alfalfa plants will get old like the rest of us and need to be rotated out. Leaving the roots to rot in the ground will sequester carbon, build topsoil, and make the soil forget that it is gravelly. Then the Ackermans will grow sorghum for a single season before seeding a new crop of alfalfa. Thus, alfalfa helped Big Bend Station bounce back, despite less water.

········· ▬· ▬·········

Not *bounce back* but *resiliency* is a term that the talking heads use now. They use it in psychology, especially for wounded soldiers; they use it in feminist theory; they use it in design, to describe stuff meant to last without taking a huger bite from Earth's resources; and they use it in ecology to encourage ecosystems that regenerate themselves. My guess is that *resilient* is a substitute for *sustainable*, a word now overused and misused enough to suggest greenwashing.

Resiliency

Resiliency is the ability to become viable again after trauma. The word comes from the Latin *resiliens*, past participle of the verb *resilire*, "to rebound."

What does it take to equip land with resiliency, and to maximize productivity and biodiversity with minimal interference? That's the question. While planners noodle over this, smaller farmers and ranchers already do it. They can't afford not to. I wanted to try. Work on and in the ground. Believe me, you don't need a farm or a degree to give this a whirl, but get ready to sweat and be thwarted. My San Diego neighbors and I recovered a creek segment near our houses. Those reconstituted wildlands may or may not prove resilient in the long run. So far, so good. Also in cities, vegetable gardens and fruit trees maximize productivity and biodiversity right in backyards, where the greatest resiliency is gardeners' stamina.

City or country, talking doesn't get the work done. Actual fixes are intensely difficult, usually requiring compromise and surprising you with unexpected consequences. For instance, reading or hearing about the well shutdowns, you might think, "Great. With less water, at least fewer farmers are growing GMO corn." That's fewer chemical inputs, fewer high-fructose corn calories, right?

Thing was, GMO corn cultivation didn't decrease. Globalization and vertical integration catapulted GMO farming to South America, where labor is cheap, water is easier to purloin, and synthetic herbicides and pesticides are less regulated or even unregulated.[3] Viewed wholly, for the sake of aggregate planetary ecosystems, shutting down American farmlands isn't an improvement; it's worse.

In the rebound, it was easy for the Ackermans to resist GMO alfalfa, a novelty that heavy dosages of herbicide won't kill. The old-fashioned alfalfa was practical, they said, because the crop didn't need all those inputs. A field seeded to alfalfa might first emerge with a cringing amount of weeds. So what? After the first cutting, the alfalfa sprang back faster than the weeds. Resilient! After the second cutting, there were even fewer weeds. By the second year's second cutting, weeds were rare. So herbicide wasn't necessary.

.........■■··■■.........

With the Ackermans I was continually humbled, made to understand that their logic about crop choices and water use was well thought through and best. When Pop died, they inherited me, a typical liberal. I could've had three nostrils caused by a failed lobotomy; I made that much sense to them. All my shoes had heels on them. I didn't even own boots! Kind enough not to roll their eyes, not to my face anyway, Dean and Ronnie patiently explained, more than once, that getting and keeping organic certification is arduous, that it exposes the methods and land to continual governmental review and interference. They said, look what listening to the government has done to us! To their mind, the less government the better.

Not yet convinced and anxious that my city friends would think I hadn't tried, I wanted to test assumptions, investigate a hypothetical. What would it take to convert even one solitary field to organic? I reasoned that the cultivation wouldn't have to change, as the Ackermans weren't using inputs. Weren't we halfway there? I strong-armed my brother into taking an outing to a large dairy operation owned by Aurora Organic Dairy, a subsidiary of Dean Foods that supplies Horizon organic milk to supermarkets near you. The idea was to explore the nearby purchasers of organically grown alfalfa, to see just how hard becoming an "organic" farm would be.

From the road, Aurora Organic Dairy's fields gushed chlorophyll. The wholesome setting masked Aurora's challenges, though. Ever since the large dairy operation received its organic certification, the question of whether its cows get enough pasture time had become "a flashpoint in a vitriolic debate over what constitutes organic."[4] Those were attacks from the Left. Large dairies that did not have organic certification were probably on the offensive too. Aurora's employees were skittish with Will and me, as if visitors were to be handled defensively. These folks didn't emanate bonhomie. The conversation was unsettling.

The biggest job of transitioning to organic, they said, had been sourcing organic grain, hay, and silage. That sounded promising to Will and me, suggesting that the dairy needed additional certified hay. More daunting was that Aurora had to be very discriminating with its purchases. We left with the impression that the only way to participate in this business would be to lease pasture to a seasoned certified grower, someone Aurora already relied on. Later, after talking with one of Aurora's suppliers, we realized the Ackermans were right—

that trying to get organic certification along these lines would subject the farm to intense scouring and a lot of paperwork, and it might pencil out in the red. So we thanked our lucky stars to have tenant experts who grow with minimal inputs and minimal tilling. We felt and feel that we are better off.

This wariness about government might change, with government and legislation truly committed to healthful food and healthful water, with a national commitment to real sustainability that flows through and perhaps even starts with consumers. Europe is trying. Here in the land of the free, though, entropy looms. Clearly, Americans aren't yet committed to keeping water on farmland . . .

Meanwhile, the government was out there, as if in a parallel universe, from the WAS well owners' perspective. My family had to rely on it, like all citizens, but nothing that had issued from the courts or legislature recently instilled confidence that the groundwater-rights holders were other than second class. It wasn't that the well owners were asking for favors. Some, like us, had water rights from the 1930s, a damn sight senior to many upstream reservoirs that were filling while our wells were curtailed. Knowing this made it difficult to understand why enforcement of the Prior Appropriation Doctrine didn't allow us to pump.

Other than being in WAS, we had no idea what to do about this. Recall that my father had paid a total of only $3,000 over the course of thirty years to keep five wells and 400 acres in operation as a member of G.A.S.P. In six years and by 2011, we'd paid Central over $18,000 in assessments for our single well (Ernesto's Well) to be part of WAS's augmentation plan. (Exertions to keep the other four wells off official "abandonment lists," tantamount to forfeiting hundreds of thousands of dollars, were yet to come.) Nothing was yet operational, because there were no accretions yet. The expense of replacement water and storage facility difficulties stood in the way. Staff at Central said that we might be able to pump, but only 10 percent of that well's historic consumptive use, in another couple of years. We couldn't pump more consumptive use than Central could replace, *even when the 1930 right was in priority, meaning that replacement wouldn't otherwise be demanded.* Based on prospective revenue from what might be future crops, it was hard to see how keeping a water right would ever be other than a loss.

The suit built on a claim of "takings," inspired by Nevadan Wayne Hage's suit against the federal government, moved ahead, but the Kobobels and Knievels were unsuccessful in their attempts to bypass Colorado's water court and get the case into civil court, as would have happened in another state. The water court turned down the plaintiffs' contention that the suddenly more restrictive state regulation amounted to a taking of their property. In appeal, the Colorado Supreme Court concurred in 2011. Only Justice Allison Eid dissented because, as she wrote, "their regulatory takings claim necessarily implicates issues of ownership appropriate for determination in district court."

·········· ▬ · ▬ ··········

Upstairs, light fell through the windows in shafts, as if into a sanctum or, alternately, a cell. To the west were croplands, corral, river, and mountains, the same view to which Gogo had committed forty years before. East-facing views were more troubling: the two-lane highway was but 300 feet away, on the other side of the cottonwoods. There, I'd marked the passing years with its changing traffic. What used to be tractors and grain trucks turned into family sedans in the 1990s. Commuter traffic subsided after the 2008 crash, and then the pall of no water fell over nearby farms and ranches. After 2010, like player substitution on a field, energy companies suddenly overtook the asphalt, joining cities and agriculture on the Platte's aqueous line of scrimmage.

Our caretaker Ernesto arrived at the door cradling a mound of buff-colored stone. In his faltering English, he explained that he'd found it down on a sandbar. Gogo eyed the round chunk and asked if she could hold it. About six inches across, it had a coronet with three flutes on one side. Her fingers moved over the flutes' rough edges. The stone was smoother than she expected. Also lighter. "Ernesto, what is it?"

"I no know," Ernesto shuffled uncomfortably, and then suggested, "Maybe a *dinosaurio.*"

"A dinosaur here?" This sounded pretty outlandish, but my mother is always up for anything.

"Maybe."

Gogo and Ernesto loaded up the car and took the discovery down to the Denver Museum of Nature & Science. From a small town in Chihuahua, Ernesto was agog before the elaborate paleontological exhibits. Gogo too, for that matter. The museum had changed a lot in her lifetime. Several paleontologists examined Ernesto's find and concluded that yes, it was a fossilized bone, a vertebra. Its size and the farm's location indicated that the fossil might be a triceratops or an Edmontosaurus bone that had sifted its way to the alluvial surface through the eons of geology. The scientists returned the fossil to Ernesto, telling Gogo that a single vertebra was too little to go on, to let them know if more turned up.

That bone was a sounding. It connected us to a creature that, like us, was made of water, that slurped the same water we now slurp before that meteor hit 60 million years ago. Now events at the same location connect us to ancient Persia, to the nitrogen cycle, to the annals of combat about water and water rights, to farmers and ranchers the world over. Hear them lapping at *your* shoreline too?

In Colorado, most of the dinosaur era, the late Cretaceous, remains buried deep beneath the aquifer in the Laramie Formation. Below the Laramie Formation, a layer of shale is all that's left of the shallow inland sea that stretched between the Rockies and the Appalachians 100 million to 60 million years ago. Those little Northern Leopard Frog wetlands that until recently speckled the prairie? They were like ghosts of a far wetter place, that Western Interior Sea (itself a later but unrelated incarnation of the Late Devonian shallow sea 200 million years earlier). While the planet dried, rock covered the dead zooplankton and other aquatic life-forms that had settled to the bottom of this muddy, brackish lagoon. Pressure and time cooked the organic matter into oil and natural gas. Such is the "Niobrara," the geologic realm extending under our land from Denver north into Wyoming, which is presently drawing wildcatters.

As I write, oil and gas interests are blitzing Big Bend Station with appeals related to our mineral rights, for energy that requires and sullies huge quantities of water, for energy that is intensely destructive to produce and burn. To the east, south, and north of us, the night sky is pierced with illuminated rigs relentlessly pounding through the Niobrara's graveyard. Who sanctions oil pipelines and wells a stone's throw from water and food supplies?

Meanwhile, passing trucks and railroad flatbeds that used to haul harvests and ag equipment now haul wind turbines. My teenage fear that the *Green Acres* lifestyle would corner me in a quilting bee pales by comparison to new nightmares. They feature desiccated cropland where hungry flocks of birds fly headlong into rotor-bladed landscapes.

To our eyes winds are invisible and to power companies they are profits, but to raptors they are a means of ready travel in view of food sources. The South Platte's eagles soar up to 70 m.p.h. above a tree line suddenly occupied by wind turbines. I'm not saying wind power won't work or isn't better, but a bald eagle— which Gogo believes is her husband incarnate—catches thermals a whole lot easier than humans catch the drift of avian flyways. Some, even most efficiencies and/or solutions have downsides. I've been startled to find so many affect rural land negatively. More and more.

This place on the Platte has always been a fulcrum, even in the Cretaceous. Who knows what happened in the millions of years between the "terrible lizards" and when westward-bound pioneers clashed with the Cheyenne here. Today the coordinates are still both the forlorn witness and the floor of the exchange. The farm is to my mind a heaven, but the transaction posed here, out the window, is a hell: *water, food, and birds for cities that never darken and machinery that never stills.*

EVADE THE REAPER

There are two spiritual dangers in not owning a farm. One is the danger of supposing that breakfast comes from the grocery, and the other that heat comes from the furnace.

—ALDO LEOPOLD, *THE GOOD OAK*

Lordy, all these knots in my stomach. Of another feather, the wild turkeys persisted, methodically, thoroughly. A reason to be grateful. Rafters of them ranged over our farm and downriver, where land was still damp. To eat, a few dozen birds at a time spread out in a line over pastures and fields. The horizontal lines of turkeys moved back and forth like windshield wipers, plucking off grasshoppers and other bugs.

Though paranoid, fixated on the species that might have been our national bird, and despite all that had happened, my family and I didn't see the incursion coming. Foolish, we might've known we were "just begging for it," like the grasshoppers, like the turkeys for that matter, if a predator so much as dared.

A deliberating water broker, in it for the money, did not sneak up on us. People who care about turkeys and grasshoppers sounded the alarm instead. It was Ducks Unlimited (DU), two years after we last spoke. Instead of Matt the biologist, DU's regional director got in touch. I was taken aback. Why the top guy?

The regional director didn't call to pony up the wetland assistance that Matt had proffered, not on our land anyway. Ducks Unlimited, he said, was a partner in a nearby wetland construction called the Haren Project. The Haren Project wasn't near the river where wetlands make sense. It was uphill to the east. Nor did it mimic ancient basins such as might have helped leopard frogs. The Haren Project was all right angles, an artificial hole in the ground, absent vegetation, made to recharge the river for augmentation, of the variety Central sought to create for WAS members like us. In fact, Central had initiated the Haren Project. We could have been part of it. When Central failed to get it together, Bob Lembke's United Water and Sanitation (United) was at the ready. The quasi-governmental district needed augmentation recharge too. As part of getting water to the recharge pond, DU's regional director had the unenviable job of telling me . . . and I could hear him pulling on velvet gloves . . . that United wanted access across our land. The plan was to put a diversion structure in the river here and then lay a big, long pipe across our alfalfa field. I was flabbergasted.

"You're kidding!" I cried together with an aspersion I now regret because, like the pope, who am I to judge? "Is this how Ducks is surviving the recession?"

And then all hell broke loose. Again.

.... ▬·▬ ....

You already know that wily Bob Lembke turned a postage stamp into United Water and Sanitation District in 2002, and that United acquires and sells water to other Colorado water providers. What you don't yet know is how many water-rights owners Mr. Lembke had ruffled since.

Mr. Lembke was so smart. Whatever you might think, he'd already thought of it.

Twenty years after the acquisitive City of Thornton tried to condemn the Farmers Reservoir and Irrigation Company, FRICO shareholders received an offer from United's client, East Cherry Creek Valley Water and Sanitation District (ECCV). The district wanted to buy but 5 percent of FRICO's water. United came at FRICO all smiles, with agreement that FRICO shareholders could continue to benefit from the infrastructure over which United assumed control. Two other ditch companies, Henrylyn and Burlington, moved water through the same infrastructure. This meant that the ECCV-United deal pulled many additional shareholders, plus the City of Brighton, into what would soon be a maelstrom.

To change the ag water to municipal use, the applicants petitioned District 1's water court. It was up to Judge Klein to determine whether the change would infringe on other water rights and if the amount of water FRICO said it owned was accurate, according to a *Denver Post* investigation. With so much at stake, more than three-dozen municipalities, districts, and private companies lined up as objectors. The objectors wanted to make sure United didn't get any more water than it was entitled to. Two cities, Englewood and Aurora, questioned the quantifications. Their numerical models, based on decree dates, demonstrated that FRICO farmers and other related parties had been overwithdrawing for more than a century! And irrigating too many acres. What a thwack across the head with a shovel for hapless ag shareholders! The finding and models were so damaging that Englewood and Aurora actually felt badly about them. Contrite and with the objective of alleviating what they knew would be catastrophic impacts to agriculture, the objectors offered an out-of-court settlement that applied only to shares changed to municipal use. Settling would have spared the farmers. Unfortunately, the attorney representing both FRICO and United refused. United's portion of the legal fees was a quarter-million dollars according to *The Denver Post* article.[1]

The Honorable Klein sided with the objectors. The Colorado Supreme Court unanimously upheld his decision in May 2011. This fiasco took nine years and cost hundreds of farmers a hunk of what they'd taken as given. Sure, United got less too. On the other hand, United got access to the South Platte through FRICO's reservoirs and canals. Both the attorney and the engineer acquired property on the 70 Ranch, which Mr. Lembke had purchased. The then general manager of FRICO said Mr. Lembke also offered to sell him eighty acres at 70 Ranch.[2] Ire about what seemed like duplicity and coercion, plus United's purchases of other ditch shares in northeastern Colorado, made local farmers and ranchers fear and detest Bob Lembke. Come to find out that United had bought shares in our Western Mutual Ditch!

Nevertheless, I could understand that the faltering economy, with shrinking donations and government funding, could force Ducks Unlimited into Faustian alliances. Population growth, water scarcity, and court cases had turned "ponds"—formerly the province of wildlife—into big business. Water rights are always junior to someone. Replace out-of-priorities where and with what?

Here, particularly given the enormous quantities of both dollars and water, is where water administration that serves cities can seem completely nuts. When one entity uses water rights out of priority, it is obliged to siphon additional water from the river and/or aquifer in a different location, to carve an artificial recharge pond where water hasn't been for millennia . . . maybe longer, and then, (using additional energy that requires water to create) to pump the additional water up-gradient into the artificial pond, on the engineered estimation that the recharge water will wiggle its way back to the river in the right spot and time to satisfy senior calls. As of 2013, there were over 500 such recharge projects in the South Platte basin, and according to Division 1 staff, as many as 300 more planned in existing augmentation plans, but yet to be constructed.[3] The "recharge pond" business was where the money was.

.... ■■ ·· ■■ ....

I told my family and the Ackermans, "Ducks says Lembke is trying to improve his image by making wetlands and giving back to farmers."

"By making recharge ponds he is legally obliged to make anyway?"

"By trenching someone else's cropland?"

"I will *not* do business with Lembke," our dear mother declared as if ready to be knighted by the queen. "The farmers hate him."

"The devil incarnate," Ronnie added, backing her up.

"Ducks only wants us to talk with him," I suggested.

"Can't a quasi-government condemn the property?" Annzo reminded us.

"Maybe we can get some replacement water out of it . . . to get the wells going," I tap-danced. I can't tell you how naive I felt. Will and I took off for Greeley to run our anxiety by the water commissioner.

The Division of Water Resources is in a 100-year-old storefront on Greeley's Ninth Street pedestrian mall. The charming old building had been fitted out with what looked like bulletproof-glass security door. We had to be rung in. Will and I looked at each other with worry. You can't imagine a place more low-key and orderly than Greeley. We guessed that the door was installed to keep irate groundwater rights owners from ending up on YouTube. Then water commissioner Bill Schneider came down to let us in personally, softening the greetings with the topic on his mind.

Snowmelt

To calculate *snow water equivalent* (SWE), two factors matter—the amount of snowpack and the melt's timing. Ablations both on the surface and within the snowpack change the way it melts. Intermittent temperature changes can produce icy sheets within the snowpack's substrate. Conditions that create columnar or platelike crystals are much more dense, for example. When the snowpack has layers of ice, the melt happens slowly, in a way that water commissioners can put greater portions to use. Trends in snowmelt, stream flow, and administration timing are correlated, all but impossible to predict, even though life worldwide hinges on snowmelt.

Almost everything about a water commissioner's job is, in one way or another, predicated on timing and quantity of snowmelt runoff, so snowmelt is one of Bill Schneider's big obsessions, particularly in an approaching spring. It's more complex than you'd think. As he spoke, my brother and I began to understand that snowpack's density, dimension, and granularity affects how fast it will melt. The Inuits' many "words for snow" have nothing on Bill Schneider's appreciation of snowmelt. Or that was our impression, anyway, as we followed him up the steps to the conference room. Once we were seated, he asked, "What can we do for you?"

"Bob Lembke approached us. Wants to put a diversion structure and pipeline across our property."

"Why?"

"For the Haren Project."

"That's those recharge ponds that Central started."

"And that United took over, with Ducks Unlimited. They say it'll connect to a pipeline, to carry water southward 70 or more miles. For South Metro water providers."

Bill Schneider looked at us with concern. "Let's see where you are on the straight-line diagram."

The straight-line diagram depicts the once mercurial South Platte as "all business," water-in and water-out, at commissioner command. It was unsettling to see the word *dry-up* just upstream of our property. Will and I were troubled anyway, but the biggest shock was seeing the Big Bend Ditch marked as no longer existing.

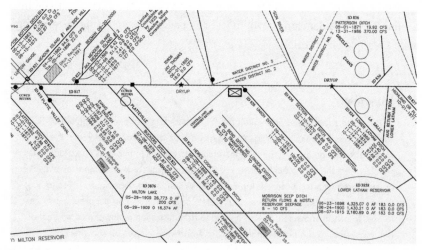

Straight-line diagram, South Platte River basin near Big Bend Station.

"You gotta get that straightened out," the water commissioner grumbled. "There hasn't been accounting on it for a long time. And that might interest Mr. Lembke."

Will and I exchanged looks, shook in our shoes. "What should we do about United?"

"Well, you could trade access for Western Mutual shares."

"What we want to do is pump. Ronnie says that trenching is going to ruin the bottom half of two fields, probably forever. It's the alfalfa field right near the river."

"I guess you could tell Mr. Lembke 'no,'" we heard. "Though, there's no sayin' what would come of that."

Will and I stared at each other as if preparing to jump off a cliff together.

When I telephoned Colorado's state oversight agency for quasi-governmental organizations, staff wouldn't discuss United Water and Sanitation with me, not at all. He said to talk to a lawyer, not to them. So much for oversight.

....

So we found Mooey Hammond, a dynamo who had been in my sister's graduating class, and then gone on to receive many honors from Harvard. I'd last seen her with a hockey stick, barreling down the high school athletic field thirty years before.

Then we called Ducks Unlimited about a meeting with United. With mounting tension, DU's regional director assured me that United looked forward to forging a relationship of mutual respect. Before the mutual respect manifested and a meeting could convene, Gogo received an unexplained thirty-three-page legal document complete with several seven-digit case numbers. Gogo found our farm in a six-page tiny-print list of recipients. Chilling. I had a fit and phoned United's attorney. Did they want to give my 5,000-year-old mother a seizure?

Miffed and nervous, Ronnie, Gogo, Will, and I pulled up to United Water and Sanitation headquarters. There, chiseled granite buildings thrust from lawn like gems from Bulgari jewelry. We unfolded from the SUV like the Clampetts. Thank God that Mooey was there to cling to. Bob Lembke, in the flesh at last, seemed as impressed with her as we were. "You couldn't have found a finer attorney," he admitted.

And the meeting couldn't have been more staged. The "uberlord" accompanied by his brother, a young engineer, and two staff from Ducks Unlimited, plus chicken salad sandwiches to grease down our guard.

"Say," opened the brother Ron Von Lembke with an air all innocence, "I heard you received some kind of documents . . ."

Gogo nodded.

"I don't know how that happened," he hedged. "Gosh, what was it?"

We stared at him silently. None of us was breathing.

With that, Bob Lembke, as polite as he was calculating, intercepted, and the game whirled forward toward a goal. He and Mooey volleyed their mutual lexicon. Except for Ronnie, who understood most of it, we other three scrambled for intellectual footing. You couldn't hear Mr. Lembke's formulations at the other end of the table, but you could watch them move behind his eyes.

What you couldn't see was a set of horns on Bob Lembke. No swishing tail with a point on it either. My impression was that he does as he does because water is challenging and because he can. Of the collateral damage, he'd probably say that's the price of supplying thirsty Coloradans. Mr. Lembke was like that Gore Vidal quote: "Beneath my cold exterior, once you break the ice, you find cold water."[4]

Mr. Lembke asked who our consulting engineer was. He rejoined by saying that the former state engineer had also worked for United. Everyone wanted a piece of Hal Simpson.

For access across our property, Mooey broached the idea of our being paid in additional Western Mutual Ditch shares, an exchange that did not appeal to Mr. Lembke. He suggested that United pay to line the earthen reaches of our Western Mutual as an alternative, but it's already lined. "We want get the wells pumping," Will said.

In fewer than three blinks, Mr. Lembke calculated that we'd need 300 acre-feet to replace corn's consumptive use on 200 irrigated acres. He had access to water at $9,000 an acre-foot, but said he couldn't do $2.7 million. Another of his ideas was to move our wells to Central's GMS. Our confidence in Central was at a low ebb. And anyway, how would United have that kind of power? United's CEO finished by announcing that his staff had to do some math to see what the district could afford, that they might have to divert from the river elsewhere. Mr. Lembke suggested that he talk directly to Mooey.

Afraid of eating their dust, I said, "No, please communicate with me."

With the meeting wrapping up, I lowered my defenses to reach for a chicken salad sandwich. That's when Bob Lembke fired his salvo: "I'd like to know what is going on with the Big Bend Ditch right."

As if zapped by Tasers, my hand dropped. Then recovering and hackles up, I hissed, "We're using it."

Just as did Misters Mullin, Lovelady, and Albee who had dug the ditch in 1873—*to grow food*. That right was not going to get plucked away and used for anything as silly as lawn!

Ronnie added, "According to its decreed use." Ronnie was like a young John Wayne. You didn't dare mess with him.

With an agreement that United would get back to us the next week, we left in a whoosh as the turkeys do, Big Bend Station's human totem. (That was two years ago, as I write. We still haven't heard from the quasi-governmental district. That doesn't, however, mean the predators are gone. *Owning a water right doesn't protect you; it puts you under siege.*)

.... ▬ ▬ ....

The next day, sooner if possible, we frantically called Hal Simpson and Bill Schneider to nail down our oldest water right. Bill Schneider asked us to narrow and clean the channel back to the headgate, so it would look less like an ice-skating rink and more like a ditch. Ronnie installed a ramp flume. (My very first flume!) Bill Schneider was kind enough to get us a free solar-powered data recorder, which transmitted the number of cubic feet per second that flowed through the flume back to the division. The neighbor Bennie Gutfelder and the pump mechanic confirmed, "No doubt about it. Your dad used the Big Bend Ditch continually all those years," and signed affidavits saying so. Ronnie and his guys reestablished the ditch to the existing pipeline above the wetland. All this happened by June so the alfalfa, our sustainable link to the Cretaceous, had irrigation. And—putting in a measuring device at the cutoff to the Yacht Club meant we'd have wetland down there for the winter and spring.

That was the end of taking the Big Bend Ditch right for granted. Additional transactional and legal cases regarding water rights, which none of us really had the time or knowhow to parse, just kept coming. They were screaming reminders that the arid West with its millions of thirsty inhabitants is in very bad straits. Even events in wetter states echoed. As they occurred, we could sometimes correlate outcomes to the situation at the farm. Sometimes not. Farmers and ranchers—they began operating defensively and in concert. Turkey medicine.

We heard that Georgian farmers, Floridian seafood producers, and Alabaman water users are in dispute due to Atlanta's booming population's water demands.[5] San Antonio's water demands, which include keeping its lucrative "River Walk" flowing, have taxed the Edwards Aquifer. The city is studying the likely effects of garnishing Guadalupe River water rights from agricultural irrigators and buying ranchland water acquired by T. Boone Pickens.[6] Again, money is winning out while decision makers fail to apprehend that human needs aren't only industrial, domestic, and landscape. We need food and biodiversity too. Looming environmental and public health crises in California's Imperial Valley, from which San Diego and Los Angeles continue to divert former agriculture water, make clear that the downsides of ag-to-urban predation are complex and devastating.

In an example near the farm, Montana took Wyoming to the US Supreme Court over shrinking waters. In the Yellowstone River watershed, Wyoming appropriators had converted from flood irrigation to sprinklers so they could irrigate more acreage. This economizing meant more crops. Good. Problem was that without furrow irrigation, deep percolation decreased, and less water percolated back into the river for Montanans to use. Bad.

Growing alfalfa in Big Bend Station's floodplain was terrific, but the higher land on the bench had only the mutual ditchwater. Ronnie had been angling for a means of getting away from furrow irrigation. It was labor intensive and only 50 percent efficient (meaning half the water went right through the soil back to the aquifer or river). Now that we had so little water and could not use the wells, why not economize? A center-pivot sprinkler was 80 percent efficient. Such were the aspirations for the big field.

The Ackermans put their ear to the farm-equipment "underground." Maybe they heard a rumor down at the seed company. Or maybe a driver gave them a lead when he filled the fuel tanks. By some buzz somehow Ronnie came into a center-pivot irrigation system and installed it on the big field. This addition increased the crop's uptake of water from the Western Mutual Ditch by over 30 percent. He hoped to fructify that bench with more alfalfa.

.... ▬ · ▬ ....

Observations on the Platte

Minus groundwater, Weld County irrigators' first inclination is to get more efficient with surface water (ditchwater). Using center-pivot sprinklers, they may make a full crop with surface water alone. However, some cropland that used to be furrow-irrigated from the aquifer is now, without that deep percolation, becoming saline. Meanwhile, some property owners have relayed concerns that high groundwater levels are damaging crops and flooding basements and septic systems. The causes of rising groundwater are manmade. Even so, water does not necessarily return to the river. The present regime radically changes the hydraulic system that worked so well for so long.

Below those revenue-producing parts of the farm, in the woods, I roamed the banks of the slough with my brother, Will, the wildlife whisperer. To damp my internal din, I tried to be "in the moment" with him, yet he was still first to point to a fat willow tree that was raw and scarified.

"What's the matter with that tree, Will? Disease?"

"A beaver's been gnawing at it."

Sure enough, I could see the tooth marks. It was a big tree, at least twelve inches in diameter. The ambition of that beaver: it made me run my tongue over the edge of my teeth. "Gosh, how long will it take the beaver to finish cutting it down?"

"Not as long as you think."

"How long?"

"Maybe three nights."

"Nights! Beavers are nocturnal?"

Will stared at me. Was I a halfwit? While *nitrogen fixation* or some other gobbledygook occupied my curiosity, this essential truth about beavers, that they are awake at night, had missed me entirely. My brother had *always* known—probably long before he subjected that other luckless beaver to taxidermy when he (not the beaver) was still pimply faced—how much happens while we're off watch, if not asleep, at least unable distinguish what is going on without cheating: a good half. To my mind this insight gave Will, and Pop who taught him, a considerable edge. As Will would say: "Duh."

I had hitherto imagined darkness in the countryside as long, placid strokes. An inert time, like daytime, but without frenzy. That a smallish animal could whittle his way through a thirty-year-old tree in three nights of industry sent that assumption packing. The witching hour rushes and fells. The beaver reminds us how much happens while our guard is down.

Will used to sleepwalk as a child, which was one thing when we still lived in Denver behind locked doors, but quite another after he, Annzo and my parents moved up to the farm, and Will's sleeping fingers could open latches. If anyone could navigate over uneven terrain in a landscape marked by trees and barbed wire in his sleep, it'd be Will. You can picture him, can't you, led by Morpheus into the company of beavers, owls, bats, and coyotes? Pop sometimes followed him, careful about disturbing him, but also disturbed himself, because he worried what would happen to Will in the dark . . . not that it was really dangerous. The real danger was everywhere else.

SPECTACLE 19

DAUGHTER IN THE DELL

If you think one voice can't make a difference,
try spending the night in a tent with a mosquito.
—ANITA RODDICK

Meet me in the leafy bower at the Platte's banks, where await additional differences of opinion.

Not long ago, I was dumbfounded to learn that many farmers get into a lather about trees. They really hate the lovely cottonwoods and willows that grow along the river.

I've heard them rant, "Them phreatophytes are suckin' up our water!" Waving a fist for emphasis, these farmers want nothing but crops along the river. Crops, period.

Phreatophyte

Phreato comes from the Greek word for springs and wells, and *phyte* is a plant. Cottonwoods, elders, and willows are common phreatophytes in northeastern Colorado.

My father was not in this category, and neither am I. From the very beginning, what Bill wanted from the Wood, which covers about a fourth of the farm, was "a park-like setting." In his mind this meant lofty cottonwoods over grassy footfall. No shrubs, no dead branches, just his own Central Park, minus the humans. And as revelations about water quality grew over the years, an upside became obvious: the Wood's vegetated buffer helped clean the nutrients from ag runoff as it made its way back to the river.

Problem was, the Wood shrank. Pop was but slightly concerned not to see cottonwood regrowth. He let Will plant saplings, with little success. Grazing deer, cattle, and horses ate seedlings. As a result, there were no new cottonwoods, not for forty years. Increasingly over the years, mature trees sloughed bark and whitened. Senescing cottonwoods lost huge branches, then finally fell over.

> **Plains Cottonwood**
>
> Scientific name: *Populus*
> *Populus deltoides* ssp.
> *Monilifera*
>
> *Deltoid* means triangular
> and refers to the leaf.

The Wood was a boneyard. To rid "Central Park" of its deceased and to keep cattle and horses from stumbling, Pop sawed and dragged the big old corpses into stacks, or asked Ernesto to do so for him. He never left the house without his lighter, so he burned the stacks, as ranchers and indeed native tribes used to, to increase grassland.[1] These blazes, he said, reflected his "pride of ownership."

"Quite a pride today, bigger than last week."

So the Wood thinned. Even though Pop considered himself a nature buff, his draconian regime didn't bother him. It did me. To my mind, the ritual burnings were loco. Pop was a pyromaniac. If the fallen branches didn't go up in smoke, there'd be protection for skyward-reaching saplings. Why couldn't the horses and cattle graze the higher ground instead? An understory of currants, roses, snowberry, and sumac might regenerate. Pop wouldn't listen to me, his position both a point of honor and the need to make a living.

After Pop died, I might have made inroads, but Will had drunk the "pride of ownership" Kool-Aid. Gogo parroted Will. Annzo stayed out of it, and the Ackermans were intransigent. Everyone channeled my father. Were they too cursing phreatophytes?

I built my case. A US Fish and Wildlife Service botanist told me that cottonwood stands provide habitat for 82 percent of all breeding bird species in northeastern Colorado. There, 245 species and subspecies of vertebrates have been recorded![2] Rotting branches add nitrogen and build topsoil. Plus, an understory would slow the "drawdown" of floodwater, keeping the ground saturated and cleaning ag runoff. These effects help cottonwood regeneration, I told anyone who would listen . . . which was no one.

In desperation, I evoked my Yoda: Matt Reddy from Ducks Unlimited. When Matt was at the farm, he saw what we all saw. Giving it to us straight, the biologist sounded as if he were wearing scrubs and a stethoscope: "I'm sorry, Tershia, your riparian forest contains a single, late seral-stage cottonwood overstory with a much depleted understory, comprised of cool-season pasture grasses with a high incidence of brome."

"Oh, no! Who wants that?"

"Brome isn't necessarily a bad indication, though there's a preponderance of herbaceous weeds."

"Well, is the case terminal?"

At this point, Matt nodded, "This condition is very common: A few old trees along the floodplain will decline . . . unless."

"Unless what?"

"Unless you reengineer the banks with cottonwood pole planting. That way the banks can overflow without causing erosion or bank collapse."

"Yes?" (I'll decipher Matt's message in a few paragraphs.)

"And I'd prescribe a grazing plan to begin the transition towards desired conditions." That Matt—he was all business.

"Such as?"

"I suspect your animals have been summer grazing here because it's cooler. That's when they'd eat and trample the cottonwood seedlings. If you want to recover, you have to change to winter and spring grazing."

I wasn't looking forward to broaching the grazing topic with the Ackermans, particularly Dean.

As it happened, the deciding factor was the river itself.

The South Platte is a "straight line" from a commissioning point of view, but the physical river dodges all over the place, never letting go of its commitment to the Missouri way off to the east. The water can't reach the Gulf of Mexico without an about-face toward the Mississippi. At our farm the river most strives to begin this turn, a striving that filled us with runnels, frogs, crawdads, and birds—a bending for which the farm is named. Since our farm and others nearby mark the Platte's big exertion, the riverbanks are regularly pummeled.

You already know of the flooding in the 1970s. Like other folks in that stretch, Pop shored up the banks with eyesores—truckloads of god-awful broken concrete and squashed vehicles. The idea was that because concrete and metal didn't erode, they'd armor the banks. Never mind that repeated impact meant water would work its way around the armor, eventually carrying off soil anyway and sometimes armor too. While some must have noticed that roots better stabilized the banks, few property owners then deliberately used plant material. People would have mocked such an idea. The word *biomimicry* didn't exist.

.... ▆ · ▆ ....

Pause here to envision two metaphorical shorelines on either side of a common water source, one representing agriculture, the opposite representing cities. For eighteen "spectacles," you've tested the near shore of my father's troubled *dérive*, a shore that strives to nurture and not to interrupt nature's intent (notwithstanding junked cars, burned wood, and chemical-intensive inputs used to produce food). There on the far shore is the urban paradigm with more people, more consumption, more waste, more entropy. You can see how the far shore has widened with population increase.

Biomimicry

Coined in 1982, the term wasn't popularized until 1997, when Janine Benyus published *Biomimicry: Innovation Inspired by Nature*. The idea is to study nature's methods, and then mimic them.

Meantime, the chasm deepens between the two shores, between ag and urban. Not just deepens, but gets more toxic, literally (more contaminants) and figuratively (more strife). The less meandering, more channelized river has less resiliency, fewer opportunities to create *shared bounty*.

Here's a topic of interest: Located between any two shores is a line called the *thalweg*. This is the truest, deepest continuous course of a river.

Students of rivers can see and follow this line, "read" the thalweg. Any reading of this book's symbolic thalweg will tell you that this acrimony between ag and urban must stop. That city folk and country folk had better realize their interdependence, better get it together.

Likewise, any reading of the *non*metaphorical and immediate thalweg at our farm would conclude (with alarm) that the Platte was intent on rejoining the

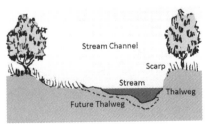 

Thalweg.

East Channel, a.k.a. the slough, even if it meant carrying away the Hundred-acre Wood for good.

The Platte hammered my father's bank-armoring approach, eventually over-banking the manmade levees and dislodging the cars. The river's next move was to saturate the immediate soil. Had the land been vegetated, had there still been cottonwoods and understory shrubs, sediment might have deposited there, building up the topsoil and the roots to stabilize the banks. But no. Not until Pop was spirited away to other realms, not until after the well shutdown, did fragments of the Wood along the shoreline, weighted with water, collapse and mix with the current to be carried off to wherever unrequited dérives flow. Maybe a sandbar for the plovers. Maybe that dead zone at the maw of the Mississippi. So in addition to dying trees, the Wood had scoured depressions in the forest floor. What a mess! The gouging had to be prevented somehow. And it had to be fixed before the snowmelt. We were in the month of March. The thaw would soon follow.

I was up to my ears in habitat restoration in California. With a lot of help, I was gradually learning to rehabilitate stream function in arid conditions. Once rain had saturated the soil, my San Diego neighbors and I gave fourth graders from neighboring schools cuttings from willow species. The children fanned out, jabbing the cuttings into stream banks in urban open space. Within weeks the cuttings burst into leaf, on their way to transforming weedy land into native habitat as well as improving water quality and stream function. This activity had made me a believer. Imagine my glee to discover a Colorado native plant nursery fifteen minutes away from Big Bend Station.

Jay Windell, an ichthyologist and professor emeritus in the Department of Biology at the University of Colorado, knows his riverbanks. Having taught trout biology, Jay is expert in riparian habitat and the insects that support fish. After retiring, he bought a few hundred acres and with his family, Brad Windell and Heidi Hynes, started a wetland nursery. Gogo, Will, a friend who prefers to remain anonymous, and I drove down a long cottonwood-lined avenue. The nursery is an encampment of hooped greenhouses, filled with seedlings to supply Colorado's riverine ecosystems. "Where's your place?" Jay inquired.

"Down on that bend south of the Big Thompson."

Whereupon Jay, who is adorable, turned to Gogo and begged, "Will you marry me?"

Gogo laughed nervously. She hadn't had that offer in a while.

For years my big vision for the Wood had been all talk and no action. I could barely wait to get planting, but planting without a watering strategy is like leaving infants unattended in tubs. We could make a maintenance contract with the Windells—*ka-ching*—or someone else. Or I'd have to stay at the farm. Gogo was getting too old to drive a water wagon . . . though she'd surprised us before. The other big hurdle was convincing the Ackermans to do the earthwork. In addition to farming, the Ackermans excavate and do site work for energy and cable companies. They have a battery of earthmoving equipment.

"Ronnie," I began tentatively, "would you mind talking with a guy who knows how to shore up banks with cottonwoods instead of riprap?" (Riprap is broken concrete.) Since Ronnie didn't answer, I finished by blurting, "He does a lot of business, I think. They have a nursery down south of Platteville." I held my breath.

"Yup, we could talk to him. Anyway, we're havin' a hard time finding riprap. What's available is expensive."

The ichthyologist's son, Brad Windell agreed to explain his approach to Ronnie. Never mind that it was eighteen below zero and the snow was up to our knees. To feed my anxiety, Dean showed up too. Dean treats me like a headstrong mare and knows better than to give me full rein.

"I'm nervous, Brad," I whispered in warning. "Dean is very conservative."

We picked our way through the drifts, the men in their Carhartts and me in cigarette jeans and knee socks worn outside. The trees had three inches of snow on them. The river was glassy. Every surface refracted light. In the quiet, our movement was as if over a blade. We stood between two basins the river had scoured in the Wood. Each had the volume of a two-car garage.

After some preliminary awkwardness, Brad Windell said, "What I would do if this were my land . . ."

Dean cut in, "Well, I'll tell you right off, those holes ain't the river. They're not jurisdictional."

"Let's hear what Brad's idea is," I interjected, breathing heavily, way out of my league. "Then you guys say what your idea is, and we'll see if we can make a plan or not."

"Okay?" Brad asked.

Ronnie nodded.

Brad continued. "I'd shove those fallen cottonwoods into the holes, to slow the river down and get some sediment in here. Then backfill it some. Then I'd bring in a bunch of willow cuttings, and lay them in the dirt, with their cut end lower. And over that I'd put more dirt."

"What about the broken concrete?"

"That's not a permanent fix. I'm betting you won't need concrete. The cotton-woods'll give you the buffer. If there's any life in them, they may well sprout."

"Really?"

"Root reinforcement of banks enhances stability. You know this yourselves, as farmers. Certainly cheaper than concrete. If the roots are strong and the surface is sufficiently rough, when the river overbanks, sediments will be deposited, not eroded away." These were the "specific treatments" Matt Reddy had alluded to.

"Ya seen this work?" Dean asked.

"The idea is to stop the bank collapse. Vegetation maintains channel stability. It also reinforces the river's gradient," Brad explained.

"Well, your dad wouldn't 've gone in for this stuff," Dean commented to me with accusation. "You know that, right?"

"Well, my dad is dead."

Brad went on to tell us how he'd seen people saw off cottonwoods, then augur holes a few feet away and lower the cut off portion into the hole. Both the stumps and the transplants grow. The more he talked, the more I felt that Ronnie might be willing to try it. Dean though? There was no telling.

By the end of about an hour, we all stared at Dean.

Dean finally said, "Well, tell ya what—ya learn something new every day."

Bursting with excitement, I ordered 800 cuttings of sandbar willow, enough to install two layers along about 250 feet. To satisfy my predilection for compli-cations and as a test, I asked the Aquatic and Wetland Company for a hundred container plants too, selections from the "cot-tonwood riparian plant community."

Yes, native plants are like all of us; they thrive best in communities.

I ran this scheme by Ernesto, bludgeoning him with my poor Spanish. To my surprise, Ernesto was excited. "I used work for the Windells! A long time, maybe seven years . . . until I hurt my back." So in Ernesto, we had a resident expert, who was familiar with the plants and where each would thrive. Not only that. He had time to water the container plants through the summer until they were established.

Maintenance problem solved!

First Planting

Three-leaf sumac (*Rhus trilobata*)

Wood's rose (*Rosa woodsii*)

Peachleaf willow (*Salix amygdaloides*)

Coyote willow (*Salix exigua*)

Box elder (*Acer negundo*)

Then, in that yin-yang of Colorado equinoxes, suddenly the snow evaporated and it got hot. One of the energy companies was giving away dirt. Ronnie's battery of yellow tractors migrating down to the Wood was a sign that the foreseen bank stabilization was today! Gogo and I took off for the nursery to pick up my willow cuttings. The Windells stored them in a cool subterranean bunker to effect sensory-deprivation, where the branches might not know the days were warming. We retrieved our share, still not leafed out.

Hastening back to the farm, we found the bulldozer, dump truck, and backhoe looming under the cottonwoods. Ronnie and his skip loader had already heaved huge downed trees sideways into the breaches, and he was covering them with soil. Gogo manned a little four-wheeler, with which she delivered the willow cuttings. Ronnie showed me the gist, then while he filled, I inserted dozens of cuttings in the banks. The idea was that some would sprout as the snowmelt filled the river.

The next day I was down there by myself. It was a furnace on the river, not a soul in sight. I began stripping off clothing. Soon it was all off, all but my new turquoise rubber wellingtons. You don't need detail. I was like one of those legendary half-women who forget or never knew civilization and travel through the forest, swinging from branches, with squirrels in their teeth. Featured that day brandishing a couple hundred willow faggots, I scaled up and down Ronnie's new bank treatment jamming them into the soil in a victory for perseverance. Oh, please let this work!

Later and more couth, I grabbed my "assistant" Gogo to complete the task. My mother was a specimen for age eighty-three, but less goatlike than her kid. Nevertheless, with a neat flick of the wrist, she could pass me willows until I moved outside her reach. I left her at the top of the levee with the willow pile, but returned a while later to find that she had tried to shimmy through a barbed-wire fence—a move accomplished successfully about a thousand times before in her lifetime. Poor little thing had become snagged and was waiting for me while poised in a "downward dog," her pants hung up on a couple of barbs. I had to tear the pants. As Gogo crawled away to recover on the grass in the fetal position, Ernesto suddenly arrived. Coming home from work at the dairy, he'd seen Gogo's entanglement from the road. He'd rushed to our aid.

While we were laughing, in a long blink a big shadow passed over us. Then another shadow and another. All three of us threw back our heads in bewilderment. Twenty or so immense white birds trailed over us along the river. They were like any number of soaring birds, except that each had a *nine-foot wingspan* terminating in elegant black remiges. The birds' size and their slow drift to the shore staged the shielding of the sun like a long series of umbrellas. Sunlight, shadow, sunlight, shadow. One by one the American white pelicans (*Pelecanus erythrorhynchos*) landed on the sandbar in front of us in a pageant of rearranged wings. Ernesto, Gogo, and I stood rapt.

I hadn't seen them since that long-ago day with Pop, during the 1973 flood. In medieval Christianity the world itself was the word of God, a belief system that might certainly make you think twice before tearing it up. The pelican was a symbol of maternal sacrifice, because people believed that pelicans stabbed themselves and fed chicks their own blood when other food was unavailable. Ernesto, Gogo and I couldn't help but feel the birds were there in approval.

Will arrived the next day, ready to get the understory container plants in the ground. And it snowed! As the plants were still dormant, this didn't stop us. We planted them hurriedly, giving each a big basin into which Ernesto could deliver water. I admit that our stretch for "resiliency" requires finessing and that only refinements over several, even many years, will show whether progress is being made.

When adjacent property owners up and across the river learned what we were up to, they too ordered cuttings and container plants. Everyone liked the wildlife, and no one wanted his or her property washed downriver. And thus the fragmented landscape became less fragmented.

PAST THE END OF OUR HOSES

Water, is taught by thirst.
Land—by the Oceans passed.
Transport—by throe—
Peace—by its battles told—
Love, by Memorial Mold—
Birds, by the Snow.
—EMILY DICKINSON, "WATER IS TAUGHT BY THIRST"

My phone rang in California at six a.m. on September 13, 2013. It was Ronnie, like a clarion.

"Your mom . . . ya gotta tell her that she needs more than the clothes on her back."

"Wait, Ronnie," I muttered, bleary-eyed. "What's going on?"

Ronnie's explanation made quick sense of snippets from my previous day: Had not my anonymous friend, whose mother lives in Denver, already mentioned flooding?

An email from Hal Simpson had warned me too: "The South Platte River is rising abruptly and the flow near Ft. Lupton is 5600 cfs and the rains are predicted to continue for two more days. You may want to check on your mom to make sure she is safe. Boulder County and Adams County under emergency operations and many roads have been damaged and closed." Hal's "5600 cfs" meant nothing to me. Boulder and Adams Counties were far away from Big Bend Station and even farther away from San Diego, where the weather was clear and dry.

We expect that everyone sees and feels what we're in the middle of. But if I've learned anything from writing about these "spectacles," it is that each of us mistakenly thinks ours is a world apart.

I didn't know that the Ackermans had spent September 12 frantically sweeping up their generators, the new data recorder, and other equipment from the headgates. I hadn't pictured them herding their horses and cattle away from lower pastures. I did receive three emails asking how Gogo was doing. I'd just spoken with her. She was fine. It wasn't raining at the farm.

Directly to the west, though, the sky had tipped over—every canyon and street a torrent, every depression overflowing, every downward opportunity a tumbling, gushing surge, and the pelting rain continued. Waters didn't stop where they fell. Descending from up-gradient, they filled new ditches, and then overbanked additional ponds, spilling then gushing forward onto roads, into new counties.

That afternoon, the day before, a mile north of our place, on the other side of the Twin Bridges, which were beginning to submerge in water, neighbors convened to try to move a national championship bull from a lowland. It's the pasture south of Jan and Gene's nursery. Belonging to a local bull-rider, the bull was worth many times more than luckless Gaddafi, as much as $200,000. He was also as big and intransigent as a rhino. They'd tried to herd him out using four-wheelers, as hurried cowboys might. Gene's idea was to put hay on the back of a quiet truck and lure him from the pasture. In the end, everyone had to give up and pray.

Ronnie had called my mother that night, "Gogo, you may have to evacuate your house tomorrow. High flood waters."

My mother later told me, "I had no idea how to respond to such a situation, so I went to bed and had a good night's sleep."

Gogo's bookkeeper, Marilyn, who had lived in Gogo's house as a little girl once told me, "We were always evacuating for floods then, but that was before your father built that dike to the south. That's high enough to stop the flow from upstream." The Crescent Dike that defined the wetland—the eight-foot dike that Arne Johnson had tried to breach—was another reason that I hadn't given the storms a second thought. Gogo either, evidently. Trusting Bill's dike to the south, she was snoozing peacefully when Ronnie called at dawn, demanding that she go to the window, not to look south, but to look out to the north. The river, usually only visible as a line of trees several football fields away, was fast and muddy, now making its way toward her across the alfalfa field.

"We didn't think the water would get this high," Ronnie managed to say, breathing heavily on the phone. "But the levee's down . . . the water is almost up to the ditch and getting higher."

"Which levee?"

"The Union," he answered with exasperation. "Not the dike. I came down to get your mom. She won't stop making the bed." When the going gets rough, the hospital corners get tighter.

"Okay, Ronnie. I'll call Gogo. And Annzo. Maybe she can mobilize the nephews."

"Well, this is bad. I have to go."

"Ronnie, thank you. Thank you so much."

"I'll send you pictures later."

And like that, everything changed. The freeways and feeder streets along the Platte and its tributaries closed, so Annzo's kids couldn't make a move. I telephoned my aunt in Greeley—Did she know any broad-shouldered men who could help? Prone to fretting anyway, and unable to help from a distance, I balled up with worry.

Ernesto's and Erminia's house is up on the bench. Ronnie's too. So they weren't in the immediate peril that Gogo was. Ernesto made Erminia stay at home when he came down with Ronnie to help my mother. He didn't want Erminia swept away! The guys hefted the Persian carpets upstairs. Not the big furniture, only chairs, could fit up the narrow, age-worn stairs. Ronnie's honey, Mindy, came along. She and Gogo concentrated on the silver, paintings, and computer. I called to remind them of the files but no one answered.

There at ground zero, Ernesto, the man born in a pueblo named "surrounded by water" eyed the approaching water now in the yard. Ernesto feared they'd be inundated inside.

"Come on, Gogo," Mindy urged. "Time to go."

"I just want to get these linens."

As they opened the kitchen door, water spilled onto the floor. Ronnie hefted Gogo, who clutched her tablecloths, Mindy grabbed Gogo's purse, Ernesto grabbed Pluck the cur who was too afraid to snarl, and they all splashed across the garden to the trucks. After loading up, too late for nostalgia, they backed quickly out the driveway, already several inches deep in water. None too soon. As they reached the highway, the piano man pulled up to rescue the Steinway (prompted by our Eaton aunt), but it was too late. He couldn't get into the driveway, which had already filled.

Excepting the 149-year-old house, everyone was safe and dry in the places that count—from the knee up.

.... ▆▆ ·· ▆▆ ....

You've read more than once that the Platte's historic path used to be wide and meandering, with rogue secondary channels like the slough. You already know that its effluent is no longer the sky-blue water of the Coors advertisements of our childhood. Rather, it is a medium used and reused, gathering substances that were treated and substances that cannot be treated many times before its flow reaches Big Bend Station. The water usually chugs compliantly through channels tamed by property owners, the state, and US Army Corps of Engineers. Usually.

Nevertheless, hydrologists will tell you that the South Platte River is still active, "modern," and flood-prone. Therefore land around the river, such as Big Bend Station, remains within a mapping designation called the "100-year floodplain." This means that, probability-wise, each year arrives with a 1 percent chance that it will flood. It's not a matter of *if* torrents will overtake the farm's lower reaches, but *when*. Development is discouraged in floodplain. Floodplain is expensive to insure. We didn't have insurance. Municipalities, counties, property owners, and mutual ditch owners spend lots of money on dikes and levees, creating what professionals call an "artifice of safety." The precautions are more commonplace than Gogo's hospital corners, but artificial, because the flood designations are based on where the river course is located at the time. The course can change.

Occasionally, discrete storms generate point-flooding in a single watershed as the deadly Big Thompson flood did. (The Big Thompson flood occurred on the exact day of Colorado's centennial, in 1976, and killed 139 people.) Every once in a while snow melts spectacularly at once as happened here in 1973. Occasional heavy rains sop many places along the Front Range simultaneously, even for several days, flooding the tributary streams. That's when the river rises most dramatically.

Precautions notwithstanding, floods are dynamic and behave unpredictably. A relatively minor event can change the river's course, moving waters to a different part of the floodplain, eroding away or flooding places that appear to be safe under the 100-year floodplain designations. All it takes is fallen trees and shrubs getting caught under a bridge. A big surge of water, which might otherwise have continued on course, will power forward in a new direction.[1]

Which is what happened.

At the northern (downstream) boundary of our property, the Union Ditch is an imposing agricultural diversion named after the Union Colony, and therefore, after the musket wielders on the Union side of the Civil War. The Union Ditch's diversion structure, built to withstand hell or high water, creates a pinch point in the river at that end of the property. When there's no downstream call on the river and the headgate is open, shareholders along the ditch use the water diverted there. In September 2013, the headgate was closed because the Union Ditch was out of priority.

Five hundred feet north, the Twin Bridges carry the double-lane highway over the Platte. The river's sluggish habits tend to deposit sand in that stretch. Long, high sandbars had raised the height of the river, closer to and under the bridge. Neighbors on both sides of the bridge had already complained to the Colorado Department of Transportation, already made themselves hoarse to the US Army Corps of Engineers. "If you don't clean out that sand," the neighbors said, "we're going to have problems." The bureaucrats were unyielding. They could not remove the sand, they said. Why? Because that might disturb the endangered Preble's meadow jumping mouse.

"Well, the mice'd better know how to swim," was the lingering sentiment.

Climate change was all over the news. Huge swathes of the Rockies had been deforested by bark beetle, the pines made vulnerable by pollution, warmer temperatures, and water scarcity. Dead trees without pine needles don't intercept precipitation, don't contribute to evapotranspiration, don't sequester carbon.[2] Their roots don't pull rainfall and snowmelt back into the ground. Deforestation on the Front Range diminished infiltration and increased erosion.

Meanwhile the paving over of everything persisted. As you already read, hardscape increased by a third between 1986 and 1998 on the Front Range,[3] and maybe a third more in the years since. Much of the land immediately along the Platte had been turned into lined reservoirs.

And land up-gradient from the Platte had been turned into recharge ponds for augmentation—500 such projects in the basin and as many as 300 more planned. Forcing G.A.S.P. out of business meant almost all augmentation

> **Infiltration**
>
> Infiltration is the process of water from aboveground entering the soil.

> **Erosion**
>
> Erosion occurs when water and/or wind dislodges soil and rock, and then transports them to other locations.

plans were recharging the aquifer, not the as-needed seasonal supplements that had functioned so well for so long. Further, unlike G.A.S.P.'s methods, augmentation ponds cannot turn off and on at will. Inundated basements, septic systems, and fields in nearby Gilcrest and La Salle made it obvious that the hydrology was awry, even without a big weather event. Why add more water to a situation already inundated?

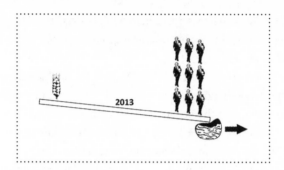

Water's highest, most valuable mission—to soak into the soil, sustain forests, grasslands, wetlands, and agriculture and/or return to groundwater—was severely thwarted. All that water.

· · · · · · · · · ▬▬· ·▬▬· · · · · · · · ·

September 2013 had arrived and with it the expectation of cooler temperatures. Only it wasn't cooler. The preceding month was the clearest of the year at the farm, and the week before blazed in the upper nineties.[4] That was the situation "on the ground."

Far above, what National Center for Atmospheric Research's Bob Henson called a "hot dome" of high pressure shifted north and east while a weak upper-low set up shop across the western United States and stayed there.[5] A plume of monsoonal moisture arrived from the Pacific and the Gulf.[6] Moist air from the Plains was driven upslope into the foothills, where it unleashed the rain. Boulder got twenty inches in four days, over nine inches on September 12 alone. In the same period of time Greeley got only 2.5 inches, but it didn't matter, because unable to infiltrate anywhere else, Boulder's rainfall was headed down the Platte in Greeley's direction. So was water from the engorged St. Vrain, James, Four-Mile, Little Thompson, Big Thompson, Cache la Poudre, and other Platte tributaries. And not satisfied to turn Boulder into an aquarium, the epic kept coming.

Rain continued, picked up fallen trees, shrubbery, debris, sheds and even houses and swept them into the Platte. The volume became *200 times* the usual autumn flow. That was a hundred years more than the floodplain designation. Overwhelmed sewage-processing plants and animal-feeding operations filled floodwaters with *E. coli* bacteria. The flow inundated industrial and oil-drilling operations. Sand and sediment from erosion and collapsing creek banks thickened the mix and increased the turbulence. Soon, downpour that impacted 450 miles of roads and 100 bridges, destroyed 1,500 homes, and damaged 19,000 others was no longer a 200-year event.[7] Now it was a 1,000-year event, Colorado's biggest storm in recorded time.[8] "Biblical."

Water boiled and frothed down the rooflines, gutters, storm drains, tributaries, and the river, jumped over itself—over 14,000 cubic feet per second at the farm—in a mad rush to mock engineers, frustrate meteorologists, and defy water-storage methodologies. Heavy rainfall might seem to have alleviated drought conditions. (G.A.S.P. would have used this storm as an opportunity to hold back on water rentals and stockpile money for other purposes, such as purchasing permanent water supplies.) The aquifer and reservoirs could hold only so much. So the water kept moving, and the situation went well beyond taunting. People were missing; people were dead. Thousands of homes were destroyed. Water-imposed isolation hampered rescue efforts. So unexpected, so out of proportion with anything that had ever been seen before, the unceasing water was brutally punitive.

Only water and gravity prevailed.

With more than 9,000 cubic feet per second (I learned that this meant 4 million gallons per minute, likewise an abstract sum) charging through and around the South Platte at the Twin Bridges north of the house, broken branches, downed trees, and other refuse piled up between the Preble's mouse habitat and the top of the bridge. That dammed the river, which wasn't going to stop anyway. The river, which was by then a flood, continued over the bridge and around the bend to the east. Water is all about shortcuts.

Slightly upstream, water raged over the Union Ditch diversion structure. But as it raged, it sopped and soaked too. As I've been saying, water's prime directive is to sop and soak, to try to get into the soil. So finally, it saturated the Union Ditch's fifteen-foot levee that protects our fields, with as much of the wet stuff as a wall of dirt can hold. Too heavy to stay upright and not held in check by tree or willow roots, the levee collapsed under its own weight, carrying the dirt off to the Mississippi Delta via the Preble mouse pileup . . .

. . . and letting the floodwaters into our property.

········· ▰··▰ ·········

So, Bill's Crescent Dike held. The house didn't flood from the south. The water surged backward from downstream. After Gogo's rescue and throughout the day, the floodwaters rose. The slurry was lapping at the windows by lunchtime. Ronnie sent photos.

Instead of worrying about people, as a more compassionate person might have done, I closed my eyes to inventory the antiques inundated downstairs.

To get a leg count, I multiplied by "4." Damaged eighteenth- and nineteenth-century legs numbered 176. The Italian walnut sofa. The French demilune game table on impossibly long legs, inlaid with marquetry of carved conches. The dining room table topped with a wood painted to resemble jade-green marble, perfectly veined in several shades. The bedroom vanity, dressers, and bed, hand-painted with rosettes. And what of their drawers lined with padded rosette brocade? Each piece of furniture represented an inspiration, the wood growing in a forest procured at who-knows-what effort, a lifetime's worth of craftsmanship, the hours, days, and months it took to make; and on top of that, my parents doing without as they stretched to afford such luxury or bought secretly for each other as gifts. I was glum. Also shallow, unlike the water.

Later in the afternoon, Gogo telephoned to say the clouds had parted. The river had encircled the farm, but Ronnie was able to drive her along the bench to see the scope of the flooding.

The sun shined on a landscape altered beyond her imagination. Our farm was, for acres and acres, a large sheet of water, with the dispersing storm clouds reflected in its surface. Of the huge 100-year-old cottonwood trees at the deep end, she could see only the scraggly tops.

No fit of spleen for Gogo. My mother sounded more cheerful than ever: "Oh, precious, you should see how beautiful everything is. It's all sparkly!"

"She's never been better, Will," I told my brother on the phone. "I'll have to think of something else to worry about." With a mad laugh, Will reminded me that it was Friday the thirteenth.

Vehicular traffic was at a standstill. Hundreds or thousands of years before, the closed byways had begun as animal trails along waterways—animal trails that turned into footpaths that turned into wagon trails that turned into roads that turned into highways that turned into freeways. And now they were all under water. Departing Montana, my brother set off for the farm. I booked an airfare. We planned to convene there two days later. We hoped highways and roads would by then be passable.

.... ■■ · ■■ ....

Every outpost along the old South Platte Trail was marooned. Those along the creeks too. The basin was catastrophically inundated for miles in every direction. The waters around Gogo's house, though, subsided by daybreak. Unbeknownst to my mother and as soon as there was enough light, Ernesto wended down to the house to confront what amounted to an Augean stables. Doing honor to his name, Gogo's caretaker methodically shoveled layers of mud from every room.

Then, after scrubbing, he brought in hoses to rinse the walls. Satisfied that the house was more presentable, he fetched my mother, la señora, from Ronnie's house on the hill. For his heroism, Ernesto deserves to be rendered in statuary.

Outside the house, Gogo thought, it was as if the inundation had never happened. The petunias along the driveway were fresh as new. Hoping for the best, my mother approached the door tentatively on Ernesto's arm. Thanks to Ernesto's ministrations, her first thought was, "Well, this doesn't look so bad."

That was before my sister, Annzo, and the broad-shouldered cousins arrived. Every drawer was a-slosh. Water poured from the opened refrigerator. Same from the oven and dishwasher. Cabinet doors were swollen shut. Veneers popped off the 176 bulging antique legs that my mother had burnished with lemon oil for decades. The lemon oil itself, as well as every bottle or jar on lower shelving, was toppled. Filled with sopping books, stationery and paper napkins, nightstands and side tables were puffed like chipmunk cheeks. Although the high-water line was but eighteen inches, the upholstered furniture was too heavy to heft because water had wicked right to the shoulder line, leaving big brown stains. Gogo's Italian sofa—with upholstery the same as Jackie Kennedy's, a decorator had told her—looked derelict, as if it had spent eons in a barn, a haven for rodents. Windows wouldn't open, and doors wouldn't close. Gogo wished it were the other way around. The scale of damage and commotion put my little mom in a daze. She didn't know what to do.

While poor Annzo rolled up her sleeves to confront the disgusting kitchen and closets, the guys carried out the furniture, then went to work on the now-bacterial carpets. Together they managed to roll up the sodden layers. As the cousins separated the heavy carpet and disintegrating padding from the floor, a cry of disgust went up. The muddy subfloor moved in place with thousands of confused night crawlers!

The woofed cousins shook their heads. It was unspeakable.

Annzo exclaimed, "Beyond revolting!"

In the oldest part of the farmhouse, which wasn't built on a concrete slab, Annzo heard the retreating river lapping at the floorboards like waves against pilings. What she sensibly thought is, *it'll be back.*

My sister and the cousins didn't think that Gogo should ever again live in the house. That morning, the consensus was, *Dig a hole in the front yard. Shove the stagecoach stop into it. Bury it.*

In the face of such a verdict, Gogo was quiet. She couldn't believe abandoning the house was her only option! This wasn't the first time in 149 years that Big Bend Station had flooded, after all. Rationalizations lapped at her like water against her floorboards. She didn't want to be thrown in the "slammer," as she referred to retirement communities. She waited until Annzo and the cousins drove away.

········ ▬ ··▬ ········

My mother lifted the sopped Yellow Pages, fat and heavy as a cement block, and then sat down on a footstool to pry it open. As she worked her way to the letter *F* pieces of paper came off on her fingers. *F* for *flood*. She needed professionals, but the disaster occurred as disasters do, on a weekend, and everyone else needed help too. Yet, without missing a beat, she dialed the company with the same name as her favorite carpet spot-remover—Service Master. There was a waiting list, they said, but she persisted and insisted. Finally, the flood damage crews agreed to come out the next day. She had been homeless for forty-eight hours thus far.

From the airport, I couldn't make it to the farm except circuitously. The scene through the window was like a zombie movie. With roads closed, parking lots and fields inundated, broken infrastructure, and other chaos, most operations were shut down. No one was on the highway. Under the sun, the wheels and undercarriages of upside-down cars steamed and upside-down animals bloated. What few people I saw were glazed over, the walking dead.

As I came through the door into the kitchen, the neighbor Gene, telephoned, "Any sign of Jake?"

"Your mule?"

"Yeah. People've heard him braying, but we can't find him. The reports are getting farther away."

"Gogo, have you heard braying? Gene's calling about his mule."

"He's welcome to come over. Tell him to ask Ronnie. How's the bull?"

"How's the bull?"

"The bull drowned. He's out there upside down. We can only see his legs."

With that Will arrived, announcing he'd seen otter bodies on the highway. "I'm betting," he said, "they probably came from above Boulder."

"That's forty miles!"

"Could've taken them less than a day."

I looked around. Ernesto, Annzo, and the cousins had faced the postdiluvian, accomplishing the grody work for which I would have had to be drinking. The night crawlers were gone. I put my ear to the living-room floor. I did not hear lapping. Funny how a "can-do" attitude sweeps over you, once someone else has done the heavy lifting.

"This house is an historic artifact," I proclaimed sanctimoniously. "We should act as stewards."

"The kitchen cabinetry isn't composite. It's solid wood," Will offered more practically. "I think it's going to be fine."

Gogo's eyes darted between the two of us.

"Gogo, what do you want?"

"I'd like to stay here."

"Let's see what the flood-response guys say."

Mold has a place in the scheme of things and that place is damp, so while I fussed over the antiques, others agonized over spores. Anyone who had time to watch the news—not us, but everyone who telephoned—had been made to fear colonies of invisible mycotoxins. The opportunistic molds—*Trichoderma, Penicillium marneffei, Aspergillus fumigatus*, and *Stachybotrys chartarum*—had for years been waiting for this moment on the Platte. Gogo, who was anyway fearless, sat on her stool and took the calls.

The spores were already among us, family members and friends told her. The dustlike reproductive cells were adrift, in the air, in the ducts, through the door, on the cur, and on us. To make mold, the spores needed only water, warmth, and organic food. This buffet was served. According to the news feed, we had forty-eight hours to avert the fungi, a second wave of disaster.

So, the race against spores hastened. In came an army of young men in tool belts, lugging extension cords, crowbars, and twenty industrial fans the size of large ottomans. With a few flicks, they wrested open the windows, and then jammed the fans into them. When the fans went on, we stopped listening. We heard only whirring. And before long, the crowbars had pried out the entire kitchen and pan-

> **Molds**
>
> In an ecosystem, molds contribute to decomposition, breaking down organic matter. Molds reproduce via spores, asexual units of reproduction that evolved both to disperse and to survive unfavorable conditions, often for a long time.

try, which the young men aborted through the small kitchen door. Bathroom fixtures too.

Meanwhile, furniture restorationists gathered up the 176 legs. Will, Annzo, and I boxed up Gogo's accumulated eighty-three years' worth of candlesticks, serving dishes, albums, photos, leather-bound books, china, spices, cutlery, bedding, nutcrackers, ice-cream makers, rags and the lemon oil—the "full Gogo." Will drove boxes over to the Hog House for storage. A lot of stuff—anything that was on the floor—met the Maker, riding Ronnie's front-end loader to a container and from there to the landfill. With those insistent spores dusting our necks, we had to work fast. It took three days.

Leaving Gogo, Annzo, and me prying apart wet business files and drying them between the ubiquitous fans, Will stopped briefly to do reconnaissance. He took off in his waders to walk the length of the river with the dogs. The peak having passed, the river gradually subsided. Will found fences buried in sand and litter. The Big Bend Ditch was silted in and the new headgate catty-wampus. Prairie Dog Town was underwater, with its former occupants either on higher ground or headed to Nebraska with mountain otters and Preble mice. Debris was everywhere. The Wood too was many inches deep, but Will said he could see the sprouting willows poking through. Our new cottonwood banks had held! Maybe finally we'd get seedlings. The exception was the Union levee, which hadn't had willows to anchor it.

Inside, to excise any material that might harbor spores, the Service Master guys hurriedly removed all wall coverings and insulation up to thirty inches high. Being ancient, the wall interiors were archaeological, containing bricks, mortar, batting, newspapers, everything but the kitchen sink, which was in any case at the Hog House by then. In the end, of the house's historic lowermost underpinnings, only the studs remained.

I found Gogo in her bedroom, doubled over, turning her head to look left and then right. "From here I can see straight through the bathroom, the dining room and the kitchen, right through to the other side. It's like the house is on stilts," she declared.

The young man who had excavated the subflooring under the oldest part of the house poked his head in to say, "Come look."

We could see right down into the mud! "Will I be able to continue living here?" Gogo asked him.

"We'll see how long it takes to dry."

And with that, the army of young men drove away.

When Will returned, we scarfed yummy club sandwiches that Annzo had brought. Ingredients raised on commodity crops. Chairs sinking into the soggy garden. Thus fortified, we decided to clear the roadside fences.

"Want to drive, Tershia?"

They lodged me behind the wheel of the sacred 1971 VW Thing—Pop's mount and the vehicle coveted by pretty much everyone who has ever laid eyes on it. This was the first time that I'd ever driven it! Gogo got in front with the cur at her feet. Annzo and Will climbed in back where Pop kept his shovel and shotgun. The old engine fired up with a low growl despite having been wet. Then, with windshield down, we bumped up onto the highway. Late afternoon and the road was ideally empty. All sorts of animal, mineral, and vegetable were stuck in the fences, the high-water detritus of a 1,000-year Colorado flood. There we pried loose the folding chair, the one Gogo leaves out by the fields so she can rest on her walks.

· · · · · · · · · ▬ · · ▬ · · · · · · · · ·

As the harvest moon surfaced in the east, we saw Annzo off to Denver. Will climbed into his van for the night, and Gogo and I ambled back to the house. "Going to sleep with me upstairs, Gogo?"

"No precious, I want to sleep downstairs alone."

"Goodnight, Gogo." I gave her a kiss.

Downstairs, my parents' four-poster—the bed she and Pop had slept in from the beginning—was the lone remaining possession in the house. The hospital corners held! Its mattress was as high as the remaining walls, so it too was on stilts. My tired mother climbed into it with her clothes on. The fans whirred. The windows were wide open, giving the impression that she and the darkness outside were one in the same. Gogo smelled wet hay. She smelled the river. The smell of wet house was all but gone.

The bed, now a raft, seemed to drift east, pulled into the mouth of the orange moon, perhaps by teams of otters and beavers, and then slowly to turn south toward Denver, where Gogo caught a glimpse of her childhood, her early marriage. She rocked toward the mountains, huge rollers to the west, the features that had always oriented her, confirmed that she knew where she was going. She fought the urge to close her eyes. The river was headed north. Through the window, the gooseberry bush and alfalfa field, the fence posts and the horizon seemed like travelers too, coasting along next to her raft as it floated toward a future uncertain. Would this be her last night at Big Bend Station? Her last night on the course Bill set for her, with his longing to be his own man, to live in the country?

Bill's wife clasped this passport tightly, that it might carry her to daybreak yet again.

The truth is always an abyss. One must—as in a swimming pool—dare to dive from the quivering springboard of trivial everyday experience and sink into the depths, in order later to rise again—laughing and fighting for breath—to the now doubly illuminated surface of things.

—FRANZ KAFKA, FROM GUSTAV JANOUCH, *CONVERSATIONS WITH KAFKA* (LONDON, UK: DEREK VERSCHOYLE, 1953).

NOTES

SPECTACLE 1

Guy Debord, *Society of the Spectacle*, English ed. (Oakland, CA: AK Press, 2006).

1. Guy-Ernest Debord, "Introduction to a Critique on Urban Geography," *Les Lèvres Nues*, no. 6 (1955), an essay of a few pages translated by Ken Knabb, accessed on June 3, 2016, http://www.cddc.vt.edu/sionline/presitu/geography.html.

2. Guy-Ernest Debord, "Theory of the Dérive," *Les Lèvres Nues*, no. 9 (1955), an essay of a few pages translated by Ken Knabb; reprinted in *Internationale Situationniste*, no. 2 (1958), accessed June 3, 2016, http://www.cddc.vt.edu/sionline/si/theory.html.

3. M. Mattes, *The Great Platte River Road* (Lincoln: University of Nebraska Press, 1987).

4. John A. Meininger, Esq., "Who Owns the Waters of the South Platte River?," accessed 2007, http://www.coloradowaterusers.com/pb/wp_e45b7c12/wp_e45b7c12.html; Dick Wolfe, *Running the River: Water Rights in the Market—Law, Hydrology and Reality*, PowerPoint prepared for September 21, 2007, Colorado Division of Water Resources, accessed June 5, 2016, http://dwrweblink.state.co.us/dwrweblink/ElectronicFile.aspx?docid=2810326&&dbid=0.

5. USGS, *Ground Water Atlas of the United States: Arizona, Colorado, New Mexico, Utah, HA 730-C,* accessed August 25, 2014, http://pubs.usgs.gov/ha/ha730/ch_c /C-text2.html.

6. Leaf, Charles, PhD, "Average Annual Water Budget 1947–1970, from Henderson to Julesburg," hydrological monograph, Merino, CO.

SPECTACLE 2

Mark Reisner, *Cadillac Desert* (New York: Viking Penguin, 1986).

1. W. H. Goetzmann, *Army Exploration in the American West, 1803–1863* (New Haven, CT: Yale University Press, 1959); 2nd ed. (Lincoln: University of Nebraska Press, 1979).

2. Goetzmann, *Army Exploration in the American West.*

3. Elliott West, *The Contested Plains: Indians, Goldseekers and the Rush to Colorado* (Lawrence: University Press of Kansas, 1998), 27–28.

4. Elizabeth Michell, "Sand Creek Massacre Site: An Environmental History," Paper written with research assistance from Julia Langfield, under the direction of Dr. Mark Fiege (Fort Collins: Department of History, Colorado State University, January 2007), 10; John H. Moore, Margot P. Liberty, and A. Terry Straus, "Cheyenne," in *Plains: Handbook to North American Indians*, vol. 13, pt. 2, ed. Raymond J. DeMallie (Washington, DC: Smithsonian, 2001), 863.

5. Moore, Liberty, and Straus, "Cheyenne," in *Plains*, 863.

6. Moore, Liberty, and Straus, "Cheyenne," in *Plains*, 863.

7. Loretta Fowler, "Arapaho," in *Plains*, vol. 13, pt. 2, 841–42; Moore, Liberty, and Straus, "Cheyenne," in *Plains*, 863.

8. Loretta Fowler, "Arapaho," in *Plains*, vol. 13, pt. 2, 840.

9. Michell, "Sand Creek Massacre Site," 17.

10. Moore, Liberty, and Straus, "Cheyenne," in *Plains*, 864.

11. Gene Gade, "The Buffalo Population and Why It Crashed," in *Plains Bison Mysteries That Remain*, pt. 1 (Sundance, WY: Vore Buffalo Jump Foundation).

12. Michell, "Sand Creek Massacre Site," 9.

13. James C. Malin, *History and Ecology: Studies of the Grassland*, ed. Robert P. Swierenga (Lincoln: University of Nebraska Press, 1984), 6.

14. Connie A. Woodhouse, Jeffrey J. Lukas, and Peter M. Brown, "Drought in the Western Great Plains, 1845–56: Impacts and Implications," *American Meteorological Society* (October 2002), accessed on August 8, 2016, http://journals.ametsoc.org /doi/abs/10.1175/BAMS-83-10-1485; *North American Drought Atlas: A History of Meteorological Drought Reconstructed from 825 Tree-Ring Chronologies for the Last 2005 Years*, Climate Data Library (a cooperative affiliation of NOAA, Columbia University's Lamont Doherty Earth Observatory, and UC San Diego's Scripps Institution of Oceanography), accessed March 7, 2014, http://iridl.ldeo.columbia.edu/SOURCES/. LDEO/.TRL/.NADA2004/.pdsi-atlas.html; C. Woodhouse et al., "Eastern Colorado

Palmer Drought Severity Index Reconstruction," International Tree-Ring Data Bank, IGBP PAGES/World Data Center for Paleoclimatology Data Contribution Series #2002-083 (Boulder, CO: NOAA/NGDC Paleoclimatology Program, 2002).

15. Woodhouse et al., "Eastern Colorado Palmer Drought Severity Index Reconstruction."

16. West, *The Contested Plains*, 67.

17. For this detail and many others, I have been helped out by my family members, Greeley's Historical Society, and Jane E. Norris and Lee G. Norris's fine book, *Written in Water: The Life of Benjamin Harrison Eaton* (Athens: Swallow Press, University of Ohio, 1990).

18. Donald Worster, *Rivers of Empire: Water, Aridity, and the Growth of the American West* (New York: Pantheon, 1985).

19. Lucy Burris, "People of the Poudre: An Ethnohistory of the Cache la Poudre River National Heritage Area, AD 1500–1880," Poudre Heritage Alliance, Larimer County, Colorado, http://www.poudreheritage.org/sites/default/files/resourceFiles /poudreethnohistory_full1.pdf; Russell Thornton, *American Indian Holocaust and Survival: A Population History since 1492* (Norman: University of Oklahoma Press, 1987).

20. John H. Moore, Margot P. Liberty, and A. Terry Straus, "Cheyenne," *Plains*, vol. 13, pt. 2, 865.

21. Berny Morson, "Forging Farm Country When Greeley Went West and Irrigation Followed," *Rocky Mountain News*, July 6, 1999.

22. Carl Ubbelohde, Maxine Benson, and Duane Smith, *A Colorado History*, 9th ed. (Boulder, CO: Pruett, 2006).

23. *The New York Times*, August 29, 1871.

24. "Greeley's Water History," City of Greeley Colorado website, accessed June 3, 2016, http://greeleygov.com/services/water/greeleys-water-and-sewer-system/water -history.

25. Stanley Schultz and William P. Tischler, "Which Old West and Whose?," in *American History 102: Civil War to the Present* (Madison: University of Wisconsin, 2004).

26. Richard White, *"It's Your Misfortune and None of My Own": A New History of the American West* (Norman: University of Oklahoma Press, 1991), 219.

27. David D. Smits, "The Frontier Army and the Destruction of the Buffalo, 1865–1883," *Western Historical Quarterly* 25, no. 3 (Autumn 1994): 312–38.

28. Kristin L. Miller, *Planning for Bison Grazing on Native Rangeland*, Rangeland Management Specialist, Natural Resources Conservation Service, USDA, April 2002.

29. Gene Gade, "The Buffalo Population and Why It Crashed," *Plains Bison Mysteries That Remain*, pt. 1 (Sundance, WY: Vore Buffalo Jump Foundation).

30. Gade, "The Buffalo Population and Why It Crashed"; quote from Andrew C. Isenberg, *The Destruction of the Bison: An Environmental History, 1750–1920* (Cambridge: Cambridge University Press, 2000), 162.

31. Kansas State Historical Society, "Grasshopper Plague of 1874," accessed August 25, 2014, www.kshs.org.

32. Frederic D. Schwartz, "Day of the Locusts," *American Heritage* 50, no. 4 (July/August 1999), http://www.americanheritage.com/content/day-locusts.

33. Carol Kaesuk Young, "Looking Back at the Days of the Locust," *The New York Times*, April 23, 2002.

SPECTACLE 3

John Steinbeck, *The Grapes of Wrath* (New York: Viking Press, 1939).

1. "Basic Beef Cattle Nutrition," Ontario Ministry of Agriculture and Food, accessed August 25, 2014, http://www.omafra.gov.on.ca/english/livestock/beef/facts/91-066.htm.

2. Maureen Ogle, *In Meat We Trust: An Unexpected History of Carnivore America* (New York: Houghton Mifflin, 2013), 226.

SPECTACLE 4

Wallace Stegner, *Angle of Repose* (Garden City, NY: Doubleday & Co, 1971).

1. Assembled Chains of Title for NE ¼ SE ¼ and SE ¼ NE ¼, Section 18, Township 4 North, Range 66 West, Weld County, Colorado.

2. This is not the attorney's real name, nor the neighboring farmer's; I have changed the names to protect the individuals.

SPECTACLE 5

Robert Penn Warren, *World Enough and Time* (New York: Random House, 1950).

1. Bob Murray, PhD, "Hydration and Health Promotion," in "Hydration and Health Promotion," supplement 5, *Journal of the American College of Nutrition* 26 (2007): 542S–547S; and Ann C. Grandjean, EdD, FACN, and Nicole R. Grandjean, PhD, "Dehydration and Cognitive Performance," in "Hydration and Health Promotion," supplement 5, *Journal of the American College of Nutrition* 26 (2007): 548S–554S.

2. As described by Justice Gregory Hobbs, email, July 8, 2014.

3. David B. Schorr, *The Colorado Doctrine: Water Rights, Corporations, and Distributive Justice on the American Frontier* (New Haven, CT: Yale University Press, 2012), quote from preface.

4. Legitimate "beneficial uses" are numerous but generally fall into four prioritized categories: domestic, industrial, irrigation, and nature and recreational.

5. Pleadings in Weld County District Court, Case #29032, *Michel v. Eaton Cattle Co.*, Findings, Conclusion, and Order, May 6, 1980.

6. Glenn Schaible and Marcel Aillery, "Water Conservation in Irrigated Agriculture: Trends and Challenges in the Face of Emerging Demands," *Economic Information Bulletin No. (EIB-99)*, September 2012, iii. "In 2007, irrigated farms

accounted for 55 percent of the total value of crop sales while also supporting the livestock and poultry sectors through irrigated production of animal forage and feed crops.
Roughly 57 million acres—or 7.5 percent of all US cropland and pastureland—were
irrigated in 2007, nearly three-quarters of which are in the 17 western-most contiguous States." United States Ag Census, 2007, "Market Value of Agricultural Products
Sold Including Landlord's Share and Direct Sales: 2007 and 2002." Glenn Schaible,
USDA Economic Research Service analyst, from 2007 US Ag Census: *"Farm Sales for
Irrigated Farms as a Percent of All Farms Sales (Percents)* [;] For 17 Western States: 60.47
percent ($83,147,363,000 / $137,494,158,000) [;] For 31 Eastern States: 21.97 percent
($34,965,743,000 / $159,155,688,000) [;] For the U.S: 39.87 percent ($118,510,873,000 /
$297,220,491,000) [;] ($137,494,158,000 divided by $297,220,491,000 = 46.25% of total
sales raised [;] in 17 western states)."

7. Russell Elliot, *Servant of Power: A Political Biography of Senator William M.
Stewart* (Reno: University of Nevada Press, 1983), 100–101, 113.

8. Congressional Record, 51st Cong., 1st Sess., 5419; Mark Panny, "The Origins of
Federal Reclamation Ideology and Irrigation in the American West" (undergraduate
thesis, Department of History, Lafayette College, Easton, PA, May 2010), presented
before his thesis committee, Professors D. C. Jackson, Emily Musil Church, and Dave
Sunderlin, accessed August 25, 2014, http://aquadoc.typepad.com/files/origins-of
-reclamation.pdf.

9. *Official Report of the International Irrigation Congress*, 1983, 109, 111.

10. T. R. Eschner, R. F. Hadley, and K. D. Crowley, *Hydrologic and Morphologic
Changes in Channels of the Platte River Basin in Colorado, Wyoming, and Nebraska: A
Historical Perspective*, US Geological Survey Professional Paper 1277-A, 1983, 39.

11. Robert Longenbaugh, "How Conjunctive Use Has Changed in the South Platte
Basin over 50 Years," presented at the Agriculture/Urban Water Interface Conflicts and
Opportunities Conference, US Committee on Irrigation and Drainage, Denver CO,
October 2013.

12. John T. Daubert and Robert A. Young, Department of Agricultural and
Resource Economics, and H. J. Morel-Seytoux, Department of Civil Engineering,
Managing an Interrelated Stream-Aquifer System: Economics, Institutions, Hydrology,
Technical Report #47, Colorado Water Resources Research Institute, April 1985.

13. Dick Stenzel, "Wells: The Final Frontier," presented at Annual South Platte
Forum, 2006, accessed August 25, 2014, http://www.cwi.colostate.edu/southplatte
/files/11132012%20web%20Dick_Stenzel_article.pdf. Mr. Stenzel is the former assistant state engineer and division one engineer for the Colorado Division of Water
Resources.

14. Richard Stenzel and Tom Cech with contributors Hal Simpson and Dick Wolfe,
Water: Colorado's Real Gold (Fort Collins, CO: Richard Stenzel, 2013).

15. W. E. Code, "Use of Ground Water for Use of Irrigation in the South Platte
Valley of Colorado," Colorado Agricultural Experiment Station, Colorado State
University, September 1943.

16. Stenzel and Cech, *Water*.

17. Only anecdotal evidence supports this assertion; however, I heard it repeatedly. Documents reinforce that "the justification to reduce the repayment burden of the farmers is that irrigation is considered not only beneficial to the farmers but also to the nation." "Irrigation costs above the water-users' ability-to-pay would be repaid through assistance from surplus power and other simultaneous project revenues [US Department of Interior, 1972, x–xiii]." Ghebreyohannes Keleta, Robert A. Young, and Edward W. Sparling, *Economic Aspects of Cost-Sharing for Federal Irrigation Projects*, Department of Economics, Colorado State University, December 1982, accessed May 21, 2015, http://www.cwi.colostate.edu/publications/CR/118.pdf. More information about these programs is available at Reclamation Act of 1939 (August 4, 1939), accessed May 21, 2015, http://www.usbr.gov/power/legislation/recproja.pdf.

18. Stenzel and Cech, *Water*.

19. USGS Colorado Water Sources Circular #28, "Hydrology of the South Platte River Valley, Northeastern Colorado," 1975.

20. Longenbaugh, "How Conjunctive Use Has Changed."

21. Water Center of Colorado State University, *Colorado Water*, 24, no. 5 (October/November 2007), http://www.cwi.colostate.edu/newsletters/2007/ColoradoWater _24_5.pdf.

SPECTACLE 6

"Cool Water," song composed by Bob Nolan in 1936, bestselling recording by Vaughn Monroe and the Sons of the Pioneers in 1948, released by RCA Victor Records as catalog number 20-2923.

1. The 1951 Colorado Supreme Court decision *Safranek v. Town of Limon* gave notice that tributary groundwater affected surface water.

2. "A Brief Timeline of Groundwater Management in the South Platte Basin," Colorado Water Institute, Colorado State University; Reagan Waskom, *A Brief Timeline of Groundwater Management in the South Platte*, Colorado State University, revised February 5, 2013, accessed on June 2, 2016, http://www.cwi.colostate.edu/southplatte /files/Reagan's%20SP%20timeline%20(brief%20history)%20revised%202-5-13.pdf.

3. The *cube* refers to the concept of "carrying capacity," discussed in Spectacle 2, "The Nuisance of Hindsight."

4. Robert Longenbaugh, "How Conjunctive Use Has Changed in the South Platte Basin over 50 Years," presented at the Agriculture/Urban Water Interface Conflicts and Opportunities Conference, US Committee on Irrigation and Drainage, Denver, CO, October 2013.

5. Author interviews and conversations with Jack Odor, in Fort Morgan, Colorado, and by telephone, November 2010–November 2015.

6. Richard Stenzel and Tom Cech with contributors Hal Simpson and Dick Wolfe, *Water: Colorado's Real Gold* (Fort Collins, CO: Richard Stenzel, 2013), 417–20; *Report to the Colorado Legislature, HB12-1278 Study of the South Platte River Alluvial Aquifer*, Colorado Water Institute, Colorado State University, December 31, 2013, 148.

7. Author interviews and conversations with Jack Odor, in Fort Morgan, Colorado, and by telephone, November 2010–November 2015.

SPECTACLE 7

Wenonah Hauter, *Foodopoly* (New York: New Press, 2012).

1. Tim Wyngaard and James Herzog, "Carter Backs Gifts to Kin Appointee," *Pittsburgh Press*, June 14, 1978.

2. Ronald Henkoff and Sara Hammes, "Oh, How the Money Grows at ADM," *Fortune Magazine*, October 8, 1990.

3. Wenonah Hauter, *Foodopoly* (New York: New Press, 2012), 65.

4. Hauter, *Foodopoly*, 66; Andrew Schmidt, *Sugar and Related Sweetener Products: International Perspective* (New York: CAB International, 2002), 33.

5. Michael Pollan, *The Omnivore's Dilemma: A Natural History of Four Meals* (New York: Penguin Publishing Group, 2006), 17–19.

6. Nina Teicholz, *The Big Fat Surprise* (New York: Simon and Schuster, 2014).

7. The 2012 USDA Ag Census counted 2.2 million American farms, but these include 1.4 million "lifestyle" farms, people whose income derives from some place other than the farmland: Timothy A. Wise, "Understanding the Farm Problem: Six Common Errors in Presenting Farm Statistics," Global Development and Environment Institute Working Paper, No. 05-02, Tufts University, March 2005.

8. US gross farm income in 2014 was $429 billion according to the USDA National Agriculture Statistics Service (see Economic Research Service's "Farming and Farm Income") statistics. "http://www.ers.usda.gov/data-products/ag-and-food-statistics-charting-the-essentials/farming-and-farm-income.aspx. US gross farm income in organic products in 2014 was $5.5 billion. https://www.agcensus.usda.gov/Newsroom/2015/09_17_2015.php $5.5 billion is 1.3 percent of $429 billion.

9. "Organic Agriculture," USDA Economic Research Service website accessed June 3, 2016, http://www.ers.usda.gov/topics/natural-resources-environment/organic-agriculture/organic-market-overview.aspx.

10. "Wild Grass Became Maize Crop More than 8700 Year Ago," National Science Foundation press release, March 23, 2009.

11. *Diamond v. Chakrabarty*, 447 U.S. 303, US Supreme Court decision (1980).

12. Pollan, *The Omnivore's Dilemma*, 41.

13. Hauter, *Foodopoly*.

14. "Freedom to Farm: A Closer Look," Environmental Working Group, February 1, 1996.

15. Brian DeVore, "Freedom to Farm, Freedom to . . . ?," *Sustainable Farming Connection* (Committee for Sustainable Farm Publishing, 1997), published online only at https://www.ibiblio.org/farming-connection/farmpoli/features/freedom.htm, accessed June 3, 2016.

SPECTACLE 8

A. B. Guthrie Jr., *The Way West* (New York: William Sloane Associates Publishers, 1949).

1. Charles Fisk, *The Metro Denver Water Story* (Fort Collins: Colorado State University, 2005).

2. Susan Mackay, Laura E. Perrault, and Vicky L. Peters, "Can States Enforce RCRA at Superfund Sites? The Rocky Mountain Arsenal Decision," *Environmental Law Reporter* 23, no. 7 (July 1993): ELR 10419.

3. *Silent Spring*, quoted in S. Labaton, "Big Courtroom for Toxic Web," *The New York Times*, November 16, 1987.

4. Matthew Green, "The Rocky Mountain Arsenal: States' Rights and the Cleanup of Hazardous Waste," in Fall 1993 Natural Resources and Environmental Policy Seminar, Conflict Research Consortium Working Paper 94-58 (Boulder: University of Colorado Interdisciplinary Graduate Certificate Program in Environmental Policy, 1994).

5. Census of Population and Housing, US Census Bureau, Colorado Decennial Census, http://www.census.gov/prod/www/decennial.html; for Thornton, Colorado population, click on "Colorado," Chapters A and B, Full Document.

6. David Olinger and Chuck Plunkett, "'Suburban Aggression,' Liquid Assets: Turning Water into Gold, Part III," *The Denver Post*, November 22, 2005.

7. Nicolas Kryloff, *Guide to the Water Supply and Storage Company Collection* (Fort Collins: Colorado State University Water Resources Archive, 2007).

8. Brian Werner, *A Brief History of How Water Influenced the Development of the Fort Collins Region* (Fort Collins: Colorado Water Institute, Colorado State University).

9. Olinger and Plunkett, "Suburban Aggression."

10. *Thornton v. Bijou Irrigation et al.*, Colorado Supreme Court, October 15, 1996.

11. Olinger and Plunkett, "Suburban Aggression."

12. Sandi Zellmer, "The Anti-Speculation Doctrine and Its Implications for Collaborative Water Management," Nevada Law Journal 8, no. 3, article 12 (April 1, 2008), http://scholars.law.unlv.edu/nlj/vol8/iss3/12.

SPECTACLE 9

Sandra Postel, *Pillar of Sand* (New York: W. W. Norton and Company, 1999), 239.

1. Janice Holt Giles, *Six-Horse Hitch* (Boston: Houghton Mifflin Company, 1969).

2. Ed Marston, "Ripples Grow When a Dam Dies," *High Country News*, October 31, 1994.

3. Michael Douglas White (White and Jankowski, LLP), "City of Thornton v. Bijou Irrigation Co.: The Thornton Northern Project Decision," *Corporate.findlaw.com*, March 26, 2008.

4. *Thornton v. Bijou Irrigation et al.*, Colorado Supreme Court, October 15, 1996.

5. *City and County of Denver v. Sherriff*, 96 P.2d, 836, 841, Colo. 1939.

6. Janet C. Neuman, "Beneficial Use, Waste and Forfeiture: The Inefficient Search for Efficiency in Western Water," *Environmental Law* 28 (1998): 919–96.

7. Scott A. Clark and Alix L. Joseph, "Commentary: Changes of Water Rights and the Anti-Speculation Doctrine: The Continuing Importance of Actual Beneficial Uses," *University of Denver Water Law Review* 9 (Spring 2006): 553.

8. *Thornton v. Bijou Irrigation et al.* prohibited any use of Colorado–Big Thompson water, acquired with the farms, outside of the boundaries of the Northern Colorado Water Conservancy District, its southern boundary not stretching past Boulder and Weld Counties—so not including Thornton.

9. § 37-92-305(3), 15 C.R.S. (1990), June 3, 2016 http://scholar.google.com/scholar _case?case=8419745857011304902&q=City+of+Thornton+v.+Bijou+Irrigation&hl=en& as_sdt=2006&as_vis=1.

10. Elizabeth Garner, "Demographic Trends: Understanding the Impact of a Changing Population on Colorado," EDCC, State of Colorado Demography Office, 2011.

11. "Free Pass for Oil & Gas," Environmental Working Group, from data purchased from IHS, Inc., 2008.

12. Charles Fisk, *The Metro Denver Water Story* (Fort Collins: Colorado State University, 2005), 298.

13. The Water Information Program, waterinfo.org; John N. Winchester, PE, "A Historical View: Transmountain Diversion Development in Colorado," Proceedings of the 2001 USCID Water Management Conference, 2001, accessed on June 3, 2016, https://dspace.library.colostate.edu/bitstream/handle/10217/46354/116_ Proceedings%202001%20USCID%20Water%20Management%20-%20Transbasin%20 Water%20Transfers%20Winchester.pdf?sequence=15&isAllowed=y. Based on the 2000 Census and the Colorado state engineer's records, the Front Range of Colorado (the East Slope, excluding the North Platte and Rio Grande basins) has 89 percent of the state's population but only 16 percent of the state's water (United States Census Bureau (USCB), 2000; State Engineering, State Engineer's Office, 2000).

14. Gregory J. Hobbs Jr., "Reviving the Public Ownership, Antispeculation, and Beneficial Use Moorings of Prior Appropriation Water Law," *University of Colorado Law Review* 84 (2013): 97–157 (no longer available online but can be accessed through the Colorado Water Institute archive); *Citizen's Guide to Colorado Water Law* (Denver: Colorado Foundation for Water Education, 2004); Daniel Tyler, *Last Water Hole in the West: The Colorado–Big Thompson Project and the Northern Colorado Water Conservancy District* (Niwot: University Press of Colorado, 1992).

15. More information about these programs is available at *Reclamation Act of 1939*, August 4, 1939, accessed May 21, 2015, http://www.usbr.gov/power/legislation/recproja .pdf.

16. Hobbs, "Reviving the Public Ownership"; Winchester, "A Historical View."

17. "Colorado Water Plan," Executive Summary, Colorado Water Conservancy Board and the Office of the Governor, 2015.

18. Western Water Policy Advisory Commission, "Water in the West: The Challenges for the Next Century," report, October 20–27, 1997.

19. Kate Watkins, *State Spending Limitations: TABOR and Referendum C. Denver: Colorado Legislative Council Staff*, 2009, accessed June 3, 2016, https://www.colorado .gov/pacific/sites/default/files/Tabor%20Limit%20and%20Referendum%20C.pdf; "The Secret Tax Explosion," Governing: Public Money, September 2013, accessed June 3, 2016, http://www.governing.com/columns/public-money/col-secret-tax-explosion .html; Colorado Department of Local Affairs, "Special Districts: A Brief Review for Prospective Homeowners," Colorado Department of Local Affairs, accessed August 25, 2014, http://redskyranchmetro.com/images/Satellite.pdf; McGeady and Sisneros, "Frequently Asked Questions about Special Districts," 2014, accessed June 16, 2016, http://www.metropolitandistricts.com/#!faq/c1stk.

20. David Olinger and Chuck Plunkett, "'A Radical New Vision': Liquid Assets: Turning Water into Gold, Part II," *The Denver Post*, November 21, 2005.

21. John Wesley Powell, *Report on the Lands of the Arid Region of the United States* [1879] (Cambridge, MA: Belknap Press of Harvard University, 1962), 53–54.

22. Mary C. Kennamer, "Rio Grande Wild Turkey," *NWTF Wildlife Bulletin* no. 3, National Wild Turkey Federation, Edgefield, SC, accessed June 3, 2016, http://indeeag .weebly.com/uploads/8/7/2/0/8720928/rio_grande.pdf.

23. US Agricultural Census, 2000; Eric Schlosser, *Fast Food Nation* (New York: Mariner, 2001), 144.

24. Highlands Ranch Community Association, History, http://hrcaonline.org /Area-Resources/Highlands-Ranch/History.

25. Courtney Hemenway and Paul Grundemann, "Ground Water/Surface Water Interactions," AWRA Summer Specialty Conference, 2002.

26. US Census Bureau, 2000 Census.

27. Colorado State Demography Office, https://demography.dola.colorado.gov /population/population-totals-colorado-substate/#population-totals-for-colorado-and -sub-state-regions.

SPECTACLE 10

Richard Stenzel and Tom Cech with contributors Hal Simpson and Dick Wolfe, *Water: Colorado's Real Gold* (Fort Collins, CO: Richard Stenzel, 2013).

1. Arnaldo Einaudi is not the seer's real name. I was unable to locate his relatives to confirm use of his story.

2. Ellen Wohl, *Virtual Rivers: Lessons from the Mountain Rivers of the Colorado Front Range* (New Haven, CT: Yale University Press, 2001) (focused on the S. Platte and tributaries, mostly in the mountains, with a combined ecosystem/historical perspective).

3. Delphus E. Carpenter's mother, Ann Hogarty, was the sister of my great-grandmother, Mary Tuttle Hogarty; Mary was the first wife of Bruce Eaton, son of Benjamin Harrison Eaton (*Descendants of Patrick Hogarty* [Fort Collins: Colorado Water Institute], accessed June 12, 2015, http://lib.colostate.edu/archives/water/dot

/hogarty.html). Richard Stenzel and Tom Cech with contributors Hal Simpson and Dick Wolfe, *Water: Colorado's Real Gold* (Fort Collins, CO: Richard Stenzel, 2013).

4. Stenzel and Cech, *Water.*

5. *Kansas v. Colorado, October Term, 1994,* on exceptions to Report of Special Master, No. 105 Original, argued March 21, 1995, decided May 15, 1995.

6. Hal Simpson, *Arkansas River Basin Water Forum: "A River of Dreams and Realities,"* Proceedings of the 1995 Arkansas River Basin Water Forum, January 17–18, 1995, Colorado Water Resources Research Institute, Information Series No. 82 (Fort Collins: Colorado State University, 1985).

7. Robert Longenbaugh, "How Conjunctive Use Has Changed in the South Platte Basin over 50 Years," presented at the Agriculture/Urban Water Interface Conflicts and Opportunities Conference, US Committee on Irrigation and Drainage, Denver CO, October 2013.

8. *Report to the Colorado Legislature, HB1 2-1278 Study of the South Platte River Alluvial Aquifer* (Denver: Colorado Water Institute, Colorado State University, December 31, 2013), 148.

SPECTACLE 11

Wallace Stegner, *Crossing to Safety* (New York: Random House, 1987)

1. Case No. 00SA211, *Empire Lodge Homeowners' Association v. Moyer*, Colorado Supreme Court, December 17, 2001.

2. Strawn, Lain, "The Last GASP: The Conflict over Management of Replacement Water in the South Platte River Basin," *University of Colorado Law Review* 75 (Spring 2004): 597–632.

3. Hal Simpson, "History of Well Regulation: South Platte River Basin," monograph, September 2006. Denver, Colorado.

4. Mary Kennamer, "Rio Grande Wild Turkey (*Meleagris gallopavo intermedia*)," *NWTF Wildlife Bulletin No. 3* (North American Wild Turkey Management Plan), National Wild Turkey Federation, November 1999.

5. Case No. 01SA56, *Board of County Comm'rs, County v. Park County Sportsmen's Ranch, LLP*, Colorado Supreme Court, April 8, 2002, accessed August 27, 2014, http://www.cobar.org/opinions/opinion.cfm?OpinionID=558.

6. Colorado Water Division No. 1, Water court, Weld County, State of Colorado, Case Number 96 CW 114, *Concerning the Application for Water Rights of: The Park County Sportsmen's Ranch*, June 1, 2001.

7. William Shakespeare, *Julius Caesar*, Act 4, Scene 3.

8. "Well Regulation in the South Platte River Basin of Colorado," briefing document for the South Platte River Task Force, Colorado Division of Water Resources, June 2007.

9. Steve Sims named these individuals from memory in a conversation with Hal Simpson, in summer 2014.

10. Robert Longenbaugh, "How Conjunctive Use Has Changed in the South Platte Basin over 50 Years," presented at the Agriculture/Urban Water Interface Conflicts and Opportunities Conference, US Committee on Irrigation and Drainage, Denver CO, October 2013.

SPECTACLE 12

1. An email from Lynn Kramer, staff at Central Colorado Water Conservancy District, sent May 15, 2014: in January 2005 there were 237 contracts totaling 25,156 acre-feet of consumptive use.

2. Reagan Waskom, *A Brief Timeline of Groundwater Management in the South Platte*, Colorado State University, revised February 5, 2013, accessed on June 2, 2016, http://www.cwi.colostate.edu/southplatte/files/Reagan's%20SP%20timeline%20 (brief%20history)%20revised%202-5-13.pdf.

3. "Water, Food and Agriculture" (Oakland, CA: Pacific Institute), accessed December, 2014, http://pacinst.org/issues/water-food-and-agriculture/.

SPECTACLE 13

Ann Oldenburg, "Salman Rushdie, Lemony Snicket support Occupy Writers," *USA Today*, October, 18, 2011.

1. "Protecting Water for Western Irrigated Agriculture: Endangered Species Act Implementation in the Western U.S. Looking for Answers to Modernize and Improve the ESA for Species and People," A White Paper Prepared by the Family Farm Alliance, April 2014. Klamath Falls, Oregon.

2. "As long as people are breaking the law and getting away with it . . . it's going to be tough" (Jim Nelson, Sidebar article, *High Country News*, October 30, 1995).

3. Tim Findley, "David and Goliath," *Range Magazine*, Summer 2001.

4. "How NWF Is Defending Our Natural Heritage," *National Wildlife*, National Wildlife Federation, October–November 1995.

5. David M. Freeman, *Implementing the Endangered Species Act on the Platte Basin Water Commons* (Boulder: University Press of Colorado, 2010), 34.

6. US Geological Survey; 2004 Federal Real Property Report, US General Services Administration, accessed May 31, 2016, http://www.nytimes.com/interactive/2012/03 /23/us/western-land-owned-by-the-federal-government.html?_r=0.

7. From the Platte River Recovery Implementation Program director, Jerry Kenny, phone call, August, 21, 2010.

8. Freeman, *Implementing the Endangered Species Act*, 179–82.

9. Mike Davis, *Living on the Ice Shelf: Humanity's Meltdown*, TomDispatch.com, June 26, 2008, accessed September 3, 2014, http://www.tomdispatch.com/post/174949.

10. J. Zalasiewicz, M. Williams, A Smith, T. L. Barry, A. L. Coe, et al., "Are We Now Living in the Anthropocene?" *GSA Today* 18, no. 2 (2008): 4–8.

11. Michael Soulé, Douglas T. Bolger, Allison C. Alberts, John Wright, Marina Sorice, and Scott Hill, "Reconstructed Dynamics of Rapid Extinctions of Chaparral-Requiring Birds in Urban Habitat Islands," *Conservation Biology* 2, no. 1 (March 1988): 75–92.

12. *State Water Supply Initiative 2010, Key Findings*, Colorado Water Conservation Board, Denver, Colorado.

13. Colorado Supreme Court, No. 10SA92, *Kobobel v. Colorado Department of Natural Resources, Division of Water Resources*, March 28, 2011, Denver, Colorado.

14. Jerd Smith, "Water Crisis Becomes Urgent amid Dry Skies, Wells," *Rocky Mountain News*, July 9, 2007.

15. "Concerning the Application for Water Rights of: Well Augmentation Subdistrict of the Central Colorado Water Conservancy District and South Platte Well Users Association, in Weld, Larimer, and Adams Counties," Case No. 03 CW 99, Findings of Fact, Conclusions of Law, Judgment, and Order of the Water Court, filing date: October 18, 2007.

16. Freeman, *Implementing the Endangered Species Act*, 443.

17. Per Hal Simpson, June 27, 2014: "This water was not made available to farmers but similar projects in the area did recharge the aquifer and the additional water was used to augment well depletions so that wells could pump. These were farmers that had been in GASP but implemented their own projects to keep pumping."

18. James L. Huffman, "Property Rights and Wrongs," *Washington Times*, June 26, 2008, accessed September 20, 2016, http://www.washingtontimes.com/news/2008/jun/26/property-rights-and-wrongs/. Huffman is the Erskine Wood Sr. Professor of Law at the Lewis & Clark Law School in Portland, Oregon, and a member of the Property Rights, Freedom and Prosperity Task Force at Stanford University's Hoover Institution.

SPECTACLE 14

Hilary Mantel, *A Place of Greater Safety* (New York: Atheneum, 1992), 98.

1. Colorado Supreme Court, November 23, 2009, No. 08SA224, *Concerning the Application for Water Rights of Well Augmentation Subdistrict of the Central Colorado Water Conservancy District and South Platte Well Users Association in Adams, Morgan, and Weld Counties: Well Augmentation Subdistrict of the Central Colorado Water Conservancy District v. City of Aurora*. No records of pumping rates from the 1970s exist.

2. Charles F. Leaf, PhD, PE, and Forrest A. Leaf, PE, *Hydrology and Well Augmentation in the South Platte River Basin: Abstract*, American Water Resources Association 2007 Annual Conference, Golden, CO; Robert E. Glover, F. ASCE, "South Platte River Flow Correlations," *Journal of the Irrigation and Drainage Division*, 101, no. IR3 (September 1975).

3. Robert Longenbaugh, email exchange with Tershia d'Elgin, June 17–19, 2015.

4. *Concerning the Application for Water Rights of Well Augmentation Subdistrict of the Central Colorado Water Conservancy District and South Platte Well Users*

Association in Adams, Morgan, and Weld Counties: Well Augmentation Subdistrict of the Central Colorado Water Conservancy District v. City of Aurora, Colorado Supreme Court, No. 08SA224. November 23, 2009.

5. Randy Ray, Central Colorado Water Conservancy District, email, June 10, 2014.

6. *Concerning the Application for Water Rights*; Division Engineer Dave Nettles of Division One, Division Colorado Water Resources, 2014.

7. Cristina Milesi et al., "Mapping and Modeling of Biogeochemical Cycling of Turf Grasses in the United States," *Environmental Management* 36, no. 3 (September 2005): 426–38.

8. USDA Census of Agriculture, 2007.

9. USDA Census of Agriculture, 2007.

10. Kevin N. Morris, National Turfgrass Research Initiative, *Golf Course Management* magazine (August 2006): "In the U.S., turfgrass covers an estimated 50 million acres, 31 million acres of which is irrigated, making turf the fourth largest crop in acreage and the largest crop that is irrigated." Also see Western Resource Advocates, *Smart Water: A Comparative Study of Urban Water Use across the Southwest* (Boulder, CO: Western Resource Advocates, 2003), chap. 4; Milesi et al., "Mapping and Modeling."

11. Eric Schechter, "Interview with John Calvert," author of *Sayyid Qutb and the Origins of Radical Islamism* and translator of Qutb's *A Child from the Village*, *Worldpress*, September 19, 2005; *The Power of Nightmares*, documentary about Sayyid Qutb, directed and produced by Adam Curtis, 2008.

12. David Olinger and Chuck Plunkett, "A Radical New Vision: Liquid Assets, Turning Water into Gold, Part II," *The Denver Post*, November 21, 2005.

13. Olinger and Plunkett, "A Radical New Vision."

14. Robert Longenbaugh, "How Conjunctive Use Has Changed in the South Platte Basin over 50 Years," presented at the Agriculture / Urban Water Interface Conflicts and Opportunities Conference, US Committee on Irrigation and Drainage, Denver, CO, October 2013.

15. Barry Mirkin, "Arab Spring: Demographics in a Region of Transition," Arab Human Development Report Research Paper Series (United Nations Development Programme, Regional Bureau for Arab States, New York, NY, 2013); "Syria: Drought Pushing Millions into Poverty," *Irin News: A Service of the U.N. Service for Humanitarian Affairs*, September 9, 2010; David P. Goldman, "The Economic Blunders behind the Arab Revolutions," *The Wall Street Journal*, July 13–14, 2013.

SPECTACLE 15

Shakti Gawain, *Creative Visualizations*, 25th anniversary edition (San Francisco, CA: New World Library, 2002).

1. *Statewide Water Supply Initiative 2010*, Colorado Water Conservation Board, accessed September 10, 2014, http://cwcb.state.co.us/water-management/water-supply-planning/Pages/SWSI2010.aspx.

2. *The Population Projections Program*, Colorado State Demography Office, accessed April 30, 2015, https://www.colorado.gov/dola/state-demography-office.

3. "Colorado Water Plan," Final 2015, Section 6.4, Alternative Agricultural Transfers (Colorado Water Conservation Board, Office of the Governor, 2015), 1.

4. D. Pimentel, B. Berger, D. Filiberto, M. Newton, B. Wolfe, E. Karabinakis, S. Clark, E. Poon, E. Abbett, and S. Nandagopal, "Water Resources: Agricultural and Environmental Issues," *BioScience* 54, no. 10 (2004): 909–18.

5. M. Kravčík, J. Pokorný, J. Kohutiar, M. Kováč, and E. Tóth, *Water for the Recovery of the Planet: A New Water Paradigm* (People and Water NGO, the Association of Towns and Municipalities of Slovakia, the community help society ENKI, and the Foundation for the Support of Civic Activities, 2007).

6. Robert Glennon, *Water Follies* (New York: Island Press, 2002), 98.

7. Glennon, *Water Follies*, 98.

8. Maude Barlow, *Blue Covenant* (New York: New Press, 2008), 64, 68, 70.

9. USDA Census of Agriculture, 2012.

10. USDA Census of Agriculture, 2012 and 1997.

11. Lester R. Brown, *Outgrowing the Earth: The Food Security Challenge in an Age of Falling Water Tables and Rising Temperatures* (New York: W. W. Norton, 2005).

12. Miles Moffeit, "Suicide Rates Show more Colorado Farmers Losing Hope: Suicide Hotlines Field Calls as Prices Fall and Money Woes Mount," *The Denver Post*, June 3, 2009.

13. L. Stallones and C. Beseler, "Pesticides and Depressive Symptoms among Farm Residents," *Annals of Epidemiology* 12, no. 6 (2002): 389–94.

14. USDA 2007 Census of Agriculture, National Agricultural Statistics Service: irrigated acres as a percent of total cropland acres (percents); for seventeen Western states: 42,336,857 irrigated acres; for the United States: 406,424,909 cropland acres 42,336,857/406,424,909 = 10.4 percent. (Glenn Schaible, USDA Economic Research Service analyst, from 2007 US Ag Census).

15. Wenonah Hauter, *Foodopoly* (New York: New Press, 2012), 33.

16. These figures reflect food trade with the rest of the world, defined as the following USDA Foreign Agricultural Service aggregations: dairy products, fruits and preparations, grains and feeds, livestock and meats, oilseeds and products, other horticultural products, planting seeds, poultry and products, sugar and tropical products, tree nuts and preparations, and vegetables and preparations (Foreign Agricultural Service, "Global Agricultural Trade System" [Washington, DC: US Department of Agriculture], accessed June 9, 2014, http://www.fas.usda.gov/gats/default.aspx). Even in the recessionary year of 2009, when import levels crashed, food imports comprised 17 percent of food consumed by Americans by volume, compared to 11 percent before NAFTA and the WTO (Economic Research Service, "Import Shares of US Food Consumption Using the Volume Method," [Washington, DC: US Department of Agriculture], 2009, accessed April 25, 2015, http://www.ers.usda.gov/media/563776/import_1.xls). This information and other startling statistics are also available at https://www.citizen.org /documents/food-under-nafta-wto.pdf, accessed June 3, 2106.

17. "Value of U.S. food imports, by food group, from 1999 to 2013," USDA Economic Research Service, Washington, DC.

18. Sophia Huang and Kuo Huang, *Increased U.S. Imports of Fruit and Vegetables*, Report of the Economic Research Service, USDA, FTS-328-01 (Washington, DC: United States Department of Agriculture, September 2007).

19. Mark Schultz (of the Minnesota-based Land Stewardship Project), "Counterpoint: If the Trans-Pacific Partnership Is So Swell, Why All the Secrecy?" *Minneapolis Star Tribune*, May 22, 2014.

20. Tennille Tracy, "WTO Rejects U.S. Meat 'Origin' Labels," *The Wall Street Journal*, May 18, 2015.

21. Seung K. Lee and Adel A. Kader, "Preharvest and Postharvest Factors Influencing Vitamin C Content of Horticultural Crops," *Postharvest Biology and Technology* 20 (2000): 207–20.

SPECTACLE 16

Noah Cross character speaking of Hollis Mulwray (character based on William Mulholland) to Jake Gittes, in Robert Towne screenplay, *Chinatown*, October 9, 1973, exterior Mulwray home at dusk, accessed June 3, 2016, http://www.pages.drexel.edu /~ina22/splaylib/Screenplay-Chinatown.htm, p. 133.

1. Communications with Dr. Lauren J. Livo regarding the amphibians mentioned took place from March 26, 2014, to July 10, 2014. Now an independent researcher, she was a postdoctoral fellow at the Ecophysiology Lab in the Department of Integrative Physiology, University of Colorado Boulder.

2. Pieter Johnson et al., "Richer Parasite Diversity Leads to Healthier Frogs, Says CU Study," *Natural Sciences, Environment Discovery and Innovation* (May 21, 2012).

3. Communications with Dr. Lauren J. Livo, March 26, 2014, to July 10, 2014.

4. Joanna Lemly, Laurie Gillian and Gabriel Smith, *Lower South Platte River Basin Wetland Profile and Condition Assessment* (Fort Collins: Colorado Natural Heritage Program, Colorado State University, April 2014).

5. M. M. Ellis and J. Henderson, "Amphibia and Reptilia of Colorado: Part II," *University of Colorado Studies* 15 (1915): 253–63.

6. Pieter Johnson et al., "Regional Decline of an Iconic Amphibian Associated with Elevation, Land-Use Change, and Invasive Species," *Conservation Biology* 25 (2011): 556–66.

7. *Regional Ecosystem Analysis for Metropolitan Denver and Cities of the Northern Front Range* (USDA Forest Service and Colorado State Forest Service, American Forests, Washington, DC, April 2001); James Falcone and Daniel Pearson, *Land-Cover and Imperviousness Data for Regional Areas near Denver, Colorado; Dallas–Fort Worth, Texas; and Milwaukee–Green Bay, Wisconsin—2001*, part of the US Geological Survey's (USGS) National Water-Quality Assessment (NAWQA) Program Effects of Urbanization on Stream Ecosystems (EUSE).

8. Laura Jamison, "Why Wetlands? Because They Clean Our Water," *BC Wetland Network*, March 1995, http://www.finnslough.com/Environment%20Pages/why_wetlands.htm.

9. Robert Longenbaugh, PE, is a consultant water engineer with over fifty-five years of experience dealing with well pumping, artificial recharge, litigation, and conjunctive use of both ground and surface water to maximize beneficial use in the South Platte River basin. A retired professor of civil engineering at Colorado State University, he was also for eleven years Assistant State Engineer for the Colorado Division of Water Resources, where he had extensive well permitting and litigation experience. Mr. Longenbaugh reviewed the manuscript during fall 2015. All quotes from him precipitate from that review and represent his extensive knowledge of ground and surface water interaction.

10. Email from Dr. Reagan Waskom, Colorado Water Institute, Colorado State University, July 2, 2014.

11. My interview with Barb Horn took place during spring 2014, and she confirmed the text by email on June 30, 2014.

12. Natural Resources Defense Council: Toxics, www.nrdc.org, http://www.nrdc.org/health/toxics.asp, April 20, 2015.

13. Charles Duhigg, "Debating How Much Weed Killer Is Safe in Your Water Glass," *The New York Times*, August 22, 2009.

14. Rachel Aviv, "A Valuable Reputation," *The New Yorker*, February 10, 2014.

15. Aviv, "A Valuable Reputation."

16. "Pesticides in the Nation's Streams and Groundwater, 1992–2001," NAWQA, USGS Online Publications Directory, #1291, accessed June 3, 2016, https://pubs.usgs.gov/circ/2005/1291/pdf/circ1291.pdf.

17. Atrazine Interim Reregistration Eligibility Decision, US Environmental Protection Agency, Office of Prevention, Pesticides and Toxic Substances, October 31, 2003, Washington, DC.

18. Duhigg, "Debating How Much Weed Killer Is Safe."

19. Tyrone Hayes, Kelly Haston, Mable Tsui, Anhthu Hoang, Cathryn Haeffele, and Aaron Vonk, "Atrazine-Induced Hermaphroditism at 0.1 ppb in American Leopard Frogs (*Rana pipiens*): Laboratory and Field Evidence," *Environmental Health Perspectives* 111, no. 4 (April 2003): 568–75.

20. Aviv, "A Valuable Reputation."

21. Melissa M. Schultz, Edward T. Furlong, Dana. W. Kolpin, Stephen L. Werner, Heiko L. Schoenfuss, Larry B. Barber, Vicki S. Blazer, David O. Norris, and Alan M. Vajda, "Antidepressant Pharmaceuticals in Two U.S. Effluent-Impacted Streams: Occurrence and Fate in Water and Sediment, and Selective Uptake in Fish Neural Tissue," *Environmental Science and Technology* 44, no. 6 (2010): 1918–25.

22. Melissa M. Schultz, Meghan M. Painter, Stephen E. Bartell, Amanda Logue, Edward T. Furlong, Stephen L. Werner, and Heiko L. Schoenfuss, "Selective Uptake and Biological Consequences of Environmentally Relevant Antidepressant Pharmaceutical Exposures on Male Fathead Minnows," *Aquatic Toxicology* 104, nos. 1–2 (July 2011): 38–47.

23. Nicholas Kristof, "It's Time to Learn from Frogs," *The New York Times*, June 27, 2009.

24. Endocrine Disruptor Screening Program, northern.epa.gov, June 3, 2016.

25. J. D. Woodling, E. M. Lopez, T. A. Maldonado, David O. Norris, and Alan M. Vajda, "Intersex and Other Reproductive Disruption of Fish in Wastewater Effluent Dominated Colorado Streams," *Comparative Biochemistry and Physiology: Toxicology and Pharmacology* 144, no. 1 (September 2006): 10–15.

26. Larry B. Barber, Alan M. Vajda, Chris Douville, David O. Norris, and Jeffery Northern, "Fish Endocrine Disruption Responses to a Major Wastewater Treatment Facility Upgrade," *Environment Science and Technology* (Boulder: US Geological Survey, Department of Integrative Biology, University of Colorado, February 21, 2012).

27. D. K. Skelly, S. R. Bolden, and K. B. Dion, "Intersex Frogs Concentrated in Suburban and Urban Landscapes," *EcoHealth* 7 (2010): 374–79.

28. Kevin F. Dennehy, *Water Quality in the South Platte River Basin, Colorado, Nebraska and Wyoming, 1992–1995* (US Geological Survey), accessed June 3, 2016, http://pubs.usgs.gov/circ/circ1167/.

29. *Targeted National Sewage Sludge Survey: Sampling and Analysis Technical Report,* EPA Document No. EPA-822-R-08-016 (Washington, DC: US Environmental Protection Agency, January 2009), accessed on June 3, 2016, https://www.epa.gov/sites/production/files/2015-04/documents/targeted_national_sewage_sluldge_survey_sampling_and_analysis_technical_report_0.pdf.

30. Tracy J. B. Yager, Edward T. Furlong, Dana W. Kolpin, Chad A. Kinney, Steven D. Zaugg, and Mark R. Burkhardt, "Dissipation of Contaminants of Emerging Concern in Biosolids Applied to Nonirrigated Farmland in Eastern Colorado," *Journal of the American Water Resources Association* 50, no. 2 (April 2014): 343–57 (as of June 3, 2016, can be accessed at http://onlinelibrary.wiley.com/doi/10.1111/jawr.12163/abstract).

31. "Research on Evaluating Endocrine Disrupting Chemicals in Biosolids (Sewage Sludge)," EPA, accessed June 3, 2016, https://www.epa.gov/chemical-research/research-evaluating-concentrations-endocrine-disrupting-chemicals-biosolids-sewage.

32. Dennehy, *Water Quality in the South Platte River Basin.*

33. Emily S. Bernhardt, Lawrence E. Band, Christopher J. Walsh, and Philip E. Berke, "Understanding, Managing, and Minimizing Urban Impacts on Surface Water Nitrogen Loading," *New York Academy of Sciences* 1134 (2008): 61–96, doi: 10.1196/annals.1439.014; "National Management Measures to Control Nonpoint Source Pollution from Forestry" (Washington, DC: USEPA, 2015), chap. 1, p. 1, accessed June 3, 2016, at https://www.epa.gov/sites/production/files/2015-10/documents/ch1.pdf.

34. Description of Gomorrah in *Zephaniah* 2:9.

35. Pieter T. Johnson, D. L. Preston, J. T. Hoverman, and B. E. LaFonte, "Host and Parasite Diversity Jointly Control Disease Risk in Complex Communities," *Proceedings of the National Academy of Sciences of the United States of America* 110, no. 42 (October 15, 2013): 16916–21.

36. S. A. Thétiot-Laurent, J. Boissier, A. Robert, and B. Meunier, "Schistosomiasis Chemotherapy," *Angewante Chemie* (international ed. in English) 52, no. 31 (June 27, 2013): 7936–56, doi:10.1002/anie.201208390.PMID 23813602. "Schistosomiasis Control Program," Carter Center, accessed June 3, 2016, abstract only: http://onlinelibrary.wiley .com/wol1/doi/10.1002/anie.201208390/abstract.

37. Johnson et al., "Regional Decline."

38. L. J. Livo, G. A. Hammerson, and H. M. Smith, "Summary of Introduced Amphibians and Reptiles into Colorado," *Northwestern Naturalist* 79, no. 1, (1998): 1–11.

SPECTACLE 17

William Butler Yeats, "The Second Coming," written in 1919, first printed in *The Dial* in November 1920, and afterward included in *Michael Robartes and the Dancer*, Yeats's 1921 collection of verses.

1. "Legume Genome Map Reveals Ancient Genes," submitted by the University of Minnesota News Service, *Land*, December 2, 2011, accessed January 2015, http://issuu. com/theland/docs/2011-1202/26/; "Genome Map of Alfalfa Reveals How an Ancient Gene Duplication Led to Plant's Unique Properties," *Discover: Science + Technology*, University of Minnesota, November 16, 2011, accessed June 3, 2016, http://discover.umn .edu/news/science-technology/genome-map-legume-reveals-how-ancient-gene -duplication-led-plants-unique.

2. "Industry Profile: Alfalfa Hay," Agriculture, Food and Rural Development pages of the Manitoba, Canada, state government website, accessed on June 3, 2016, https:// www.gov.mb.ca/agriculture/crops/production/forages/industry-profile-alfalfa-hay .html.

3. Members of the Wheat, Feed Grains, Rice, and Oilseeds Interagency Commodity Estimates Committees, "Grains and Oilseed Outlook," USDA Agricultural Outlook Forum, February 26, 2016, accessed June 3, 2016, http://www.usda.gov/oce /forum/2016_speeches/GO_AOF2016_FINAL.pdf.

4. Andrew Martin, "Organic Dairy Agrees to Alter Some Practices," *The New York Times*, August 30, 2007.

SPECTACLE 18

Aldo Leopold, from an essay titled "The Good Oak," in *A Sand County Almanac* (Oxford: Oxford University Press, 1949), 6–18.

1. Karen E. Crummy and Eric Gorski, "Lawyer Had Dual Role in Deal that Cost Weld, Adams Farmers Water Rights," *The Denver Post*, July 17, 2011.

2. Crummy and Gorski, "Lawyer Had Dual Role."

3. *Report to the Colorado Legislature HB12-1278 Study of the South Platte River Alluvial Aquifer* (Fort Collins: Colorado Water Institute of Colorado State University, December 31, 2013), 10.

4. Charles McGrath, "Gore Vidal Dies at 86; Prolific, Elegant, Acerbic Writer," *The New York Times*, August 2, 2012, accessed on June 3, 2016, http://www.nytimes.com /2012/08/01/books/gore-vidal-elegant-writer-dies-at-86.html?_r=0.

5. Stacy Shelton, "Water Wars: GOP Shift New Reality as Tri-State Talks Begin," *Atlanta Journal-Constitution*, Atlanta, GA, January 6, 2003, retrieved March 21, 2011.

6. Robert Glennon, *Water Follies* (New York: Island Press, 2002), 98; Maude Barlow and Tony Clarke, *Blue Gold: The Fight to Stop the Corporate Theft of the World's Water* (New York: The New Press, 2004).

SPECTACLE 19

Dame Anita Lucia Roddick, a human rights activist and environmentalist, who founded The Body Shop, is often credited with this observation.

1. David L. Lentz, ed., *Imperfect Balance: Landscape Alterations in the Pre-Columbian Americas* (New York: Columbia University Press, 2000), xviii–xix.

2. Charles A. Segelquist, Michael L. Scott, and Gregor L. Augle, "Establishment of Populus Deltoides under Simulated Alluvial Groundwater Declines," US Fish and Wildlife Service, National Ecology Research Center, Fort Collins, Colorado, *American Midland Naturalist* 130, no. 2 (October 1993): 274–85.

SPECTACLE 20

Emily Dickinson, "Water Is Taught by Thirst," *The Complete Poems of Emily Dickinson*, edited by Thomas H. Johnson (Boston, MA: Little, Brown & Co., 1914).

1. Colorado Geological Survey geologist Dave Noe, telephone conversations, confirmed by email, between March 19, 2014, and August 18, 2016.

2. M. Kravčík, J. Pokorný, J. Kohutiar, M. Kováč, and E. Tóth, *Water for the Recovery of the Planet: A New Water Paradigm* (People and Water NGO, the Association of Towns and Municipalities of Slovakia, the community help society ENKI, and the Foundation for the Support of Civic Activities, 2007).

3. *Regional Ecosystem Analysis for Metropolitan Denver and Cities of the Northern Front Range*, USDA Forest Service and Colorado State Forest Service, American Forests, Washington, DC, April 2001.

4. Historical Weather for 2013 in Greeley, Colorado, weatherspark.com.

5. Bob Henson, "Inside the Colorado Deluge: How Much Rain Fell on the Front Range, and How Historic Was It?" *NCAR/UCAR AtmosNews*, September 14, 2013.

6. US Drought Monitor; Henson, "Inside the Colorado Deluge."

7. Bobby Magill, "Uncertainty a Big Hurdle in Colorado Climate Planning," *Climate Central*, January 29, 2014.

8. Scott Cuthbertson, PE, Colorado deputy state engineer, "Colorado Engineer 2014," presentation to American Council of Engineering Companies of Colorado.

GLOSSARY

100TH MERIDIAN. This line of longitude is 100 degrees west of Greenwich and runs through central Nebraska, figuratively represents the line between our country's moist East and its arid West. The Union Pacific Railroad reached and marked the 100th Meridian in 1868.

ACEQUIA. Translated from the Spanish, *acequia* is an irrigation ditch. The Arab word for *acequia* is *assaquiya*.

ACRE-FOOT. Equivalent to one acre, a foot deep in water, which equals 325,851 gallons.

ADJUDICATION. The legal process for obtaining, in this case, a water court decree. This is the legal means of legalizing a water right (conditional or absolute), a finding of reasonable diligence, an exchange, an augmentation plan, or a right to withdraw nontributary water.

ALLUVIAL. A geologic term meaning composed of sand, soil, and gravel, deposited by running water.

AQUIFER. A subsurface geological area capable of storing and yielding water to springs, waterways, and wells.

GLOSSARY

ARTIFICIAL RECHARGE POND. A human-made pond, located at such place and distance that water within it is expected to recharge the river in time to offset depletions caused by out-of-priority water use.

AUGMENTATION. Replacing water to a specific river or stream system, such that a water user can withdraw water out of priority without injuring a senior water-right holder.

AUGMENTATION PLAN. A court-approved plan to replace water in a specific river or stream system, such that a water user can withdraw water out of priority without injuring a senior water-rights holder.

BASIN. A topographic region in which all water drains to a common area, such as a river.

BENCHLANDS. As used in this book, the long terrace above the floodplain, defining the former path of the river.

BENEFICIAL USE. Lawful appropriation that employs reasonably efficient practices to place water to use. Uses deemed "beneficial" have evolved in response to changing economic and community values.

BIG AG. The few powerful multinational corporations that control the agricultural supply chain, from, in and around farms and ranches in the United States and abroad. They do this by virtue of development and exertion of intellectual property rights over seeds, chemical inputs (herbicides, pesticides, and fertilizers), milling, feedlots, and processing. These corporations also exert enormous influence over legislation, trade agreements, and financial markets. This influence determines the content, price, and availability of what we eat. Big Ag's sway extends beyond edibles to other products—such as clothing, fuel, packaging, cosmetics, and pharmaceuticals—because they contain agricultural commodities. These corporations also influence the seed stock to which farmers have access and the markets to which farmers and ranchers can sell.

BIG FOOD. The few powerful multinational corporations that control the food supply chain, from farms and ranches through processing to markets in the United States and abroad. These corporations also exert enormous influence over legislation, trade agreements, and financial markets. This influence determines the content, price, and availability of what we eat. These corporations also influence the seed stock to which farmers have access and the markets to which farmers and ranchers can sell.

CALL. Demand for administration of water rights, such that one can use the water. A call results in the water commissioner shutting down water use by undecreed and junior water rights sufficient to meet the call.

CARRYING CAPACITY. The maximum population size of the species or multiple species that the environment can sustain, given the food, habitat, water, and other necessities available in the environment.

CFS. Cubic feet per second as a flow rate. One cfs is 448.8 gallons per minute or 648,000 gallons per day, approximately two acre-feet per day.

COMMODITY. A raw material or primary agricultural product that can be bought and sold.

CONDITIONAL WATER RIGHT. A right to perfect a water right with a certain priority upon the completion, of an appropriation to a fresh use.

CONE OF DEPRESSION. A depression of the water level in the aquifer, caused by pumping groundwater from a well. The time it takes for the well pumping drawdown to reach the river and reduce flow is called "lag time."

CONJUNCTIVE USE. The use of groundwater and surface water, from the same basin, so that both sources can be used more efficiently. In wet years, surface water is used and also recharges aquifers, from which it can be withdrawn and used in dry years.

CONSUMPTIVE USE. The amount of water permanently withdrawn from its source, because it has been consumed by plants, livestock, or people; evaporated; or been transpired by plants.

DEPLETION. Net quantity of water (consumptive use) diverted through a headgate or pumped from a wellhead minus the return flow to the stream, river, or aquifer.

DÉRIVE. As used by Guy Debord, French revolutionary of the mid-twentieth century, the French word *dérive* is a personal deviation from absolutes imposed by convention. Departing on a *dérive*, a person follows his or her instincts.

DESERTIFICATION. Land degradation in which relatively dry region becomes more arid, typically losing its bodies of water as well as vegetation and wildlife. Climate and/ or human activities can cause desertification.

DIVERSION. Removing water from its natural location by means of a ditch, pipeline, pump, reservoir, or well.

ECOSYSTEM SERVICES. The dollar value ascribed to ecosystems, before development, as they pertain to water availability, water quality, air quality, storm-water infiltration, human quality-of-life, biodiversity, and other environmental factors. The cost is calculated by measuring the cost of redressing pollution, disease, water quality, and other internalities and externalities that are the result of ecosystem destruction.

ENDOCRINE DISRUPTORS. Chemicals that may produce adverse developmental, reproductive, neurological, and immune effects in both humans and wildlife.

ENTROPY. A gradual decline into disorder brought about by decreased availability of a system's thermal energy for conversion into productivity.

EROSIONAL RUNNEL. A narrow channel in the ground, formed by erosion.

EVAPOTRANSPIRATION. The combined water evaporation (from soil, canopy, and water bodies) and plant transpiration to the atmosphere.

EXTERNALITY. A cost that a party, who did not choose to incur that cost, incurs.

GROUNDWATER. Water below the soil surface that is in an aquifer.

HARDSCAPE. Impervious surfaces such as roofs, driveways, sidewalks, walls, streets, highways, malls, and parking lots, which cannot absorb water. Lawns and turfgrass are sometimes considered hardscape, because tight growth and short roots do not encourage water infiltration, and most water slides off.

IMPERVIOUS SURFACES. Surfaces that are hard and resist water. Surfaces that are not porous. Impervious surfaces deflect water infiltration and work against aquifer recharge. By limiting where water can go, impervious surfaces may increase flooding.

INJURY. In prior appropriation water doctrine, an action that deprives owners of a more senior water right to suffer a loss of water at the time, place, and amount to which they are entitled.

INTERNALITY. A cost a buyer incurs in the long run that was not taken into account at the time of purchase.

JUNIOR RIGHTS. In prior appropriation water doctrine, water rights that were decreed later (nearer in time to now) than senior water rights and therefore are lower in priority. Senior rights must be met—in time, place, and amount—before junior rights can be fulfilled. As an example, a 1909 decreed water right is junior to an 1876 water right.

OUT-OF-PRIORITY USE. Use of water, not in order of priority, according to decreed water rights. For instance, pumping from a well that was adjudicated as a 1933 right may later create a depletion in the conjoined river. If this depletion occurs when an 1876-decreed water right needs water, the well pumper will be out of priority and must replace that water in the system, by augmentation.

POST-PUMPING DEPLETION. The amount of depletion (amount pumped minus return flow) impacting a stream or river at a point in time after pumping occurs. The interval until the impact of pumping causes a "depletion" in a nearby stream or river is a function of the well's distance from the stream and the aquifer's transmissivity.

PSYCHOGEOGRAPHY. As coined by Guy Debord, French revolutionary of the mid-twentieth century, the innate ability to navigate over the ground on which we live, knowing Earth's forms and intuitively navigating them. In today's terms this would exclude GPS, maps, sidewalks, traffic lanes, and so on.

RIPARIAN. Related to or situated on the banks of a river.

RUMINANT. Mammals that acquire nutrients from grass, by fermenting it in a specialized stomach prior to digestion, principally through bacterial actions.

SENIOR RIGHTS. In prior appropriation water doctrine rights that were decreed earlier (longer from now) than junior water rights and therefore are higher in priority. Senior rights must be met—in time, place, and amount—before junior rights can be fulfilled. As an example, an 1876 decreed water right is senior to a 1909 water right.

STREAM DEPLETION FACTOR. Also known as SDF, a semianalytical method for quantifying stream depletion caused by groundwater withdrawals in alluvial aquifers.

SUBSTITUTE WATER SUPPLY PLAN (SWSP). This water-replacement plan identifies sources of water that are either owned or leased and can be introduced into the same water body from which water is withdrawn, in a location that prevents more senior water-rights owners from being negatively affected by the out-of-priority withdrawal.

SURFACE WATER. Water visible on the surface of the land, as in rivers, streams, ditches, reservoirs, ponds, and so forth.

SURFICIAL AQUIFERS. A groundwater repository near the soil surface, which consists of unconsolidated sand and limestone that may date to the Pliocene-to-Holocene periods. Water there is otherwise unconfined and moves along the hydraulic gradient from areas of recharge to rivers and streams.

SWSP. See Substitute water supply plan.

USUFRUCT. The right to use and enjoy another's property without destroying it.

WATERSHED. An area of land whose topography drains to the same stream, lake, or wetland. Many smaller watersheds are within a river basin.

WELL CALL. An as-yet unapproved means that would allow groundwater appropriators to call on the groundwater, a "well call" would be administered as a "bypass" to the calling reservoir in the winter, and would be senior to recharge projects. A well call would demand closer administration of the groundwater appropriations, which the state engineer's office claims it cannot provide.

ACKNOWLEDGMENTS

This project took shape only by the grace of the following, arranged alphabetically, not by measure of bloodletting:

Dean Ackerman
Ronnie Ackerman
Judy & Roger Alexander
Jon Avery
Deborah Axton
Maude Barlow
Grace Bell
Dave Buchanan
Laura Burnett
Cheryl Brantner
Julie Castiglia
Ned Daugherty
Mike Davis
Kathi Diamant
Winkie & Gene Dines
Phyllis & Larry Eaton
Ron Ehrlich
Peggy Ford
Laura Furney
Betty Fussell
Laurie Gillian
Bill Gladstone
Winifred Golden
Dita Guery
Bennie & Betty Gutfelder
Selby Hickey
Justice Greg Hobbs
Louis Hock

John Hollow
Barb Horn
Steve Ilott
Dana Ivers
Fabio Kacero
Jan & Gene Kammerzell
Dana Kolpin
Rebecca & Tom Kourlis
Chuck Leaf
Joanna Lemly
Kelly Lenkevich
Lauren Liven
Robert Longenbaugh
Jean Lowe
Diego Lynch
Kim Macconnel
Nina Macconnel
Sonya Manes
Maranda Miller
Alice Mitchell
Jeanne Thomas Moore
Kitty & Owen Morse
Dave Nettles
Gayle Newhouse
Dave Noe
Jack Odor
Beth Ann Parsons

Jim & Barb Peugh
Ellen & Jim Phelan
Annzo Phelps
Bill Phelps
Dorothy Thomas Phelps
Kate & Primo Phelps
Daniel Pratt
Peter Quinlan
Randy Ray
Matt Reddy
Silvina Retrevi
Patricia Rettig
Leslie Ann Ryan
Carrie Schneider
Hal Simpson
Michael Spooner
Lorann Stallones
Charlotte Steinhardt
Donald Strauss
Beth Svinarich
Erminia & Ernesto Varela
Sally Van Haitsma
Alice Waters
Bob Wilder
Kit Wilkins
Frankie Wright
Pamela & Steve Wright

May each of you live awash in your hearts' desires.

With bottomless thanks from the depths of me, Tershia

ABOUT THE AUTHOR

TERSHIA D'ELGIN is a social activist with deep Colorado roots and a special interest in water policy, water conservation, and the tension between agricultural and metropolitan claims on water. A San Diego–based writer and water resources consultant, she also oversees a working farm on the South Platte River in Colorado with her family.